The 1889 Flood In Johnstown, Pennsylvania

By Dr. Michael R. McGough

Thomas Publications
Gettysburg, Pa.

The 1889 Flood In Johnstown, Pennsylvania

Copyright © 2002 Dr. Michael R. McGough

Printed and bound in the United States of America

Published by THOMAS PUBLICATIONS
                    P.O. Box 3031
                    Gettysburg, Pa. 17325

All rights reserved. No part of this book may be used
or reproduced without written permission of the author
and the publisher, except in the case of brief quotations
embodied in critical essays and reviews.

ISBN-1-57747-082-6 (softcover)

ISBN-1-57747-090-7 (hardcover)

Cover design by Ryan C. Stouch

This book is dedicated to the memory
and honor of the families of:

Raphael Francis McGough, Sr.
&
Mary Elizabeth (Franchic) McGough

And

George Alton Gordon
&
Blanche Mae (Shull) Gordon

Contents

Foreword

In 1989 the centennial observance of the Johnstown Flood was a celebration of the triumph of the human spirit. The tragedy that struck the Conemaugh Valley in 1889 and those it claimed were remembered. Those who survived and the generations that followed were remembered and honored for their efforts to rebuild the city at the confluence of the Stony Creek and the Little Conemaugh.

The human spirit that made Johnstown what it was in the nineteenth and twentieth centuries still exists today. When asked to provide some perspective on present-day Johnstown for this book on the town's greatest tragedy, Dr. Donato B. Zucco, Mayor of Johnstown spoke of the strength of those who call Johnstown and surrounding communities home.

> The residents of the City of Johnstown have recovered and prospered after floods and other adversities because this community is made up of resilient, creative and persistent individuals. The heritage of our population goes back to the immigrants seeking a better life with a willingness to surmount obstacles and make sacrifices to live their dreams.

> I believe the residents in our area continue with the mindset that you make the best of the challenges and opportunities presented to you. There is a diverse ethnic population in our community and it is our ability to rise above our differences, to create opportunities, to provide for our children, which is in my opinion at the core of what makes Johnstown unique.

> As we begin the 21st Century we have almost $200 million worth of projects underway, which when completed will set the stage for a renewed downtown. Our efforts to strengthen the core city and promote the region while being secure with the quality of life we enjoy and the need to create jobs has energized us all.

Dr. Donato B. Zucco, Mayor
May 22, 2001

Acknowledgements

I want to thank the following for their assistance in the research and writing of this book:

My wife and my children for their endless help and support. Their research assistance, proofreading, suggestions, and willingness to listen were absolutely essential and will forever be appreciated.

My mother for being an excellent Johnstown guide, for ongoing assistance with local research, proofreading and editorial suggestions. Her help was invaluable and most sincerely appreciated.

My father, for creating in me an early interest in the Johnstown Flood and an appreciation for those who survived and rebuilt a town, which continues to prosper more than a century later.

Douglas Richardson of the National Park Service for his kind and knowledgeable assistance, support, suggestions, and proofreading. Doug's willingness to share his vast knowledge of the Johnstown Flood, the Victorian era of American history, and the South Fork Fishing and Hunting Club was absolutely invaluable.

Robin Rummel of the Johnstown Area Heritage Association for her research assistance, support and proofreading. Robin's kind and patient assistance was nothing short of essential.

Richard Burkert, the Executive Director of the Johnstown Area Heritage Association, for his editorial review and suggestions.

Dr. Raymond K. Reichwein, MD, the Milton S. Hershey Medical Center, for his part in a medical miracle.

James E. Vedock, the Director of the Grandview Citizens' Cemetery Association for his assistance and direction in researching and locating numerous gravesites at Grandview.

Tim Skertich, a good friend and fellow flood hiker, for assistance locating the remains of the Sang Hollow railroad tower and related artifact and photographic research.

James E. Thomas, of Thomas Publications, for his help in putting this book together.

Thelma and Belinda Galbreath for sharing the story and photographs of their family's connection to the Johnstown Flood.

Mrs. Virginia Anthony Soule, granddaughter of Louis S. Clarke, for permission to use photographs from her grandfather's collection from the South Fork Fishing and Hunting Club.

Dr. Donato B. Zucco, the mayor of the City of Johnstown for his assistance with the introduction to this book.

Dr. Douglas Cook of the Shippensburg University Library for archival research assistance.

Congressman John Murtha for his reflections and insights included in the epilogue.

Martha Frick Symington Sanger, the great-granddaughter of Henry Clay Frick, for sharing information from the Frick Archives and her personal insights and perspectives.

Adda Lee Hoskinson, the granddaughter of Frank Shomo, for sharing her recollections of her grandfather, his eulogy and family pictures.

Ann E. Bartholomew, the registrar of the American Red Cross Museum in Washington, DC, for her research assistance concerning Miss Clara Barton and the Red Cross.

The archives and libraries of:

The University of Pittsburgh at Johnstown
Millersville University
Pennsylvania State University
Shippensburg University
York College of Pennsylvania
Gettysburg College
University of Pennsylvania
Cambria County Library System
Office of the Coroner, Cambria County
Office of the Recorder of Deeds, Cambria County
Pennsylvania State Archives
Cambria County Historical Society
Pennsylvania Historical and Museum Commission
The Johnstown Tribune Publishing Company
Pennsylvania Department of the Carnegie Library
The Petoskey Title Company
Archives of the Conemaugh Valley Memorial Hospital.
The Frick Archives
Manuscript Division of the Library of Congress

Introduction

Few natural occurrences are more devastating than a flood. At a weight of about eight pounds per gallon, moving water has tremendous force and carrying capacity. Floodwaters have the power to drown, damage, destroy and carry off virtually anything. Floods spread disease, spawn fires, and generally leave a sense of human hopelessness in their wake.

The city of Johnstown, Pennsylvania gained a permanent place in history as a result of a flood that swept through the city and surrounding towns and boroughs on May 31, 1889. The Johnstown Flood, a natural disaster so horrible that it was said to be of biblical proportions, remains one of the most devastating natural occurrences ever recorded. In all 2,209 victims perished, most of the estimated 27,000 survivors of that region were homeless, and property damage approached the $30 million mark.

The flood and the events surrounding it have been the subject of study, research and investigation for more than a hundred years. No single cause or explanation has been identified, and no specific combination of events or occurrences is generally accepted as the irrefutable explanation. Instead, the prevailing theory holds that this flood was the result of a tragic combination of human error and natural occurrence that converged with devastating consequences. Human error, although not directly responsible, most definitely set the stage upon which natural events played out a deadly drama. Man and nature unwittingly formed an alliance that produced lethal consequences in and around Johnstown in 1889.

There were those who had concerns about Johnstown and the potential for flooding in and about that region. A man-made dam high above the town was a particular concern. Men of power and rank in the community were anything but shy about voicing their fears, but unfortunately, the warnings they offered went largely unheeded.

The full drama and all of the compelling details of the Johnstown Flood will never be told. Like most historical incidents, too much of the story disappeared with those who did not survive, and much more was never recorded by those who did survive. However, through the accounts, records, histories, and images that have been preserved, much of the story of the devastation, recovery, survival, and rebuilding of Johnstown can be retold.

It is not the purpose of this book to affix blame. Neither blame nor liability was definitively determined in 1889, and attempting to do so now would be pointless. Instead, what follows is a historical account of various aspects of the tragic story of Johnstown's flood of 1889.

The research involved in the development of this book made it necessary to reference numerous sources. Historical documentation and specific source identification is offered within the text to support the story, add relevant detail, and permit continuous reading without the need to check specific source listings.

Quoted passages are included herein just as they appeared in the original sources. As a result there are frequently inconsistencies in punctuation and spelling, but the meaning of the quoted material is not affected. Information added to quoted passages is added within brackets [ ]. Explanatory notes needed to clarify the meaning of a word or phrase within non-quoted text are provided within parentheses ( ).

In describing locations at the South Fork Dam, various accounts use different directions. For ease of understanding the author used the directions east and west. In some of the original sources that are herein quoted the eastern end of the dam is referred to as the northern end or the north abutment, and the western end is referred to as the southern end or the south abutment.

Chapter 1

Johnstown, Pennsylvania

Any attempt to chronicle the Johnstown Flood of 1889 must begin with a brief history of Johnstown, Pennsylvania. Such a historical review provides background and a sense of perspective for the tragic events of 1889. The historic storm of late May 1889 permanently altered the Conemaugh Valley, with no single borough being more affected than Johnstown. To understand Johnstown after the flood, it is essential to have some appreciation for the town and its municipal neighbors before May 31, 1889.

The history of early settlement in Johnstown was not well documented. In fact, credible accounts of this period in the townís history are at best sketchy. Many believe that Indian villages may once have dotted the area between the Stony Creek and the Little Conemaugh rivers. These villages may have been those of Delaware Indians known to have lived in the area. When interest in early Indian settlement became popular, numerous stories and legends were created by imaginative historians and writers detailing Indian settlements in and around Johnstown. Unfortunately, a general lack of records and written histories renders many of these accounts more fiction than fact.

The journals and correspondences of many explorers, traders and frontiersmen indicate that at one time or another they passed through the area that later became Johnstown. Following the signing of the Treaty of Fort Stanwix in November 1768, efforts to claim and settle lands in the Conemaugh Valley increased markedly. As a result of these settlement endeavors, whatever Indian presence there had been in the area began to decline.

Numerous individuals took out patents and tried to secure deeds to lands in and near present-day Johnstown. Notable among these efforts were those made by James Dougherty, Charles Campbell, James Wilkins, Jacob Stutzman and the Adams brothers, Solomon and Samuel. For the most part these were land claims that resulted in settlements, most of which were no larger than individual homesteads.

The most notable attempt at early settlement at the junction of the Stony Creek and the Little Conemaugh came during the second administration of George Washington in the early 1790s. Joseph Schantz, more widely known as Joseph Johns, began building the settlement that ultimately became Johnstown.

Johns initially named his settlement Conemaugh Old Town. He was an Amish farmer who had come to America from Switzerland, where he was born in 1750. Along with his wife and four children, he worked to develop a settlement that he hoped would grow and prosper. Securing his charter was the first step.

The charter for John's town, which referred to the town simply as Conemaugh, was drafted in Somerset County on November 3, 1800, and officially recorded the following day by John Wells. The witnesses were Abraham Morrison, John Berkey, and Josiah Espy. The charter declared that Joseph Johns laid out his town on seven basic principles and conditions. These included:

1. The town was named Conemaugh.

2. Individuals who purchased lots in Conemaugh would be granted a deed free and clear of all encumbrances except a $1.00 annual land rent to be paid each year on or before October 1.

3. A market square and several roads, highways and alleys were identified on a plot plan of the town, and their *undisturbed* use was guaranteed permanently to the inhabitants of the town.

4. Lands on Market Square and Chestnut Street were granted to the residents of Conemaugh for the purpose of building schools and churches.

5. On May 1, 1801, Johns and any other lot owners who cared to participate would lay out a public *burying grounds* on land granted by Johns for that purpose.

6. On the plot plan, lots number 49, 50, 51, and 52 were reserved for a county court house and other public buildings that were to be granted to the county *...as soon as the said town becomes a seat of justice....*

7. A parcel of ground known as the *point* and *...lying between the said town and the junction of the two rivers or creeks...*was reserved as a commons area for *...public amusement....*

At the time the charter was granted to Johns, his town, then situated in Quemahoning Township of Somerset County, contained 141 lots, ten streets, six alleys and one market square. It was to be known as Conemaugh, and it was *...situated in the forks of, and at the confluence of Stony Creek and Little Conemaugh River....*

Johns and others believed that as the population of the area increased, a new county would be formed in the Conemaugh Valley. It was clear from condition number six of the charter drawn up by Johns that he intended for his town to become the county seat. This, however, was not to happen. When Cambria County was established in 1804, Ebensburg, a town north of Conemaugh, was selected as the county seat. It remains the county seat today.

To all People to whom these presents shall come. Joseph Johns of Quemahoning township in the County of Somerset in the Commonwealth of Pennsylvania, woman sends Greeting: Whereas the said Joseph Johns hath laid out a Town on the tract of Land whereon he now lives (situate in the forks of, and at the confluence of, Stony Creek and Little Conemaugh river, known by the name of Conemaugh old Town) in the township and County aforesaid which said town contains at present one hundred and forty one Lots, Ten streets six alleys and one Market Square, as by the plan thereof will more fully and at large appear. Now know ye that the said Joseph Johns hath laid out the said town on the principles and conditions following Viz. 1st the said town shall be called & hereafter known by the name of Conemaugh ...

The charter for the town of Conemaugh was recorded in Somerset County, Pennsylvania on November 4, 1800. It was recorded in the hand of John Wells.

Johns sold his town in 1807, and he and his family left Conemaugh. They moved to Somerset County where Johns died in 1813. The charter for Conemaugh passed through several hands between 1807 and 1818. One of those owners was Peter Levergood. He bought it for $8,000 in 1811, then sold it in 1813 for more than $12,000. Levergood, a German from York County, Pennsylvania, remained interested in the area, and when he again had the chance to buy the town in 1818 he did so at a fraction of the cost he had paid in 1811.

When Levergood bought Conemaugh a second time, it was little more than a frontier trading post. He actively promoted his town and remained one of the town's most prominent residents until his death in 1860. As a result of Levergood's active promotion, the opening of the canal era, the arrival of the railroad, and the coming industrial revolution of the mid-19th century the town grew.

Many changes had come to Conemaugh since 1800. Among those changes was a new name. As a result of an action taken by the Pennsylvania General Assembly in 1834, the name Conemaugh was changed to *Johnstown*. This change was welcomed by the residents, since they had already been calling their town Johnstown for many years.

This bust of Joseph Johns (Schantz) is part of a memorial to him in Johnstown's Central Park which recognizes the part he played in establishing the town which came to bear his name. The monument was erected by Johnstown's citizens of German decent on June 16, 1913.

As the transportation system of Pennsylvania developed, Johnstown became an important town along the Main Line Canal. The Main Line was a transportation system that combined rail and canal passages to move both people and products across Pennsylvania. The steep inclines of the Allegheny Mountains were conquered by means of a system of inclined planes that moved canal boats and railroad cars. Johnstown became the western point of the system from which products and passengers began to move through the mountains of western Pennsylvania by way of the Allegheny Portage Railroad. Portions of the Allegheny Portage Railroad are still visible today. One of the more unique features of this early transportation system that survives today is the Staple Bend Tunnel. This tunnel is located near the town of Mineral Point. Although no longer in use, it stands as a true engineering marvel of its day.

The Lemon House, a tavern and resting place near plane number six was one of many establishments to serve the needs of travelers. Built by Samuel Lemon and his wife Jean in the early 1830s, the Lemon House, as it came to be known, served both passengers and workers of the Allegheny Portage Railroad. Taverns of this style sprung up along the various transportation routes of nineteenth century Pennsylvania. Today, they serve as timeless monuments to the early transportation endeavors of the Commonwealth.

One of the many difficulties associated with Pennsylvania's canal system was the seasonal fluctuation in the water supply upon which the canal depended. Those responsible for the canal felt a dam might enable them to better deal with these unpredictable water levels. Toward this end a site was selected, surveyed and plans for a large earthen dam were drafted. Initial progress on the project was slow, but by 1853 work was completed on what was named the Western Reservoir of the Pennsylvania Main Line Canal System.

The canal system, although never a highly profitable venture, had served the needs of Pennsylvania well for about 20 years by the time the Western Reservoir was completed. However, when the Pennsylvania Railroad successfully completed a rail line across the state in 1854, the canal system was rendered obsolete almost overnight. Pennsylvania was now part of a new era in transportation. Fortunately, Johnstown was one of the towns along the new rail line. The massive reservoir that had been built near South Fork, some 14 miles away from, and slightly more than 400 feet above Johnstown, was no longer needed. It was part of a transportation system that had become obsolete.

At about the same time that the Pennsylvania Railroad linked eastern and western Pennsylvania, the Cambria Iron Company came to Johnstown. The arrival of Cambria Iron immediately established Johnstown as a major industrial town, and Johnstown quickly became a leading iron and steel-producing center in the post-Civil War industrial age. The natural resources needed for iron and steel production, and a plentiful supply of both skilled and unskilled labor were readily available in and around Johnstown. Immigration to the Johnstown area had been brisk since the 1840s. Johnstown had become a typical industrial town that attracted immigrants from countries around the world. If the United States was becoming the great melting pot of the world, Johnstown was contributing significantly to the process.

The Cambria Iron Company was not the first iron-producing endeavor to be established in Johnstown. There were crude forges in the area in the late 18th century. These operations were quite small, and the iron produced was of limited quantity and quality. One of the first serious efforts to manufacture iron in the Conemaugh Valley was started by Peter Levergood, in 1808. He called his operation the Cambria Forge. Several other foundries and furnaces were soon built in the area. It was not, however, until the establishment of the Cambria Iron Company that Johnstown had a major iron and steel producing facility.

This section of the Allegheny Portage Railroad, depicted in a 19th century painting by George Storm, is located along U.S. Route 22. The Lemon House atop Cresson Mountain provided food and lodging for travelers and workers along the Main Line. (Picture courtesy of the State Museum of Pennsylvania, Pennsylvania Historical and Museum Commission)

The canal era was short lived in Johnstown. However, it helped to establish Johnstown as an important link in the transportation routes across the Commonwealth. The canal ran directly through Johnstown. By the time this picture was taken the canal was no longer in use, but portions of the canal wall were still visible.

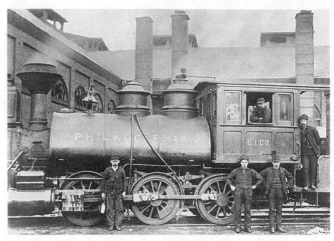

As the demand for iron and steel increased, the Cambria Iron Company's operations in Johnstown expanded to meet the demand. As the company grew so did its need for support industries like mines and railroads. To protect their local interests, Cambria Iron Company had their own mines, railroad system, and farms.

George S. King, a local businessman, was granted a charter for the Cambria Iron Company in 1852. King, the father of iron making in Johnstown, wanted to develop a large-scale iron production facility. He personally tried to tend to all aspects of his endeavor, from prospecting for local deposits of iron ore to securing capital for the new company. The Cambria Iron Company did not prosper under his leadership and passed through several hands before it was leased in 1855 to Wood, Morrell and Company of Philadelphia. By 1862, Wood, Morrell and Company purchased the facilities in Johnstown for a little more than $150,000, which represented about 10 percent of the value of the company's stock. They retained the name Cambria Iron Company.

As the mills, mines, railroads and related support industries grew to meet the expanding demands for iron and steel, the need for both skilled and unskilled labor continued to grow. Following the Civil War, the flow of immigrants to the United States grew each year. Many immigrants found their way to Johnstown, settling together in small communities such as Cambria City, Conemaugh, East Conemaugh, Prospect, Millville, Morrellville, and Johnstown. The Johnstown area boasted a rich and diverse blend of nationalities. English, Irish, Welsh, and German immigrants were among those who traveled great distances for the promise of a new life in America. In the decade prior to the flood, small clusters of Croatians, Hungarians, Polish, and other eastern

European immigrants also began to appear in Johnstown. Cultural diversity made Johnstown what it was in 1889, and the long-term traditions and implications of that heritage are still evident in Johnstown today.

Not everyone who lived in Johnstown in the late 19th century labored in the mills or the support industries. Like other towns, Johnstown had its professionals who provided a wide range of services, civic and governmental leaders, and independent businessmen, in addition to those who managed the thriving industrial interests of the area. Johnstown had both a working class and a professional class. The undisputed leader of Johnstown's professional and management class was Daniel J. Morrell, the general manager of the Cambria Iron Company from 1855 to 1884.

Daniel J. Morrell arrived in Johnstown in 1855. He had been sent to manage the Cambria Iron Company by Wood, Morrell and Company of Philadelphia. Under his skillful leadership, which spanned almost thirty years, Cambria Iron prospered, and as Cambria Iron prospered, so too did Johnstown. Few people understood this relationship better than Morrell. Of the partners of Wood, Morrell and Company, Morrell was the only one to live in Johnstown.

Morrell, a merchant prior to his entry into the iron and steel industry, quickly learned and mastered his new trade. As a merchant he had long known the basics of business and the respective roles of the producers and consumers in a market economy. He understood and took seriously the obligations workers had to their employers, but just as well he knew the responsibilities management owed to their workers. He represented the

Daniel J. Morrell was the general manager of the Cambria Iron Company in Johnstown for 29 years (1855-1884). During that time the company and the town both prospered under his watchful eye.

interests of the Cambria Iron Company well, and their Johnstown facility prospered under his careful and purposeful leadership.

One of the newest and most promising innovations to hit the steel industry after the close of the Civil War was the Bessemer conversion process. The process was named for its inventor, Sir Henry Bessemer (1813-1898), a British metallurgist. In the Bessemer process, molten iron was subjected to a blast of compressed air, which burned off excess carbon and a number of other impurities. Steel produced through this process was of significantly higher quality than steel produced through traditional, less efficient methods.

Shortly after Morrell's arrival in Johnstown the large pear-shaped vats used to treat iron in the Bessemer conversion process became part of the Cambria Iron facilities. To assist with the development of new technologies in iron and steel production, Morrell brought industrial leaders like William Kelly, the Fritz brothers, and William R. Jones to Johnstown. The introduction of the Bessemer process was but one example of Morrell's ongoing efforts to make the Johnstown facilities of Cambria Iron as modern and efficient as possible. Under Morrell's management Cambria Iron grew steadily in Johnstown. From their initial investment of approximately $150,000, the holdings of the Cambria Iron Company grew to more than $50 million by 1889, making it one of the larger steel producing operations in the world.

Because of Morrell's reputation and his tireless energy very little missed his careful eye. For example, he watched with great interest as efforts began to establish a mountain retreat around an abandoned canal reservoir in the mountains above Johnstown. The retreat, which was being developed under the leadership of Benjamin Ruff, was designed to provide a summer respite from the heat, smog and dirt of industrial towns like Pittsburgh.

Like all industrial centers of the late 19th century, Pittsburgh lived off of the wealth of industry, and at the same time suffered the numerous ill effects associated with those large industries. Among the more noticeable of those ill effects were the rude and foul interruptions to nature's order. Clean air and clean water were often among the most serious shortages produced by rapid industrial growth and development. Unfortunately, those who were responsible for that growth and development and thus the problems created, usually enjoyed the lion's share of the wealth generated. And with the personal financial resources they could accumulate they were also best prepared to distance themselves from the more unpleasant aspects of their industries. As a result they were less likely to be sensitive to the problems for which they were most responsible.

The project of the Pittsburgh industrialists, which was incorporated in 1879 as the South Fork Fishing and Hunting Club, was some fourteen miles from Johnstown. Even so, Morrell and others feared the consequences that could result from a collapse of the Club's dam.

The Cambria Iron Company was the centerpiece of the town's thriving economy. The iron company mines, railroads, and allied industries that supported it provided the vast majority of the employment in and around Johnstown. Iron and steel from the mills of the Cambria Iron Company were well known for their quality. They were widely used both nationally and internationally. Johnstown had truly become an industrial town of the post-Civil War industrial age, thanks largely to the Cambria Iron Company.

As the last decade of the 19th century approached, Johnstown became a prosperous town with a bright future. There was every reason for the townspeople to be optimistic about life and what the future held for them. The local economy was good, and since the demand for Cambria Iron products seemed to grow each year, the long-term prospects for Johnstown seemed bright.

Yet life was not easy in Johnstown. Industrial safety and general working conditions in mines, mills, and factories of the late 19th century were not priority concerns. Workers assumed a great deal of personal responsibility for their own welfare and safety. A wage necessary to provide a family with even a modest existence required a ten- to twelve-hour work day, five to six days a week.

From all outward appearances Johnstown, Pennsylvania in 1889 was not noticeably different from numer-

Few photographs demonstrate the financial impact the Cambria Iron Company had on Johnstown more vividly than this payday scene, photographed on April 24, 1886.

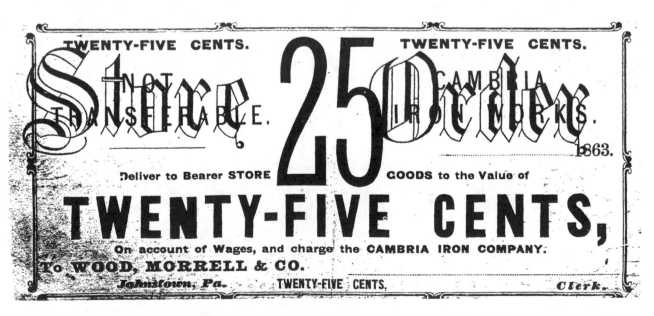

Cambria Iron workers were not always paid in cash. Often wages were paid in the form of a store order payable to the company store, Wood, Morrell & Company.

ous other industrial towns during America's post-Civil War industrial era. To those who lived and worked there, it was a unique town; it was their home. Many of Johnstown's 1889 residents had been born there, while many others had come to Johnstown in search of work in the mills and related industries. Many who came to Johnstown had once called other parts of Pennsylvania, other states, and numerous foreign countries home.

In 1889 Johnstown was actually a collection of boroughs with Johnstown Borough being the largest and most centrally located. In 1889, the residents of Johnstown Borough numbered about 10,000. Their town contained a large number of churches. Many of these churches had distinctly ethnic backgrounds and could be found in neighborhoods that had similar ethnic identities. Services were offered in native languages, and the churches became the center community life in Johnstown's ethnic sections. Many of these congregations still exist and preserve the rich cultural heritage of Johnstown.

As the numerous churches of Johnstown and the surrounding area sought to win and maintain the souls of the folks who lived there, saloonkeepers and prostitutes provided sources of diversion. Johnstown's neighborhoods were dotted with a wide variety of churches in 1889, but more than 120 bars and saloons could be found in those same neighborhoods. These establishments ranged from the somewhat sophisticated saloons along Main Street, which catered to a professional and management clientele, to the dingy, makeshift bars found in back alleys that served the less privileged locals. Prostitution was part of the local economy, just as it was in most towns of the era. Because of the distinctly quiet nature of such business, there is no way to know how prevalent it was in 1889. However, the mention of Prospect Hill or Frankstown Hill, for those who frequented such places, would conjure up images of the more unsavory side of life in Johnstown in 1889.

The Quicksteps, Johnstown's hometown baseball team, entertained the locals during the spring and summer months. In 1889, the team got off to a rather slow start, but that did little to weaken the support showed by the locals. The account of the game on May 28, 1889, carried in the Pittsburgh Times on May 29, 1889 read as follows:

The Game at McKeesport Yesterday
The McKeesport County League Club defeated Johnstown, of Western Pennsylvania League, at McKeesport yesterday. The game was very one-sided. Johnstown had no show at all. Williams knocked a home run over the right-field fence, the first one ever sent over that place. The batting of Torreyson, Provins, and Smick was particularly fine.

The score by innings is as follows:
McKeesport ... 2 4 0 6 4 3 4 2 2—27
Johnstown .... 0 1 0 1 3 2 0 0 2—9

Like most teams the Quicksteps had both good and bad games, and good and bad seasons. There was a sense of local pride in the Quicksteps, and following the team provided an opportunity to share in that pride.

Johnstown had a police force and a jail. Both were needed and both were used. Not unlike current crime reporting, more serious crimes quickly became front-page news. A headline from the February 28, 1889 edition of the *Johnstown Tribune* read, "Murder Most Foul." The story which appeared under this headline provided the details of the murder.

Information was brought to this city this morning about half-past 9 o'clock by Mr. Sipe, a huckster, that Herman Umberger, a farmer living on the Jenner Pike, about three miles this side of Jennertown (about sixteen miles from Johnstown) was murdered and robbed last night.

Johnstown's crime statistics from the late 1880s would not set the town noticeably apart from any town of similar size, either positively or negatively. Every town had its good and bad in 1889, and Johnstown was no exception.

Plans to bring the several boroughs in the area together as a city had been discussed time and again. Such plans surfaced anew early in 1889. However, local politics, competing taxing structures, established ways of conducting neighborhood affairs, and politicians who feared the loss of positions and the power those positions afforded, stalled such efforts. Ethnic pride, which was prevalent in many of the boroughs, also seemed to inhibit efforts to consolidate. In the spring of 1889, there was not a compelling need to do so, but by the end of the year that changed.

Beyond local politics, the influence of Johnstown was felt in the workings of the state legislature in Harrisburg. Early in 1889, for example, the Ways and Means Committee of the Pennsylvania House of Representatives voted to amend a revenue bill so as to provide an exemption for businesses that exclusively produced iron, steel, cotton and woolen products. This was excellent news for Johnstown and the Cambria Iron Company. Cyrus Elder, the solicitor of the Cambria Iron Company, was instrumental in securing this exemption. As a result, Cambria Iron was credited by many as having more influence than any other single manufacturer in the Commonwealth.

In 1889, Johnstown had an opera house, several local bands and musical groups, a night school, a library, a company hospital, and a new railroad station. Two

This picture shows one of several crews that worked the mills of the Cambria Iron Company in Johnstown. The workers pictured in this photograph were members of the Bessemer 4:00 o'clock crew. Cambria Iron was particularly proud of the Bessemer process used at its Johnstown facility. Steel produced in Johnstown through the Bessemer process helped to set a standard of excellence throughout the industry. The skilled labor force in Johnstown took pride in the products of their labors.

Peace, security and safety in Johnstown were the primary responsibilities of the local police force. The force expanded throughout the latter years of the nineteenth century, as the need for such services expanded with the continual growth of Johnstown and neighboring boroughs.

opera houses, one on Main Street and a more prestigious one on Washington Street, brought the entertainment and culture of the stage to Johnstown. Patrons had the opportunity to see many of the major shows and performances that were touring the country. Local bands provided entertainment on spring and summer nights and performed for special celebrations and events throughout the year.

Public schools were well established in Johnstown in 1889. So too were the public library and a night school for those who chose to continue their education as adults. Rail service to Johnstown had grown since the close of the Civil War to a point where a second railroad station was built to meet the demands of the town.

Merchants in and around Johnstown provided a wide variety of both foreign and domestic goods to local consumers. There was plenty of competition in the local marketplace, which helped to maintain competitive prices and expand the variety of goods available to the consumers of Johnstown. For example, the Economy Clothing Company ran an advertisement in the May 29, 1889 edition of the *Johnstown Tribune* that offered one, three and four-button cutaway Prince Albert Suits. The headline for this advertisement declared, *COMPETITION SWEPT AWAY BY THE ECONOMY'S TIDAL-WAVE OF LOW PRICES.*

Social, religious and fraternal organizations were common in Johnstown. Each in its own way added to the community. Each attracted a certain membership. Collectively they demonstrated the diversity of the people who lived in Johnstown in 1889, and served as

WODD, MORRELL & CO., Limited,

WHOLESALE AND RETAIL DEALERS IN

GENERAL MERCHANDISE.

In our immense building, which consists of **TEN STORES** in one, can be found at all times a bountiful supply of anything in the following goods, which are first-class in every respect:

Groceries, Provisions

GLASS AND QUEENSWARE,

BOOTS AND SHOES,

HATS AND CAPS,

CLOTHING, GENTS' FURNISHING GOODS

CARPETS, OIL CLOTHS, WALL PAPER,

DRY GOODS AND NOTIONS,

MILLINERY AND TRIMMINGS.

We sell only HONEST GOODS and sell them only for what they are. By means of Low Prices, Fair Dealing and an earnest desire to please, we will endeavor to MERIT PUBLIC PATRONAGE.

WOOD, MORRELL & CO., Limited.

As shown in this ad, which appeared in the 1889 edition of C. B. Clark's Johnstown Directory and Citizens' Register, *Wood, Morrell & Company offered Johnstown shoppers a wide variety of goods.*

The Johnstown Reed Band was one of several musical groups that had been organized in Johnstown. In addition to periodic concerts, such community bands performed at local ceremonies and during holiday celebrations.

an excellent example of the sense of community that existed in Johnstown as the twentieth century approached.

By 1889, modern conveniences were making their way into the homes of the working class. Electricity and natural gas service were common. Streetlights extended nightlife in Johnstown. The telephone had come to town several years earlier, and each year more and more subscribers became part of the local phone network. Indoor plumbing was also quickly becoming the norm in Johnstown. A wide variety of convenience and timesaving devices were available. For example, the Singer Sewing Manufacturing Company, long a producer of sewing machines for clothing manufacturers, was offering a new electric powered model to fit the needs of the homemaker.

The *Johnstown Tribune*, the competing *Democrat*, the *Weekly Herald* and the German *Freie Presse* brought the news of the world to readers in Johnstown. In 1889 newspapers told of such events as the World's Fair in Paris and the opening of the Oklahoma land rush. In that same year, Coca-Cola was first advertised for sale, and Captain Frederick Pabst established his brewery in Milwaukee. From his Menlo Park laboratory in New Jersey, Thomas Edison announced that he had invented the kinetoscope, the first motion picture machine. A patent was also given in 1889 for the first coin operated pay telephone.

In the June issue of the *North American Review*, Andrew Carnegie first published his essay *The Gospel of Wealth*. In it Carnegie asserted the obligation of those who profit most from the free enterprise system to serve as trustees of that wealth, sharing it in ways that will enhance the public welfare. In 1889, Andrew Carnegie, a Pittsburgh industrialist, held a share in the South Fork Fishing and Hunting Club, situated in the hills above Johnstown.

In 1889 four states joined the Union. They were North and South Dakota, Montana and Washington. Drs. William and Charles Mayo, brothers, opened the Mayo Clinic in Rochester, Minnesota. *Collier's Weekly* announced the first All-American football team, and bare knuckle boxing gave way to boxing with gloves under the Marquis of Queensberry rules.

In June of 1889 there was a single news story that captured and held the attention of the world for several months. It was the story of a disaster, a disaster more horrible than any other folks could remember. It was the story of a disaster that was at the same time natural and manmade. The loss of life and destruction of property were almost more than one could imagine. This disaster, which is still seen as one of the most awful in recorded history, and the worst ever to result from the bursting of a dam, was the Johnstown Flood.

Chapter 2

The South Fork Fishing and Hunting Club

The Western Reservoir had originally been built to serve as a feeder for Pennsylvania's Main Line Canal system. Summers in western Pennsylvania were often times of low water. In an effort to better provide and regulate the water supply available for the canal system, the Western Reservoir was built. At various points in its history it was also known as the South Fork Dam, the Old Reservoir, Three Mile Dam, and finally Lake Conemaugh. When completed in 1853, the dam was an impressive work. Because of its proximity to the town of South Fork, it quickly became known as the South Fork Dam by the locals. It was fed by six streams and was believed by many to be the largest manmade body of water in the United States.

According to an account provided in the June 29, 1889 issue of *Scientific American*, in an article titled "The Johnstown Disaster," the South Fork Dam was not the largest manmade body of water in the United States. When the reservoir was full the South Fork Dam held approximately 3,600,000,000 gallons in check, which is approximately 480,000,000 cubic feet of water or an estimated 20 million tons of water. Larger manmade bodies of water included the following:

Croton Dam—NY	5,000,000,000 gallons
Dam at Oakland—CA	5,000,000,000
Sweet Water Dam—CA	6,000,000,000
Bear Valley Dam—CA	10,000,000,000
Dam at San Mateo—CA	32,000,000,000
Quaker Bridge Dam—NY	37,500,000,000

(under construction in 1889 at the site of the Croton Dam)

Even though it was not the largest manmade body of water in the United States, the South Fork Dam was impressive. Two engineers of the Pennsylvania Main Line Canal System were responsible for selecting the site of the reservoir and designing the dam that would impound the water. Sylvester Welsh selected the site and supervised the clearing of approximately 400 acres of land, and William Morris, who was responsible for the system's western division, designed the dam and supervised construction.

The first appropriation of funds for the project were passed by the Pennsylvania General Assembly in 1836.

Preliminary surveys at the site may have been made as early as 1834. Several other appropriations would be needed to complete the project. The work of actually preparing the site near South Fork for the building of the dam began in the spring of 1840. The land area was divided into seven lots and individual contracts were awarded. The cost per acre ranged from a low of $33.00 to a high of 73.00. This initial step in the development of a reservoir near South Fork would have been no small undertaking. Most of the land area included in the site selected was heavily wooded at the time.

James Moorhead* of Pittsburgh and Hezekiah Packer of Williamsport, Pennsylvania were awarded the construction contracts, which were dated January 31, 1840. David Watson was the supervisor of the project for the canal commissioners. Samuel Kennedy was awarded a contact for the ironwork on the sluice pipes for the dam. For cast iron he would be paid 3.75 cents per pound and for wrought iron he would be paid nine cents per pound. Barr & Pennington received a contract for just under $800 for the construction of a stone house and stable at the reservoir site. The work of construction at the dam site began in April of 1840 and continued through 1841. Between 1842 and 1851, work on the Western Reservoir was stopped due to a lack of funds, wavering interest in the project, and even a feared cholera epidemic.

The dam at South Fork was an earthen and stone structure. On its interior or upstream side, it was made of horizontal layers of clay and earth covered with a thin surface of stones. The upstream surface of the dam was constructed with a two-to-one slope. Each of the clay and earth layers was approximately two feet thick. The layers were well packed and rammed or pounded into place, then skimmed with water before the next layer was placed. Once skimmed with water they were left to sit for a time so as to make the surface watertight. This construction technique is known as "puddling." Puddling of the layers caused them to settle into place, adhere to each other and harden. Puddling dramatically increased the overall strength of the upstream portion of the dam, and made it far more watertight than if the clay and earth had simply been dumped or piled as one solid mass. The upstream portion of the dam was the watertight portion of the structure. Its interior surface was then covered with a layer of small stones and rocks to protect the clay and earthen layers. This protective layer is known as "riprap."

---

* James Moorhead was the father of Maxwell Kennedy Moorhead who was a member of the South Fork Fishing and Hunting Club. After attending Western University, Maxwell assisted his father in the construction of the Western Reservoir.

This view of the interior surface of the dam shows the smaller riprap that was used on the upstream or reservoir side of the dam. The small footbridge in the upper left portion of this view runs across the spillway cut into the rock of the mountainside to which the eastern end of the dam was joined.

Directly behind the clay and earth portion of the dam was a core of broken slate, shale and other small rocks mixed with earth. The core was designed to provide extra weight and thus enhance the total strength of the structure. The downstream or exterior portion of the dam was made up mostly of large rocks with earth filling in the spaces between the massive stones. Some of the rocks used to create this outer surface of the dam weighed more than ten tons. The downstream or exterior surface of the dam was constructed with a slope of one and one-half to one.

The massive boulders used on the outer surface, which also formed a riprap, were intended to secure the other two layers and help hold the entire structure in place. If water flows over the top of an earthen dam, a process known as "overtopping," serious erosion is sure to result. The riprap on the exposed surfaces of the dam was intended to protect the fragile clay and earthen core from erosion, which is the most serious threat to the stability of such a structure.

Five cast iron pipes, each two-feet in diameter, were laid completely through the base of the dam. These pipes ran through a rock culvert and were fitted with valves. The valves could be opened and closed from a wooden control tower situated inside the reservoir. These cast iron pipes would permit control of the level of water in the dam. During periods of high water, excess water could be harmlessly discharged through the base of the dam, thus reducing the possibility of overtopping. The system of discharge pipes also provided a means of lowering the level of water in the reservoir, if repairs to the dam became necessary.

A spillway for the dam was constructed along its eastern end. It measured slightly more than 70 feet wide and was approximately ten feet below the top of the dam. It was cut into the natural rock layers of the hillside to which that side of the dam was anchored. As with the cast iron pipes, the spillway was designed to provide a safe outlet for excess water in the reservoir before it could reach a level where it would overtop the dam. With the bottom of the spillway approximately ten feet lower than the top of the breast of the dam, the possibility of overtopping, even during the worst storm of a century, was remote.

The superstructure of the dam was as impressive as it was massive. The overall length of the dam was just over 931 feet. At its base the dam's thickness was measured at a little more than 270 feet. The distance from the river bed to the top of the dam was 72 feet. At the top the dam was 10 feet wide. Depending on the level of the water maintained in the reservoir, estimates of the surface area of the lake ranged between 400 and 450 acres. The perimeter of the lake was estimated at approximately seven miles, when the dam was full. There was an estimated 20,000,000 tons of water in the Western Reservoir when it was at capacity.

Although all of the work at the dam was not completed until the following year, it was deemed ready to retain water in June 1852, so the sluice gates were closed. By August the dam was retaining a body of water that had reached a depth of forty feet in spots. Engineers responsible for the dam decided not to fill it to capacity initially. They wanted to allow the dam to adjust to the pressure behind it, while providing an opportunity to observe its structural integrity without a full head of water behind it. If repairs had to be made, doing so with less water behind the dam would make the work easier. Also, if the dam did prove to have structural imperfections, a break with the dam only partially full would greatly reduce damage from flooding down stream. This decision proved to be a prudent one. Within the first two years some minor leaks did appear. A quantity of water was released from the dam, and the necessary repairs were made.

By the spring of 1853, the dam was deemed complete and slightly more than 400 acres of the reservoir

THE SOUTH FORK DAM

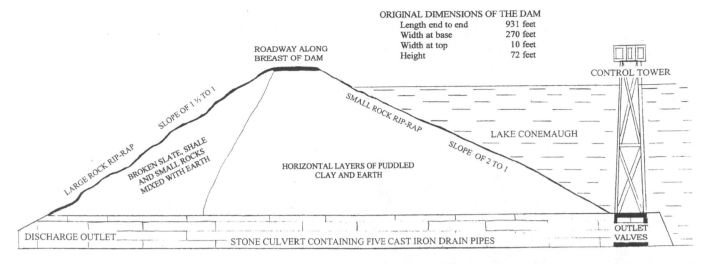

ORIGINAL DIMENSIONS OF THE DAM
Length end to end   931 feet
Width at base   270 feet
Width at top   10 feet
Height   72 feet

CONTROL TOWER

ROADWAY ALONG
BREAST OF DAM

SLOPE OF 1½ TO 1

SMALL ROCK RIP-RAP

LAKE CONEMAUGH

SLOPE OF 2 TO 1

LARGE ROCK RIP-RAP

BROKEN SLATE, SHALE
AND SMALL ROCKS
MIXED WITH EARTH

HORIZONTAL LAYERS OF PUDDLED
CLAY AND EARTH

DISCHARGE OUTLET   STONE CULVERT CONTAINING FIVE CAST IRON DRAIN PIPES

OUTLET
VALVES

This drawing represents the basic characteristics and general dimensions of the South Fork Dam, as it was originally designed.

The larger boulders used to riprap and secure the downstream surface of the dam were so large that, according to eyewitness accounts, it took as many as three teams of horses to move some of them into place.

Portions of the stone culvert through which the five cast iron discharge pipes ran are still visible on the floor of the reservoir, as is a small portion of the base of the wooden control tower from which the valves were controlled.

This view of the eastern abutment of the dam shows the slope of both the upstream (right) and the downstream (left) surfaces of the dam. It also shows a cross section of the portions of the original structure that still exist today. In the upper right portion of this picture is the footbridge that today crosses the spillway. The building in the extreme upper right portion of the picture is the visitor center of the National Park Service.

bed was under water. The dam was approaching its intended level. In spots the water was already more than fifty feet deep. Various cost estimates of the project put the total at a little more than $160,000 for the Western Reservoir. From the approval of the initial state appropriations until it was finished, this project took nearly seventeen years to complete. It was an impressive structure, well designed and equally well built, with the capacity to more than fulfill the purpose for which it had been built. However, other events would soon diminish and ultimately render the Western Reservoir useless.

Local interest in the building of the reservoir near South Fork passed through a number of phases, but was generally difficult to measure. There were times, particularly during construction, that there was much interest. When construction was halted, which happened often, interest would quickly fade. There were periods when the locals believed that the reservoir would never be completed. When it was finished, there were those who saw it as a wise investment in the future of the towns along the Main Line. They saw it as an essential piece of the system that would keep their town on one of the most active transportation links in the East. There

were others who saw little or no value in the massive structure. However, among both its supporters and critics, there were people who saw the reservoir as a threat. Situated high above the numerous towns and villages along the Little Conemaugh between South Fork and Johnstown, the Western Reservoir appeared to some to be a disaster waiting to happen. If the reservoir broke, there was nowhere for the water to go but downstream, and many feared the potential consequences if that ever happened.

The rapid expansion and growing popularity of the railroad quickly put an end to the canal era in Pennsylvania. The Commonwealth was left holding a public transportation system that was of little or no value either in the present or in the foreseeable future. Three different times between 1854 and 1857, the Commonwealth tried to sell its rail and canal system. Finally in 1857, the system was purchased by the Pennsylvania Railroad for $7,500,000. The Pennsylvania Railroad abandoned the canal at points where it had tracks, and where needed new tracks were laid. The Western Reservoir was of no use to the Pennsylvania Railroad.

During the next decade, the Western Reservoir was all but ignored. Locals hunted the area and fished the lake and the streams that fed it. The level of the lake was kept well below capacity. Several pockets of water supported enough fish to attract local anglers. Those who farmed the area grazed their livestock along the edges of the old and now abandoned reservoir. Many of the initial fears that folks below the dam had had were quieted by the uneventful passage of time.

In July of 1862, there was a period of high water brought on by unusually heavy rain. A break occurred near the center of the dam. The *Cambria Tribune* in its August 1, 1862 edition, under the heading "Local Miscellany," offered a brief account of the break.

> The Reservoir dam, the precarious condition of which we noticed two weeks ago, gave way on Saturday morning last, and emptied its water into the Conemaugh. The announcement of the breaking of the dam caused considerable alarm in town, but owing to the low stage of water in the creek the flow from the Reservoir produced but an inconsiderable rise, and the excitement and the flood both soon subsided. No loss or damage was sustained by anybody so far as we can learn, except the carrying away of about two hundred dollars worth of bridge timber belonging to Wood, Morrell & Co., which was being floated down the creek, and the overflowing and washing away of a few rods of the railroad track at South Fork, which detained the morning train from the East until late in the afternoon.—Many people were badly scared about the breaking of the Reservoir, but nobody was hurt by it.

It has been estimated that a section of the dam that may have measured as much as 200 feet wide washed out near its center. A portion of the stone culvert that housed the sluice pipes had collapsed, which is believed to be why the section of the dam above it washed out. Unprofessional and undocumented speculation as to why the section of stone culvert failed covered a wide range. There were those who concluded that the break was an act of purposeful vandalism. Others concluded that locals had for years been stealing stones from the culvert and lead from the sluice pipe joints, thus weakening the entire structure. Still others concluded that the collapse of the culvert was the result of natural deterioration resulting from the gradual drying out of the dam's puddled layers, because the intended level of the reservoir had not been maintained. Shortly after the 1862 break in the dam, a fire destroyed the wooden tower from which the dam's sluice pipes were controlled.

The level of the dam was low at that time, and the valley below the dam was in a dry season. The sluice pipes at the dam were opened, which helped to reduce the pressure behind the dam. Even though there was great alarm at the time, this break actually had a calming affect on many who had feared what might happen if the dam broke. There was a certain level of comfort generated by the fact that the 1862 failure of the dam rendered no serious damage to the valley below. As a result fears and concerns related to the dam, and the threat it held for Johnstown and other towns below it were quieted, at least for a time.

Those comforted by the minimal damage brought about by the 1862 break in the dam failed to realize the circumstances that surrounded the incident. Collectively, these factors made the 1862 break anything but a fair gauge of the devastation a break in the South Fork Dam could bring to Johnstown and every other town between there and South Fork. No photographs were taken and the state did not conduct an investigation. After all, the reservoir had been abandoned for a decade at the time of the break. As a result there are no reliable records of the 1862 break. The failure of the state to investigate the 1862 incident left estimates of the potential damage that could result from a similar break in the future to local conjecture and unprofessional speculation. Twenty-seven years later, even the direst conjecture and the gravest speculation could not begin to estimate the horror that such a break would cause throughout the valley below.

Congressman John Reilly bought the Western Reservoir from the Pennsylvania Railroad in 1875. Although the reason for his interest in the property has never been positively determined, it is believed that it was a speculative land venture. Reilly was a one-term

congressman from Pennsylvania and had previously been in a management position with the Pennsylvania Railroad. Reilly, who was from nearby Altoona, paid $2,500 for the property. Although no one is certain, there is reason to believe that it was Reilly who had the five, two-foot sluice pipes removed from the damaged stone culvert that ran through the base of the dam. The pipes were reportedly sold for scrap. He also completed some repairs, minimal and inadequate as they were, to the 1862 break. During his ownership the reservoir was never brought up to its capacity level. The Western Reservoir continued to stand as a quietly abandoned vestige of the bygone canal era.

It is believed that Reilly's plan was to purchase the property, hold it for a time, and then find a buyer willing to pay more for the property than he had. In 1879, he found a buyer, but he failed to realize a profit. In that year he sold the property to Benjamin Ruff, a railroad tunnel contractor from the Pittsburgh area. Ruff saw great potential in the Western Reservoir and the land surrounding it.

The industrial revolution of the late nineteenth century was transforming the nation. Powered by growing demands for American products from both foreign and domestic markets, the growth of industry in America seemed as though it would have no end. Industrial expansion continued through the decade of the 1880s unabated. Industrial towns and cities grew up around these industries. Those towns and cities responded to the needs of their specific industries and tolerated the excesses and the problems they caused.

There were many demands on the natural resources of an industrial region. Frequently, those demands generated subtle yet catastrophic disturbances to the natural balance of the area. Industrial operations also created by-products that impacted the environment in a harsh and unrelenting manner. The full extent and many of the consequences of the late nineteenth-century industrial era were not known or even anticipated until well into the twentieth century.

Among the most bothersome and noticeable by-products of the industrial era, which followed the Civil War, was smoke and soot that fouled the air. The atmosphere around many industrial towns was often so affected, that the rays of the sun were partially blocked. When snow was on the ground, the various discharges were clearly visible against the white background. Buildings, regardless of the materials used in construction, often took on the gray cast of the air laden with industrial wastes.

Rivers and streams were also victims of the industrial age. They frequently served as convenient drainage systems and open dumps for all manner of industrial waste, both liquid and solid. Even more troublesome was the practice of filling in riverbeds to expand the land area near the river for further industrial growth. Such a change in the natural character of a river had dramatic impact on the riverbed, its capacity to carry water and the area around it. Since industrial towns and cities depended on their industries for their livelihood, they were usually somewhat tolerant of the unpleasant conditions associated with those industries. Management of natural resources, efforts to protect the environment and related ecological concerns were initiatives that would not become common until well into the twentieth century.

Iron and steel operations were among the worst offenders when it came to resource management and pollution. The rivers and streams around these plants quickly took on a yellow to murky-brown hue from the industrial wastes discharged into them. The air around iron and steel plants was constantly clouded with the steam, smoke, and soot vented from the smokestacks. Pittsburgh, Pennsylvania had become a leading center for iron and steel production in America and a prime example of the ill effects such plants could and did bring to an area. Johnstown, although on a slightly smaller scale, had witnessed the same growth and encountered similar environmental concerns. When the production figures from Johnstown and Pittsburgh were combined, western Pennsylvania was clearly the center of iron and steel production in America. Had statistics for environmental pollution been kept during this era, the Johnstown-Pittsburgh area would again have been a leader.

The various health-related issues associated with heavily industrialized areas were just becoming a public concern in the 1880s. The unhealthy effect of air fouled with industrial wastes was one such concern. An advertisement, which appeared in the April 10, 1889 edition of the *Johnstown Tribune*, attempted to capitalize on the growing concern regarding the ill effects of polluted air.

The Population of Johnstown

Is about thirty thousand, and we would say at least one-half are troubled with some affection of the Throat and Lungs, as those complaints are, according to statistics, more numerous than others. We would advise all our readers not to neglect the opportunity to call on their druggist and get a bottle of Kemp's Balsam for the Throat and Lungs. Trial size free. Large Bottle fifty cents and one dollar. Sold by all druggists.

Not surprisingly, cleaning up the industries was a low priority when solutions were proposed. The technology to accomplish this was still in the future. The easiest solution, particularly for those who owned and managed the various industrial interests of the day, was to avoid the foul air of the city and escape to the mountains or the seashore. Such escapes also provided relief from the oppressive heat of the inner city during the summer months. Unfortunately, this solution was available only to those who had the time and the money to escape the city.

Advertisements appeared in many eastern papers for summer resorts and retreats. They spoke of clean air and a relaxing environment that would provide relief from the heat, smoke, and clamor of industrial cities. Several of the major railroad lines offered a wide range of summer vacation opportunities. Some retreats were in the mountains, while others were seaside resorts. Cresson Springs, in Cambria County, Pennsylvania was an example of a mountain resort. An advertisement in the July 3, 1863 edition of the *Cambria Tribune* referred to Cresson Springs as a "...delightful summer resort immediately on the line of the Central Pennsylvania Railroad, located on the summit of the Allegheny Mountains, 2,300 feet above the level of the sea,....." In describing the various attractions of the resort, the ad spoke of the results of careful analyses done by three Philadelphia professors. The ad boasted that, "The water and air at this point possess superior attractions." Andrew Carnegie was a frequent guest at Cresson Springs, as were others from the Pittsburgh area who could afford such a respite. Although popular, Cresson Springs and other resorts that did not afford immediate access to a body of water of sufficient size for fishing, swimming and boating held far less appeal than resorts that did. Accessibility to water, whether ocean, lake or stream, seemed to be a desired prerequisite for those who frequented resorts and retreats of the late nineteenth century.

Life in the Victorian era afforded the average, working-class family few luxuries. For those of more substantial means luxuries of a constantly expanding variety were readily available. Both foreign and domestic producers flooded the marketplace with new and improved products faster than retailers could offer them to the public. As a result the mail-order industry witnessed unprecedented growth. Specialty stores and private suppliers who catered only to the wealthy also became far more numerous. It was increasingly easier for the rich to separate themselves from the middle class and the poor.

Andrew Carnegie's "Gospel of Wealth," an essay published in 1889, discussed the inequities created by a free enterprise economic system. Carnegie, who undoubtedly had mastered such a system, asserted that those who profit most from free enterprise had an obligation to use the power and influence of their profits for the public good. By doing so they would, at least to some degree, reduce the overall inequities of the system and thus reduce the inequities of life within such a system. This line of thought was not well received by other industrial and business leaders. His was not the prevailing thought of the day. Such sentiments would win wider appeal in a later more benevolent era.

During the Victorian era the privileged and wealthy had no reason to feel shame or guilt for what they had already acquired and their potential for future acquisitions. In America, the land of equal opportunity, a man could and should gain for himself all that he could; it had become the American way. The business of America was business, competition was healthy for business, and what was healthy for business was healthy for America. As a result of competition there were bound to be winners and losers. Along the continuum of winners and losers one could reasonably expect to find industrialists and capitalists who powered industry with their money, daring and ingenuity at one end. They had earned the right to live as opulently as they could afford. That opulence was an outward symbol of their success, and one should be proud of his successes. At the other end there was a working class that powered industry with their brawn, blood and sweat. Workers were maintained as economically as possible. They were as expendable as any other commodity that industry required. The working class lived on the edge of poverty, and their limited-opportunity way of life was seen as a natural by-product of an industrialized society.

Benjamin Ruff saw the potential of the abandoned Western Reservoir, if properly developed and marketed. He struck a deal for the purchase of the dam, the reservoir and the land around it with Congressman Reilly. The agreed upon price for the transaction was

$2,000, which was $500 less than Reilly had paid for it in 1875. Ruff was speculating that with the proper amenities, he could turn this abandoned property into a first-class resort. He wanted to attract the attention and gain the support of those who could afford to get away to a mountain retreat.

It is not known exactly when or where Ruff and Reilly agreed on the terms for the sale of Ruff's property in Cambria County. Discussions were held and

Benjamin Ruff was the founder and first president of the South Fork Fishing and Hunting Club. When local concern over the project in South Fork increased, Ruff assured all that they had nothing to fear from his venture.

The Pittsburgh industrialists who were attracted to the mountain retreat being organized by Benjamin Ruff included such wealthy notables as Andrew Carnegie (left) and Henry Clay Frick (right). By the time they became members of the South Fork Fishing and Hunting Club, they were two of the richest, most influential and powerful men in America.

terms were probably set prior to the spring of 1879, since the South Fork Fishing and Hunting Club was incorporated on May 19, 1879. It is difficult to imagine that Ruff would have sought members and prepared a Charter of Incorporation unless he had reasonable certainty that he could gain title to the property in South Fork.

As Ruff set out to sell shares in his South Fork Fishing and Hunting Club, he had to go no further than Pittsburgh and neighboring Allegheny City. There he quickly found fifteen men of means who were willing to purchase shares in his vision of what the Western Reservoir could become. Their names are listed as part of the Charter of Incorporation.

From the very title of the corporation, the South Fork Fishing and Hunting Club of Pittsburgh, it was clear that it was their intention to establish a club in South Fork, Cambria County, while retaining the right to conduct their legal affairs in Pittsburgh, Allegheny County. The fact that they were permitted to do so would be the topic of serious question a decade later, since the laws governing the granting of corporation charters in Pennsylvania clearly called for a corporation to be chartered in the county where its place of business was located. In the case of the South Fork Fishing and Hunting Club of Pittsburgh, that would have appeared to be Cambria County, since that was where their major holdings at Lake Conemaugh were located. However, it must be noted that in May 1879, the Club did indeed own no land. And since all of the members, to a man, were from Pittsburgh or Allegheny City, it is not difficult to imagine that they could have viewed Pittsburgh and thus Allegheny County as their place of business. Even after the Club was established, the "business" affairs of the Club were transacted from the office of E. A. Myers, the Club Secretary, located at 49 Fifth Avenue, Pittsburgh.

An application for a charter for the South Fork Fishing and Hunting Club of Pittsburgh was filed on November 15, 1879 in the Court of Common Pleas No. 1 of Allegheny County, Pennsylvania, the county seat of which is Pittsburgh. Howard Hartley, one of the original members of the Club appeared before Thomas Leggett, a Notary Public, that same day to have the application notarized for presentation to the Court. This application was recorded in Allegheny County Charter Book Volume Six, starting on page 232.

To the Honorable, the Judges of the said Court:
The undersigned petitioners, Citizens of the Commonwealth of Pennsylvania, having associated ourselves together under the provisions of the Act of the General Assembly entitled "An Act for the Incorporation and regulation of certain Corporations," approved April 29th, A.D. 1874, and having made the following Certification of organization as "The South Fork Fishing and Hunting Club of Pittsburgh," do respectfully pray your Honorable Court to approve the same and order the recording thereof and to declare that the undersigned persons and their associates and successors shall be a body corporate under said Articles of Association, in accordance with the above entitled Act of Assembly, and we will ever pray, &c.

C. A. Carpenter	Howard Hartley
D. R. Euwer	Wm. S. Dunn
W. F. Fundenberg	H. C. Frick
B. F. Ruff	A. V. Holmes

Due notice of publication was made in two Pittsburgh papers regarding the petition of the South Fork Fishing and Hunting Club of Pittsburgh. Those papers were the Post and the *Commercial Gazette*. That same day Benjamin Ruff, Howard Hartley, and A. V. Holmes, all three members of the South Fork Fishing and Hunting Club of Pittsburgh, appeared before the Recorder of Deeds for Allegheny County, Ralph J. Richardson, to have their charter recorded. Two days later, Judge Edwin H. Stowe of the Court of Common Pleas of Allegheny County issued the following regarding the petition of the representatives of the South Fork Fishing and Hunting Club of Pittsburgh:

And now to wit: November 17th, 1879, the within petition and certificate of Organization having been presented in Open Court and due proof of the notice by publication required by the Act of Assembly entitled "An Act to provide for the incorporation of certain Corporations," approved April 29th, 1874, having been made and the said Certification of Organization having been perused and examined by the undersigned Law Judge, and the same having been found to be in proper form and within the purposes named in the first class specified by the second section of said Act of Assembly, and the same appearing to be lawful and not injurious to the community, it is ordered and decreed that the said Charter is hereby approved and that, upon the recording of the same and this order, the subscribers thereto and their Associates and successors shall be a Corporation perpetually for the purposes and upon the terms therein stated.

The above statement from Judge Stowe was formally recorded on November 18, 1879, and attested to by B. F. Kennedy, the prothonotary for Allegheny County. The Charter of Incorporation for the South Fork Fishing and Hunting Club of Pittsburgh, containing eight separate articles, was duly approved and recorded in accord with the judge's order issued on November 17, 1879.

CHARTER OF INCORPORATION

First.   The name and title of the organization shall be the "South-Fork Fishing and Hunting Club of Pittsburgh," incorporated under and in pursuance of the provisions of an act of General Assembly of Pennsylvania, approved April 29, 1874, entitled "An Act, etc."

Second.   This association shall have for its object the protection and propagation of game and game fish, and the enforcement of all laws of this State against the unlawful killing or wounding of the same.

Third.   This association shall have its place of business in the city of Pittsburgh, county of Allegheny, State of Pennsylvania.

Fourth.   This association shall, as such, exist perpetually from the date of its incorporation.

Fifth.   The capital stock of this association shall be ten thousand dollars, divided into one hundred shares of the value of one hundred dollars each.

Sixth.   The names and residences of the subscribers hereto, with the number and value of the shares held by each, are as follows:

Name	Residence	Shares	Value
B. F. Ruff	Pittsburgh	8	$ 800
F. H. Sweet	Pittsburgh	2	$ 200
Chas. J. Clarke	Pittsburgh	2	$ 200
Thomas Clarke	Pittsburgh	2	$ 200
W. F. Fundenberg	Pittsburgh	2	$ 200
Howard Hartley	Pittsburgh	2	$ 200
H. C. Yager	Pittsburgh	2	$ 200
J. B. White	Pittsburgh	2	$ 200
H. C. Frick	Pittsburgh	6	$ 600
E. A. Meyers	Pittsburgh	2	$ 200
C. C. Hussey	Pittsburgh	2	$ 200
D. R. Euwer	Allegheny	2	$ 200
C. A. Carpenter	Allegheny	2	$ 200
W. S. Dunn	Pittsburgh	2	$ 200
W. L. McClintock	Pittsburgh	2	$ 200
A. V. Holmes	Pittsburgh	2	$ 200

Seventh.   The number of Directors shall be five and their names and residences for the first year are: C. C. Hussey, Pittsburgh; W. S. Dunn, Pittsburgh; C. A. Carpenter, Pittsburgh; Howard Hartley, Pittsburgh; W. F. Fundenburg, Pittsburgh.

Eighth.   The officers of this association selected for the first year, with their residences are as follows: President, B. F. Ruff, Pittsburgh; Secretary, E. A. Meyers, Pittsburgh; Treasurer, W. L. McClintock, who are to serve until the next annual election.

As noted in the charter, 100 shares of stock were initially available, each of which had a value of $100, for a total capitalization of $10,000.00. Ruff held eight of the 42 shares initially sold, and Henry Clay Frick held six. The other fourteen charter members of the Club each owned two shares. It is interesting to note that by 1889, when the roster of the Club's membership contained 61 names, only five of the original sixteen members were still Club members. They were, C. J. Clarke, H. C. Frick, E. A. Meyers, W. S. Dunn, and W. L. McClintock.

Just a little over a year after the Charter of Incorporation was approved, the members of the South Fork Fishing and Hunting Club acted to double their capital stock and make provisions for future development. Their formal application for an amendment was presented to the Court of Common Pleas Number One of Allegheny County for the March 1881 term. This application had been approved at a formal meeting of the South Fork Fishing and Hunting Club of Pittsburgh, held at their office on Fifth Avenue in Pittsburgh, on November 29, 1880 at 7:30 P.M.

In their application, recorded in Allegheny County Charter Book Volume 6 page 452, their stated rationale for the amendment was, "...that under its charter the capital being limited it cannot receive new members or carry out the purposes for which it was created unless it be allowed to increase its capital stock or membership." The amendment as proposed and approved by the membership would allow the Club to immediately expand its capital stock by an additional one hundred shares, each share having a value of $100, as established under the terms of the original Charter of Incorporation. The amendment would also, if approved, allow the Club future capital stock expansion up to four hundred shares. On March 19, 1881, Judge Collier of Allegheny County formally approved the amendment.

Annual dues for membership in the Club were initially $25. For the last two years that dues were collected, 1888 and 1889, the annual rate was $50. At the direction of the Board of Directors notices for the payment of annual dues were sent to members announcing the current amount of the annual dues and the date by which payment was to be received.

With their Charter of Incorporation approved, the Club was ready to begin securing a deed to their property near South Fork, Pennsylvania. On January 17, 1880, John Reilly and his wife Anna, who lived in Altoona, which is in Blair County, appeared before Blair County Alderman, B. F. Rose to "acknowledge their Indenture," for the sale of their property in Cambria County to the South Fork Fishing and Hunting Club of Pittsburgh. (An indenture is an agreement to sell which becomes the deed of the buyer once recorded in the county where the property is located.) According to the indenture, the Reillys had already received the $2,000 that was to be paid for the property.

Formal transfer of the property did not take place until March 15, 1880, when the deed was recorded in Cambria County. When the property was transferred from Reilly, it was titled to the "South Fork HUNTING and FISHING Club of Pittsburgh," instead of the South Fork FISHING and HUNTING Club of Pittsburgh, which was the correct name of the corporation. This property transaction is recorded in Cambria County *Deed Book* Volume 43, beginning on page 319. It conveyed a parcel of ground containing 500 acres and 54 perches. (A perch equals one square rod of land. A rod equals 16.5 linear feet. There are 160 square perches in an acre.) On March 2, 1880, the Reillys again appeared before Alderman Rose to complete a second indenture, which corrected the name of the South Fork Fishing and Hunting Club of Pittsburgh. For this correction the Club paid a consideration of one dollar. As with the first deed, it was recorded in Cambria County *Deed Book* Volume 43. It begins on page 322.

This is the handwritten entry marker for the initial deed between the Reilly's and the South Fork Fishing and Hunting Club.

This notice was sent to Henry Clay Frick for the 1887 season; the last year that the annual dues were $25.

These receipts were provided to Henry Clay Frick for the payment of his 1887 and 1888 dues.

In all the South Fork Fishing and Hunting Club was involved in nine land purchases. The last purchase was made on January 20, 1887. At that time the Club bought a parcel of ground measuring 4 acres and 128 perches from Colonel Elias J. Unger, a member of the Club who also owned adjoining properties. In 1889, Colonel Unger was the President of the South Fork Fishing and Hunting Club. The total land holdings of the Club, including the lake, never exceeded 600 acres.

The first order of business associated with the development of the old reservoir site was the repair of the dam. With the exception of the removal of the five two-foot cast iron pipes that ran through the base, nothing remarkable had been done to the dam since the 1862 break. The section of the dam that had been damaged in that year, approximately two hundred feet at the very center of the dam, accounted for more than twenty percent of the dam's total length, which was slightly more than 931 feet. Such a repair was no small undertaking and demanded at least the same care and attention afforded the construction of the original dam. As the president of the Club, Benjamin Ruff was charged with the responsibility for seeing to these repairs.

Without the body of water the dam was designed to hold back, the Club would have nothing more to offer its members than other mountain retreats such as Cresson Springs. Lake Conemaugh, as the Club named it, was to be the centerpiece of their resort. Boating of all manner, fishing, and swimming were among the most enticing of the pleasurable pursuits that awaited Club members, their families and guests. All of these activities required a lake, and if there was no dam there would be no lake.

The lake that Ruff needed for his South Fork Fishing and Hunting Club did not need to be nearly as large as that proposed in the original design for the Western Reservoir. Initially, his plan was to reduce the total size of the man-made lake. To accomplish this he planned to lower the overall height of the existing dam and cut the spillway down to provide a means for excess water to run off. Ruff quickly learned that cutting the spillway down was all but impossible, because it had been cut into the solid rock surface of the hillside to which the eastern end of the dam had been attached. He opted to leave the spillway as it was. By doing so the dam could be and ultimately was filled to its originally intended capacity.

Even though he was not able to lower the level of the spillway, Ruff went ahead with his plans to cut down the top surface of the dam to widen the carriage road that traversed it. Ruff and others agreed that one of the more impressive views of the Lake was from the breast of the dam. Club members generally came to South Fork by train and were then chauffeured to the club house or a private cottage by carriage. The view of the lake from the breast of the dam was magnificent and would create a memorable first impression. The original width of the top of the dam was as narrow as ten feet at spots. So that wagons and carriages could pass each other along the breast of the dam, it was widened to at least twenty feet and in some spots as much as thirty feet. The increased width of the dam was achieved by cutting the level of the dam down approximately two to three feet. By original design the bottom of the spillway had been ten feet lower than the top of the breast of the dam. Without an equal reduction in the level of the existing spillway or the installation of another spillway, cutting the level of the breast down two or three feet, reduced the effectiveness of the spillway to prevent water from overtopping the dam by twenty to thirty percent.

The general public first became aware of renewed interest in the Western Reservoir as a result of a story that appeared in the *Johnstown Tribune* on October 14, 1879. In that edition it was reported that there were rumors to the effect that the "Western Game and Fish Association of Pittsburgh" was considering the old Western Reservoir as a possible site for a summer resort. Although there was no organization by that name, the rumor was obviously true, but the group considering the site was the South Fork Fishing and Hunting Club of Pittsburgh. This was the first of many times that the *Tribune* and other papers misstated the name of the Club. The following day, a brief ad appeared in the *Tribune*, calling for men to begin the work of repairing the dam.

WANTED—FIFTY MEN to work on the Dam on South Fork of Conemaugh—the Old Reservoir. Inquire of DANIEL KAINE, Contractor of the Work.

Ruff selected Edward Pearson, who worked for Haney & Company, a freight hauling firm from Pittsburgh, to be the site foreman at the dam. Daniel Kaine was retained as the project contractor. Neither Ruff nor Pearson had any engineering experience of which to speak. Yet they had an anxious desire to get started. Work began even before the land was formally transferred on March 15, 1880. There were reports that some initial work was done to accomplish repairs to the dam during November and December 1879. Heavy rains during late December were reported to have caused some damage to the dam on Christmas Day of 1879, particularly in the area of the washout from 1862. Work was suspended until the following spring, when a period of heavy rain again washed out repairs that had recently been made.

The work of repairing the dam was not done under the careful and professional eye on an engineer. Ruff had engaged a civil engineer from Pittsburgh, Nathan McDowell, but his onsight participation was very limited. There is but one reference placing him in South Fork. That was during the visit made by officials of the Cambria Iron Company. No care was taken to puddle the area being repaired, as had been the practice when the dam was constructed. The openings where the sluice pipes had been removed years before were simply filled in. Hay and branches were placed on the outside of the dam surfaces and stones were used to hold them in place to prevent leaks and seeping. Almost any manner of fill available, even several wagonloads of manure, was used to close the gap between the existing sides of the dam left after the 1862 break. An earthen dam is only as strong as its weakest point.

Renewed interest in the all but abandoned Western Reservoir and the work of rebuilding it awakened old concerns regarding the structural integrity and relative safety of the dam. The potential consequences of a break that would send the water of the reservoir down the valley to Johnstown were virtually unthinkable to many. Folks who had lived through the break in 1862 reminded themselves that that incident caused little damage. However, as work began and continued at the Old Reservoir, local concerns grew.

Few people, if any, feared a break in the dam at South Fork more than Daniel J. Morrell did. This was understandable since no one had more to lose, at least in a material sense, than Morrell and the Cambria Iron Company. Although centered in Johnstown, the various facilities of Cambria Iron, which included mines, a railroad system, forest lands, offices, stores and various mills, dotted the valley of the Conemaugh. The industrial complex of the Cambria Iron Company was valued at an estimated $50 million when Benjamin Ruff began to establish the South Fork Fishing and Hunting Club. To one unfamiliar with the topography of the land between South Fork and Johnstown, it may have been difficult to see or understand the relationship between the ventures of Benjamin Ruff and Daniel Morrell. To one familiar with that topography, which Daniel Morrell most assuredly was, the relationship was extremely close and beyond question.

The privacy of the work being done near South Fork during the spring of 1880 was troublesome to Morrell. It was troublesome because he had no idea what was happening and thus no inclination of the possible effect the venture of the South Fork Fishing and Hunting Club would have on the Conemaugh Valley. On a more personal front, Morrell would have been troubled because he was not used to being in the dark, particularly in

matters regarding Johnstown and the surrounding area. If ever a man earned the nickname "City Father," it was Daniel Johnson Morrell.

In addition to his business and industrial interests, Morrell also had political aspirations. Of particular interest to Morrell were tariffs that protected American manufactures. To further those interests, he ran for and won a seat in Congress, serving from 1867 to 1871. After his time in Congress, and in recognition of his mastery and leadership in the iron and steel industry, he was elected president of the American Iron and Steel Institute. Even though his interests ranged far beyond Johnstown and the Cambria Iron Company, neither was ever far from his thoughts. Morrell realized the importance of the relationship between the future of the Cambria Iron Company and the future of Johnstown, and he was protective of both. He had a genuine interest in the town and could influence everything that happened in and around Johnstown.

His presence in Johnstown was large by any standard. He stood slightly under six feet tall and his weight was probably in excess of 200 pounds. If he favored something, such as the iron business, he really favored it. He gave it his strength, his energy, and his undivided attention. If he opposed something, such as the abuse of alcohol, it received no less of his strength, energy, and attention. By 1880, Morrell had established himself, the Cambria Iron Company, and Johnstown through a tough, no nonsense approach. It should have come as no small surprise to anyone who knew him, that he would be concerned about the goings on at South Fork. Unsatisfied with information shared through hearsay and rumor, Morrell sent John Fulton, his trusted assistant, to South Fork in November 1880 to inspect the work at the reservoir site and report back. Fulton, who had training and experience in matters of engineering and geology, was a prudent choice for such an assignment. His interests in Johnstown and the Cambria Iron Company were second only to those of Morrell. Upon Morrell's death, it was Fulton who became the general manager of the Cambria Iron Company in Johnstown.

Once in South Fork, Fulton met with at least three representatives of the Club. They included Colonel Elias J. Unger, C. A. Carpenter, and Nathan M. McDowell. Colonel Unger, who later became president and manager of the South Fork Fishing and Hunting Club was not a charter member. He was one of the earlier members who was still on the Club's membership roster at the time of the flood. ("Colonel" was an unearned title, as Unger did not serve in the military.) C. A. Carpenter was a charter member of the Club, but by 1889 was no longer listed as a member. He was a Pennsylvania Railroad freight agent.

Nathan M. McDowell, the civil engineer from Pittsburgh retained by Ruff, was supposedly there to inspect the dam site and make recommendations concerning the repair work. Critics would later speculate that McDowell's only purpose was to rebuff questions and counter any concerns raised by Fulton. Some accounts indicate that an assistant named W. A. Fellows may have accompanied Fulton. Particulars of the inspection tour are not known, but through the written report provided by Fulton to Morrell, his findings are clear. John Fulton's initial report, which was provided to Morrell on November 26, 1880, initiated a series of letters between Morrell and Ruff.

John Fulton, the general manager of the Cambria Iron Company in June 1889, held the following letters that had been exchanged by Morrell and Ruff in 1880. Fulton provided the letters along with a brief introductory letter to the *Johnstown Tribune*. They appeared in the June 18, 1889 edition under the headline "OLD CRITICISMS OF THE RESERVOIR."

Letters from Mr. John Fulton
and Hon. D. J. Morrell
dated Over Eight Years Ago—
Faulty Construction Condemned
The following correspondence, furnished by Mr. John Fulton, fully explains itself, and will be read with great interest at this time:

Cambria Iron Company
John Fulton, General Manager
Johnstown, June 15, 1889
To the Editor of the Johnstown Tribune.

Sir: I have been quite busy during the days that have passed since the great calamity that wrecked this part of the Conemaugh Valley.

I have only just learned that some adverse criticisms have been made from an incorrect basis that the writer, in a report, gave his assurance of the stability of the South Fork Dam about the year 1880, at the close of the repairs then being made. Such is not the fact.

I condemned the method of repairs as clearly as I could do so in plain English language. To show this I have copied the original report, with the criticisms of Colonel Ruff on my report; also the letter of the late Hon. D. J. Morrell, General Manager of the Cambria Iron Company, at the time these reports were made.

I have been unable to put my hands on the reports of A. J. Whitney, Esq., who was at the time resident Engineer of the Pennsylvania Canal Company, and who is an expert in these matters.

The material facts, however, are given in my report. It is well to understand, in this time of excitement, that the main cause leading to the breaking of the dam was the choking by lumber, brush, and logs of the overflow on the north side of the dam, which was originally seventy feet wide. This caused the water to flow over the central portion of the dam—the portion that had been repaired—making the break that has caused such a terrible disaster to the Conemaugh Valley.

After I had submitted my report to Mr. Morrell the matter was considered here, and I think it was decided that we had no legal means of arresting the repairs of the dam. I may add that Colonel Unger appreciated the value of the report which I had made, and had very considerable work done afterward in strengthening the part of the bank that had been assumed to be completed.

Very respectfully,   JOHN FULTON

———

JOHNSTOWN, November 26, 1880
Hon. D. J. Morrell, General Manager Cambria Iron Company, Johnstown.

SIR: As you instructed, I met a representative delegation of the "Sportsmen's Association of Western Pennsylvania," at the old reservoir dam fork of the Conemaugh River, two and a half miles southeast of South Fork station, on the Pennsylvania Railroad.

This delegation, consisting of Colonel Unger, C. A. Carpenter, Esq., Secretary of the Board of Directors, and a number of gentlemen, brought with them N. M. McDowell, Esq., C. E., [civil engineer] of Pittsburgh, to examine the dam in company with your engineer.

This dam is seventy feet high and 884 feet long. It was originally constructed by the State authorities, during the canal epoch, as a reservoir for storing water for use during the dry season of boating. It is designed to hold a body of water sixty feet deep, covering about six hundred acres of land, and containing, at an average depth of thirty feet, nearly six thousand millions of gallons of water.

It was built mainly with rocks and faced with earth on its upper or pool slope, and covered with a riprap of stones. About the middle of the dam a cut stone, arched culvert was constructed, in which a large discharge pipe was placed with connections with a wooden bulkhead. On the north end an ample overfall has been cut through the rock, seventy feet wide, to discharge surplus water during rainy seasons.

After the disuse of the reservoir, the wooden bulkhead was burned down and the dam neglected. The consequence was that the water, under its full pressure, with no repairs to dam, found its way through the masonry of the culvert, and the result was the washing out of a triangular notch of the dam, two hundred feet wide at the top and forty feet deep. The resultant flood past South Fork and down the Conemaugh did some damage, the extent of which I have been unable to learn. The break occurred during a time of low water in the streams, which very greatly modified its action.

During the past season the Sportsmen's Association of Western Pennsylvania, which now owns this property, has put a force at work to repair the breach in the dam, so as to raise the water to its maximum hight of sixty feet. The repair force began by placing large rocks in the breach, facing these with hemlock boughs and hay, and covering the whole with earth and shale. The facing of earth is being made with carts, the material dumped down a slope from the line of the top of the dam, thus gravitating the coarsest materials to the lowest depths—just the opposite of the result demanded in this case.

It did not appear to me that this work was being done in a careful and substantial manner, or with the care demanded in a large structure of this kind.

When this work shall be completed to the full section of the old dam, the entire embankment will contain 262,241 cubic yards, or 316,094 gross tons.

The pressure of water—sixty feet deep—on the slope of this dam is 73,782 gross tons. The weight of the dam, is therefore, 4 2/10 times that of the pressure of the water against it.

It is evident, therefore, that the water cannot overturn, or slide, the dam, en masse.

There appear to me two serious elements of danger in this dam: First, the want of a discharge pipe to reduce or take the water out of the dam for needed repairs. Second, the unsubstantial method of repair, leaving a large leak, which appears to be cutting the new embankment.

As the water cannot be lowered, the difficulty arises of reaching the source of the present destructive leaks. At present there is forty feet of water in the dam. When the full head of sixty feet is reached, it appears to me to be only a question of time until the former cutting is repeated. Should this break be made during a seasonal flood it is evident that considerable damage would ensue along the line of the Conemaugh. It is difficult to estimate how disastrous this flood would be, as its force would depend on the size of the breach in the dam with proportional rapidity of discharge. The stability of the dam can only be assured by a thorough overhauling of the present lining on the upper slope, and the construction of an ample discharge pipe to reduce or remove the water to make necessary repairs.

Very respectfully,   JOHN FULTON
General Mining Engineer   Cambria iron Company

NOTE: Fulton mistakenly referred to the Club as the Sportsmen's Association of Western Pennsylvania even after his visit. Although the Sportsmen's Association of Western Pennsylvania was a Pittsburgh organization that did exist at the time and did share some common members with the South Fork Fishing and Hunting Club, they were two distinctly separate entities.

———

PITTSBURGH, Dec. 2, 1880.
Daniel J. Morrell, General manager.
DEAR SIR: have had your favor with report of your engineer for some days, and they would have received attention sooner, but I have been sick. Knowing your large interest in the Conemaugh Valley, I am not surprised that you feel some anxiety, and shall therefore briefly review your engineer's report.

In the first place he was not met by a delegation of the Sportsmen's Association of Western Pennsylvania. It is owned by the South Fork Fishing and Hunting Club.

In the second place he is wrong in saying that the dam was originally built mainly of stone; exactly the reverse being true. The face on the lake was not riprapped, but covered with a slope wall.

In the third place the large arched culvert did not contain a single pipe, but three conduits, and, instead of terminating in a wooden bulkhead, were embraced within the base of a wooden tower, which stood out in the lake, extending above the highest water level, to protect rods from ice and drift, connected with valves on the conduits, by which the flow of water was regulated.

He is in error in saying the burning of the wooden bulkhead was the primary cause of the destruction of the dam. Its destruction by fire, while the dam stood, was simply impossible, and it stood many years afterward, and only has been burned a few years. The dam was destroyed by the arch culvert giving way about the center of the embankment. This danger we have avoided by making it solid throughout. He is grossly in error in saying that it resulted in carrying away a notch two hundred feet long and forty feet deep. The fact is that it swept it clear to the bottom, carrying everything before it, slope wall, embankment, and all the arch but a section of about thirty feet long, embraced in the riprap on the lower side. You can have some idea of its extent when I tell you it took over twenty-one thousand yards of material to fill in. We did not put hemlock boughs and hay on the rock. We put them in the notch, but put more than ten thousand yards of material over them before using the hay, etc.

He objected to our throwing material over the face of our embankment, because the coarser went to the bottom. This is just what we wanted to do, and were putting a riprap of coarse material over our earth face, to protect it from the action of the water direct. We positively deny that there are dangerous leaks in our new work. He makes the amount of water in our lake about 2,000,000 gallons more than it really contains. He says we have ample overfall, also more than four times the weight necessary to resist the pressure it was to sustain. We know we have the first and six times the latter. We consider his conclusions as to our only safe course of no more value than his other assertions. I submit herewith the report of our engineer, feeling certain you and your people are in no danger from our enterprise.

Very respectfully,
B. F. Ruff, President.

———

CAMBRIA IRON COMPANY
JOHNSTOWN, Pa, Dec. 22, 1880
B. F. Ruff, Esq., President South Fork Fishing and
Hunting Club, Pittsburgh,

DEAR SIR: Your esteemed favor of the 2nd inst., with accompanying report of your engineer, Mr. N. M. McDowell, was duly received and handed to our engineer, Mr. John Fulton, for consideration and report.

Mr. Fulton handed me some time since his letter of the 18th, with the communication marked "A," from Mr. A. Whitney, engineer, to which he refers, and also a report made to him by his assistant, Mr. Walter A. Fellows, who had more recently examined the South Fork dam. Pressure of business and absence from home has prevented my sooner writing you. I note your criticism of Mr. Fulton's former report, and judge that in some of his statements he may have been in error, but think that his conclusions in the main were correct.

We do not wish to put any obstructions in the way of your accomplishing your object in the reconstruction of this dam; but we must protest against the erection of a dam at that place, that will be a perpetual menace to the lives and property of those residing in this upper valley of the Conemaugh, from its insecure construction. In my judgement there should have been provided some means by which the water would be let out of the dam in case of trouble, and I think that you will find it necessary to provide an outlet pipe or gate before any engineer would pronounce the job a safe one. If this dam could be securely reconstructed with a safe means of driving off the water in case any weakness manifests itself, I should regard the accomplishment of this work as a very desirable one, and if some arrangement could be made with your Association by which the store of water in this reservoir could be used in time of great drought in the mountains, this Company would be willing to co-operate with you in the work and would contribute liberally toward making the dam absolutely safe.

I herewith return Mr. McDowell's report presuming that you will wish to preserve it.

Yours truly,   D. J. MORRELL
General Manager

The written exchanges between Morrell and Ruff, although brief and to their respective points, clearly indicate the positions of each. Morrell contended that the upper valley of the Conemaugh was in danger, and Ruff totally disagreed. Morrell sought to strike a deal, and Ruff wanted no part of it. Morrell's offers of help, both advisory and financial, were flatly declined, which should not have come as much of a surprise to anyone. The South Fork Fishing and Hunting Club wanted as little contact with the surrounding communities as possible. Why would a club, the members of which were among the wealthiest men in America, accept advice or financial support from the Cambria Iron Company or anyone else for that matter? However, anyone who was even remotely familiar with Daniel J. Morrell and his longstanding presence in the area, should not have been surprised that he tried to form a beneficial relationship with the Club. It was only natural that Morrell wanted information more reliable than rumors and hearsay about a potentially menacing enterprise that threatened Johnstown, its people and their main industry. If there were any additional correspondences between Morrell and Ruff, or if they had any informal meetings is unknown. The Cambria Iron Company did purchase a membership in the South Fork Fishing and Hunting Club. It was purchased in the name of D. J. Morrell.

According to the guest book from the South Fork Fishing and Hunting Club, currently in the hands of the Johnstown Area Heritage Association, Morrell visited the Club on September 7, 1883. Cyrus Elder, the solicitor for the Cambria Iron Company, and Charles H. Read, Morrell's second assistant at Cambria Iron, accompanied him. The guest book is at best a sketchy and incomplete record, as numerous pages have been removed. It is not known if Morrell was a frequent visitor at the Club, but it is unlikely. He did however, have access to the goings on, and his knowledge was based on more than rumor and hearsay. Near the back of the guest book, a list of sixty members was recorded sometime in 1886. D. J. Morrell is listed among the members, even though he had died in August 1885. Following his death, the membership of the Cambria Iron Company was transferred to Cyrus Elder. The Cambria Iron Company held a membership in the Club on May 31, 1889.

Daniel Johnson Morrell died on August 20, 1885 at about 8:00 A.M. at his home on Main Street. The *Johnstown Tribune* carried a brief description of community reaction to Morrell's passing in the Monday, August 24, 1885 edition, which opened with the following paragraph:

The depth of the sorrowful feeling of this community over the passing away of Daniel J. Morrell can scarcely be fathomed. There have been no outward, visible signs of mourning, not even upon the house of mourning itself, for the deceased was an exponent of the tenets of the Friends (Quakers), who frown upon all ostentation; but on every hand there have been quiet evidence of public grief and of private, personal loss. The full realization of our bereavement has not yet come, however. Although Mr. Morrell had been failing for years and gradually withdrawing himself from active participation in the conduct of affairs, we still had him with us; his familiar face was occasionally seen upon the streets, and the feeling of security inspired by his presence remained to the last. The awakening was rude.

Less than four years later, the town and surrounding communities that Morrell cared so much about would face another rude awakening. The concerns he had expressed over the affairs of the South Fork Fishing and Hunting Club became a stark reality on May 31, 1889. His warnings and the offers of assistance that were rebuffed and refused were clear reminders of both his desire and ability to protect Johnstown and the Cambria Iron Company.

By the spring of 1881 Lake Conemaugh was filling and the dam was holding. The resort was ready for the season. The repair work to their dam had reportedly cost the Club a mere $17,000. The initial and possibly the only stocking of Lake Conemaugh attracted considerable attention. On June 4, 1881, the *Johnstown Tribune* carried the following story under the title "Bass for the Reservoir":

> One thousand black bass brought from Lake Erie, were dumped in the "Old Reservoir," near South Fork, yesterday, by Col. E. Unger, and a party of other gentlemen, all belonging to the Western Game and Fish Association. A palace car was chartered for the accommodation of the fish, which were transported in iron tanks, to which were attached air pumps for supplying oxygen. The cost of the fish when safely in the dam was estimated at $750. Only three fish died, one of which was a huge old chap, weighing over three pounds.

In an effort to protect their investment and retain the black bass in their lake, a weir was added across the spillway. This weir was a series of metal screens attached to the wooden piers of the bridge that had been constructed across the spillway. Although these screens did permit water to pass through, they restricted the totally free flow of water over the spillway as did the wooden piers of the bridge. The restrictive effect of the weir was exaggerated when the screens became clogged with debris such as leaves and twigs from the lake. Sometime later several logs were added around the spillway to help prevent debris from clogging the fish weir. Although this addition seemed both purposeful and harmless at the time, it would later become a key point of the controversy surrounding why the South Fork Dam gave way on May 31, 1889.

The *Johnstown Tribune* carried an article titled "Western G. and F. Association (South Fork Fishing and Hunting Club) Branching Out" on March 22, 1881. This article provides an excellent summary of the plans of the Club as it was about to begin its first summer.

> During the spring and summer a hotel-building will be erected for the accommodation of the stockholders who purchased the property, as well as invited guests, and it is anticipated that fishing will prove one of the pleasurable sports in that body of water the coming season, as it has been well stocked from time to time with bass, etc. It is also in contemplation to erect a narrow-gauge railroad from South Fork to the reservoir during the present year.

The railroad spur was never finished, but had the Club survived past 1889, chances are that one would have been completed. The earliest section of the "hotel-building," which became known as the clubhouse, was completed for the summer of 1881. The clubhouse accepted guests for the first time on July 28 of that season. The first guest to register at Lake Conemaugh was John D. Hunt of Pittsburgh. Hunt was not a charter member of the Club, but was an early member who was still listed on the Club's roster in 1886. He was no longer listed as a member in 1889. Little is known of Hunt other than that he was a member of the Club, had served as the Club treasurer for a time, and that he lived in Pittsburgh. And as the writer of the March 22 article anticipated, fishing was indeed a most popular pastime of those who came to Lake Conemaugh. It remained one of the most popular attractions of the Club through the final season of 1888.

Specifics regarding the physical development of the facilities of the South Fork Fishing and Hunting Club are very limited. It is known that construction of various buildings began as early as 1881 and continued through 1888, the last summer season at the Club. It is reasonable and likely to speculate that if the dam had not broken in 1889, new construction would have continued as well as ongoing improvements to the property. In fact, during the spring of 1889, work had begun on a sewer system. A brief note in the April 10, 1889 edition of the *Johnstown Tribune* stated, "The work has begun at the Conemaugh Lake of laying sewers from the cottages down to the breast of the dam. There are about twenty Italians working and a number of country boys."

Research into the physical facilities that existed at Lake Conemaugh prior to the breaking of the dam in 1889 indicates that there were fourteen cottages, a clubhouse, an annex to the clubhouse, and several boathouses along the shore of the lake. Records indicate that there were horses and mules at the lake, as well as a number of wagons and carriages for use by the owners and guests, so there may also have been a barn, a stable and some storage buildings. Today the largest section of the clubhouse, the clubhouse annex, and eight of the original cottages are still standing.

The buildings of the South Fork Fishing and Hunting Club were situated along the southeastern shore of the lake. The boathouses were directly adjacent to the lake, with the cottages, the clubhouse and the clubhouse annex just a short distance back from the lakefront. Al-

This is a reproduction of the initial entries from the original guest book of the South Fork Fishing and Hunting Club. The original book is currently part of the collection of the Johnstown Flood Museum of the Johnstown Area Heritage Association.

though the exact locations of a barn, a stable or other storage buildings has not been determined, it is believed that they were situated further back from the lake, possibly in a wooded area behind the row of cottages. A service road ran behind the clubhouse and the ten cottages southeast of the clubhouse. There were boardwalks, floating and stable docks, a number of stone and dirt paths, a few springhouses and a number of privies scattered among the cottages. The paths ran among the cottages and wooded areas behind them. The boardwalk started at the clubhouse and ran southeast in front of the ten cottages in that direction. The largest section of

boathouses was situated in front of the clubhouse. There is reason to believe that there were also at least two sections of boathouses south of the clubhouse and one section north of the clubhouse.

The clubhouse was the largest and most prominent of the structures at Lake Conemaugh. It is believed that the clubhouse was built in two sections. The first, a rather small cottage-like structure, was completed and ready for guests in 1881. The much larger section was joined to the original clubhouse and was connected with a grand porch that fronted the lake. The larger portion of the clubhouse was completed prior to the 1885 sea-

The South Fork Fishing and Hunting Club In 1889

This plot plan of the South Fork Fishing and Hunting Club shows the holdings and principle features of the Club and their relative locations in 1889. It is not necessarily to scale, nor does it represent the actual shapes of the various structures and fixtures.

(Adapted from the Conjectural 1889 Site Plan of the Historical Structures Report of the National Park Service)

This is a plot plan of the facilities of the South Fork Fishing and Hunting Club.

This view of the clubhouse shows both the original section, which was completed for the 1881 season (far left) and the much larger section, which was ready for the season of 1885. The clubhouse was the centerpiece of the Club's facilities.

Today only the larger portion of the clubhouse is still standing. It is listed on the National Register of Historic Sites.

son and increased the number of guest rooms from seventeen to forty-seven.

In an article that appeared in on June 25, 1889 in the *Johnstown Tribune*, W. Y. Boyer, the superintendent of the lake and grounds of the Club described events at the dam on May 31, 1889 just prior to and following the breaking of the dam. Boyer had contacted the *Era*, a newspaper in Salem, Ohio, by letter and shared his story. In his account he included the following description of the facilities of the South Fork Fishing and Hunting Club.

Perhaps it would interest you to know what we had in the way of a summer resort. In the first place there is a fine clubhouse or hotel with forty-seven bedrooms, well furnished; a nicely furnished office, a dining-room 40 x 60 feet, a well-furnished kitchen, bakery, cooling-rooms, milk room, vegetable room, and everything to be found in a well-furnished hotel. We also have sixteen cottages, in one of which lived

Cottage #1 is no longer standing. It was the cottage that was furthest from the clubhouse along the boardwalk. Today, the only remnants are a few stone steps and foundation stones.

four families and in another two families, two fine steam yachts; four sailing boats, and about fifty sailing canoes and row boats. Of course none of them are of any use up here now.

Although his description seems to be generally accurate in character and intent, he overestimated the size of the rooms. The main portion, and definitely the larger portion, of the clubhouse is still standing today. The largest room in the existing clubhouse structure measures 26 x 38 feet. The smaller original clubhouse structure was destroyed by fire in the 1930s. Also, there were almost certainly never more than fourteen cottages at Lake Conemaugh.

Accounts as to the number of cottages built at Lake Conemaugh, when they were built, and who owned them vary greatly. As noted earlier, the Club succeeded to a marked degree in keeping its business private and out of the view of the locals. As a result, little is known about the singular or collective history of the cottages at Lake Conemaugh.

By almost any standard, these were far more than cottages. Although there is no single architectural style that dominated, their design and construction represent the good taste and comfortable style to which the Club members would have been accustomed. There is some evidence, through land deeds, that the land on which the various cottages were built was leased, not sold, to the cottage owners by the Club. There is also reason to believe that the Club may have built some of the cottages as a way of expanding the facilities of the early clubhouse. Notations in the Club's guest book indicate that certain parties were put up in cottages upon their arrival at Lake Conemaugh. Today, eight of the original cottages are still standing along what was once called "cottage row."

The Suydam cottage was built by Moses Bedell Suydam. Suydam was the founder of M. B. Suydam & Company of Pittsburgh. The company manufactured white lead and a variety of paints, oils, and varnishes. Shortly after the close of World War II, M. B. Suydam and Company became a subsidiary of Pittsburgh Plate Glass Company. In 1889, M. B. Suydam was listed as an active member of the Club.

Maxwell K. Moorhead, the man who may have built and owned cottage #3 was a Civil War veteran who established himself in Pittsburgh and Soho in the iron and steel business. His principal business, Moorhead and Company, was purchased by Pittsburgh Iron and Steel

This cottage is most often referred to as the Suydam Cottage. In this photograph, the giant porches that surrounded the living quarters on three sides are clearly visible. So too is the portion of the boardwalk that ran from the clubhouse southeast to the ten cottages in that direction.

This rare interior view was taken in the main room of the Suydam cottage. Notice the ornate stained glass window built into the chimney of the fireplace.

Although there have been modifications both to the exterior and interior of the Suydam cottage, it still retains the elegant, yet simple, charm of the cottages of Lake Conemaugh.

Manufacturers in the mid-1890s. He also served for a time as president of the Monongahela Navigation Company, and as a director of several other Pittsburgh companies. Moorhead died in 1897. At the time of the flood in 1889, he was listed as a member of the Club. As noted previously, he was actively involved in the original construction of the dam at South Fork, working with the construction company owned in part by his father.

Cottage #4 was known for years as the Knox cottage, since Philander C. Knox was believed to have been the owner. Recent research into the history of this cottage proves that in fact it belonged to the James W. Brown family. J. W. Brown had established himself in the iron and steel business of Pittsburgh through his associations with Hussey, Howe and Company Steel Works Ltd. and the Crucible Steel Company. He was also a trustee of Dollar Savings Bank. Brown was elected to the United States House of Representatives and served from 1903 to 1905. In 1889 he was listed as an active member of the South Fork Fishing and Hunting Club.

Cottage number six was the cottage of the Clarke family. Charles J. Clarke was one of the original members of the Club, having bought two shares. When the

South Fork Fishing and Hunting Club was organized, Clarke was among the most influential men in Pittsburgh. It surprised no one that he was offered shares and took the opportunity to join such a venture. Charles Clarke had entered the family transportation business after completing college in 1852. Following the death of his father he became the president of what was then known as Clarke & Company. After early retirement from his business interests, Clarke engaged himself in a number of philanthropic endeavors, several of which centered on educational opportunities for women.

The guest book from the Club indicates that the Clarkes were frequent visitors to Lake Conemaugh. There were six children in the Clarke family, but none appears to have enjoyed their time at Lake Conemaugh any more than the second son, Louis Semple Clarke. Although never named as such, Clarke was the unofficial Club photographer. He was responsible for creating more photographic views of the Club, its facilities and the activities of members and guests than anyone else.

Cottage number nine is still standing today, although it has undergone significant changes both inside and out. Although there is no credible evidence to prove owner-

This view shows cottages one through five (from left to right) of cottage row. Cottage #4 was the Brown cottage. Shown in this view on the extreme right, is cottage #5 that was demolished sometime after 1920. Also visible is a portion of the boardwalk, a section of boathouses and one of the Club's many rowboats.

Cottage number six was the Clarke family cottage. In this scene the young Louis Semple Clarke is seen sitting along the shore of Lake Conemaugh in front of the family house.

Cottage number seven (left) was destroyed sometime between 1920 and 1955, while cottage number eight (right) was destroyed prior to 1907, because it does not appear on local maps drawn at that time. Today a church occupies this site.

This panoramic view shows cottages six through ten and a portion of the clubhouse. Also featured are several of the Club's boats.

This is the only known view of cottages 12 through 14. It was a shot taken of one of the neighboring farmers, which shows the cottages from across Lake Conemaugh.

ship, it was long assumed that Robert Pitcairn at one time owned this cottage. Pitcairn, a native of Scotland, was the superintendent of the Pennsylvania Railroad's Pittsburgh Division. His signature appears numerous times in the guest book of the Club. It is not known if this meant that he stayed in the clubhouse, or if he was simply signing in.

Because of their desire for privacy while the Club existed and because of the Club's rapid demise after May 31, 1889, there is very little credible history of the South Fork Fishing and Hunting Club. Much of what is known is the product of imagination, rumor and pure conjecture. On occasion, and these were rare occasions, guests were invited to the Club. Usually these were people of means who were above sharing their pleasurable experiences with the press or locals. What the locals saw of the Club, its members and their activities, was what could be seen from a distance. More often than not locals attracted to the grounds and feeder streams were seen as unwelcome intruders. Those who owned property that adjoined the lands of the Club had some level of access, but they too were clearly informed that they were not members and did not have the rights and privileges of members or their invited guests. When trespassing and poaching were suspected, the management of the Club often made threats. Even though they were seldom carried out, such threats did serve notice on the locals that privacy was a luxury Club members were not willing to sacrifice.

Although rare, there were occasions when visitors were invited to Lake Conemaugh and the press was allowed a glimpse of life at the Club. One such event was reported in the *Johnstown Tribune* on June 4, 1884. The story was titled "Sportsmen at the Old Reservoir."

The Sportsmen Association of Pittsburgh were yesterday the guests of the South Fork Fishing and Hunting Club. Lunch was served to seventy persons about 2 o'clock. Afterward there was a shooting match, in which seventeen crack shots participated. Three hundred and fifty birds had been provided, and about two hundred and forty were killed. The match for a silver cup was won by a man named Carpenter, who shot at twenty birds and killed nineteen. A man named Crawford killed eighteen out of twenty. Several others killed eleven and twelve. In the handicap match, in which clay pigeons were used, D. C. Hostetter shot at ten and broke them all. To-day there was to be a glass-ball contest for a silver medal.

If the South Fork Fishing and Hunting Club was established to provide members, their families and guests an opportunity to escape and relax, it most definitely achieved its intended purpose. Although not nearly as opulent as other more upscale resorts of that era, the Club afforded a host of leisure activities in a relaxed, and decidedly private setting.

One of the richest sources of what may be termed the lifestyle of the South Fork Fishing and Hunting Club is the photograph collection of Louis Semple Clarke. Clarke was thirteen when his father bought two shares in the venture at South Fork being proposed by Benjamin Ruff. In the spring of 1889, Louis S. Clarke, then 22 years old, became a member of the Club himself. The photographs taken by Clarke during his family's frequent visits to Lake Conemaugh were stored away for nearly a hundred years. A granddaughter, Mrs. Virginia Anthony Soule of New Hampshire, discovered the collection of pictures among some family albums.

There was great interest in the photographs as they provided a glimpse into life at the Club and broke a cloak of secrecy that had surrounded the Club for nearly a century. Charles Guggenheim, who had produced an Oscar-winning documentary on the Johnstown Flood, was asked to produce a longer version of the film. He became aware of the photographs and in his search for more material he contacted Mrs. Soule who made the collection available. The photographs have also been generously shared with both the National Park Service and the Johnstown Area Heritage Association.

Even though Mr. Clarke made only meager notes on his individual photographs, they are collectively among the most reliable sources of information about the South Fork Fishing and Hunting Club. The photographs that follow, the vast majority of which are from the Clarke-Soule collection, all but speak for themselves.

According to the "South Fork F. & H. Club Rules and Regulations," published in 1885 or later since it refers to the "new part of the Club House," there were ten rules and regulations for members and visitors. They were as follows:

In this photograph (Left) from the Clarke-Soule collection, Louis is sitting in the lower left corner with the shutter-release bulb from his camera in his hand.

(Below) Several pictures in the Clarke-Soule collection show groups dressed in costumes. Based on these pictures it is assumed that small pageants, plays and some informal summer theater were part of the activities which visitors to the Club enjoy either as active participants or part of the audience.

Many visitors to the Club enjoyed walking through the wooded areas that surrounded the lake. In this scene, taken while wild flowers were in bloom, each of the ladies is holding a bouquet. A picnic lunch was often part of members' sojourns as they enjoyed the grounds around Lake Conemaugh.

Judging from the various pictures in the Clarke-Soule collection, the unofficial dress code at the Club was rather formal and represented the best fashion of the day. Agnes Clarke, the youngest sister of the photographer, is in the center.

(Below) One of the favorite spots around the lake was the spillway. Cut into the hillside to which the eastern end of the dam was anchored, water that flowed out of the dam cascaded over a series of natural rock ledges before flowing into the Little Conemaugh.

Although most attractive to the younger guests, Lake Conemaugh provided ample opportunities for swimming. Notice the makeshift diving board elevated on a sawhorse.

Music was part of the entertainment offered to members and guests. In this picture, a four-piece band is entertaining guests seated on the steps of the clubhouse. It is not known if the musicians in this picture were guests performing for other guests, or musicians invited to the Club to entertain. The young man in the center of the picture seems to be holding out his hat to receive something from one of the young ladies seated on the steps. This may suggest that the musicians are playing for tips. Note the boathouses visible directly behind the musicians.

Many of the activities at Lake Conemaugh brought the various families and their guests together. There were also ample opportunities for families to enjoy the quiet solitude of their own company, particularly if they happened to own one of the fourteen cottages. In this scene the Brown family is shown on the porch of their cottage, which was completed in 1888.

The very name of the club bespeaks the popularity of fishing. Even though Lake Conemaugh had been stocked, at least once with 1000 black bass, many of the Club's anglers preferred pursuing native fish in the various feeder streams that emptied into the lake.

At Lake Conemaugh one could enjoy a ride in one of the Club's two steam powered yachts. These yachts were known as the Captain Eads *and the* Mountain Belle. *The man standing to the left in the sailing outfit is Louis Semple Clarke.*

This is one of four large sailboats available to Club members.

The facilities at Lake Conemaugh were available year round. Here a young man is shown sailing across the frozen lake.

Self-powered or rowing boats of a variety of sizes and designs were also available to Club visitors.

1. The Club House being especially for the accomodation of members, guests can only be furnished with rooms at such times and for such periods as will not interfere with members desiring accomodations.

2. Any member in arrears for assessments or fines, or for bills rendered against him for repairing property of the Club injured by him, for the space of sixty days after notice of the same shall have been mailed to his address, shall stand suspended of the privileges of the Club until all arrearages are paid.

3. Members entertaining guests (visit family and friends) at the Club House or on the premises of the Club, shall be held responsible for the conduct of such person or persons, and for any damage done by them to the property of members, or of the Club.

4. No non-members, except families of members of the Club shall have the privileges of the Club more than three separate times, and for more than ten days altogether during any one year, unless quartered in a private cottage.

5. A member's wife, parent, unmarried children, and any permanent resident of the household, shall be entitled to member's rates. Unmarried members under these rules shall be considered heads of families.

6. Fishing, shooting, or playing of any kind of games on Sunday, strictly prohibited, under penalty of fifty dollars.

7. No family, whether guests' or members', shall occupy more than one front room in the Club House, unless occupying four or more rooms in all, when they shall be entitled to two front rooms.

8. No bill or charge will be made against any except members of the Club, who will in all cases be responsible for the expenses of all persons or guests invited by them.

9. Members or guests having any cause or complaint, or knowing of any matter demanding attention, will please communicate the same promptly to the chairman or some other member of the House Committee.

10. Servants will not be permitted to occupy rooms in the new part of the Club House.

The "Schedule of Rates" as published by the South Fork Fishing and Hunting Club offered reasonable rates, well below what members could easily have afforded.

For members living in cottages, boarding at
Club House .... $1.20 per day
Visitors at cottages, boarding at
Club House .... $2.00   "
Members boarding and rooming at
Club House .... $1.60   "
Visitors boarding and rooming at
Club House .... $2.50   "
Children over 12 years, at regular table, full price.
Children under 12 years, a regular table, half price.
Nurses at regular table same as other adults.

Members rooming and boarding in
cottages .... $ .25 per day
Visitors rooming and boarding in
cottages .... $ .33   "
Children under twelve years of age, rooming and boarding in cottages, one half price.
Servants rooming in cottages and eating at
Club House .... $ .60 per day
Servants rooming and boarding in
Club House .... $1.00   "
Five per cent will be taken off all bills for more than two weeks, and less than a month.
Ten percent will be taken off all bills for a month or more.
Billiards per game, 10 cts. Per hour; 30 cts.
For use of Boat, 25 cents per hour, and 10 cents for each additional hour or portion of an hour.
Coach Fare, for each passenger 25 cents, and 25 cents for each trunk, average size. Larger trunks and special packages to be charged for according to size and weight.

The "Time of Meals" at the South Fork Fishing and Hunting Club was listed as follows:

BREAKFAST— Servants ...... 6 to 7   a.m.
            Guests .... 7 to 9 1/2   "
DINNER—   Servants ...... 12 to 1   p.m.
            Guests .... 1 to 2 1/2   "
TEA—   Servants ......5 1/2 to 6 1/2   p.m.
            Guests .... 6 1/2 to 8   "
            SUNDAY THE SAME

As noted previously, the activities available to Club members, their families and guests were many. There was, however, no annual event bigger than the Regatta and Feast of Lanterns. Held in two parts, this annual event usually took place during the latter part of the summer season. The festivities began with a regatta that featured competitions and races of various boat types. These competitions were divided into classes by age and sex. Following the regatta, there was the Feast of Lanterns.

The Feast of Lanterns began at Locust Point on Lake Conemaugh. According to the program for August 22, 1885, the procession would feature fifty boats, each illuminated by five lanterns. One of the Club's steam yachts, the *Captain Eads*, pulled the procession around the lake. During the procession there was a fireworks display from the center of the lake. The final event of the day was a party held in the parlor of the clubhouse, where prizes for the various categories were distributed.

Those who founded the South Fork Fishing and Hunting Club wanted to do so without fanfare, attention, or public notice. Once established they wanted their Club, its members, families and guests, and their activi-

South-Fork Fishing and Hunting Club

CONEMAUGH LAKE,

REGATTA AND FEAST OF LANTERNS

TO BE HELD ON
Saturday Afternoon and Evening, August 22, 1885.

✦Part·I··Regatta.✦

BEGINNING AT 2:00 P. M.

Canoes, and other Boats Under Sail.

Open to all except Yacht "Mountain Belle."

C. F. HOLDSHIP,	G. I. HOLDSHIP,	W. E. WOODWELL,
T. M. McKEE,	J. B. SHEA,	J. J. LAWRENCE, Jr.
	B. S. HORNE,	

Double Sculls, with or without Coxwain.
ONE MILE.

T. M. McKEE,	AND	J. J. LAWRENCE, Jr.
J. B. SHEA,	AND	B. S. HORNE,
JAS. H. WILLOCK,	AND	FRANK S. WILLOCK.

Canoes with Double Paddles.
ONE-HALF MILE.

J. J. LAWRENCE, Jr.	T. M. McKEE.
C. F. HOLDSHIP,	GEO. E. SHEA.

Single Sculls, for Ladies.
WITH OR WITHOUT COXWAIN. ONE-FOURTH MILE.

Miss A. M. LAWRENCE,	Miss M. B. SHARPE,	Miss R. E. HENDERSON,
Miss M. G. HUSSEY,	Miss E. B. SUYDAM,	Miss CLARA HUSSEY,
Miss LILLIE RANKIN,	Miss T. M. LAWRENCE,	Miss M. S. LAWRENCE,
Mrs. SEMPLE,		Miss N. B. McINTOSH,

Double Sculls, for Boys under 14 years.
ONE-FOURTH MILE.

DICK SUYDAM	AND	HARRY IRWIN,	Coxwain, J. K. CLARKE,
O. McCLINTOCK	AND	FRANK SEMPLE,	Coxwain, HART McKEE.

Single Sculls, for Girls under 15 years.
ONE-FOURTH MILE.

ALICE HOLDSHIP,	ANNIE SEMPLE.
IDA IRWIN,	BELLE SHARPE.

Double Sculls, for Boys under 16 years.
ONE-HALF MILE.

HART McKEE AND	ED. S. MULLINS,
BEN. WELLS AND	WALTER McCLINTOCK.

Single Sculls, for Boys under 16 years.
ONE-HALF MILE.

JOHN SEMPLE,	HARRY RANKIN.

Upset Canoe Race, 200 yards.

J. J. LAWRENCE, Jr.	T. M. McKEE.	J. B. SHEA.

Hurry-Scurry Canoe Race, 100 yards.

J. J. LAWRENCE, Jr.	T. M. McKEE.	J. B. SHEA.

Tub Race, 60 yards.

ED. S. MULLINS,	OLLIE McCLINTOCK,	HART McKEE,
JAMES F. KEENAN,	BEN. WELLS,	HARRY IRWIN,
JNO. S. CLARKE,	JAS. K. CLARKE,	DICK SUYDAM.
	HARRY RANKIN.	

✦Part·II··Feast·of·Lanterns.✦

BEGINNING AT 8:00 P. M.

FIRST—Line to form off Locust Point.

SECOND—Procession of fifty boats, illuminated by five lanterns each, drawn around the lake by Steam Launch, "Capt. Eads."

THIRD—Pyrotechnic display from the center of the Lake during procession.

FOURTH—Landing and assemblage in Parlor for distribution of Regatta Prizes.

---

ties to remain as private as possible. In this endeavor they were, to a marked degree, highly successful. Life at the South Fork Fishing and Hunting Club began as a virtual unknown to everyone except members, their families and guests, and it ended in much the same way. Many have tried through conjecture and speculation to explain the Club's insistence on insulating itself from local contact. That conjecture and speculation has been both kind and unkind over the years. It remains, however, little more than conjecture and speculation. Until accounts heretofore unknown and undiscovered are brought to light, the South Fork Fishing and Hunting Club and life at Lake Conemaugh from 1881 through 1888 will remain largely a mystery.

(Left) This is the program from the Regatta and Feast of Lanterns held on Lake Conemaugh on August 22, 1885.

The last Regatta and Feast of Lanterns held at Lake Conemaugh by the South Fork Fishing and Hunting Club, was held in 1888. The winners of one of the categories in that competition, shown in this photograph, were James King Clarke, son of member C. J. Clarke, and Dellie Suydam, son of member M. B. Suydam. Both the Clarkes and the Suydams owned cottages at Lake Conemaugh.

Chapter 3

Failure of the South Fork Dam

Memorial Day was a time to celebrate in Johnstown. Under the headline "WHAT WILL BE DONE HERE TO-MORROW" the May 29, 1889 edition of the *Johnstown Tribune* reported the following plans for May 30, 1889:

> To-morrow the ceremonies incident to Memorial Day will engage the attention of surviving veterans and, to a greater or less extent, of all patriotic citizens. As far as possible the ordinary affairs of every-day life will be set aside, and the holiday will be given over to the purposes of its institution. During the earlier hours of the day the various cemeteries will be visited by detachments of the Grand Army and the graves of the sleeping soldiers will be indicated by the national colors, so that, in the afternoon, when those charged with the duty of depositing flowers upon the mounds shall visit the burial places, they will be enabled to perform their work in a speedy and satisfactory manner.

Little did the writer of this copy know that following Memorial Day 1889, the "...ordinary affairs of everyday life...," would be set aside in Johnstown for many months.

The Johnstown Flood of 1889 was the result of the convergence of several unusual factors in a relatively short period of time. Heavy snowfalls during the late winter and early spring of 1889 left much of the region saturated by spring thaws. A front-page story of the April 6 edition of the *Johnstown Tribune* reported a story from Pittsburgh under the headline "PENNSYLVANIA SNOWED UNDER."

> The heaviest snowstorm of the season is prevailing in this section. It began about 10 o'clock last night and has been snowing ever since. The snow fall is about eight inches up to 10 o'clock this morning, but in the mountains the railroad men report from eighteen inches to two feet. Trains are all behind time, but no accidents have been reported. The storm seems to be confined to the western part of this State.

April and May both witnessed heavier than usual rainfalls further saturating the area. On May 30 and 31 a storm system, the likes of which no one could bring to mind, visited the area with unprecedented rainfall amounts. At a time when the regional landscape was unable to handle the water already dumped on it, it witnessed one of its heaviest storms. The resulting run off was significant.

Just as the conditions of this natural flooding had surpassed any pervious periods of high water, a new and even more devastating set of circumstance continued to unfold. In addition to all of the water nature could dump on the area, 20,000,000 tons of water from a man-made reservoir was suddenly added to the already flooded valley of the Conemaugh. The collapse of the South Fork Dam and the release of Lake Conemaugh combined with the water already in the valley to create one of the greatest inland floods ever recorded and the greatest flood ever to result from the failure of a single dam.

Flooding in Johnstown was not an unusual occurrence. In fact, flooding was a problem that had plagued the town from its earliest days and would continue to do so for many years to come. Johnstown had been established on a flood plain, so periodic flooding was to be expected. By 1889, flooding did not significantly raise the level of concern among the locals. They had seen flooding before and anticipated that they would certainly see it again. They tended to react accordingly with a calm resolve.

A History of Flooding in Johnstown
(In each of the following years, Johnstown experienced one or more floods.)

1808	1816	1817	1818
1819	1820	1837	1847
1859	1861	1867	1875
1880	1881	1883	1884
1887	1889*	1936*	1977*

* denotes major floods

The sun rose behind a cover of clouds on the morning of Thursday, May 30, 1889, with the promise of rain on the horizon. By late afternoon the rains began to fall, but not early enough or heavy enough to seriously interrupt either the planned events of the day or numerous impromptu gestures to honor the town's veterans. Memorial Day festivities in Johnstown would not be diminished by a little rain. The fraternal organizations, social clubs, ethnic associations, local musical groups, red-white-and-blue clad school children, and members of the Grand Army of the Republic were not to be deterred in the pursuit of their patriotic duties. Memorial Day, known more commonly as Decoration Day since it was a day to decorate the graves of veterans with flags and flowers, had become an important day in Johnstown. By May 30, 1889 the patriotic citizens of Johnstown had been decorating many of these graves as part of their Memorial Day remembrance for almost a quarter of a century.

This flood scene, taken during the flood of 1887, shows one of the town's billiard halls and an insurance agency. Although not one of the more pleasant aspects of living in Johnstown, periodic flooding was to be expected. This picture also provides a glimpse of what the streets of Johnstown may have looked like on the morning and early afternoon of May 31, 1889, prior to the breaking of the dam in South Fork.

Once assembled near the center of town, those in the procession and those who followed paraded east out of town up the Stony Creek River to Sandy Vale Cemetery, the final resting place of many local Civil War veterans. In Sandy Vale and other cemeteries around Johnstown the graves of fallen veterans were marked with small flags so that later in the day, when it came time to decorate the graves of those who had served in the military, they could be easily identified.

The storms that brought the rain to the Johnstown area were part of a massive weather system affecting much of the country. "Weather Indications" offered in the May 30, 1889 edition of the *Johnstown Tribune* had predicted the heavy rains that swept across the region.

> Rain will prevail in New England, the Lower Lake region, Southern Michigan, and thence southward to the South Atlantic and East Gulf Coast, with severe local storms in the Middle, South Atlantic, and East Gulf States and the Ohio Valley, followed by colder weather in the Atlantic Coast Friday. Warmer, fair weather is indicated for the States west of the Mississippi River.

The Conemaugh Valley and several other areas throughout Pennsylvania and surrounding states were quickly thrown into flood conditions by this storm system. Although the attention of the nation and the world was clearly focused on Johnstown and vicinity, flooding of dramatic proportions was indeed visited on a wide area. The following are brief excerpts from the *Chicago Tribune* of June 1, 1889, detailing the flooding spawned by the regional storm that brought flooding to Johnstown:

Tyrone, Pa., May 31.—The Juniata River has overflowed its banks at this place and flooded the entire southern portion of the city, causing great destruction to property and the streets. People living in the flooded districts had to be removed from their homes in wagons to places of safety. All the railroads centering in this place are greatly damaged by the flood. The water was never known to be so high at this place.

Altoona, Pa., May 31.—The highest and most destructive flood that has visited this place for fifty years occurred today. It has been raining continuously for the last twenty-four hours and the rain is still falling. The Juniata River is ten feet above low water mark and is still rising.

Williamsport, Pa., May 31— Heavy rain has been falling here almost continually since yesterday evening. Reports from up the river announce a twelve-foot flood near Clearfield and high water in Sinnemahoning indicating a bigger flood than that of 1863.

Harrisburg, Pa., May 31—This city had been in the middle of a deluge all day long. There has been a steady down-pour since before daylight this morning, and up to 10 o'clock tonight four and a half inches of rain had fallen. Danger of a disastrous flood in the Susquehanna River is imminent.

Piedmont, W.Va., May 31—This place had been visited with the greatest flood since 1876. In began raining yesterday and continued until noon, also rained some this afternoon. Two hundred families living near the river were forced to leave their houses and fled to the hills.

Martinsburg, W.Va., May 31—[Special]—The rains here are the heaviest since 1873. It is feared the long iron bridge at Harper's Ferry will be washed away. All the smaller streams are out of banks and still rising.

Hagerstown, Md., May 31—A terrific storm passed over the Potomac River district of Washington County yesterday afternoon. It seemed to follow the course of the river, leaving destruction in its tracks and blowing down buildings, trees and fences, and ruining growing crops.

Richmond, Va., May 31—[Special]—Today the James River is rising at an almost unprecedently rapid rate. All day long a fearful rain and wind storm has prevailed and the evening papers have had long accounts of tornadoes in all sections.

The Monday, June 3 edition of the *Chicago Tribune* announced "THE POTOMAC IS ON A SPREE, WASHINGTON PEOPLE GO ABOUT THE STREETS IN BOATS." The story beneath the headline described an all but submerged city.

Washington, D.C., June 2—Boats plied along the avenues near the Pennsylvania Railroad Station and through the streets of South Washington, and things wore aspect faintly resembling descriptions of scenes in cities built on canals. A carp two feet long was caught in the ladies' waiting room at the Baltimore & Potomac station, and several others were caught in the streets by the boys.

The city has been shut off from communication with the West and South for two days, and there will be a scarcity of milk and other supplies until the roads are repaired sufficiently to allow railroad trains and wagons to enter the city.

The regional storms that struck Johnstown and vicinity pelted the area with rains that were all but continuous from the late afternoon of Thursday, May 30 through much of Friday, May 31. The rains, by numerous accounts, were the heaviest anyone cared to remember. By Friday morning the Stony Creek and the Little Conemaugh were rising at a rate approaching eighteen to twenty-four inches per hour. Schools were closed, mills and factories were either shut down or manned by skeleton crews, so workers could tend to their families and homes. Business owners across town did what they could to move stock and equipment beyond the destructive reach of the rising waters. By mid-afternoon this had indeed become the worst period of high water anyone could recall, but even so there was no real sense of wide spread panic. There was instead a somewhat calm resignation to the reality that if you lived in Johnstown, such was to be expected from time to time.

As the rains continued throughout the morning of May 31 the level of the rivers rose and more and more of Johnstown was submerged under murky, brown floodwater. A growing sense of urgency began to grip some of the locals. Those people who were among the more concerned would later recall that they sensed a difference in this particular period of flooding. Others, possibly fearful over the old rumors about the dam in South Fork, also moved themselves and what they could carry to higher ground. They would later recall that they never had trusted that dam. These folks, those whose fears caused them to act, unfortunately were relatively few in number. Those whose sense of concern caused them to leave Johnstown were dramatically fewer in number than those whose lack of concern caused them to simply hold on in the hopes of waiting out what they thought was just another spring flood.

Through the late morning and early afternoon several bridges had been washed off their foundations, basements and cellars were flooded throughout the town and surrounding areas, trains were being held up due to track washouts and mud slides that blocked roadbeds, and there had already been one drowning with others reported but unconfirmed.

The single confirmed drowning victim was Joseph Ross. Ross was a driver for Jacob J. Strayer who operated a planning mill. Ross, who lived in Conemaugh on Gautier Street, was in Johnstown attempting to help those in need. The mule on which he was riding stepped into an excavated site where some new construction had begun. Ross was thrown from the animal and drowned. The mule survived. Even though most folks in Johnstown in 1889 had been through other floods, Ross was, at least as far as anyone could recall, the first to die as a result of a flood.

The towns and villages surrounding Johnstown were not faring much better than Johnstown since mid-day on May 30. This was a regional storm system, and the entire region was suffering its effects. One eyewitness claimed that a bucket left outside near South Fork, Pennsylvania during the night of May 30 through the morning of May 31 had eight inches of water in it.

W. Y. Boyer was the superintendent of the lake and grounds for the South Fork Fishing and Hunting Club. In a report that appeared in the June 25, 1889 edition of the *Johnstown Tribune*, Boyer offered a description of the local weather on the last two days of May in 1889 from his vantage point in South Fork.

On Thursday (the day before the breaking of the dam) it commenced raining about 4 P.M., but did not rain very hard until about dark, when it commenced to blow and rain, and all that night it rained very hard. It not only rained, but it poured, and in the morning when I got around I told the guests that I thought the dam would run over that day, of course not being sure at that time. The water rose ten inches an hour.

Unconfirmed sightings led to reports that one or more waterspouts were associated with the weather system that gripped the region of the Conemaugh Valley. The June 1, 1889 edition of the *New York Times* carried the following three-segment headline on page one in bold, uppercase print:

HUNDREDS OF LIVES LOST
A WATERSPOUT'S DREADFUL WORK IN PENNSYLVANIA
THE CITY OF JOHNSTOWN SWEPT COMPLETELY AWAY.

True to its headline, the story reported that the dam near South Fork, Pennsylvania broke, "...just as it was struck by a waterspout.... " Although there were reports of high winds associated with this weather system, there were no reports of waterspouts in that area. Although a waterspout, a mini-tornado over water, could have been associated with this weather system there is no reliable evidence to indicate that one was.

One of the better summaries of the weather event that surrounded the Johnstown Flood was offered in the July 6, 1889 edition of the *Johnstown Tribune*. The headline read, "THE HISTORIC STORM" and was followed by a sub-headline which read, "The Extraordinary Atmospheric Conditions Which Proceeded It."

A specialist writing in the Pittsburgh Dispatch, says that the Johnstown calamity has so overshadowed all else in the public mind that but few comprehend the extraordinary atmospheric phenomena which culminated in the storm of May 30th and 31st, the prodigious rainfall accompanying it and the wide area of country devastated by its floods. He finds three areas of low barometer or storm centers, one moving from the west, another from the southwest, and still another from the southeast, met in a dire embrace upon the summits of the Allegheny Mountains. Simultaneously an area of high barometric pressure (30.20) extended on the Atlantic Ocean, from the Bermudas to Newfoundland, and thence westward to the lakes and the Allegheny Mountains.

The three united storm centers, held in check on the east by this wall of high barometric pressure, stood as if anchored above the crests of the Alleghenies, and for thirty-six hours discharged an amount of rainfall unprecedented in the history of this region. From the reports, which have slowly come to hand, it is considered by experts as being now quite clear that the headwaters of the north and south forks of the Conemaugh were in the center of this gigantic atmospheric disturbance, and that the phenomenal downpour of rain extended along the Alleghenies for a distance of one hundred miles in either direction from this point.

If anyone will examine a good map he will notice that, although the greater part of the watershed of the forty square miles, contiguous to these two mountain streams, drains toward the west into the Conemaugh Valley, yet, within the same area, will be found the mountain divide, from which the waters flow north into the west branch of the Susquehanna, east into the Juniata, and south into the Potomac. It is an interesting fact, to be noted in this connection, that all of these streams received floods from the storm now under consideration only less disastrous than the portion which devastated Johnstown and the Conemaugh Valley.

The June 14, 1889 edition of the *Johnstown Tribune* carried a front-page story that detailed the flooding in Johnstown prior to the bursting of the dam in South Fork. Titled "Before the Reservoir Came" the story described conditions in Johnstown at 3:00 p.m., just prior to the breaking of the dam in South Fork.

At 3 o'clock the town sat down with its hands in its pockets to make the best of a very dreary situation. All had got out of reach of the flood that could and there was nothing to do but wait; and what impatient waiting it was any one who has ever been penned in by a flood and has watched the water rising and night coming on, can imagine.

That same article reported that there had been a call to the *Tribune* office from the local telephone switchboard that the Johnstown freight agent for the Pennsylvania Railroad, Frank S. Deckert, had been notified that the dam at South Fork was becoming more dangerous by the hour, and there was serious concern that it may break. At the time that call was received at the office of the *Tribune*, 3:15 p.m., the dam had already broken and the waters of Lake Conemaugh were rushing toward Johnstown. Two similar warnings had been received earlier in the day, but they were afforded little attention and no general alarm or calls for evacuations were sounded.

In his Pennsylvania Railroad Testimony* railroad freight agent Deckert described what appears to have been the prevailing attitude of locals regarding warnings about the dam at South Fork and the likelihood that it

_____

* In the months following the flood the Pennsylvania Railroad conducted extensive interviews to ascertain information regarding the unusual weather of the spring of 1889, the breaking of the dam in South Fork, and the subsequent flooding of the Conemaugh Valley. In anticipation of litigation and culpability, since the reservoir had at one time been owned by the railroad, and there had been several reports that the railroad had provided periodic inspections, it was certainly in the best interests of the railroad to gather as much credible information as possible. With few exceptions, the testimony was gathered in the question-and-answer format of a typical legal proceeding. Excerpts from the transcripts of that testimony are available through the website of the Johnstown Flood National Memorial of the National Park Service (www.nps.gov/jofl). Any references drawn from this bank of testimony will hereafter be referenced as "Pennsylvania Railroad testimony."

was about to give way. Deckert recalled two warnings coming through his office on May 31, the first of which arrived about noon. Deckert lived with his wife and children on Iron Street in Millville, less than a block from the Pennsylvania Railroad depot. In May 1889, there were five people living in the Deckert home at 20 Iron Street. None of the Deckerts were lost in the flood.

Q. *When did you get the first one?*
A. I didn't receive the first one. When I saw it or heard of it, it was about 12 o'clock, I suppose?

Q. *Tell me what you know about it.*
A. I didn't know anything in regard to it. I saw it but didn't read it. It was in regard to the dam; that there was some danger of it breaking.

Q. *That was what time?*
A. 12 o'clock, or in that neighborhood.

Q. *You don't know who that was from?*
A. No, sir.

Q. *What did you do when you heard of that? Did you give any notice of it to the people?*
A. No, sir, we did not. It came through the ticket office in the first place, and I believe that is the way the message reached our office; that is, the ticket man brought it up to our office.

Q. *Was it a telegraphic message?*
A. It was written on Penna. Railroad telegraphic paper.

Q. *Do you know where that came from?*
A. No, sir, I don't.

Q. *Did it create any alarm in your mind?*
A. Oh no.

Q. *For what reason?*
A. Well, we had had that alarm before. We had had it every high water we have had there.

Q. *That was the reason, was it?*
A. Yes, sir, it was a common subject of remark that the dam might come out, in times of high water.

Q. *And you didn't take any interest in it?*
A. No, sir, I did not, or I wouldn't have left my family, or remained in the house.

The *Tribune* editor, George T. Swank, one of Johnstown's more prominent Main Street residents, was in his office at 92 Franklin Street, just off of Main on the afternoon of May 31. As he watched the flood scene develop around him he wrote, "It is idle to speculate what would be the result if this tremendous body of water—three miles long, a mile wide in places, and sixty feet deep at the breast at its normal stage-should be thrown into the already submerged Valley of the Conemaugh." The time for speculation had already passed when he penned those words, for a brutal, ugly reality was on its way to Johnstown.

For some weeks there had been an expanding level of activity in and around the property and facilities of the South Fork Fishing and Hunting Club. As usual, everything was being done to accommodate the personal wishes and demands of the Club's management and its members in anticipation of their summer visits. Colonel Elias Unger, the president of the South Fork Fishing and Hunting Club, was the person chiefly responsible for the preparations for the 1889 season. Unger had likely become the president of the South Fork Fishing and Hunting Club in 1887, following the death of Benjamin Ruff, the Club's founder and first president. His assistant, Mr. W. Y. Boyer, was often referred to as the superintendent of the property and grounds. When asked to define his relationship to the Club during his Pennsylvania Railroad testimony, Boyer said, "I was there to look after their property. I suppose to protect it, and board people coming up there."

Needed repairs were being made to the clubhouse, the boathouses, and the private cottages surrounding Lake Conemaugh. Loose boards along the several boardwalks were being re-nailed as needed. Broken limbs and branches from the heavier than usual winter snow fall were being cleared away. Here and there a fresh coat of paint was being applied, supplies were being purchased and delivered, and boats of several types were being readied after standing idle all winter. The telephone line, which connected the clubhouse with the small town of South Fork, had yet to be restored after being disconnected at the end of the previous season. The wagons and teams of horses used to move guests and their trunks between the railroad station in South Fork and the Club had been running for some time, accommodating a number of pre-season visitors and those having business with the Club. Beyond the routine work of maintaining the grounds and facilities of the Club, there was the addition of the system of sanitary sewers. When completed it would bring the convenience of indoor plumbing to the members of the Club and their guests. In general the work of getting the Club in its best condition for its ninth season, a season that held the promise of being a excellent one, were progressing nicely.

During the last week in May 1889, a few members of the South Fork Fishing and Hunting Club had come up from Pittsburgh. One of those at the Club for the rainy Memorial Day holiday was D. W. C. Bidwell, who had been a member of the Club for two years. His business firm, D. W. C. Bidwell & Company of Pittsburgh, sold explosives, particularly the type of powders and charges used in mining operations. He left Pittsburgh for the South Fork Fishing and Hunting Club on Wednesday, May 29. On Friday morning he decided to return to Pittsburgh, but was unable to because the trains in and out of South Fork were not moving. When the dam broke, Bidwell was among those in South Fork who witnessed the rush of the torrent.

Caught in the throes of the regional storm system that gripped Johnstown and vicinity, fears among those at the South Fork Dam regarding the potential effects the rapidly rising waters could have on the earthen dam heightened by the minute, during the early morning hours of May 31, 1889. There had been some concerns raised the previous evening, but there appear to have been no efforts to act on those concerns. In fact as late as 8:30 a.m. on the 31st, when Bidwell and Boyer crossed the breast of the dam on their way to South Fork, Colonel Unger did not register any serious concerns with them regarding the potential stability of the dam. However, as the morning progressed the situation at the dam deteriorated quickly and dramatically.

During his Pennsylvania Railroad testimony, Colonel Unger described the situation at Lake Conemaugh on the morning of May 31 and the initial efforts to deal with the circumstances that so seriously threatened the dam.

Q. *(Col.) Unger, I wish you would state whether you were up at the South Fork dam in the latter part of May, and I wish you would state about what time it commenced to rain, and what was the character of the rain?*

A. I was there on Thursday evening; there w as [sic] no rain then, but it was cloudy, and thewater [sic] was very low, but on Firday [sic] morning, when I got up at six o'clock, the valley below me seemed to be all under water, and I couldn't understand what all that meant.

Q. *You slept in a house near the dam, did you?*

A. Yes, sir, 200 yards off. I got my gum coat and gum boots on and went down, and found it was rising at the rate of about ten inches an hour in the dam, and was pretty well up then; within four or five feet of the top of thebreast [sic] of the dam. I saw the way it was rising, it wouldn't be very long until it would get full. I couldn't tell how much water was coming; I came to the conclusion that I would cut an extra waste way, and sent for the Italians and the tools and went right to work.

Q. *How many Italians had you up there?*

A. About 20, but I only put about 13 on this work; they were all I could use. They were up there engaged in building a sewer. I sent for them and soon got them to work.

Q. *Which side of the dam?*

A. The west side. The face of the embankment there was solid ground, and I knew it couldn't wash that out right away. The people there protested against it; they said "If you cut that waste weir there, you will ruin the whole business"; and I said, "It won't matter much; it will be ruined anyhow if I can't get rid of this water."

By several eyewitness accounts the level of Lake Conemaugh had risen to within four feet of the top of the dam by 8:00 a.m. Shortly before noon, the level of water in the dam had reached the top of the breast, and continued rising. The reality that the waters of Lake Conemaugh would top the dam which held them in check was no longer a matter of if, but was instead a question of when. Those familiar with the construction of earthen dams, such as the South Fork Dam, knew that any significant amount of water passing over the top of the dam had the power to wash away the dam's outer surface. Any reduction in or major disturbance to the outer surface of the dam would dramatically weaken its overall stability. As the stability of a dam is reduced so too is its ability to resist the force of the water behind it.

Those responsible for the South Fork Dam, namely Unger and Boyer, were aware of the potential danger to the Conemaugh Valley if their dam burst and let go all at once. They were also undoubtedly aware of their responsibility to the Club and its members. Without the dam there was no lake, and without Lake Conemaugh, theirs was nothing more than a collection of cottages, a Clubhouse, an annex, a few outbuildings and some useless boathouses. On the morning of May 31 their goal was to prevent the water of the reservoir from spilling over the top of the dam. They began working toward that goal early on Friday morning, and even though their work was vigorously undertaken from the start, it was initially tempered, at least to some degree, by their desire to save the dam and the prize fish in it.

The man in charge of the work at the breast of the dam was Colonel Unger. John Parke provided suggestions and helped to keep work progressing, but clearly it was Colonel Unger who was directing the work. An engineering student from the University of Pennsylvania in Philadelphia, Parke, a civil engineer by training, had been hired by the South Fork Fishing and Hunting Club to oversee the installation of their new sanitary sewer system. In the years following 1889 it was also frequently reported that he had been engaged by the Club to oversee repairs to the dam as well. There is no documentation to support this assertion.

The November 1, 1933 edition of the *Pennsylvania Gazette*, carried an article that detailed the life and career of John Grubb Parke, who had died the previous

January 30. In that article it was reported that, "In 1889 he was in charge of a corps of men engaged in strengthening a dam near Johnstown owned by a Fishing Club, when the dam broke, causing the terrible disaster known as the Johnstown Flood."

At the time Parke had just turned twenty-three. His prior work experience had been with the Pennsylvania Railroad in their construction division. His uncle, Major-General John G. Parke, for whom the young Parke was named, had won distinction as a Union commander during the Civil War and in 1889 was the superintendent of the United States Military Academy at West Point.

The most organized effort to prevent the overtopping of the dam at South Fork was provided by the crew of workmen engaged in the sewer project at the Club. Numerous accounts put several locals on or near the breast of the dam during the morning and early afternoon of the 31st as well. The locals were engaged, to varying degrees, in helping, watching and predicting what was about to happen. Undoubtedly there were those among the locals who had known for years that "that dam was gonna go some day." Just as certainly there were locals on hand that morning who hoped against hope that it would stand just one more period of high water. After all, "there hadn't been no real problem at the dam since 1862."

The work at the dam site, which became increasingly frantic as morning turned to afternoon on May 31, focused attention on several specific initiatives. These included digging an auxiliary spillway to relieve some of the pressure on the dam, trying to remove a mass of floating debris that had clogged the spillway, and raising the level of the breast, particularly at the center where it sagged slightly. The goal of all of these efforts

John Grubb Parke, Jr.

was to prevent water from spilling over and washing away the outer surface of the dam. Unfortunately, as the work at the dam continued throughout the morning and the afternoon, the level of the water behind it rose unabated.

When a secondary spillway was opened on the western end of the dam, rushing waters quickly cut through the embankment, but only to the level of the rock which made up the embankment. This new spillway provided little if any relief. The six streams that normally fed Lake Conemaugh plus numerous new streams of runoff from the surrounding hillsides continued pouring water into the lake at a phenomenal rate. Digging further through the solid rock was impossible, so this initiative quickly failed. Speculation by several engineers years later holds that a secondary spillway on the western side of the dam may have been part of the original design. There are those who believe that Unger or Parke may have either been aware of this fact or at least speculated that a secondary, emergency spillway was provided in the original construction and were trying to open it. For a time consideration was given to opening a small notch in the breast at one of the ends to allow water to escape more slowly than it would if the entire embankment were to give way all at one time. That proposal was not carried out because of fears that water rushing through an opening big enough to be of any value would quickly cut through and collapse the entire dam.

The fish screens across the spillway and the V-shaped, floating structure designed to catch and hold debris to prevent it from clogging the fish screens quickly rendered the spillway all but useless. Early on the morning of May 31, it was suggested to Unger that the screens and the debris catcher be removed from the front of the spillway. Fearing that the fish would wash over the spillway, Unger failed to act on this suggestion. Removing the screens would prevent the debris that had washed into the lake and flowed toward the spillway from obstructing the flow of the spillway. Obviously, an unobstructed spillway would have carried off more water from the lake. By several accounts from the morning and early afternoon of May 31, any degree of obstruction at the spillway was too much. However, whether an unobstructed spillway would have reduced the level of water in the dam enough to prevent the water from flowing over the top of the dam is not certain.

Later in the morning Unger reconsidered his earlier decision about the fish screens and the debris catcher, but by then they were so heavily entangled with limbs branches, small trees, and other debris that they could not be budged. The heavy metal screens, which were securely attached to the support posts of a foot bridge that crossed the spillway, now not only kept fish in the lake, but they also dramatically reduced the only means for the rapidly rising waters of the Lake Conemaugh to escape without rushing over the breast of the dam that held it in place.

Although not particularly noticeable to the naked eye, the breast of the South Fork Dam sagged slightly in the center. Estimates as to exactly how much the dam sagged at its middle range between two and five feet. If that sag was only two feet, the bottom of the spillway was just five to six feet higher. The weakest point of an earthen dam is its center and should be the last place water is permitted to run over the dam. In the case of the South Fork Dam, the center was the lowest spot along the breast and would thus be the first spot where water from the reservoir would begin to rush over the top. The cause of this sag was the removal of the cast iron sluice pipes and much of the stone culvert that had once run directly through the mid-section of the dam. This sag was made worse by the inadequate repairs made to that section of the dam following its purchase by Benjamin Ruff. Ruff's repairs to the dam were not accomplished to the same standard as the original construction of the breastwork. Even though Ruff consulted with Nathan McDowell, there is no evidence to indicate that McDowell or any other qualified engineer was responsible for planning, supervising or later inspecting the repairs.

On the morning of May 31, little could be done to prevent this sag from becoming a point of particular weakness along the dam. Someone suggested running a plow across the top of the dam several times to turn rows of dirt up. Dirt and stones were also hauled onto the breast and piled in small rows along its length with emphasis on the middle. Although this may have raised the height of the dam, the increase was so slight as to be virtually insignificant.

The net effects of the sag at the middle of the dam, the clogged spillway, and the lack of any sluice pipes to run water off without it going over the dam were all made more serious by the fact that the total height of the dam had been reduced when Ruff bought the property. As mentioned previously, Ruff wanted to widen this cart way to allow two carriages or wagons to pass along the breast of the dam. He wanted members and guests to be able to stop along the breast and not be hurried by another wagon or cart wishing to use the cart way. Even though the level of the dam was lowered, it is doubtful if it would have been wide enough for two wagons to pass. The only thing Ruff accomplished by lowering the dam was to dramatically reduce its capacity to retain water before overtopping began.

Between noon and 1:00 p.m. water had begun running over the top of the dam. Even though it did, the level of the water in the reservoir continued to rise, and since it did, it would continue to flow over the breast at an increasing volume, cutting into the exterior surface of the dam as it did. As overtopping began to occur, layer after layer of the outer surface of the earthen dam was washed away. The inevitability of the collapse was only a matter of time once overtopping began.

By noon, those involved in the frantic efforts in South Fork realized that they were fighting a battle they could not win. Although their labors to stem the tide of the rising waters were carried out in earnest, they accomplished little more than prolonging the inevitable. An

In this modern view, a wooden footbridge crosses the spillway approximately where a similar footbridge would have crossed in 1889. In the upper right portion of this scene is the rehabilitated farmhouse of Colonel Unger. The larger building to the left is a reconstruction of Unger's barn, which serves as the visitor center of the Johnstown Flood National Memorial of the National Park Service.

answer to the decades of speculation regarding the effects of a sudden release of water from the South Fork Reservoir into the valley below was at hand.

With a growing awareness of what was to come, warnings were sent down the valley that the dam was in a dangerous state. Accounts and recollections differ as to exactly how many warning notices were sent, to whom they were sent, and exactly how the information was received and shared. However, one fact is unfortunate yet unmistakably clear; the warnings that were received did not generate enough concern to cause the residents of Johnstown, a town already partially submerged under flood waters, to engage in a general evacuation of the area. The *Johnstown Tribune*, later contended that the residents of Johnstown and other towns between there and South Fork were struck without "a moment's warning." By all accounts warnings were indeed sent, but by those same accounts, they went unheeded but by a cautious few. The *Tribune* carried the following in the Friday, June 14, 1889 edition:

Thousands of happy homes and thousands of joyous and useful lives were blotted out of existence without a moment's warning. The pestilence that walketh at noonday and the fire that consumes great cities have some pity for poor human hearts, for the former give notice of its coming and the latter spares life and takes property; but the flood of that terrible 31st of May came unheralded, and it was insatiate, rapacious, and remorseless. No shipwreck that ever happened will compare with it in the suddenness of its coming, for shipwreck gives time at least for a last prayer on earth, while many shipwrecks could not engulf so many victims as went down in that Conemaugh flood.

By stark contrast, a story carried in the Sunday, June 2, 1889 edition of the *New York Times* tabbed the victims of the Johnstown Flood "Victims of Incredulity." Under the sub-headline which read, "AMPLE WARNING GIVEN OF THE IMPENDING DANGER" the following story appeared:

New Florence, Penn., June 1.— The vast cataclysm that overcame the city of Johnstown and the string of villages and towns up the South Fork Valley from that point yesterday was as singular as it has proved to be calamitous. It is now very evident that more lives have been lost because of foolish incredulity than from ignorance of the danger.

For more than a year there have been fears of an accident of just such a character. The foundations of the dam were considered to be shaky early last spring, and many increasing leakages were reported from time to time. According to the statements of the people who live in Johnstown and other towns on the river, ample warning was given to the Johnstown folks by the railroad officials and by other gentlemen of standing and reputation. In dozens, yes in hundreds of cases, this warning was utterly disregarded, and those who heeded it early in the day were jeered for their timorousness by lips that are now cold.

From the Pennsylvania Railroad testimony and numerous other eyewitness and first-person accounts, it appears reasonable to assume that no less than three messages came from South Fork regarding the deteriorating condition of the dam of the South Fork Fishing and Hunting Club. What follows are excerpts of this testimony which describe efforts to warn Johnstown and other towns and villages between there and South Fork.

According to the testimony of Frank Deckert, a portion of which was presented previously, he had knowledge of two messages received in Johnstown.

Q. *Do you recollect whether on the day the dam broke there had been any messages received at Johnstown in relation to the South Fork dam, who received them, and what was in the message?*
A. I received a message dated at 2.44; it was between that time and 3 o'clock that I got it.

Q. *Who was it from?*
A. t was from J. C: W. ; I don't know who that is; I suppose it was an operator.

Q. *Do you think it was the initials of the operator at South Fork or at Conemaugh?*
A. It was dated at South Fork; from the telegraph station at South Fork. I had the message quite a little while.

Q. *What was in that message, as near as you can tell?*
A. Itwas [sic] that the dam was getting serious, and would possibly go.

Q. *To whom was that sent?*
A. That was addressed to me. The signature was, I think, J. C. W. or J. S. W. I kept it for quite a —— while, but I have lost, or mislaid it.

Q. *Do you know, from any conversation you had with Walkinshaw since, whether he sent that message?*
A. No, I never asked him about it.

Q. *Did the dispatch disclose how they had received the news of that fact about the dam, or how the news had got to South Fork?*
A. No, sir.

Q. *That was at 2.45, you think?*
A. The message was dated 2.44. I remember distinctly about the time.

Q. *How do you happen to remember the exact time?*
A. I don't know, except that I looked at the time after I got it.

Q. *How long was it after you got that dispatch until you had to clear out?*

A. I had gone out to the office, and telephoned it over to the central office, and they received it all right, and I went down to the house—

Q. *How long do you suppose it was?*

A. Oh I suppose half an hour?

Q. *I understand you telegraphed that to whom?*

A. To the central office.

Q. *What central office?*

A. Johnstown.

Q. *The telegraph office?*

A. No, sir, the telephone office.

Q. *The Company's telephone?*

A. No, sir, the public telephone. The Company don't have one.

Q. *What request did you send along with it to make it known? Did you request the operator to make it known?*

A. I did.

Q. *Who was that man?*

A. I don't know; there is a lady there in day time, and I suppose she had left the office.

Q. *Was it a man's voice?*

A. Yes, sir.

Q. *Did you receive any other dispatch than that?*

A. Well, I saw a dispatch; it wasn't addressed to me; it was addressed to other parties.

Q. *What other parties?*

A. I don't remember now.

Q. *You have given us a statement here of a dispatch you got and telephoned to the central office. Was that the second or first one?*

A. That was the second one.

Q. *When did you get the first one?*

A. I didn't receive the first one. When I saw it or heard of it, it was about 12 o'clock, I suppose?

Mr. C. P. Dougherty was the local agent for the Pennsylvania Railroad in South Fork, a position he had assumed on November 21, 1887. Excerpts from his testimony to the Pennsylvania Railroad provide a summary of how information came into South Fork about the deteriorating condition of the dam, and how that information was sent out from South Fork.

Q. *When did you hear, if you did hear at all, anything about the condition of things up at the dam that morning?*

A. The first information I got from the dam was by a Mr. Boyer about 8.45, Mr D. W. C. Bidwell, and two other gentlemen whose names I don't remember, who came to take Pacific Express from there, and I inquired from this party about the extent of the flood. That was the first information I had.

Q. *Now, tell (m)e what the information was that they gave you.*

A. I asked Mr. Boyer if the water was high in the dam, and he said it was pretty high. I asked him then if there was any likelihood of its running over. He said he thought not, that it was perfectly safe. I then inquired of Mr. Bidwell afterwards, and he informed me that the water would have to riise [sic] four feet from the time he left the dam until it would run over the breast, and that there was no danger of it running over. He also informed me that they were engaged in digging a trench on the far side (that is, speaking from the roadside) in the solid ground, that would be sufficient with the regular waste weir to release all flood that would come, so that it would be impossible for it to run over, and I understood that there were quite a number of men there—

Q. *Now, what time of day was it you had this conversation with Bidwell and Boyer?*

A. About 8.45 I was talking to Boyer, and it might have been ten or fifteen minutes later I was speaking to Mr. Bidwell.

Q. *Did you know what time, or do you know what time they left the dam?*

A. No, sir, not exactly. I would suppose they left there not later than 8 o'clock.

Q. *Now, did you have any conversation with anybody else as to the condition ofthat [sic] dam other than you have stated?*

A. Not until sometime in the afternoon.

Q. *What time?*

A. I couldn't be positive as to the exact time

Q. *Give it approximately, or as near as you can remember.*

A. As near as I can recollect, it was about 1 o'clock.

Q. *Now, just go on and tell me what that was.*

A. The gentleman who told me was Dan Sibert [sic]. He was sent to the dam purposely to find out what was the danger of the water running over.

Q. *Who sent him?*

A. Mr. J. P. Wilson.

Q. *Who is he?*

A. The Superintendent of the Argyle Coal Company at South Fork. Mr. Seibert said it was running over at the far side, and also in the middle. He supposed it was about ten feet wide in the middle.

Q. *Just go on and state what he said to you, and you said to him.*
A. That was all the conversation I had with Mr. Seibert.

Q. *Did he state to you whether there was much of a stream or volume of water going over the dam?*
A. He thought apparently it had just commenced to run over.

Q. *What did he say as to the probability of the dam breaking? Did he express an opinion?*
A. No, sir, he gave no opinion.

Q. *Did he seem to be alarmed about it?*
A. No, sir, he was perfectly cool about it. As I understand, he was sent by this gentleman, Mr. Wilson, to get information as to the situation of it, and return as soon as he could, and that, I heard him state as what he had seen of it viewing it from a short distance below the breast.

Q. *Do you know what report he made to Mr. Wilson?*
A. No, nothing more than what I heard him say.

Q. *Was there anything in that that would lead you to believe that it was dangerous?*
A. Yes, sir. I considered it was dangerous after finding it was running over.

Q. *What did you do then? Did you communicate that to any officer or anybody connected with the Penna. Railroad Company?*
A. Yes, sir, I made an attempt to do so at once. Mr. Wilson asked me if Mr. Pitcairn had been notified, and I told him that I had been trying to get the circuit, and had been to the office several times, but the circuit could only be had to Wilmore east, and Mineral Point west. The lines were down. I said to him " I will make another effort, and I will take Elmer Paull (?) with me", another operator who lives just above the station, "and see if he can get the circuit" . My reason for that was because I thought he had more experience probably than the regular operator who was at the tower, and he might possible [sic] be able to get the circuit. This gentleman and I started for the telegraph office, and after a few minutes there, he informed me, after testing the wires, that the line was down west of Mineral Point.

Q. *How far is Mineral Point from South Fork?*
A. Mineral Point tower, I suppose, is in the neighborhood of four miles from South Fork. He then told me that he could get a message to Pittsburgh by having it conveyed from Mineral Point to "AO" tower, the next telegraph office west of Mineral

Point. I told him then to go ahead and write a message and send it; and he wrote the message, and the regular operator sent it.

Q. *Did you see the message?*
A. Yes, sir.

Q. *Did you write the message?*
A. I saw him write it, and sign my name to it.

Q. *What was in it?*
A. I am not positive about it, but I think I can give you nearly the wording of it: "From all information we can get from the South Fork dam, it is running over at the west side and middle, and is now becoming very dangerous"; that is about the wording of it, an near as I can recollect. I understood he got that message to Mineral Point to direct, and operator Paull informed me that the operator at Mineral Point had started a man, or agreed to start a man at once to carry the message to "AO" tower. I then left the office.

Q. *What time of day was this?*
A. As near as I can tell, it was somewhere near about 1.45, probably later, when we effected this. I wouldn't be positive as to the time.

Q. *What is the distance of "AO" tower from Mineral Point?*
A. I don't know exactly. I would judge about one mile.

Q. *What was your plan of getting a message to Mr. Pitcairn from there? That there was telegraphic communication from that tower to Pittsburgh?*
A. We were informed so. The operator said he could get Pittsburgh and all points west.

Q. *Do you know in point of fact whether that message did get to Pittsburgh?*
A. No, sir, I don't know for certain. I never inquired.

Q. *Did you send, or attempt to send any other message than that?*
A. Not after that.

Q. *Did you before that?*
A. Yes, sir, I was there several times at the office making inquiry, and found that they were unable to get the circuit, and unable to get any information as to where the trouble was, or any way to get a message through, and I gave up the idea of sending it. I was willing to and ready to, and wished to, but could not get the circuit.

Q. *Then you made this third effort afterwards, and got this message off?*
A. That was what they informed me. Of course, I'm not an operator, and don't know anything beyond what the operator told me+ [sic] that he had sent it.

Q. *I understand that. You did all in your power after you learned the water was up over the dam, to notify Mr. Pitcairn and others connected with the Company?*

A. Yes, sir.

Q. *What was the name of that operator that sent the message down to Mineral Point?*

A. It was the regular operator, Miss Emma Ehrenfeld.

Q. *And who is the operator at Mineral Point?*

A. I am informed, Mr. Pickerell.

Q. *Well, I understand then, from you, as Agent there, you did everything in your power to keep the officers of the company advised as to the state of things at South Fork dam?*

A. Yes, sir; that is, everything that I could see that lay in my power to do.

Miss Emma Ehrenfeld was the telegraph operator in South Fork at the time of the flood. In her Pennsylvania Railroad testimony, she described her efforts to get information from South Fork to Johnstown.

Q. *Miss. Ehrenfeld, just commence now in your own way, and tell me where you were employed in May last, and by whom.*

A. I was working at South Fork in the telegraph tower. I went on duty at 7 o'clock in the morning. It was raining very hard when I went down. I found orders there to hold all trains east for orders. No. 20 was there, and I got orders for them, and they went on east to Sonman. There was an A Extra, and I got orders for them also to go east. The 1167 was on South Fork middle siding, and the 1163 was just west of the tower on the Argyle siding, for orders. Limited came there at 8.46, ten minutes late. They were there, I judge until between 1.30 and 1.45 when they pulled over the bridge to the station. The conductor came to me, and said he thought it best to go to the station on account of the water, and the danger of the bridge going out, and in case I got orders for them , they would be there. Of course, that was the last I saw of Limited, after they went to the station. Then, about noon, I judge it was, a man came in very much excited; he says "Notify Johnstown right away about the dam". He says, "Its raising very fast and there's danger of the reservoir breaking I said "Who told you all this?", and he says, "There's a man cmae [sic] from the lake, and he told me". We didn't have any wires then; our wires were all down, and I couldn't work with Johnstown direct.

Q. *Who was that person?*

A. I think his name was Wetzengreist, or something like that. I didn't know the man personally. He is a man that people generally don't have much confidence in, and for that reason, I scarcely knew what to do under the cirsumstances [sic]. Had it been a person I knew very well, or if he had given me a message, it would have been different, but he just told me this in a very excited manner, and I scarcely knew what to do; but of course, I knew the water was high in the river, and thought I would do the best I could, so I called the operator at Mineral Point; he was the only one I could work with west; and I told him, and we fixed up a message, and I asked him to send it. He said he could send it west from there with one of the division men. So we fixed up a message; I don't know how it was worded, but anyway, that there was danger at the reservoir. It was directed to the agent at Johnstown and the Yard Master at Conemaugh. He was to send it by a man to the next office west, and they were to forward it to Conemaugh and Johnstown by wire. Whether it ever reached Johnstown, I am unable to say. About 1.30 or 1.45, the Agent cmae [sic] and he gave me a message addressed to Mr. Pitcairn here in Pittsburgh. I told him about the wires, and the only things I could do was to send it just as I did the other one.

Q. *Have you that message?*

A. No, sir, they were all taken away with the tower.

Q. *It was swept away, was it?*

A. Yes, sir.

Q. *What were the contents of it, as near as you can recollect?*

A. I really couldn't tell you. It was about the reservoir, about the water rising, and there was danger apprehended. I can't just give the exact words. I sent that at once on that wire; just a short signal wire: then Mr. Wilson came in between 2.20 and 2.25, and he gave me one, something to the same effect. He told me Mr. Pitcairn had notified him that whenever the reservoir was in danger, he should let him know. I told him I would do what I could to send it, and I sent it just as I did the other ones.

William Hilary Pickerill (in the transcripts, he is mistakenly referred to as P. N. Pickerell) was the telegraph operator for the Pennsylvania Railroad at Mineral Point. In his testimony for the Railroad he was able to support his memory of the messages that came through his tower with copies of the original messages.

Q. *What dis patch [sic] did you(g)get [sic], as operator, after you went on duty, as to the condition of the South Fork dam?*

A. Well, the first tidings that we received from the dam was a party, I understood from the operator, had been out on horseback; I heard the persons name, but I can't reco llect [sic] the name;

Q. *What operator?*

A. The lady operator at South Fork. And this party he came in to South Fork somewheres between the hours of 11 and 12 o'clock, and stated to the lady operator there that the dam was in a critical condition, and he thought the people in Conemaugh and Johnstown ought to be notified to be on the look-out,that [sic] it might break any time; and if I understood her right, and recall to memory, it was then within about two feet of the top.

Q. *This is the conversation youm [sic] ad [sic] over the wire with her?*

A. Yes, sir, and she inquired of me to know whether I could get a message to Conemaugh or Johnstown. I told her I couldn't, because all communication was cut off, supposed to have been caused by the poles falling in the river. You know the river far enough to catch the poles, and some of them were down at that time west of my office; and I told her the only salvation would be to take the message, and try to dispatch it to Conemaugh by foot messenger, if I could catch one coming along. She said to take it and do the best I could. I told her to go ahead with the message, and she said she had no message from this party; that he just chanced to come in and told her, and she didn't know whether to give it any credit or not. I told her that I thought it was a thing that there oughtn't to be any risks taken on, and she asked if we couldn't get together and make a message, and send it down. I told her I could, and she told me to go ahead and make a message, and I done so.

Q. *Who did you direct that message to?*

A. I addressed it, I think, to the Yard Master or Despatcher at Conemaugh, and to R. P. at Pittsburgh. That was the way I had it addressed.

Q. *What was in that message?*

A. To the best of my recollection it read something like this: That the reservoir was reported as being in a critical condition, and it would be well to notify the people of Conemaugh and Johnstown to prepare for the worst, and I signed "Operator" to it. I wrote the message up, and repeated it to her and asked her if that would do, and she said that was splendid; to send it that way. I doubled the message and waited and waited, and after while there was a track man came up to flag a washout that had been caused west of my office, and I pressed him into service to take this message to the first telegraph office, to sendd [sic] it to Conemaugh and Pittsburgh.

Q. *What was that person's name?*

A. I think that man's name is William Reichard.

Q. *Do you know whether he did it or not?*

A. He started with the message and he got down to where this washout was, and he met the division foreman, Rushor, and he turned the message over to Rusher, and Rusher said he would take the message back and see that itt [sic] w as [sic] sent, and would also notify the people in Conemaugh and Johnstown that they had better go to higher ground, and this man Reichard returned to my office again, and took charge of his flag, to flag the track, and he hadn't been there but a short time until I got a second message;

Q. *Who from?*

A. The second message was signed by C. P. Dougherty, Agent at South Fork.

Q. *What time of day was that, as near as you can tell?*

A. I received that message from the South Fork operator over No. 4 wire at 2.24 p. m.

Q. *Now did you fix upon the time?*

A. I fixed upon the time from the message I have on file in my office.
(Here, the witness discovers he has made a mistake in the time of the receipt of the message, which he corrects, as follow s; [sic])
The C. P. Dougherty message was received at my office at 1.52

Q. *How do you know that fact?*

A. I know by the message I have on file in the office. The message is hanging there on a hook.

Q. *What was in it?*

A. I have a duplicate of it; I can show you th [sic] exact copy.
Witness produces copy which reads as follow s:
"South Fork, May 31, 1889.
R. P.
OD via MP &AO.
 The water in running over the breast of Conemaugh lake in the center and west side end is becoming dangerous.
C. P. Dougherty"

Q. *What route was that message to take in order to reach R. P. and did it take?*

A. That message was sent from my office by this young man Reichard, on foot. He started away from there just shortly after I got it.

Q. *What time?*

A. I got it at 1.52 p.m% [sic] and just as quick as I got it fixed up, I started him right off.

Q. *Where did you send him to?*

A. To AO office, the tower immediately west of No. 6 bridge. That was the first office I understood that had communicatin [sic] with Pittsburgh, the wires being broken down between my office and his office.

Q. *Did he get that message to the destination?*

A. Yes, sir, that message reached the destination, so I understand; the operator himself told me he had received it and sent it; he didn't tell me he sent it; I suppose he did.

Q. *Did you get any other message that day?*

A. Yes, sir, I got one more. That message was sent by the operator at South Fork to me over No. 4 wire. I have a copy of it here.

Q. *Read the copy.*

(Witness produces copy and reads as follows:)
"South Fork, May 31, 1889.

R. P.

OD

The dam is becoming dangerous and may possibly go.

J. P. Wilson."

He is the Superintendent of the Argyle Coal Works.

Q. *Have you the original of that dispatch in the office?*

A. I couldn't say whether I have the original there or not. I copied that dispatch off from emmory [sic] without looking for the original among the oth r [sic] messages. I don't know whether the original is on the hook or not.

Q. *Are you sure that is the contents of the message?*

A. Yes, sir, I could be qualitfied [sic] on that.

Q. *What time did you get that message?*

A. 2.25 is the time I received the message from the operator. The time I got it to Conemaugh is on the back of it; 2.35. There was only ten minutes elapsed between the time I got it and getting it to Conemaugh over the wire. We got a circuit by some unknown cause; the operator and I had a communication over a wire that was crippled for a long while there before, and all at once the wire came all right. We can't account for it in any other way unless the wire raised up from the river and cleared it out of the water. I had a circuit with the operator about 2.20, I think it was, and we were trying to get a line opened to get communication between Conemagh [sic] and South Fork, but we couldn't do it. I sent him thc mcssage at 2.35 and the operator signed his signal "jo"; he signed for the message.

Q. *You know that he did receive it?*

A. Yes, sir, to the best of my knowledge; the sign he gave, and everything indicated that the message was received in as good faith as any I ever sent. He answered fari and plain [sic] for it and signed his office call, which indicated that he had got it.

Q. *How long after that ^[last] message was received was it until the flood came?*

A. It was about, I should say, somewheres between 30 and 35 minutes. That is, after I got it in to Conemaugh.

Q. *How far was your t ower [sic] from Conemaugh?*

A. My tower is located from Conemaguh [sic] to 3.3 miles east.

Q. *Did you get any other than th se [sic] messages?*

A. No, sir that is all the information I got in regard to the flood.

Mr. J. P. Wilson, the superintendent of miners for the Argyle Coal Company of South Fork, had both a self-interest in the condition of the dam and a shared interest based on a promise he had made to Robert Pitcairn some years earlier. In his Pennsylvania Railroad testimony, he described two visits made to the dam site between noon and the time of the break. He described how he warned Emma Ehrenfeld just minutes before her tower was destroyed by the flood wave. Wilson also makes reference to John Baker who made a trip to the dam and came back to South Fork with a report that carried a message of imminent doom. Baker's father owned and operated the Lake Hotel in South Fork at the time of the flood.

Q. *Just go on in your own way, and describe what took place on Friday, when the dam broke, where you were, and the whole thing.*

A. About half-past twelve o'clock on Friday with that tremendous rain that we had, I had some doubts about the dam, and I got Mr. Sibert, who drove team for me, to take the horse and ride up to the dam;

Q. *What time?*

A. It was about half-past twelve when he left South Fork on Friday. He came back in less than an hour, and he told me that the water was then running over the top near the middle of the dam, and I knew then that it was dangerous, and just when he came back, the Agent at South Fork, Mr. Dougherty, was standing close by when I got this news, and I turned to him, as I supposed he was the proper party to give warning to Mr. Pitcairn, and I asked him if he would not go to the tower, and notify Mr. Pitcairn of the condition of the dam. He hesitated, and said that there was trouble getting a message through, and I supposed at first that he didn't like to take the responsibility upon himself to do it, and I just replied that Mr. Pitcairn had told me some three years before if I ever saw any appearance of danger, to notify him at once, and I said "If you don't like to use your own name, use mine", and he then stated that it was on account of the wires being down that he hesitated in trying to send a message, but he went and endeavored to send it, and I believe he did. I waited in South Fork then until about 2 o'clock, and a second messenger that had went up to the dam, came back.

Q. *Who is he?*
A. I think his name is John Baker.

Q. *Who sent him out?*
A. Nobody. I know of nobody sending him out. When he came back, he reported that the water was running over, and that there was a hole some twelve feet below the top through which the water was coming. I then started for the tower, some four or five hundred yards, I think, and I said to the lady operator, (I just gave her a verbal message; I really don't remember what it was) but it was to Mr. Pitcairn stating that the dam was breaking, or something to that effect, and to look out for it. She told me then that the wires were down between Mineral Point and the tower west, the one near deep cut, I think it is termed "AO" tower, and that there was trouble in getting the message through, but the operator said he had sent it with some person who was in the tower.I [sic] waited a few minutes, and warned her in regard to the danger; that h [sic] she had better keep a look-out up the creek, and whenever she saw the water coming, to get out of the tower. Just when I went to leave, I asked her if the message had got through yet and hse [sic] said she asked the operator at Mineral Point tower, and he said the messenger hadn't returned yet, and he didn't know. I went out of the tower, and got, I suppose 150 feet from it when I saw the water coming. I then turned and saw the lady at the windown [sic] and motioned to her to run. I had told her where to go to get out of danger, and she went where I told her, and I went up and watched the water until it came and took the tower away.

The Pennsylvania Railroad testimony of Mr. J. C. Walkinshaw centered on the positions of the various trains in the East Conemaugh yard just prior to the rush of the floodwaters. Walkinshaw was the yard master at East Conemaugh. He had been employed by the Pennsylvania Railroad in East Conemaugh in one capacity or another since 1866. In his testimony he also makes reference to a message that reached him at East Conemaugh just prior to the arrival of the flood wave.

Q. *Who was the message sent by?*
A. I don't know; I didn't look at the signature.

Q. *What was the purport [sic] of the message, and where did it come from?*
A. I didn't look where it was from; I understood the operator to say it was from "AO" tower. "AO" tower is about a mile and three quarters, I judge, east of Conemaugh. I don't know whether it came from Mineral Point or "AO" tower. That message that Conemaugh Lake had filled up, and was running over, and was liable to break at any moment.

Q. *What time did you get that message?*
A. That message was handed to me, as near as I can remember, between 3.30 and 3.35 in the afternoon. I handed the message to Mr. Trump, and while he was looking at it, the operator called down from the tower where we were standing, and told me that the tracks east of the big cut were washed out. The big cut is two miles east of Conemaugh. I asked Mr. Trump how far he was going east, and mentioned to him about these tracks being washed out east of the deep cut. He remarked that they would go on east as far as they could, and see what damage was done. His train started away, and Local Freight came up just after his train left. I went out and put that train on one of the sidings out of the way, and went back into the office and looked up at the clock, and it was then fifteen minutes to four o'clock. I sat down and wasn't in the chair more than a minute until I heard a whistle blow. (One of our work trains had been ordered to Wilmore, but they got up as far as the deep cut, or this washout, and they couldn't get any further, and they were turned back, and there was a slide on No. 4 and No. 3 tracks about five or six hundred yards east of Conemaugh, and they stopped there on their way back to clean it off). That train was standing there, and while I was sitting there in the chair, I had just sat down about a minute, I heard a whistle blow, and I knew it was the engine that was up there. She gave four or five long blasts. That meant to me that there was danger. I jumped off of my chair, and as soon as I heardd [sic] the second blast, I ran out and hollowed [sic] for every person to go away off the road and get on high ground, and I started up the track. Just as I left the office, I saw the rear end of this work train backing around the curve. I started up toward the train, and the minute I saw the train stop, I saw the engineer jump off and run for the hill. Just at that minute, I saw a large wave come around the hill. When I saw it, it was a body of water in a swell, apparently to me about four feet higher than the track where I was standing. As soon as I saw it come every person was making for the hill, and the distance I had to go, I started to save myself, and I saved myself, but I was in very close quarters when I got out.

Q. *All the information you got then from the message was the fact that the water was running over the South Fork dam, and that there was danger of it breaking?*
A. That was all.

Q. *It didn't tell you whether any portion of the dam had given way, nor how much water was running over the dam?*
A. No, sir.

Q. *Now, from the time you got that message until you saw this body of water coming, how long was it?*

A. Well, it wasn't over 15 minutes.

Q. *Now, when you got that message about the water running over the South Fork dam, had the water gotten outside of the river bank at all up opposite where these trains were staniding [sic] ?*

A. No, sir.

Q. *How far was it below the level of where these trains stood?*

A. Three or four feet below the level.

Q. *Where is that dispatch you say your son gave you?*

A. After I read it, I laid it down on the desk in the office, (the Yard Master's Office) and everything was washed away. That message was swept away with the office.

Q. *You don't know where the message your son gave you came from?*

A. No, sir, I couldn't say whether it came from Mineral Point or "AO" tower, but it came from one of those two places.

In addition to the three messages referred to in the testimony gathered by the Pennsylvania Railroad, there were several other accounts of telegrams sent down to Johnstown. One for example, was a message that a coal miner named Hartman claimed he sent to Johnstown when he heard from W. Y. Boyer that the water was nearing the top of the dam. There is no credible evidence to support any claims that any messages other then those referenced in the Pennsylvania Railroad testimony were sent to warn any location in the Conemaugh Valley about the pending danger of the dam in South Fork.

In the immediate aftermath of the flood, much was made of how many warnings were sent down the valley, who sent them, who received them, how the information was dispersed, and how folks reacted to it. A careful review of available information indicates that three messages were sent down the valley on May 31, 1889, warning of the dangers of the dam of the South Fork Fishing and Hunting Club.

The Pickerill-Ehrenfeld message was the first of the three warnings sent to Johnstown. It was based on information brought to South Fork by John G. Parke, between 11:00 a.m. and noon. Pickerill and Ehrenfeld discussed the reliability of the information they had received, crafted a message and sent it on to the yardmaster in East Conemaugh and Robert Pitcairn in Pittsburgh. Because of damaged lines this message was carried part way along the line by hand. Between noon and 1:00 p.m., Walkinshaw in East Conemaugh, agent Deckert in Johnstown, and Robert Pitcairn's office in Pittsburgh had

also received this message. Upon receiving this news Robert Pitcairn made the decision to come out and have a look for himself.

The second of the three messages was based on information provided by another visitor to Lake Conemaugh. Dan Siebert, a driver for J. P. Wilson, was sent to Lake Conemaugh to make an assessment. When he returned and reported that water from the lake was flowing over the breast of the dam, Wilson, working with C. P. Dougherty, put out a dispatch that indicated that the condition of the dam in South Fork was worsening. This message provided the first news that water had begun to flow over the top of the dam. The second message, or the Dougherty message, also had to be carried part way by hand because of downed wires. It was received in East Conemaugh, Johnstown, and Pittsburgh.

The third and final message may have been prompted by the report of John Baker, a boy from South Fork who had been up to the dam for a look. It does not appear that he had been sent to the dam, but instead went because of his own curiosity. His observation was that a portion of the dam's breast, near the center, had been washed away by the water as a result of overtopping of the earthen embankment. Based on Baker's account, J. P. Wilson himself went to Emma Ehrenfeld, dictated the message to Robert Pitcairn and waited to see if it at least made it as far as Mineral Point. This message made it through. Agent Deckert in Johnstown recalled receiving this message a 2:44 p.m. Based on this message, Deckert decided to notify Hettie Ogle, who ran the telegraph office of Western Union and the local telephone switchboard. In the June 14, 1889, edition of the *Johnstown Tribune*, Editor Swank reported that he had received a call from the telephone office at about 3:15 p.m. regarding Wilson's assessment that the condition of the dam in South Fork was worsening and may soon give way. At that time, it already had!

In 1889 Alexander Graham Bell's telephone was already more than a decade old. Most cities and towns had telephone exchanges, but general use was somewhat limited to those who had a direct need, such as doctors, or those who could afford to indulge their desire to own the latest technology. As a result, the telephone had yet to come into wide spread use and was still something of a novelty. The telegram, on the other had, was the workhorse of electrical communications. With a wire connecting two points, regardless of the distance, instant communications were available. There were, however, times, places, and circumstances that rendered the telegraph useless. In such cases, word had to be carried from one point to another just as it had been for thousands of years: in person.

There were numerous stories told following the flood of brave and heroic rides to spread the word that the dam had broken and peril was on the loose. Although somewhat interesting and dramatically heroic to say the least, each of these stories is little more than a marginally plausible figment of an inventive imagination. The fact that the stories were so widely circulated is due largely to the almost hysterical search for details and related stories following the flood. In many instances, if a story could be reduced to words and could conceivably have occurred, it was fair game. It was not until sometime after the flood that the line between fact and fiction could be distinguished with any degree or reliability.

The most popular of the "Paul Revere" stories is the story of Daniel Peyton. Interestingly enough, it is also the most fictitious of the lot. According to the various accounts of Peyton's ride, he and his trusty steed rode from South Fork to Johnstown, via the "turnpike" just ahead of the wave of flood water from the collapsed dam. Once they arrived in Johnstown, supposedly just prior to the flood wave, they rode throughout the town warning all to take to the hills. Just as horse and rider were about to heed their own warning, the wave overtook them and they both perished.

The June 11, 1889, edition of *The Star and Sentinel*, the weekly paper of Gettysburg, Pennsylvania, reported the following under the headline "THE HERO'S BODY FOUND":

> JOHNSTOWN, June 4—The body of the Paul Revere of the Valley and the first man to go down at the call of the demon of death on Friday, was found beneath the mass of broken trees at the base of the hill west of Johnstown this afternoon. It was horribly disfigured and the features of the man who sacrificed his life that thousands of his fellow beings might live, were almost beyond recognition. Daniel Peyton's name will go down to history among the greatest of heroes. He it was by whom the message, sent from South Fork by John G. Parke to the effect that the dam was about to burst was conveyed.

A few simple facts have long compromised this story, rendering it a handsome piece of fiction and rendering Peyton an imaginary hero at best. There is no "turnpike" or single road along which a horse and rider could travel from South Fork to Johnstown. With every road flooded or mud-swamped by the heavy rains a trip of some fourteen miles in well under an hour would have been essentially impossible. The streets of Johnstown were already submerged at the time Peyton was to have arrived, seriously compromising his ability to ride the streets of Johnstown at great speed warning everyone who would listen. No one between South Fork and Johnstown had any recollection of a horse and rider galloping past in advance of the flood wave giving warning of what was coming. And possibly the most compelling piece of information, the lack of which refutes this story totally and completely, is that there simply was no Daniel Peyton. There is no record of a Daniel Peyton having lived in South Fork, Johnstown or anywhere else in that vicinity, and no one had a recollection of a person by that name. The creators and purveyors of this story held that both Peyton and his horse died in the end. Was it their purpose to add a touch of the ultimate drama to the story, or was their intent to make the story impossible to verify?

The second Paul Revere was none other than John G. Parke, Jr., the engineer recently employed by the South Fork Fishing and Hunting Club. According to most reliable accounts, it was indeed Parke who made the first trip into South Fork carrying the message that the dam's condition was worsening steadily and that the dam might collapse. The first telegraph message sent from South Fork west seems to have been based largely on the information provided by Parke. Parke was at the dam on May 31, 1889, he did ride a horse from the dam toward South Fork, and he did carry a warning that the condition of the dam was worsening. These details were not enough, however, to satisfy the inventive and imaginative wit of those who fancied and admired Parke beyond what he had actually done. As a result, his story was easily embellished, almost to mythical grandeur. The January 31, 1933, edition of the *Pittsburgh Post-Gazette*, carried a summary of Parke's life and notification of his death the previous day. The headline of the story read, "Paul Revere of Flood Dies." The following are excerpts from the account of Parke's efforts following the breaking of the dam:

> The "Paul Revere" of the Johnstown flood is dead. The man who is credited with spreading the alarm through the streets of Johnstown on horseback before the flood struck the city in 1889, died at his home here at the age of 67.
> He is reported as the one who warned the people that the dam was going to break. As soon as the accident occurred Parke mounted a horse, sped down the hill overlooking Johnstown, rode through the main streets spreading the news of the flood which was fast approaching the city. His gallantry saved the lives of thousands of persons, who fled to the hills.

For basically the same reasons why Peyton's ride was impossible, so too would have been such a ride for Parke. Also, it was Parke who provided one of the better eyewitness accounts of the final collapse of the dam.

So, unless he had mastered the art of being two places simultaneously, his ride through Johnstown was virtually impossible.

A third and final "Paul Revere" account is that describing the efforts of John Baker. As previously noted, Baker made a trip to the dam during the day on May 31, 1889. Based on his observations and the word he brought back from the dam, the third and final message was sent down the Conemaugh Valley from South Fork. It was received in Johnstown at 2:44 p.m., at least twenty minutes before the dam gave way. There are those, who for years, credited Baker with waiting until the dam actually broke, then riding just in front of the wave to warn South Fork. The time that the warning was received in Johnstown would make this impossible, since the dam broke at 3:10 p.m.

It is true, based on several eyewitness accounts, that he did ride a horse both to and from the dam, and he did carry news about the condition of the dam. What is not true is that he stayed at the dam site until the dam burst, then galloped in front of the churning waters of Lake Conemaugh screaming "My God the dam has burst."

It is interesting to note that in McNutt's published history and souvenir booklet, he says, "No one rode through Johnstown giving warning." However, regarding Baker's ride he says, "John Baker rode from the dam to South Fork, a distance of two miles, just ahead of the avalanche and gave warning to the inhabitants of that village." McNutt, although not to the degree of many others, still sensationalized actual events to create a hero of fiction rather than of fact.

Regardless of how many warnings were sent from South Fork on May 31, 1889, and how many gallant rides were or were not made, the dam that held back the 20 million tons of water of Lake Conemaugh broke at 3:10 p.m. The worst fears of Daniel J. Morrell and others regarding the endeavors of the South Fork Fishing and Hunting Club were realized. A giant wall of water, the force of which was compared to that of Niagara Falls, was unleashed when the dam broke. It took about forty-five minutes for the lake to totally empty itself into the valley below. The elevation of Johnstown was just about 400 feet below that of Lake Conemaugh, and the distance from Lake Conemaugh to Johnstown was nearly fourteen miles. In less than an hour the almost total destruction of Johnstown and several towns between there and the broken dam was a reality of epic proportions that was difficult to comprehend and almost impossible to describe.

Randolph McNutt and numerous other entrepreneurs and promoters quickly sought to turn a quick buck on the public interest generated by the flood. McNutt created a scenographic reproduction of the flood, which he set up in Atlantic City, New Jersey on the Boardwalk. His was a black and white slide show which was often referred to as a "magic lantern shows." On the cover of a souvenir publication from this production was a likeness of John Baker making his famous ride.

JOHNSTOWN FLOOD

A HISTORY AND A SOUVENIR

"MY GOD THE DAM HAS BURST"
JOHN BAKER'S RIDE

Chapter 4

The Flood

At 3:00 p.m. on May 31, 1889, Johnstown, Pennsylvania was experiencing the worst flood in its history, and the entire area of the Conemaugh Valley was trapped under similar conditions. Flooding throughout much of Pennsylvania, Ohio, Maryland, West Virginia and Virginia, Delaware, New Jersey and New York was far worse than anyone could recall. In Johnstown, the waters of the Stony Creek and the Little Conemaugh Rivers met in the streets of the town. Water had reached a level of eight to ten feet on some of the city streets in the lower districts of the town, making evacuation by any means other than boat impossible. Although some of the residents of Johnstown and surrounding towns did evacuate the area, most of the residents did what they had become accustomed to doing during other periods of flooding; they quietly resolved to wait out the high waters.

Mr. Trump, the assistant superintendent of the Pittsburgh district of the Pennsylvania Railroad, was in Johnstown during the early afternoon, prior to the bursting of the dam at South Fork, on May 31. He provided the following description of the flooding in and around Johnstown as part of his Pennsylvania Railroad testimony:

Q. *Now, Mr. Trump, please state why you left Pittsburgh in the latter part of May, where you went, what you did, etc.*

A. I got up on Friday morning, May 31st, at home in Pittsburgh; the Train Despatchers [sic] called me up on the telephone, and advised me that we were having considerable trouble at Lilly on account of the tracks being washed out. I came to the office, and after arrival there, found there was great danger of our telegraph line being washed out, and our communication cut off. I then began to hunt up Mr. Wierman, whom I found at home, sick. I gave him the situation, and I then sent for our Master Carpenter, Mr. Webb, and about 11 o'clock, and we left with engine 266 (?) and one coach, and Mr. Wierman, Mr. Webb, Mr. Sheaffer, and a telegraph operator, and a gang of telegraph repairmen, with the intention of going as far as Lilly and repairing any damage that might be done to the telegraph

line. On arrival at Wilkensburg, we picked up John Stewart, Train Despatcher [sic], and took him along. We had no further reports of the situation until we arrived at Johnstown; [sic]

Q. *What time?*

A. The train sheet shows that we arrived at Johnstown at 2.27, after which there is no record of the run of this train. On arrival at Johnstown, we found the town flooded:-

Q. *To what extent do you judge the water was up on the houses?*

A. Well, the water, as far as I could see from the track, was up about to the second floor, almost within a foot of the second floor, and the people were all in the second stories of their houses, including our Agent's family at the station, and right at the station, the water was up at the top of the fence there, which was about four feet high, and that portion of the town is considerably higher than the balance of the town, so that I judge the water in the main part of the town must have been eight or nine feet deep. We stopped at the bridge, and found Mr. Hays' work train at that point, and we got out, made an examination of the abutments—

Q. *You are speaking now of the stone bridge below Johnstown?*

A. Yes, sir;— and we found there was a considerable amount of timber, such as logs, etc., coming down from the Johnstown Lumber Company's boom, and lodging against the bridge. The boom which had already broken, was hanging through the piers at that time. We then arranged for the work train gang to go down, and see what they could do to keep the drift passing through the piers. We then pushed on to the telegraph tower.

When the dam at South Fork broke at 3:10 p.m., flooding of an entirely different nature was soon to be upon Johnstown. Flooding that is the result of water that rises over a period of time provides some level of predictability and thus offers some degree of warning. However, when a man-made body of water, particularly one of the largest bodies of water ever contained by an earthen dam, goes on a rampage sending an avalanche of water down a valley with a fall of 400 hundred feet in just fourteen miles, predictability and danger warnings are far less likely.

The immediate cause of the failure of the dam at South Fork was the steady deterioration of its outer surface, brought on by water rushing over the breast. Most eyewitnesses reported that the dam held for just about three hours after overtopping had begun eating away at the dam's outer surface. When the pressure of the water being held in check by the dam was greater than the dam's weakened capability to hold, a massive section of the middle of the dam moved away. Having witnessed the breaking of the Club's dam, Colonel Unger collapsed.

Although there are numerous accounts of the breaking of the dam, certain elements seem to be common among them. Most who witnessed the failure of the dam speak of it as a gradual process that began early in the day and progressed through the afternoon hours. The level of water in the reservoir rose steadily, exerting ever-increasing pressure on the dam. Once the overtopping began, it continued unabated and as such wore away the outer surface of the dam in the same unabated manner. Once sufficiently weakened, the center section of the dam pushed out and the reservoir began its rampage. What follows is an overview of the course the flood wave took from South Fork to the Conemaugh River below Johnstown.

Many in the Conemaugh Valley claimed to live in the shadow of the South Fork Dam and in a manner of speaking maybe they did. However, George Lamb, George Fisher, and their families lived in the shadow of the dam in a far more literal sense. Their homes were just below the breast of the mighty earthen structure, and when it broke, they were the first two properties affected. Ironically, the Fisher property sustained relatively minimal damage. Fisher, a local milkman, had tried to move some of his equipment to higher ground but failed in his efforts to do so. Lamb, concerned for his pigs, remained at his property until the very last minute, and was spared only with the help of some friends. The Lamb property was not spared by the wave of water from the dam.

The first victim of the flood was Michael Mann of South Fork. Mann was a coal miner who had come to the United States from England. He was also a self-pro-

In this historic view, the center section of the great earthen dam in South Fork which gave way is clearly visible. Both the east and west abutments survived this initial failure and still stand today. As noted on the photograph, the breast of the dam was roughly 72 feet above the streambed.

In this modern view the east (left) and west (right) abutments of the dam are still visible. The center section of the dam which gave way on May 31, 1889 is also still well defined. Following the flood the town of Saint Michael was established in what had been the lakebed of Lake Conemaugh.

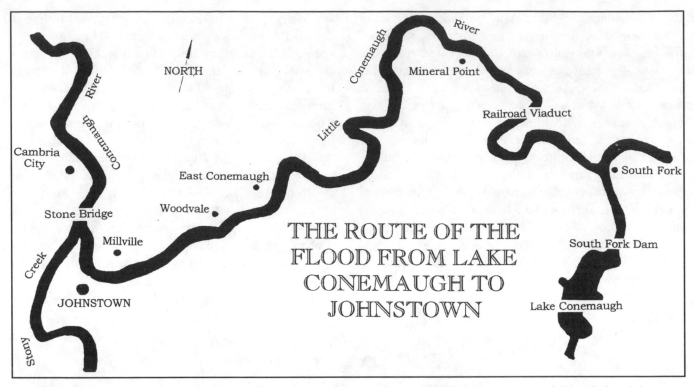

This map indicates the route taken by the floodwaters from Lake Conemaugh through to the Conemaugh River below Johnstown.

claimed minister. A reference to Michael Mann, age 41 of South Fork, appears in the records of the dead compiled by James Murtha, (see reference in Chapter 6 to Murtha) and may be among those buried in the unknown plot at Grandview Cemetery.

Contrary to Murtha's account, there are those who believe that Michael Mann's body was not among those seen by Murtha, but was instead found by some of Mann's friends and buried in an unmarked plot near South Fork. Including Michael Mann, four deaths occurred in the South Fork area. South Fork, even though it was the closest town to the dam, was spared the full force of the flood's destructive wave, since it was built on a hill, which kept it beyond the reach of the torrent of water from Lake Conemaugh.

As the water surged from the dam, it began picking up debris, a process that continued all along the fourteen-mile path to Johnstown. The debris in the wave of rushing water significantly increased its destructive force. At various points along the course that the floodwaters took, the valley grew narrow. This narrowing only served to increase the force of the water. Such an increase occurred just before the waters struck a stone viaduct just below South Fork. This massive stone viaduct had originally been built as part of the Allegheny Portage Railroad. The viaduct provided a bridge for the railroads that passed through South Fork. It was made of sandstone and stood approximately seventy-five feet above the bed of the stream that ran below it.

By the time the wave of water rushing from the dam hit the viaduct, it had picked up a great deal of debris. That debris quickly collected behind the massive stone structure and created another dam. Briefly, the waters of Lake Conemaugh were again contained, but as the pressure of the water behind the viaduct increased, it collapsed. The destruction of the viaduct just below South Fork began what would become almost a total destruction of the transportation and communication systems of the Conemaugh Valley. The viaduct had withstood floodwaters numerous times, but never before had it been put under the stress of 20,000,000 tons of water already laden with additional tons of debris. With the collapse of the viaduct, the surging waters of Lake Conemaugh continued, with renewed force, what was to be an unabated rush to Johnstown.

The wildly churning water ripped trees out by the roots, quickly and dramatically altered the natural course of the streams which flowed through the valley, and continued gathering speed as it rushed along the 400-foot decent toward Johnstown. Virtually nothing in its path was spared. Eyewitnesses would later claim that whole sections of hillsides simply vanished and were stripped to bare rock.

Following the collapse of the stone viaduct, a wave with the force of Niagara Falls began making its way to the village of Mineral Point. In 1889, Mineral Point was a prospering town, the economy of which was centered around a saw mill and a small furniture factory. At the

These photographs are of the Fisher house and were taken before (left) and after (right) the failure of the dam.

The entry for Michael Mann in the Murtha book reads, "Mann, Michael 41 South Fork Found Wife & 2 Survivors."

Mangus, Martha	?	?	Found	
Mann, Michael	41	South Fork	Found	Wife & 2 survivor
Marbourg, Dr. H. W.	56	42 Market St	Found	Wife survivor

This view shows the viaduct prior to its destruction by the flood. As originally constructed it had only a single arch.

This current view shows the reconstructed viaduct. In the days and weeks following the flood a wooden, trestle-style bridge was quickly constructed to re-establish the rail lines east and west.

time of the flood, there were nearly 200 residents living in Mineral Point. When the wall of water struck Mineral Point nothing there altered its course. By the time the water had passed, nothing stood in its wake. Full houses and railroad locomotives were caught by the wave of water and moved right along with it. Mineral Point seemed to vanish, and sixteen residents were dead. The death toll in Mineral Point was smaller than it might have been had there not been heavy stream flooding during the morning and early afternoon. The water had been rising in Mineral Point all day, and most of the residents had sought refuge on higher ground.

In an early report of the flood, a resident of Mineral Point, Abraham Byers, read an account of his own death and that of his mother. In a letter written by Byers that was carried in the June 20 edition of the *Johnstown Tribune*, he reported that it was instead his wife and her mother who had been claimed.

According to Byers' account, his wife and their six children made it safely out of the house. His mother-in-law, for some unknown reason, did not leave the house when warned that the floodwaters were approaching. In an effort to save her mother, his wife went back into the house. As Byers reported, "That is the last I ever saw of her." The oldest son escaped on his own, and Byers managed to save the other five children. Regarding the loss of his wife and her mother Byers said, "I would willingly devote the balance of my life to slavery if it would have saved the two lives that went down with that house."

The next town along the path of the floodwaters was East Conemaugh. East Conemaugh was home to a large railroad yard and a railroad station. As the water moved toward East Conemaugh, it sent an eerie warning ahead. The force of the water and the debris it was carrying created a rushing sound punctuated continually with the groaning and crushing sounds of the destruction it was causing.

John Hess, a railroad engineer in the East Conemaugh railroad yards, heard the sounds and knew exactly what had happened. In an effort to provide some warning to the residents of East Conemaugh, which included his family, Hess tied down the whistle of his train as he headed down the tracks toward East Conemaugh. Engineers typically had a number of signals that they could send with the whistles on their locomotives. However, the signal Hess was sending, a continual blast from the locomotive whistle, was an unmistakable warning of danger. Hess, a true hero, is credited with saving many lives in East Conemaugh.

The following is an excerpt from the testimony of John Hess before the officials of the Pennsylvania Railroad:

Q. *Now, just commence and tell us what you did on Friday with your train, where you were, and what you saw.*

A. well, in the morning we started; I went as usual to take my engine, and the conductor was there, and coming down out of the telegraph office, he says "We will go to Cambria; there's a small slide down there, and we'll go down and take it up. I had my engine ready and all, and we coupled on and started down to Cambria % [sic] We worked there until somewhere between 10 and 11 o'clock, when we got an order to leave there, and go to one mile west of Wilmore to a land slide, and as soon as we could get out of there, which was very soon; as soon as the men could get on the train, we started and went up the main south track to Johnstown. No. 8's were laying at Conemaugh, and we couldn't pass Johnstown as the block was red, as it always is on an occasion like that. We laid there some 15 to 20 minutes, and finally we got an order to go ahead under green, and I had a hand-full of other messages and orders, that it took me from Johnstown almost to Conemaugh to get them all read. There was some five or six different ones. We went to Conemaugh and No. 8 was laying on the main track, and of course we couldn't pass. We laid there some 20 or 25 minutes more, and we got more orders there, and among the orders we got at Conemaugh was one to go on to the trouble one mile west of Wilmore, and to report from each telegraph office we came to the condition of the track we passed; how it was, you know. We started from there then, and we didn't get out of Conemaugh more than 500 yards untilw [sic] we found one track in the river, the track next to the river. We found it in the river, I suppose nearly 100 feet.

Q. *What time was that?*

A. This was nearly 1 o'clock; between 12 and 1 somewheres. We went on to "AO". My conductor w as [sic] new up there, and he says to me when we left Conemaugh, he says, "You will have to hunt the road; I don't know it." He was off of his division at that time. He belonged on Hays' Division. He says to me "You'll have to tell me when we come to" such and such a place; so I says to him, "Here's "AO"!" Have you anything to report?" and he says "No, we'll not report anything from here; we'll go on." We started on again, and didn't reach more than 200 yards more until there was a flagman: I stopped to let him on, and he says "You can't go any further", and I asked him why, and he says, "The north track is in the river and I don't believe the one you're on is safe", and I says "Whereabouts?" [sic] and he says "Right through the big cut". We went through the cut to where the washout was, and seen it was badly washed, and

Someone, probably a niece or a nephew, made a note on this photograph which shows John Hess and his engine, which was number 1124.

John Hess is buried in Johnstown's Grandview Cemetery among family. An inscription on his tombstone bespeaks his role in the Johnstown Flood. It reads "There is but a step between me and death."

I says to the conductor "I guess we'll have to take it afoott [sic] from here, and see where it is safe." The conductor is an old experienced man, and he looked at the track we were on, and he says "It isn't safe; I won't run you over that." It was washed up to the endso [sic] of the ties and underneath the track, and undermined it; the ballast was still sticking to the ties; the ties seemed to be holding it up. He says "That isn't safe at all", and we walked on up to Mineral Point, the next tower, and were going to report there, but the operator told us he had no communication except with South Fork, so we knew it was no use to stay there, and we went b ack [sic] to "AO" tower. We could get communication there by some wire, and my conductor reported the condition of the track that he had seen. This was after one o'clock, and we had no dinner yet; we hadn't had time to eat dinner, and while he was waiting on an answer what to do, we ate our dinners, and I suppose by the time we got our dinners eaten, it was two o'clock. By that time, there was an answer there telling him to come to the trouble east of Conemaugh, to that slide about four or five hundred yards east of Conemaugh. We came down there and found the track that we had went up on—the [sic] conductor thought at first it was unsafe, and we walked down over it and left the engine above it, and he suggested to cut a couple cars of—we [sic] had 7 empty flats and the cabin ahead of our engine, and he suggested to cut off a couple cars and run them over to see whether it was safe, and probably we could bring the rest over. So we sent a man with two cars down over this dangerous place, and the bank didn't appear to slip down much, and I brought the engine and rest of the train over. That left us on the Conemaugh side of this washout. I went down and

the brakeman coupled up those cars that they had sent down ahead, and the conductor took the men with their shovels and went back to the slide about one hundred yards back of where we were laying. There had been a small slide come down over the bank, and he was taking it off, and I don't suppose we had laid their more than 20 minutes until we heard the flood coming. We didn't see it but we heard the noise of it coming.

Q. *What was the noise of it like?*

A. It was like a hurricane through a wooded country. It was a roar and a crash and a smash; I can't tell what it was like, but the first thing I heard was a terrible roar in the hollow and the next thing was a crash something like a big building going to pieces, which I think w as [sic] the Company house that stoodd [sic] right up around the curve, and the trees and brush hid it from our sight. I couldn't see it, but there was people told me after wards [sic] that that house crushed together just about the time we left. We saw no flood; we saw a drift of lg [sic] logs in the river, but the river was no higher then it was twenty minutes before that. I pulled the whistle wide open, and went into Conemaugh that way.

Q. *How far were you away from Conemaugh?*

A. Four or five hundred yards.

Q. *Did you keep ahead of the flood?*

A. Oh yes, I kept ahead of the flood down as far as I could go. I couldn't go through Conemaugh on account of the tracks below me being washedin [sic] the river; of course I didn't know it att [sic] that time, but I didn't know where No. 8's were, and it occurred to me that they might be pulling No. 8's up on higher track, and I was a little dubious about going down, though we had ourselves protected and had a full right to go down that was because our flagman was down there.

Unfortunately, not everyone in East Conemaugh was able to escape the wrath of the floodwaters from South Fork. A passenger train waiting there for clearance to continue along its run was destroyed. More than fifty people died in East Conemaugh, the railroad station was destroyed, and the railroad yard was in shambles. Eyewitnesses recalled watching as the wave of water pushed railroad locomotives, weighing more than 50 tons, around with ease. More than forty homes and two hotels were lost. Like Mineral Point, East Conemaugh was destroyed.

Lou S. Dallmyer was a passenger on one of the trains engulfed and destroyed by the flood at East Conemaugh. His account, which appeared in the June 11 edition of *The Star and Sentinel* of Gettysburg, Pennsylvania, was vivid and clear. He described the brief lapse of time from when they heard the continuous blast of a locomotive whistle, possibly that of John Hess, and the frantic calls of the conductors and trainmen, until the flood wave was upon them. He recalls seeing railroad cars and locomotives being lifted from their tracks and tossed around, "...as if they had been paper toys." Dallmyer recounted a mad rush to escape the oncoming wave of water and debris that was nothing short of mass hysteria.

Many of the passengers in their mad, frantic efforts to release themselves dashed their hands and faces against the windows, the broken glass cutting gashes from which the blood flowed in streams. Some of the men succeeded in climbing to the tops of cars, only to be dashed off into the water when the former would strike against some obstacle.

Frank Trout, a resident of East Conemaugh, was on his way to work when he was caught by the wave. Trout was employed by the Johnson Company at their Woodvale facility. He tried to escape the rushing water by crawling on top of the ticket office of the East Conemaugh fair grounds. From there he managed to climb up a telegraph and telephone pole that was soon broken off by the flood wave. Attempting to remain above the wave, he grasped onto another pole and finally clung to one of two logs between which he was almost crushed. Trout managed to remain upright on the log, riding it into Johnstown as far as the Stone Bridge before being washed back up Main Street as far as the Presbyterian Church. From there he made his way to Alma Hall, where he spent the night.

The next town in the path of the flood was Woodvale. Woodvale was sort of a model town established in part by the Cambria Iron Company. Woodvale had a woolen mill owned by Cambria Iron, and there was a privately owned tannery there as well. In a matter of minutes, the surging waters of Lake Conemaugh were upon this fashionable town and everything, except a single span of railroad bridge was gone. The residents of Woodvale had no warning that the dam had indeed broken, and more than 300 people perished. It has been estimated that one out of every three people living in Woodvale on May 31, 1889, died. In one stable almost ninety horses were claimed by the flood. The destruction of Woodvale, which left the town little more than a muddy plain between the mountains, took less than ten minutes.

Although the destruction of Woodvale appeared to be all but complete, the small settlement of New Austria remained after the wave of destruction passed. It was saved only because it was perched on high ground just north of Woodvale. The homes in this small settlement numbered approximately thirty at the time of the flood.

The single span of roadway (railroad) bridge, which withstood the flood wave, was the object of a story that appeared in the June 6, 1889 edition of the *Lebanon* (Pennsylvania) *Daily News*. The Headline of the story was "A Solitary Monument of Ruin."

The windows of the playground where a giant force played with masses of iron as a child might play with pebbles, begin with a bridge, or piece of bridge, about thirty feet long, that stands high and dry upon two ordinary abutments at Woodvale. The part of the bridge that remains spans the Pennsylvania tracks. The tracks are gone, the bridge is gone on either side, the river is gone to a new channel, the very earth for 100 yards around has been scraped off and swept away, but this little span remains perched up there twenty feet above everything, in the midst of a desert of ruins, the only piece of a bridge that is standing from the rail bridge to South Fork is a light iron structure, and the abutments are not unusually heavy. That it should be kept there when everything else was twisted and torn to pieces, is one of the queer freaks of this flood.

As the floodwaters continued their downward rush toward Johnstown, tremendous additional force was generated. Friction at the bottom of the wave of water and debris that at times reached forty feet caused it to move slightly slower at the bottom than at the top. As a result the wave kept rolling over itself, causing a tremendous crushing action as the debris-filled water continually thundered down on top of itself.

The caption across the bottom of this picture reads, "But one building withstood the Flood and one span of Roadway Bridge July 15, 1889."

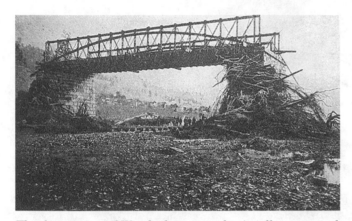

The devastation of Woodvale was made visually more stark by the solitary bridge span left standing.

At 4:07 p.m., slightly less than an hour after the South Fork Dam broke, the destructive wall of water neared the end of its fourteen-mile run as it struck Johnstown. Within fifteen to twenty minutes Johnstown was virtually destroyed. A dark mist rose ominously just in front of the flood wave. Those who saw it and lived to recall what they had seen referred to it as the "death mist." It was a combination of dirt, dust, smoke and steam, much of which came from the Gautier wire works between Woodvale and Johnstown. The Gautier works also contributed miles of barbed wire to the mass of debris being carried to Johnstown. Efforts to clean up after the flood were hampered by the miles and miles of barbed wire that entangled the debris.

The floodwaters also announced their arrival with a rumble that echoed off the mountains that surrounded the town. To some it sounded like the approach of a giant train, while others likened it to the roll of thunder that precedes a great storm. Mixed with the sounds of the wall of water and debris that was estimated by many

to be between thirty and forty feet in height when it struck the town, were factory and shop whistles, and church bells. Exactly which whistles and bells called out warnings as the floodwaters approached the town is not known, but there were numerous stories of such last minute efforts. The Monday, June 17, 1889, edition of the *Johnstown Tribune* offered one such account:

> When word was received that the Reservoir had broken, Mr. Charles Horner, aged eighteen, employed at Harry Swank's machine Shop, blew the whistle as a warning to residents of the Fourth Ward, and continued the good work until the fires were extinguished by the water and the building floated a square away. Then he coolly walked from raft to raft until he reached a place of safety. It is known that a number of people saved their lives by fleeing to the hills upon hearing the whistle.

As the water struck Johnstown, it appears to have broken into several different torrents, the largest of which followed Washington Street and struck Westmont Hill, known as Yoder Hill at the time. The waters hit the hill with such force that a secondary or ricochet wave was sent up the Stony Creek, all but destroying the villages of Kernville and Moxham.

The Methodist Church on Franklin Street split another of the torrents of water, significantly reducing its destructive force. Although heavily damaged, the substantial stone church withstood the onslaught of the floodwaters and lessened the damage to buildings in front of it. For this reason suggestions to raze the church during the rebuilding which followed the flood were never acted upon.

The low plain, an area of approximately thirty acres that was Johnstown on May 31, 1889, was submerged under floodwaters that were eight to ten feet deep in spots, even before Lake Conemaugh poured into the town. Shortly

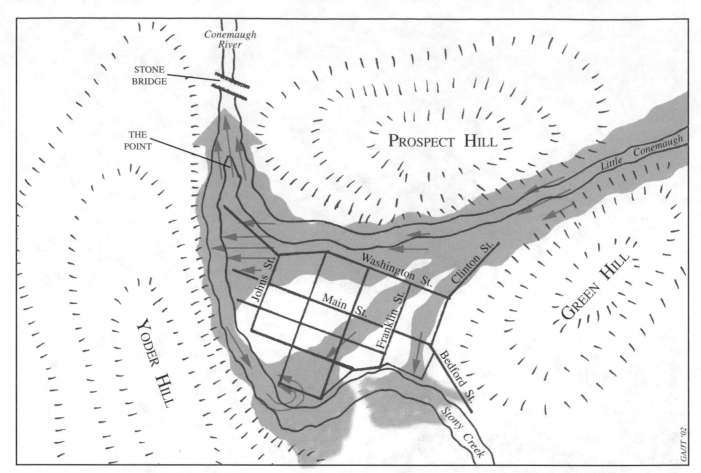

As the flood wave hit Johnstown it split into several sections. One portion of the wave flowed in the direction of Clinton Street toward the Stony Creek. Another flowed through the center of town. The largest portion of the wave continued along Washington Street until it crashed into Yoder Hill. Rebounding off that hill, this wave deposited tons of debris on Johnstown and caused a surge up the Stony Creek River before finally following the Conemaugh River out of Johnstown. The shaded areas only represent the paths of the flood wave from South Fork. This was in addition to the water that was already eight to ten feet deep in places.

after 4:07 p.m., flood levels in Johnstown ranged from ten to thirty feet. Johnstown was at that time under Lake Conemaugh. The Stone Bridge (a railroad bridge) just below the point where the Stony Creek and the Little Conemaugh join to form the Conemaugh River, quickly clogged with the debris. The Stone Bridge was the first structure the floodwaters encountered since the viaduct just below South Fork that was formidable enough to interrupt its rush. Even though the massive Stone Bridge held, it could not contain the floodwaters for long. Cutting channels around the bridge, the surge of water continued on through Millville and on to Cambria City. With only slightly reduced force, the floodwaters from Lake Conemaugh brought their wrath to these two communities just below Johnstown. Brownstown, a small community perched on a hillside was spared, but anything that came within the angry reach of the muddy torrent suffered the same fate as those villages and boroughs between Johnstown and South Fork.

Below Cambria City, where the Conemaugh River widens to a marked degree, the destructive force of the water from Lake Conemaugh was finally reduced. Bod-

The Methodist Church on Franklin Street was a key landmark in Johnstown. It stood as a recognizable point of reference amidst the destroyed town.

This illustration shows the Stone Bridge and the Cambria Iron works just before the Flood.

(Below) After the tremendous flood wave had passed, an almost unimaginable mountain of twisted and tangled debris was left in front of the Stone Bridge.

The Stone Bridge was credited by some with preventing many from being carried down the Conemaugh River to almost certain death. It still stands today as a stark reminder of the role it played in the flood of 1889.

ies and debris from Johnstown were carried along with the floodwaters, but the broad valley below Johnstown provided a release for the tremendous surge of the floodwaters.

The situation in Johnstown at 4:30 p.m. on the afternoon of May 31, 1889, was well beyond anything the average citizen could have imagined or anticipated. Nothing they had experienced before could have prepared them for the circumstances that now confronted them. Even after the deluge of water had spent its force, Johnstown stood under as much as thirty feet of water in certain locations. The level of water in Johnstown receded, but slowly. The Stone Bridge and the mass of debris that had collected in front of it served as a dam that held the waters in Johnstown. The mass of wreckage that clogged the Stone Bridge covered acres. It was a twisted and tangled mountain of houses, railroad cars, trees, animals, and most tragically, human bodies. Both living and dead were among those trapped at the Stone Bridge.

As night drew closer and the horrors of the day had scarcely been realized, fire broke out in the debris field at the Stone Bridge. Hot coals and ashes from stoves and furnaces, oil and kerosene from lamps and heaters, and ruptured natural gas lines ignited anything that would burn amidst the debris deposited in front of the Stone Bridge. Many who had survived the initial wave of water and debris, now fell victim to an enormous fire that immediately raged beyond control. Those who witnessed this scene were helpless to do much more than look on in dazed horror.

In 1889, prior to daylight savings time, night fell shortly before eight o'clock. The electric and gas service of Johnstown had been destroyed. The town was covered with water and shrouded in darkness. The blaze at the Stone Bridge produced a glow that grew throughout the night. Efforts to save those trapped in the wreckage proved futile in all too many cases, due in part to the fact that the condition of the rescuers was more often than not little better than those they sought to help.

Throughout the valley of the Conemaugh and particularly in Johnstown, those who had survived were engaged in a desperate struggle not to become victims themselves. Some managed to escape to hillsides and higher ground surrounding Johnstown, while others gathered in attics and upper floors of buildings that had not been toppled or crushed by the rushing waters. Family members and friends desperately sought to learn of the fate of loved ones. As evening gave way to night the panic of desperation began to give way to the agony of reality. The flames of the ravaging blaze before the Stone Bridge cast an orange glow on the night sky that many could never forget.

On October 5, 1900, during Johnstown's centennial year, the cornerstone for the new City Hall building at the corner of Main and Market Streets was laid. A bronze plaque identifies the High Water Mark from May 31, 1889. The high water mark from 1889 measures 21 feet.

The typical sounds of the town were gone. A silence pierced by periodic screams of fear and cries for help replaced the routine sounds. Many who the day before had attended Memorial Day festivities at Sandy Vale Cemetery or enjoyed the evening performance of the New York comedy production *A Night Off* at the opera house on Washington Street had since passed from this life. Many others tenuously clung to life having been seriously injured. Those who had only lost a home, a business, their church, their school, or all of their possessions now counted themselves among the most fortunate.

The desperate struggle to survive filled the air with screams and shrieks that lingered in the minds of survivors for the remainder of their days. Whole families were swallowed up in an instant, others families survived only in part, while still others miraculously survived intact. Statistics made available through the Johnstown Flood Museum of the Johnstown Area Heritage Association indicate that 99 entire families were lost. The loss of children under the age of ten amounted to 396, while 568 children lost one or both of their parents in the flood. Following the flood, 198 men were widowed and 124 women had lost their husbands.

The story of the Johnstown Flood of 1889, like any good story, is best told through the accounts of those who were part of it. The following stories are a sampling, and only a small sampling, of the informal collection of stories associated with the events of May 31, 1889, in Johnstown, Pennsylvania and vicinity. Newspaper reporters and correspondents, who brought the news of the Johnstown disaster to the nation and the world, recorded some of these stories. Others were recorded in the numerous books written in the months and years following the flood. The accuracy of the stories and the details associated with them are virtually impossible to document positively. However, their value goes far beyond their absolute accuracy and their many details. Collectively, these stories provide a vivid account of Johnstown's tragedy. In a strange way, they tend to authenticate each other. They are valid accounts not because of the details they offer, but instead because of the contribution they make to the larger story of which they are a part.

Through the Johnstown Flood by a Survivor, a book written by Reverend D. J. Beale, includes the detailed account of the escape of the Alfred Easterbrook family. The Easterbrooks, father, mother, two sons and a daughter, lived on Union Street in Johnstown. They were among the more fortunate families.

At about 4 o'clock we were all frightened by the cries of the people on the neighboring hills, and before we could realize what had happened, we saw our neighbors' houses floating toward us. I rushed for the attic, and then dragged my wife and children up after me; we did not all reach the attic before our house was afloat, but at last I succeeded in getting my children up, when all at once the flue of my house fell out. I then rushed to get out, and I succeeded. Then my eldest son got out of the attic window, on to the side of the house. The house turned over again, and parted in the centre, and my daughter shot out of the house, just as she was half way out, the house was forced together again. Holding her fast, by a great effort we released her from this position. All this time my wife and youngest son were under the water. I then saw my youngest son coming toward us. I reached out, caught him, and by dragging him out, and my wife having a hold of him under the water, I happened to see her hair floating on the water, and I caught it and dragged her out. Once more we were all together. We then began to consider which way we could reach the hill. At last the ruins gorged together, and we climbed from one thing to another over the debris and were then near enough the hill to be drawn up with ropes.

As the level of the Stony Creek and the Little Conemaugh continued to rise most of the day on Friday, folks were busy moving valuables to higher ground. Jeremiah L. Smith, a stonemason by trade, feared for the safety of his family and it was them who he chose to move. Smith lived with his wife and three children at 202 Stony Creek Street. He made arrangements for them to stay at the Hulbert House, a relatively new and substantially built hotel on Clinton Street. He saw them safely to the Hulbert House then returned to their residence to weather the flood and care for the property as best he could. When the wave from South Fork struck the town, the four-story, brick Hulbert House crumbled in an instant. Among those killed were Mrs. Smith and her three children. Mr. Smith survived.

David Creed operated a grocery store at the corner of Washington and Franklin Streets. For years that particular corner had been known as Creed's Corner. The six members of the Creed family made their home at the same address, 200 Washington Street. The flood claimed Mr. & Mrs. Creed, their three daughters Maggie, Kate, and Mamie, but spared the only son, Edward, who was working when the flood struck Johnstown. Edward was a clerk at the company store of Wood, Morrell and Company, just below his parents' store on Washington Street.

Even though it was a well-built and substantial structure, the Hulbert House fell shortly after being struck by the wave from Lake Conemaugh. It is interesting to note that the wave that hit the Hulbert House was but a portion of the total wave that had swept down the valley from South Fork. There were an estimated sixty people in the Hulbert House shortly after 4:00 p.m. on May 31st. Only nine survived.

Mr. Charles Murr ran a cigar manufacturing business and lived at 162 Washington Street. His home and business were swept away by the flood wave that followed the course of the Little Conemaugh to the Point. At the time of the flood, Murr lived with his wife and seven children. Only Mrs. Murr and one of the children survived.

At 224 Washington Street, George Heiser and his wife, Mathilde, ran a grocery store and lived above the store with their sixteen-year old son Victor. Like most grocery stores of that time, the Heiser's offered a good deal more than groceries. George, like many other men his age, had fought in the Civil War. Following the Battle of Fredericksburg, Virginia, he was taken prisoner and held for a time at Libby Prison. In the flood, both George and Mathilde were killed, but young Victor was spared.

Victor's survival, an ordeal of dramatic proportions, was recounted in the first chapter, "Just Short of Eternity," of his 1936 autobiography, *An American Doctor's Odyssey Adventures in Forty-Five Countries*. Just before the flood wave struck the Heiser property on Washington Street, Victor's father had asked him to go to the stable and untie a team of horses. Hearing the rush of the coming wave, Victor looked toward the house to see his parents standing at an upper window, motioning him to get to higher ground. He would never again see his parents alive. Sensing what was about to happen, the sixteen-year-old looked at his pocket watch. In an interview conducted many years later, Heisen recalled that he had looked at his watch because he wanted to know how long it would take to get to Heaven. According to Heiser's recollection, the time was 4:20 p.m.

Like numerous others, he rode the merciless wave of water and debris for some time before being able to escape its grasp. His ride on the wave of debris that leveled his world took just about ten minutes. He spent the night in an attic with several others who had managed to hold their own against such a powerful force. Shortly after the flood, Heiser found one of his family's wardrobes several blocks from where their home had been. Inside he found his father's Grand Army of the Republic Uniform and a single penny in one of the pockets. This was his total lot in life and what he would later call "the sum of my inheritance."

In 1889, Mr. C. T. Schubert was the editor of the *Freie Presse*, Johnstown's German newspaper. The *Freie Presse* was one of a limited number of papers for German-speaking residents in that region of Pennsylvania. Mr. Schubert was the only member of his family to be lost. He was thrown from the roof of the house upon which the family had gathered. It was reported that Mr. Schubert had a life insurance policy in the amount

A captivating display in the main hall of the visitor center of the Johnstown Flood National Memorial in St. Michael, features this life-size likeness of Victor Heiser riding out the wave of the floodwater from South Fork, just after seeing that wave destroy his home and claim his parents.

of $7,500 with Masonic Mutual Relief, making him the exception rather than the rule when it came to personal insurance policies.

Squire Richard Jones and his family lived at 283 Maple Avenue in Woodvale prior to the flood. After the wave struck their home, the former Justice of the Peace in Conemaugh and his entire family were lost, save one child. Myrtle Viola, a daughter who was believed to be about five at the time, was found several days later wandering about in the hills above Woodvale. Like many children orphaned on May 31, 1889, Myrtle Viola was taken in by another family.

Few stories in the aftermath of the Johnstown flood were more heart wrenching or more widely told than the story of the Fenn family. John and Anna Fenn lived with their seven children at 223 Locust Street. Mr. Fenn operated a stove, tinware, and hardware business on Washington Street. During much of the day on May 31, 1889, John had been helping friends and neighbors move valuables to upper floors. As the wave from South Fork arrived, he was attempting to make his way to his home. He was swept away before making it. At the time, Mrs. Fenn and all seven children were at home. The flood wave engulfed the Fenn house and tore it from its foundation in an instant. All were lost except Mrs. Fenn.

When the first edition of the *Johnstown Tribune* was published after the flood, June 14, 1889, the story of the Fenns was one of many recounted under the headline "The Fate of Some Families."

Mrs. John Fenn lost her husband, her seven children, her home, and her husband's tin store. A young woman, a domestic in the family, was also drowned. Mr. Fenn had left his store on Washington Street for his home on Locust Street. The water was too high on Franklin Street to permit him to take that route, so he started around by Clinton Street. He got as far as the residence of Mr. Woodruff on Locust Street and had barely time to get in the house when the deluge made its descent. His refuge fell before the torrent and he and Mr. Woodruff's housekeeper, Miss Mollie Brindle, of Conemaugh Borough, were lost. Mrs. Fenn and children were at home.

The account in the Johnstown paper may well have left this store as nothing more than another indistinguishable tale tangled amidst the larger story of the Johnstown tragedy. However, the accounts that appeared in the New York, Chicago and numerous other papers dramatized the story, which quickly and permanently set it apart from most, if not all, of the Johnstown family stories. After the press arrived in Johnstown, the tragic story of the Fenns was among the first reported to the nation and the world. The story of the Fenns appeared in the June 3 edition of the *New York Times*, the *Chicago Tribune* and countless other papers.

An utterly wretched woman named Mrs. Fenn stood by a muddy pool of water trying to find some trace of a once happy home. She was half-crazed with grief, and her eyes were red and swollen. As the writer stepped to her side she raised her pale and haggard face and remarked:

They are all gone. My husband and my seven dear little children have been swept down with the flood and I am left alone. We were driven by the raging flood into the garret, but the waters followed us there. Inch by inch it kept rising until our heads were crushing against the roof. It was death to remain. So I raised a window and one by one placed my darlings on some driftwood, trusting to the Great Creator. As I liberated the last one, my sweet little boy, he looked at me and said: "Mamma, you always told me that the Lord would care for me; will He look after me now?" I saw him drift away with his loving face turned toward me, and with a prayer on my lips for his deliverance he passed from sight forever. The next moment the roof crashed in and I floated outside to be rescued fifteen hours later from the roof of a house in Kernville. If I could only find one of my darlings I could bow to the will of God. But they are all gone.

Dr. Samuel C. Poland had a dental practice, which he operated from an office at 93 1/2 Franklin Street. Dr. Poland, his wife, and two sons, Walter and Freddie, lived at 76 Market Street. When the torrent hit their home, Dr. Poland grabbed the boys in an attempt to carry them to safety. They were washed into the floodwaters and carried more than a block away. Although he managed to hold onto them, both of the boys drowned in the debris-filled flood wave. Dr. Poland suffered two broken ribs, and Mrs. Poland was so bruised and crippled that

The portrait of the seven Fenn children, probably taken in December of 1888 just prior to Christmas, shows all seven children. Inserted in the upper right corner are portraits of Anna and John Fenn. At the time of the flood John Fulton (standing left) was 12; May Fleming Miller "Daisy" (seated holding the baby) was 10; Genevieve (standing right) was 9; George Washington (seated far right) was 8; Ann Richmond Virginia (seated second from right) was 6; Bismarck Sullivan (reclining in front) was 3; and Queen Esther (on Daisy's lap) was 16 months old on the day of the flood. Mrs. Fenn was pregnant at the time, and lost that baby as well.

family members found it difficult to recognize her. Both of the Poland boys were buried in Grandview Cemetery. Dr. & Mrs. Poland later relocated to Philadelphia.

An article titled "The Worst Not Told" that appeared in *The Evening Bulletin* of Philadelphia, June 1, 1889, included the account of one Cambria City survivor. Even though the great Stone Bridge at the point in Johnstown temporarily broke the momentum of the flood wave, areas below the bridge were devastated nonetheless.

The home I was in was soon smashed to pieces and I managed to jump on to a cellar door. In a few seconds I was rushed off into the flood and when I looked back where Cambria City stood there was nothing but a great lake of water. It looked to me as if every house had been raised or covered over. The vast sheet of water was full of floating timber, roofs of houses, rafts, boards and other articles. The scene was indescribable. The cries of the men, women and children were fearful, and I suppose I added my own yells to the shrieks of the unfortunate. I think not less than 1,500 people were lost in the flood. This estimate may be too high, but I am afraid it is too low. I passed Paddy Madden's wife, my son's wife and a man clinging to the roof of a house. I called to them and bade them good-bye. In a short time I was caught by the water and turned under every once in a while.

I went into a whirlpool and more than once almost lost my grip on the cellar door. I saw people ahead

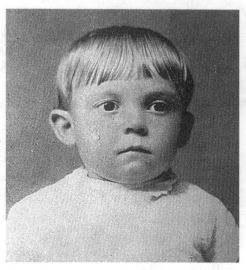

Freddie Poland was one of two children of Dr. & Mrs. Poland who died in his father's arms during the flood.

The brothers Freddie and Walter Poland were buried in a private plot in Grandview Cemetery.

of me and all around me. Many of them were struck by the crashing timbers and killed outright. They were so badly hurt that they fell into the water and were drowned at once. A Mrs. Boyle was also rescued at Lockport. The poor woman was moaning and crying and would not be comforted. Her children and her husband are supposed to be drowned.

For some, the Stone Bridge was a refuge. The family of J. H. Wright was reportedly saved when their house came to rest there. When the wave struck Woodvale, they had moved to the attic where they stayed. Once deposited by the floodwaters at the Stone Bridge, they managed to climb across the debris to the safety of a nearby hillside. In this same house a domestic and another couple named Buchamer were also saved.

Shortly before the floodwaters struck, Gertrude Quinn, the six-year-old daughter of James Quinn, received a scolding from her father for disobeying him and coming outside of their house on the upper end of Main Street. Gertrude later recalled that she had wanted to watch the rising water. Her father was a partner in the dry goods establishment of Foster & Quinn with his brother-in-law, Andrew Foster. Their place of business was located on Clinton Street, just a block from their home. Earlier in the day he had warned all of his children to stay in the house. No sooner had Mr. Quinn taken Gertrude back into the house than the crushing sound of the wave from South Fork could be heard in the near distance.

Of the seven Quinn children, only four were at home at the time of the flood. Mrs. Quinn and two of the children were in Scottdale, Pennsylvania having remained there after a visit earlier in the week. A sister-in-law of

the Quinns, Abbie Geis, and her infant son, Richard, were visiting at the time. The Quinns also employed a young girl who helped with the children. Her name was Libby Hipp.

Sensing the coming danger, James Quinn managed to grab three of his children and make a run for high ground on Green Hill, just two blocks east up Main Street. Gertrude, Aunt Abbie, her baby, and Libby, against the hastily shouted orders from James, did not follow but remained in the house. The impact of the wave destroyed the house, tossing it down and crushing it. Miraculously, Gertrude was thrown free. The other three who stayed in the house were not as fortunate. Sixteen-year-old Vincent, the oldest of the seven Quinn children, was trying to make his way back from the family store when he was swept away by the current and drowned.

By the description Gertrude later gave, she may well have been carried a distance of more than two miles by the angry waters from Lake Conemaugh. As she was being carried by the rushing waters, first on a mattress, then on a tin roof, she was moving ever closer to the Stone Bridge. However, before she was thrown into the wreckage that had accumulated in front of it, she was rescued by Maxwell McAchren, and became a temporary guest in the home of the Metz family. The next day, with the help of Barbara Foster, James Quinn's sister, father and daughter were reunited.

In 1936 Gertrude Quinn Slattery wrote an account of her experiences and those of her family during the flood. She titled her work *Johnstown And Its Flood*. In telling the story of her family, she, by necessity, told much of the story of the town and many others who

This photograph of Gertrude Quinn was taken shortly before the Flood.

James Quinn managed to get three of his children to higher ground before the wall of water from South Fork destroyed their home.

shared the experiences of the 1889 disaster. She closed with a passage that described both the attitude and resolve of many who survived the Johnstown horror.

> The heart and mind while scarred are ever filled with love and hope, and while we drained the cup of bitterness to the dregs, we learned early in life that looking backward would not help, so with faces to the east, we took our places in life, as I like to think to myself, each one to her easel or tapestry to use the colors in such a way that when completed, it is viewed as a finished picture worthy of the material at hand and the love and care our parents exerted, so that it may hang on memory's wall, a credit to them, and an inspiration to our children.

The Monday, June 17, 1889 edition of the *Johnstown Tribune* featured a front-page article titled "Drift From the Flood." As a part of this article the survival of a Johnstown notable, "Old Kelly," was described:

> "Old Kelly," the aged colored man, who has been a familiar personage on the streets of Johnstown for a generation or longer, still lives. He has survived murderous assaults, frosts, fires, and floods innumerable, and does not look much older than when, twenty odd years ago, the late Alvar Akers, who lost his life in the recent flood, picked him out of the gutter in front of the Methodist Church one cold winter morning frozen still and almost lifeless. He had been murderously assaulted the night before by a lawless character then about town, beaten nearly to death, and left lying in the gutter to die from his injuries or freeze to death. This would certainly have been his fate but for the timely appearance of Mr. Akers at an early hour on his way to market. (Mr. Akers was a partner in the grocery business of Akers & Baumer located at 86 and 88 Franklin Street.)

Mrs. Mary McNally had passed away on the morning of May 30, 1889. She was not a victim of the flood that struck Johnstown the following day, but she did nonetheless figure into the drama of the day. Her funeral had been planned for the morning of May 31. As planned, the family gathered in St. John's Catholic Church on Clinton Street for the service. Burial following the service was to take place in the Lower Yoder Cemetery. At the conclusion of the service, it was decided that the body could not be safely moved to the cemetery so it was left in the church. The June 14 edition of the *Johnstown Tribune* reported that the body was still in the church, which had been severely damaged by the flood wave before catching fire. It was later learned that the body had been washed from the church. The March 8, 1890 edition of the *Johnstown Tribune* reported that the partially burned corpse and coffin of Mary McNally had been found in Kernville.

W. Horace Rose was one of Johnstown's more prominent and respected citizens. He lived with his wife and five children at 131 Main Street. He was engaged in the practice of law and had his office at 64 Franklin Street. Rose had served in the military during the Civil War, had been the district attorney of Cambria County, and served in the Pennsylvania General Assembly.

During the morning hours, Rose and his sons passed time trying to help other families along the lower end of Main Street. Rose checked his office on Franklin Street and moved valuable papers above where he thought the waters of the Conemaugh and the Stony Creek might reach. In 1887, there had been about a foot of water in his office. On his way back to his home, Rose met a neighbor, John Dibert. They chatted briefly about the

During the Civil War, W. Horace Rose served with the 54th Pennsylvania Volunteer Infantry Regiment.

inconvenience of the spring flooding, and the need to have Cambria Iron Company remove years of manufacturing waste from the riverbeds. If Cambria Iron would do so, the channels of the rivers would be significantly increased, which would increase their carrying capacity, thus reduce the level of the water during spring floods. Rose returned to his house before lunch, prepared to wait out yet another spring flood.

When the torrent from South Fork struck the town, the Rose house, like so many others was totally destroyed. In an account dictated by Rose, which appeared in the book *Through the Johnstown Flood by a Survivor*, by Rev. David J. Beale and published in 1890, the following excerpts outline his experiences in his own words:

> So unsuspecting of danger was I that, from the time we removed the furniture to the second floor, until within fifteen minutes of the final catastrophe, I amused myself by shooting rats from an upper window, or joking with my neighbors, Squire Fisher and Mr. Hamilton, across the street.
>
> I walked to a window, raised it, and called to Bessie Fronheiser, a neighbor's child, who stood at an opposite window, and asking her to come over, she laughingly said: "I can't." I then told her to come to a window in the front part of the house and I would give her some candy; a minute after, she and her mother appeared at a window directly opposite one in our house, where the distance between the houses was about five or six feet. I took a broom; some member of my family poured a lot of mixed candy on it, and I passed the same across the open space to Bessie and her mother; as she took the candy from the broom, Mrs. Rose said to Mrs. Fronheiser, "You are not looking well—wait till we hand you some coffee; we have made some on the grate." She then handed me a tin-cup of coffee, which was placed on the broom and passed to Mrs. Fronheiser, who took it and raised it to her lips. She never tasted it. There came a crash; she lowered the cup and exclaimed: "My God! What is that?" My daughter said: "Our fence is breaking down!"
>
> I heard loud screams, the sound of breaking timbers, the alarm of a bell, and the loud scream of a steam whistle. I said: "Something awful has happened!" and rushed to the third floor of the building followed by all who were in the house.
>
> Several persons were floating directly down Main Street, in front of me; a large frame building, directly opposite me, careened at the attic windows of which I saw a number of ladies, one of whom held an infant in her arms; there was a crash, a sensation of falling, a consciousness that I was in the water, and all was dark.
>
> I was laying on my left side, perhaps twenty to twenty-five feet distant from where my wife, daughter and son were struggling, the skin torn from the right side of my face, the blood flowing profusely from the wound, the skin torn from the back of my left hand, my right collar-bone broken, my shoulder-blade fractured, the ribs crushed in upon my lung, my right arm from shoulder to waist lying limp on my side, powerless to give aid or assistance to my loved ones.
>
> I saw a stout roof floating on the outer edge of the mass of debris; I told my family that if that roof could be reached, there was a chance to escape, as the roof might drift to the hillside, where escape was possible; we were then slowly drifting down the stream toward the stone bridge; we all reached the roof in safety, my boy assisting me to gain it.
>
> A cold and pitiless rain poured down upon us, causing me to have frequent and severe chills. At this time the spire of St. John's Catholic was on fire, and as we floated about we were in plain view of the flames as they leaped up the magnificent spire and consumed the emblem of Christianity which graced its lofty top.
>
> I shall not attempt to describe the terrors of the following night, with its thousand and one alarms, as the crash of buildings was heard as they settled in the water or were crushed by the weight from above, suffice it to say, it was a night of awful terror, and over all was the ghastly and lurid light that came from the burning debris at the stone bridge below.
>
> By four o'clock on Saturday, my two sons, who had been separated from us in the flood, rejoined us, and we found all had safely escaped with life and limb, I alone being injured. From my injuries I have not yet recovered, and am only able to dictate this narrative, which fact must be excuse for any want of directness and polish.

Although the Rose family survived, the names of several of their neighbors were later to appear on the lists of victims. Squire Fisher and his family, who lived at 142 Main Street, were all lost. John Dibert, who refused to leave his home at 141 Main Street, was lost. His wife survived and later moved to Philadelphia. Dr. James J. Fronheiser, who was the general superintendent of Cambria Iron, a daughter, a son, and a three-month-old baby were saved. She only survived two weeks, having been weakened by exposure and near drowning during the flood. She was buried in Grandview Cemetery on June 18, 1889. Mrs. Fronheiser and daughter Bessie were lost. Their home, located at 127 Main Street, was one of the last to crumble under the pressure of the flood wave as it struck the lower end of Main Street.

An account of the Fronheiser story, which first appeared in the June 8 edition of the *New York Times*, was later carried in part in the June 20 edition of the *Johnstown Tribune*. The account of Dr. Fronheiser's rescue of his twelve-year-old daughter Mamie and teenaged son Jacob, with the help of others, clearly illustrated the horror visited upon the children. This story, along with countless others, were dramatized a little more each time they were told. Even though the basic facts may have been accurate, embellishments were colorful, dramatic and numerous. Where details were missing or weak, the

Bessie and her mother were among the victims of the flood who lived at the lower end of Main Street, near the Stony Creek.

imagination of the reporters and writers covering the greatest news story of the day were plentiful and vivid:

> He [Dr. Fronheiser] caught Mamie, but she cried; "Let me go, papa, and save Jacob. My leg is broken and my foot is caught below." When he told her he was determined to rescue her, she exclaimed: "Then, papa, get a sharp knife and cut my leg off, I can stand it." The little fellow cried to his father: "You can't save me papa. Both my feet are caught fast and I can't hold out any longer. Please get a pistol and shoot me, but don't let me drown."

Rev. David C. Phillips was the pastor of the Welsh Calvinistic Church located at 115 Vine Street. He was also part owner of a notions and dry goods business with his brother Seth, which they operated at 233 Main Street. Rev. Phillips and his family also lived at 233 Main Street. His brother and his family lived on Conemaugh Street.

The family of David Phillips was trapped in their home on Main Street. Phillips believed their fate in that building to be questionable. He believed that he and his family would be much safer in a neighboring building. With no other way out, Reverend Phillips used a hatchet to chop a hole through the wall of their house and opened a passage into the neighboring J. A. Larkin & Company, a jewelry store. According to the account provided by Reverend Phillips, he had only chopped a small hole when his grip on the hatchet failed and he lost it. He completed the work with his hands. He succeeded in making a hole large enough for his family to escape. After crawling into the Larkin building, they were able to make their way out onto Main Street and safety.

The flood demonstrated numerous times that a turn of fate could either be a blessing or a curse. Many who may well have been in Johnstown, but for some reason were not, were spared the ravages of the flood. Many others who were there by chance alone were among those claimed by the catastrophe.

On June 4 Mrs. Lew Wallace was listed among those reported as missing. It was believed that she had been a passenger on one of several trains destroyed as the flood ravaged East Conemaugh. Lew Wallace, a celebrated Civil War general and the author of *Ben Hur*, was in Washington at the time. According to the June 5 edition of the *Chicago Tribune*, Wallace was "greatly alarmed" to learn that his wife was listed among those who were "certainly dead." Brainard Rovison, a close personal friend of President Harrison from Indianapolis, had provided the information about Mrs. Wallace. As it turned out, Mrs. Wallace had not been on that particular train, but had instead taken another train. She was safe in Altoona, Pennsylvania.

Frank B. Felt and Sidney McCloud arrived in Johnstown on Thursday evening, May 30. They checked into the Hulbert House. Mr. Felt was the superintendent of the Calumet Iron Company. Both Felt and McCloud lived in Chicago. At the time the floodwaters surged up Clinton Street, they were not at the Hulbert House, but were instead in a restaurant that was also on Clinton Street. They were at Charlotte Kast's at 112 Clinton Street, next door to the Hulbert House. Just ahead of the wall of water from Lake Conemaugh, they saw people dashing down the street in desperate attempts to escape the torrent. Although heavily damaged, Mrs. Kast's restaurant and saloon withstood the force of the flood wave, permitting Felt and McCloud time to escape. Leaving by way of a back door, they ran directly toward Green Hill and the safety of higher ground, which was only a few blocks behind Kast's. Once on safer ground, they were involved in the rescue of several people overtaken by the flood wave.

Andrew C. Young lived with his wife and six children at 195 Broad Street. Young was one of the butchers for Wood, Morrell & Company. Two of the children of the family, Harry and Pearly, were visiting relatives in Indiana County, Pennsylvania. All of the family members in Johnstown at the time of the flood perished. Harry and Pearly were spared because they were in Indiana County.

Sometime during the early spring of 1889, John R. Day and his daughter Hannah Grace made a trip to Indiana County, Pennsylvania. Grace, as her family and friends knew her, and her father left Prospect, Maryland to visit relatives in the town of Saltsburg. According to the family story, John was taking his daughter to western Pennsylvania to put some distance between her and a boyfriend who was not totally acceptable to the family. In Saltsburg the Days stayed with Mr. Day's nephew, Harry H. Robinson. Robinson was a Saltsburg pharmacist.

Exactly when the Days arrived in Saltsburg is not known. While there, they enjoyed the company of family and visited a number of local points of interest. By the end of May, the Days decided to return home to Prospect. For the first leg of their return trip, they boarded a Pennsylvania Railroad mail train on May 31 shortly before 9:00 a.m. It was raining heavily at the station in Saltsburg. After a short trip, they transferred to another train that was, ironically, called the *Day Express*. At Blairsville they boarded the first section of this train. Even though there were heavy storms in the region, there is no reason to believe that the trip east was at all eventful or out of the ordinary, until they reached the train yards at East Conemaugh in Cambria County.

Submerged and washed out tracks, bridges that were in tenuous condition, and a general lack of definitive information about general conditions along the miles of track that lay to the east, caused their train to be held in East Conemaugh. When the floodwaters from South Fork hit East Conemaugh, the *Day Express* was virtually destroyed. The Days were passengers on the first section of the *Day Express*. Although there were numerous survivors, more than 35 perished from the *Day Express*. Both John R. and Hannah Grace Day were listed among those who were killed.

Fearing the fate that may have befallen his Uncle John and his cousin, Harry Robinson left his home in Saltsburg and made his way to Johnstown to search for his relatives, hopefully among the survivors. After several trips to the flood-stricken district, he learned that both his uncle and cousin were not among the survivors. In a letter to his Aunt Mattie (Martha), dated June 13, 1889, Robinson carefully detailed his efforts and informed her of his sad find. Grace's body had been recovered, identified and prepared for return to Prospect. The body of nineteen-year-old Grace arrived back in Prospect for burial that same day. John's body was bur-

These photographs of John and Grace Day, and an original letter detailing their tragic story were donated in 1999 to the Johnstown Area Heritage Association by the family of Grace Day Galbreath, who was a second-cousin of John Day.

The Day Express *was one of several trains held at East Conemaugh because of dangerous conditions east of that point. The car in which the Days were riding can be seen just behind the destroyed locomotive.*

The Day gravesite is in a small country cemetery outside of Prospect, Maryland. In memory of the untimely death of Grace, at least one member of the family in each generation has had the name Grace as part of her name. One of the members of the family so named is Belinda Grace Galbreath, who is a fourth cousin of Hannah Grace Day. The family member most recently named in memory of Hannah Grace is Elizabeth Grace Galbreath born in 1995.

ied initially at Grandview Cemetery in Johnstown among the unidentified. In December, his brother and a friend went to Johnstown, and after reviewing descriptions of numerous unknown victims, had a body exhumed which they quickly and positively identified. The body was returned to Prospect for burial next to his daughter.

At the corner of Washington and Market Streets, at 150 Washington Street, John Coad operated the Exchange Hotel. Coad, his wife, and children occupied the residence portion of the building that stood on what most locals called Coad's Corner. John operated a small saloon out of one of the rooms of the building. His daughter also ran a small shoe business at the same location. Mr. and Mrs. Coad, their daughter, a granddaughter, and a son were killed in the flood. Their home and business were totally destroyed. Three other sons, John, Thomas, and Peter, were not at home at the time and thus survived. At the time of the flood, Peter was a student in the seminary at Mount Saint Mary's College in Emmitsburg, Maryland.

Miss Carrie Deihl of Shippensburg, Pennsylvania was in Johnstown visiting a friend, Miss Jennie Wells, formerly of Tioga County. Jennie was a teacher at Johnstown High School. Miss Deihl, who was to turn twenty-five on July 19, had completed two terms of course work at what is today Shippensburg University during the 1884-1885 academic year. She was preparing for a career in teaching. She was engaged to be married to William H. Ocher of Philadelphia. Ocher was a salesman for a Philadelphia wholesale company. Upon learning of the disaster in Johnstown and knowing that Carrie was there, Ocher made his way to Johnstown, first by train, then on foot. Learning of the total destruction of the Hulbert House, where both Deihl and Wells were staying, he began checking the morgues. He located his fiancé's body in the morgue set up in the Fourth Ward school. He personally escorted the body back to Shippensburg. A funeral service was held in the home of Miss Deihl's father followed by burial in Shippensburg's Spring Hill Cemetery.

Flood stories were as numerous as the newspapermen and freelance writers who flocked to Johnstown to cover one of the biggest stories of the century. Even a summary review of the newspapers of the day leaves little doubt that there was no shortage of survivors willing to provide the particulars of their story. In time many of these stories have faded into the collective whole that is the story of the flood. Others, for a variety of reasons, seem to endure as veritable benchmarks of the horror that struck Johnstown. They stand out and they stand alone. The story of a child washed as far as the bridge at Bolivar, well down river from Johnstown is just such a story. This story, or one of its many versions, appeared in countless newspapers, magazine accounts and most of the books written following the flood.

The Saturday, June 1, 1889 edition of *The Evening Bulletin* of Philadelphia, carried the story as part of its coverage of the Johnstown disaster. It appeared under the headline, "The Worst Not Told," which was the paper's lead article:

A little girl passed under the bridge just before dark. She was kneeling on a part of a floor and had her hands clasped as if in prayer. Every effort was made to save her, but they all proved futile. A railroader who was standing by remarked that the piteous appearance of the little waif brought tears to his eyes. All night long the crowd stood about the ruins of the bridge, which had been swept away at Bolivar. The water rushed past with a roar, carrying with it parts of houses, furniture and trees. The flood had evidently spent its force up the valley. No more living persons were being carried past. Watchers with lanterns remained along the banks until daybreak, when the first view of the awful devastation of the flood was witnessed.

Like many folks who were visiting in Johnstown and fell victim to the flood, Miss Deihl's body was returned to her hometown for burial. The burial service was held on June 6, 1889, one week after the flood. This memorial identifies the Deihl family plot in the Spring Hill Cemetery.

This illustration appeared opposite the opening paragraph of chapter seventeen of the book The Story of Johnstown, *written by J. J. McLaurin in 1890. (McLaurin was the editor of the newspaper, the* Harrisburg Telegram.) *The title of this chapter is "Slaughter of the Innocents." The opening sentence of this chapter reads, "Perhaps the saddest feature of the disaster was the dreadful slaughter of the children."*

Chapter 5

Destruction, Debris and Death

During the long night of May 31 and June 1 the corridor of destruction from South Fork to Bolivar was strewn with victims, survivors, and those whose fate had yet to be determined. There were many who clung to life in solitude, having been isolated by the flood. Others had the advantage of sharing their dreadful situation, for whatever advantage such sharing might have brought. Where possible, those spared by the flood gathered in groups in substantial buildings, on hillsides or in other locations that provided some reasonable hope of enhancing the odds of making it through the night. Rains, heavy rains, continued falling during most of the night. Those who found some shelter were among the more fortunate.

The massive blaze at the Stone Bridge lit the night sky with an orange cast. Smaller fires, like the one at St. John's Catholic Church, also burned throughout the night. The intensity of the fires changed from time to time. However, numerous accounts hold that there were extended periods when the light was so bright that reading a newspaper would have been possible virtually anywhere in town. Buildings creaked and groaned as they began settling under their own weight and from the damage that had been done to them.

The darkness made searching for family and friends impossible, and added to the anguish and agony of what the light of day would reveal. There were many, like Victor Heiser, who would never again see family members alive. Others were more fortunate. The June 14 edition of the *Johnstown Tribune* reported the reunion of a husband and wife on the road beside the wreckage near the Stone Bridge. "Each had thought the other had been lost and at the sight of each other they embraced, sinking on their knees and offering a prayer of thanksgiving for their safety."

The most basic of needs could not be met during the night of terror in Johnstown. Food, clothing, blankets, medical supplies, even clean water was simply not available. Several buildings in Johnstown became gathering places and makeshift shelters. Alma Hall, located on Main Street across from Central Park, was such a place. As a large, substantial brick building, its very appearance offered a sense of safety in the midst of pure calamity.

James M. Walters, one of the more prominent attorneys from Johnstown, spent the night in Alma Hall. His account of that night provides a picture of what many of the survivors faced. It is interesting to note that Walters was at his home at 135 Walnut Street when the floodwaters struck the town. He and his family were separated. Adrift in the floodwaters, Walters managed to stay afloat on a piece of one of the buildings that had been destroyed. As he was washed onto Main Street, Walters was hurled against the Alma Hall and thrown directly into his own law office located in that building. He remained there throughout the night, and was one of the key players in maintaining order in the building and providing what little relief was possible.

Although the lower floors of Alma Hall were flooded, the upper floors provided refuge during the night. Some immediate safety measures were determined and strictly enforced. For example, no fires were lit because of fears of natural gas leaks, and all alcohol was confiscated to prevent inappropriate use and to reserve it for medicinal purposes. Dr. W. Edgar Matthews became a hero during the night for his actions in Alma Hall. He had himself sustained two broken ribs, but nonetheless cared for the sick and the injured as well as conditions would permit. Although accounts vary, it was reported that two babies were born during that night in Alma Hall.

Reverend David Beale, pastor of the Presbyterian Church on Main Street had led a group of survivors into Alma Hall. During the night he frequently led the group in prayer. He later said, " That was, indeed, a solemn and impressive occasion. In this service Jews and Gentiles, Catholics and Protestants, Africans and Chinamen united.... It is doubtful if anyone in that entire building on that awful night refused to pray to his Master."

Reverend Beale quoted two of Johnstown's veterans in his book regarding their thoughts on the comparison between the Civil War battlefield and what they witnessed in Johnstown. He wrote about a conversation he had with Colonel Jacob Higgins and Major Robert Litzenger in which they assured him that, "...nothing occurred in their army life to compare with the horrors of the evening and night of the 31st of May, 1889."

Saturday, June 1 dawned gray and cloudy. There was a damp chill in the air that provided no relief to those who had survived. The normal sounds of the prosperous towns in the Conemaugh Valley were gone, for most of what had made those sounds just the day before was gone. The frightful destruction in the corridor that extended from South Fork to where the Conemaugh River enters the Conemaugh Gap was of a magnitude well beyond any natural disaster that had previously visited that area. There were countless locations where trees and

In this view, taken shortly after the flood, Alma Hall can be seen at the extreme right of the picture.

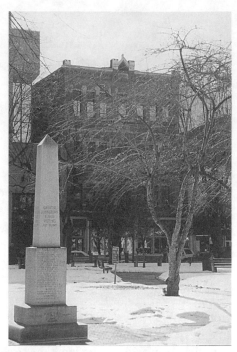

In this modern view, Alma Hall is seen in the center of the picture. The monument in the foreground is to those lost in Johnstown's 1977 flood.

other natural vegetations were washed completely away. In places the earth had been scraped clean to bare rock. The wall of water and debris devoured, destroyed, or carried away virtually everything in its path. Although the area of destruction ranged well beyond Johnstown, it was Johnstown that felt the most destructive blow of the flood, and most of the attention that was focused on the flooded district in the weeks and months that followed was focused on Johnstown.

Exactly when and through whom word of the devastation of the Conemaugh Valley got out to the world has never been determined, but most reliable sources credit Robert Pitcairn. Pitcairn, a member of the South Fork Fishing and Hunting Club and the Superintendent of the Pittsburgh Division of the Pennsylvania Railroad, had multiple interests in the happenings in the Conemaugh Valley on May 31. Learning of the heavy natural flooding he left Pittsburgh shortly after noon to survey damages to tracks, bridges and telegraph lines. Arriving at Sang Hollow just below Johnstown, shortly after 4:00 p.m., he saw the initial wave of debris the waters of Lake Conemaugh had sent around the Stone Bridge. Realizing what had happened he got word back to Pittsburgh, which was quickly shared with the city's newspaper editors. Within hours reporters were making their way toward Johnstown. Although Johnstown faced numerous shortages during the first week of June in 1889, there was no shortage of newspapermen.

Which paper was first to have a man on the scene has long been a point of contention. Numerous papers claimed this distinction. William Connolly, the agent of the Associated Press in western Pennsylvania, Claude Wetmore, a free-lance reporter, and Harry W. Orr, a telegrapher for the Associated Press, are generally recognized as being the first on the scene. They arrived on one of the trains that had been chartered from Pittsburgh. Wetmore was sent to Johnstown as the correspondent for the *New York World*. The *Harrisburg Telegram* claimed to already have had a man in Johnstown on another assignment. The General Manager of the Associated Press, William H. Smith, was a passenger on the Day Express. Having seen the flood first hand in East Conemaugh, he filed an account of what he had seen shortly before midnight on May 31 from Ebensburg. The following day he made his way back to Johnstown.

Special trains were chartered in Pittsburgh to carry writers and sketch artists to Johnstown. They made it only as far as Bolivar, some twenty miles from Johnstown, between 10:00 and 11:00 p.m. on the 31st. The rest of their journey to Johnstown, approximately twenty miles, was a trek over the mountains and through the valleys of that area. The terrain that they covered was unknown to them and was still saturated from late spring snows and the current rainstorms, making their progress all the more difficult. The endless mud, heavy rains and darkness complicated their movement, but they pushed on until they reached Johnstown during the early morning hours of June 1. The descriptions provided by Pitcairn were little more than gross underestimations compared to the scenes they saw in the early light of day.

Upon their arrival in the flooded district, establishing a means for getting the news out became a first priority. Several of the newspapermen helped to string a telegraph wire back down the valley. On the hillside just above the Stone Bridge the newspapermen gathered in an old coal shed and a brick kiln. Such would be their quarters for several weeks to come. During the initial two days of their work in Johnstown, their efforts were hampered for want of more telegraph lines and telegraph operators. This situation was dramatically improved by Monday. The reporters and artists who came to Johnstown labored tirelessly to provide the world with details of a story the likes of which had not been seen since the end of the Civil War.

Members of the press initially received a cool welcome in Johnstown. They would be just another drain on what the locals feared would be a scarce food supply, while contributing nothing. It was not until some time after the flood that the role of the press in getting the story out was credited with the swift and overwhelming generosity that was to be shown to Johnstown and surrounding boroughs. In his book, *The Story of Johnstown*, J. J. McLaurin, the editor of the *Harrisburg Telegram*, summed up the service of the newspapermen this way.

> The occasion had come to put to the severest test the mettle of the press, nor were heroes lacking to use it to the best advantage. Provided the facts be told, what matter that hardships be experienced? Little cared the pencil-pusher that his food was the coarsest, his seat the hard side of a brick pile, his resting place in the open air, his desk a coal shovel! The true newspaper man never fails to respond to the call of duty, and just then duty was summoning him with a trumpet voice such as earth has seldom or never heard.

Even though the disaster in Johnstown did indeed "test the mettle of the press," their collective experience was not without its humorous moments. One of the many New York papers covering the story sent a young reporter. Imbued with a certain sense of poetic license he is reported to have sent the following back to his editor for publication: "God looked down from the hills surrounding Johnstown today on an awesome scene of destruction...." As the story goes, the editor back in New York, watching over the receiving telegrapher's shoulder as he penciled the words from the Johnstown correspondent, told the telegrapher to break in and send the following reply: "Forget flood. Interview God."

Of the newspapermen who came to cover the story in Johnstown, there was none more colorful than Richard Harding Davis (1864-1916). Although he was not among the early arrivals in Johnstown, his presence quickly became known when he did arrive. In fact, he became the subject of some newspaper stories himself. Davis, the son of a Philadelphia family that had made a name for itself in literary circles, was used to a comfortable life. When he arrived in Johnstown, the harsh conditions he found did not deter him from seeking the comforts to which he had become accustomed. In the midst of the calamity that was Johnstown in early June 1889, Davis afforded the other members of the press corps some humorous interludes with his highbrow antics, but provided the *Philadelphia Press* readers with some of the most detailed and insightful accounts of the flood and its aftermath.

Although on assignment to cover the biggest news story of the day, it is not surprising that the newspapermen took part in some of the less professional pursuits that engaged many throughout the flooded district. For example, they too gathered relics while in Johnstown. The July 29 edition of the *Johnstown Tribune* carried a story that had previously appeared in the *New York Graphic*. The story was titled "They Too Carried Things Away."

> With very few exceptions, all the New York 'boys" of the press who did duty at Johnstown brought back relics of the eventful trip. Among a collection which I happened to see was a gravure type of the Madonna. The flood had evidently torn the picture from the frame, but the face was not marred in the least. The relic was pasted upon a large white sheet of cardboard, and the whole piece framed so that the ragged and torn edges were visible. Among the same collection was a marble which had been taken from the little hand of a dead child which the reporter had stumbled over the first night he spent on the site of the desolate village.
>
> A more interesting souvenir, but one fraught with more sad recollections, is the silver half dollar wrapped in a piece of brown paper, upon which was written the following sentences: "Three and a-half pounds of brown sugar, one pound of starch; yeast cake." The handwriting was that of a woman, and the coin and paper were tightly clenched in the hand of a twelve-year-old girl, whose body was found half buried in the sand.

On the first anniversary of the flood, a group of Pittsburgh newspapermen returned for a visit to Johnstown. A brief note in the May 31, 1890 edition of the *Johnstown Tribune* described their visit.

> A special train of four coaches and a baggage car brought a large number of newspaper men and their guests—including many ladies from Pittsburgh to Johnstown this morning about half-past 10 o'clock.

A monument to the Flood Correspondents Association stands on the point of land where the Stony Creek and Little Conemaugh meet just above the Stone Bridge. This monument was erected by the school children of the Conemaugh Valley. It serves to commemorate efforts to control flooding in Johnstown, and is dedicated to the correspondents from the flood of May 31, 1889. The monument was dedicated on May 31, 1940, the fifty-first anniversary of the flood.

They strolled about town until noon, when they had a banquet in the cars, after which they again looked about town and visited the cemeteries. At 3 o'clock they left for South Fork. At 5:10 they left that place on their return to Pittsburgh, where they will arrive at 8:20. The newspaper men were mostly of the number of those who did such valuable service here during the flood.

One of the major tasks to which the writers devoted considerable attention was trying to provide their editors and thus their readers with the number of casualties. As honest as their efforts may have been, it soon became clear that estimates of the loss of life in and around Johnstown were dramatically exaggerated or markedly underestimated. This was due to a lack of credible information and no means to do anything to gather better data. It is interesting to note, however, that some of the earliest estimates turned out to be the most correct in the end. For example, the first accounts to appear in the *New York Times* on June 1 reported the estimated death toll to be 1,500. The source quoted was a dispatch received from Philadelphia on Saturday, June 1. In the days and weeks following the flood, it was not uncommon for the same paper to offer several conflicting accounts of the death toll in the same edition of their paper. The June 2, 1889 edition of the *New York Times* offered all of the following estimates:

> Pittsburg*, June 1. —The first direct communication by wire with Johnstown was opened at 2:30 o'clock this afternoon. A dispatch was received, saying a careful estimate placed the number of drowned and missing at 2,000.

> Pittsburg, June 2. —1 A.M. Dispatches just received from Johnstown indicate that the death list from that city alone will run up to 10,000.... At Bolivar, New Florence, Nineveh, and other towns below Johnstown 2,000 dead bodies have already been recovered.... It is believed that 5,000 lives have been lost in the towns above Johnstown. The valley is laid waste for a distance of more than twenty miles.

> Sang Hollow, Penn., June 2—The first reports of loss of life were entirely too low. It is believed that at least 8,000 persons have perished; of these 700 to 800 were burned in the fiery furnace at the viaduct. Two thousand coffins have been ordered for bodies already rescued.

Most of the early estimates of the death toll, and they were most certainly estimates, were based more on overall perceptions of the horrible scene of devastation that was Johnstown in early June 1889, rather than any effort to accurately calculate the number that would ultimately be part of the list of victims. The June 4 edition of the *New York Times*, reported that General Hastings, Pennsylvania Adjutant General and the person in charge in the flooded district, had reported to Pennsylvania Governor Beaver that the death toll would reach at least 8,000. Burgess Horrell of Johnstown (reported as Mayor Morrell in the *Times*) and A. J. Moxham, who was at the time heading the relief efforts, believed that Hastings had underestimated the loss by at least 2,000 bodies. Within three days, the *Lebanon* (Pennsylvania) *Daily News* reported to its readers, under the headline "Scenes of Woe," datelined from Johnstown, June 7, that General Hastings had then estimated the casualty figure as nearly 15,000, with many other people suggesting that it may well reach 20,000. *The Star and Sentinel* informed its

---

* This was the accepted spelling of Pittsburgh in 1889.

readers in its June 4, 1889, edition, under the headline "Greatest Disaster of Modern Times," that an accurate estimate was impossible.

Yesterday's dispatches state that while hundreds of bodies of the victims of the terrible flood in the Conemaugh Valley have been recovered and identified, it is still impossible to estimate with any degree of accuracy the number of lives lost. Railroad officials and those in authority at Johnstown vary greatly in their estimates, the lowest being 5,000 and the highest 10,000.

One of the first efforts to arrive at an accurate figure was that of the *Pittsburg Commercial Gazette*. This estimate was picked up and carried by a number of papers. It appeared in the New York Times on Saturday, June 8:

ONE ESTIMATE OF THE LOSS
From the Pittsburg Commercial Gazette

There is reason to believe that the number of those lost in the Conemaugh flood has been subjected to the same sensational exaggeration as has been applied to other incidents of the dreadful catastrophe. The estimate of 15,000 made in one of the papers yesterday, is clearly preposterous.

The population whose settlements were in or close to the track of the Conemaugh flood were as follows, the figures being those of the census of 1880 and the last Presidential election:

	1880 Population	1888 Voters
Cambria Borough	2,223	454
Cambria Township	1,047	245
Conemaugh Borough	3,498	714
Conemaugh Township	437	114
Coopersdale Borough	409	116
East Conemaugh Borough	756	217
Johnstown Borough	8,380	2,238
Lower Yoder Township (including Morrellville)	957	494
Millvale	2,409	532
Mineral Point	134	26
Woodvale Borough	639	240
Total	20,889	5,390

At the usual basis of computation of five to a voter, the vote cast at the last Presidential election would indicate that the population of that region had increased to 26,950 since 1880, and this includes all those on safe high ground as well as those on low.

It is known that the settlements below the lake had three hours' warning so that at the village of South Fork the people were able to move out not only themselves, but their furniture. It is known, moreover, that comparatively few were lost at other settlements between Johnstown and the lake. The loss centered in Johnstown and the settlements clustered around— Cambria City, Millvale, Morrellville, Woodvale, hav-

ing a population of 21,015 as computed on the basis of the last Presidential vote. This represents the total population within corporate limits, and, although the flood swept across the business and principal residence portions of Johnstown, yet the populated area exposed to the rush of the flood will not exceed two-thirds of the whole, or 14,010 according to the method of computation or, say, 15,000 in round numbers.

Up to 8 o'clock last night the number of survivors registered at Johnstown was 13,000, and it is conceded that this registration is very incomplete, many of the survivors having gone away or else have failed to report. Moreover, the registration is taken at Johnstown and does not include survivors at other points, unless they have come to Johnstown. It is pretty evident on the basis of this registration that the death roll cannot possibly number above 5,000, with a probability that it will be a good deal less. The number of bodies so far gotten out, it turns out, are only about 1,200, and the ruins have been pretty thoroughly explored, with the exception of the jam at the bridge.

Anyone who followed the story closely quickly realized that exact numbers simply were not possible. In June 1889, any credible count, or even close estimate of the total losses was still months away. Arriving at an accurate count was further complicated by several other factors. Visitors in the town, those just passing through, new residents who had yet to be made part of population figures, and residents who for any number of reasons were not in town on May 31 all affected the count. In the face of what had happened to the area, an accurate count was just not possible, and in fact was a rather low priority to those in and around Johnstown. Their efforts were focused on rescuing and supporting those who could be saved rather than counting victims who were then beyond such earthly needs.

In the aftermath of the flood, the aid and relief needed in Johnstown were tremendous. Johnstown and surrounding boroughs needed everything in large measure. Fortunately, the nation and the world responded. Relief efforts began even before the waters had receded. In the end, those who responded to Johnstown's needs after the flood set a standard that has yet to be surpassed in generosity or sheer volume. There were, however, those who felt that this may have been due, at least in part, to the exaggerated stories and casualty reports that came out of Johnstown in the early hours and days following the flood. Few were callous or certain enough to level such charges, but the innuendo of several editorials and stories was unmistakably clear. In short, there were those who believed that accounts, related stories and numbers of the Johnstown disaster were intentionally exaggerated to attract more attention and thus more support than was actually needed.

In a story that reads more like an editorial, the *Johnstown Tribune* answered these charges. Leveling a countercharge of "ignorance" at some of the "Eastern papers," the *Tribune*, in its June 14 edition attempted to explain the basis for the figures that had been and were continued to be released:

UNJUST FIGURING

Some of the Eastern papers have been exposing their ignorance and at the same time treating Johnstown very unfairly. They insist that our loss, both of life and property, cannot be anything like so great as has been reported; and as to property loss, they prove it by comparing Johnstown with places of eight and ten thousand population where valuations have been made.

They either forget or do not know that the population of Johnstown as given in the census reports is not the population of Johnstown at all, and that instead of ten thousand, as the census of 1890 would give the place, the actual population is over twenty-nine thousand, for Johnstown is made up of many boroughs and villages, all dependent upon the same mills and factories and separated only by imaginary lines, and the greater portion of all is swept away.

The direct track of the flood was through a population of not less than twenty-five thousand—the best portion of the city. Base your calculations on that fact, and include the costly mills. There is no disposition here to exaggerate. It is bad enough to tell the awful, crushing truth.

In the same edition of their paper, the *Tribune* offered its own estimate in a story titled "The Number of Lost." The assertions of the article were clear. The estimate was made based on a total population of Johnstown and surrounding townships and boroughs, which they set as just under 30,000. Allowances were made for those who lived in places like Brownstown, Franklin, Walnut Grove, Moxham and the hill portions of the various boroughs that were struck since they were virtually untouched by the floodwaters. The Office of Registration was headquartered in a building at Main and Adam Streets, which was also the temporary post office. There were branches set up in the outlying boroughs with a number of canvassers attempting to register those who had survived. As of June 11 at 6:00 p.m. there were 15,578 people registered. There was recognition of the fact that many survivors had as of yet failed to register, and many had left town without notifying anyone of their fate. Taking all that was then known into account, the *Tribune*, a paper at the very heart of the disaster, said a full two weeks after the flood, "It will scarcely fall short of 5,000 and may go higher."

If the *Johnstown Tribune* was still offering a figure that approached 5,000 two weeks after the flood, is it any wonder why papers around the world were unable to be more accurate? It is interesting to note that one of the first dispatches from Johnstown, as reported in the *New York Times* on June 1, set the estimate of casualties at 2,000. Although no single number is considered irrefutably correct, the final casualty count has been set at 2,209.

The suspected horrors of the night, in all too many cases, became the reality of the day when the first light of dawn broke on the morning of June 1. Slowly people began moving from places that provided refuge during the night. Periodic screams and groans of agony pierced the air. The field of destruction made many parts of the town impossible to identify. People who had lived a lifetime in Johnstown had to look for familiar landmarks to find their way. There was a general movement to get the women and children out of low areas and onto hills that surrounded Johnstown. Many of the survivors made their way to Green Hill at the upper end of Main Street. Others went to Prospect Hill, while still others sought refuge on Yoder Hill and in Brownstown. As they did, they passed men heading into the lower, flooded areas of the town to begin the dreadful task of searching for survivors and gathering the dead. During the early morning hours there was no plan, but instead a helpless sense of confusion and hopelessness. In many cases the lives and in even more cases the possessions of thousands now littered the low plain between the Stony Creek and the Little Conemaugh like so much refuse.

A simple yet profound musing carried in the July 3 edition of the *Johnstown Tribune*, illustrated with unintentionally callous truth the magnitude of the numbers associated with the disaster in the Conemaugh Valley.

There could be no better evidence of the stupendousness of our calamity than the fact that only today is the complete list of the lost and saved at the Hulbert House printed for the first time by any paper. Forty-eight men, women and children swept into eternity from under the same roof, yet the destruction of life that would have been appalling under other circumstances is passed by as a mere incident of the overwhelming disaster!

Johnstown on the morning of June 1 was a scene of utter destruction and desolation. The level of the water had receded to some degree, but fires were visible throughout the flooded area. Fires at the Stone Bridge and several other locations continued to burn at varying levels of intensity. Several of the smaller fires burned and smoldered for days. The major blaze at the Stone Bridge, which claimed many lives that had been spared

This is a view of Johnstown following the flood from Green Hill. Notice the spire of the Franklin Street United Methodist Church.

by the flood wave, was brought under control by Sunday evening. It smoldered in numerous spots for days and periodically small pockets of fire would break out. Gaining control of the fire at the Stone Bridge, which many referred to as a funeral pyre, is credited to the fine work of the firemen who came in from Pittsburgh.

The threat of disease became an immediate issue. The rivers in Johnstown and virtually anything touched by the floodwaters was contaminated and posed a serious public health threat. Warnings of pestilence were numerous and created much concern. Decaying human and animal flesh, stagnant pools of filthy water, and waste and debris of all manner were critical concerns. Physicians generally agreed that it would be highly advisable to allow the fires that had been burning around the town to continue to do so. This, however, did not meet with public approval. Suggestions to allow the fires, particularly the one at the Stone Bridge, to continue burning so as to purify the ruins quickly gave way to public sentiment that the recovery of victims was the preeminent issue. Before the fire at the Stone Bridge could be extinguished, it claimed numerous victims. In the June 14 edition of the *Johnstown Tribune* it was reported that an estimated seventy charred bodies had already been pulled from the debris field in front of the bridge. Undoubtedly this number increased as the work at the Stone Bridge continued.

The fears that typhoid fever might spread through the stricken area were realized by mid-June. The number of cases reported in Johnstown was slightly more than 200, while in the surrounding areas, almost 250 additional cases were reported. Death attributed to typhoid amounted to some forty individuals by the end of the

summer. All things considered, this was remarkably low. The June 14 edition of the *Johnstown Tribune* carried an article on the somewhat surprising state of the public health of the town. It was reported that, "Even the chronic invalids are on their feet, and the doctors smile when they tell of men and women who had long been under their care, suffering from all sorts of obscure diseases, but whom they now find 'roughing it' like anybody but an invalid." The brief article concluded with some reminders to the good citizens of Johnstown to protect their own health. "It should be the duty of each individual, therefore, to take all precautions, eating regularly of wholesome food—for there is plenty to be had—taking needed rest, and observing cleanliness even if they cannot obey the Health Department's amusing recommendation of a daily bath."

Buildings and mountains of debris that would shift, move and collapse provided ever-present dangers for those who began the search for survivors. The destruction along Main Street was dramatic and is representa-

This scene shows a victim being removed from the debris field.

tive of the general condition of the town. The June 3, 1889 edition of the *Chicago Tribune* carried the following description of Main Street in Johnstown:

> It is impossible to describe the appearance of Main Street. Whole houses have been swept down this one street and become lodged. The wreck is piled as high as the second story windows. The reporter could step from the wreck into the auditorium of the opera house. The ruins consist of parts of houses, trees, saw logs, and reels from the wire factory. Many houses have their side-walls and roofs torn up, and you can walk directly into what had been second-story bedrooms or go in by way of the top. Further up town a raft of logs lodged in the street and did great damage. At the commencement of the wreckage, which is at the opening of the valley of the Conemaugh, one can look up the valley for miles and not see a house. Nothing stands but an old woolen mill.

The first task that faced the survivors was to organize themselves to begin the recovery process. Although ill prepared to do so considering the events of the previous twenty-four hours, the citizens of Johnstown organized in remarkable fashion to begin caring for themselves and their town. By the early evening of Saturday, June 1, the process of recovery and rebuilding had begun. An initial meeting was held in the Adams Street or Fourth Ward School at 3:00 p.m. Arthur J. Moxham, one of the town's leading citizens, presided at the meeting.

Moxham, although able in his own right, presided at the meeting only because John Fulton, the General Manager of the Cambria Iron Company, could not be located. He was presumed dead, but was in fact out of town. This meeting of what came to be known as Johnstown's Citizens' Committee was called for the purpose of drafting a number of sub-committees to address specific tasks deemed immediately essential. Among the things destroyed by the flood was the local government, with many officials, killed, missing, or incapacitated. As Johnstown was organizing itself, so too were other local boroughs.

Moxham, who had come to Johnstown in 1886 as the president of the Johnson Steel Street Rail Company located in Woodvale, had made a good name for himself and developed a positive reputation. In 1888, Moxham purchased land south of Johnstown along the Stony Creek. He established a small town, which was promptly named "Moxham," and built a large rolling mill there along the river. At the same time the name of the company was changed to the Johnson Company.

The subcommittees organized under Moxham clearly indicate the chief concerns as seen by those who found themselves in the very midst of the flooded dis-

trict. As listed in the June 14 edition of the *Johnstown Tribune*, the following subcommittees were organized:

Committee on Local Distribution of Supplies
Committee on Finance
Committee on Teams and Messengers
Committee on Information and Transportation
Local Commissary Committee
Committee on Removing Dead Animals
Morgue Committee
Committee for Removal of Debris
Committee of Timekeeping and Books
Committee on Dangerous Buildings
Police Committee
Fire Committee
Committee on Employment
Sanitary Committee
Registration.

Unfortunately not everyone in town shared the noble goals of the Citizens' Committee. In fact, there were those who saw the present situation as the perfect opportunity to act in ways that showed the worst side of man's nature. Difficult as it was for many to comprehend, there were those who robbed and pillaged with impunity. Business houses and homes left vacant by families that had fled or were now among the dead were their targets. Anything that could be carried off was fair game. In some cases, although limited, individual corpses were reported to have been stripped of personal possessions. Fighting and drunkenness were prevalent. The situation in Johnstown was far beyond anything the local police force was prepared to handle, because of their limited size and the impact of the flood on individual members of the force. The only officer of the Johnstown police to perish was Samuel Eldridge. The police chief, John T. Harris, suffered the loss of his wife and five of his six children. David, a surviving son who was eight at the time of the flood, was sent to stay with relatives in Braddock, Pennsylvania.

Because the new community of Moxham was largely beyond the reach of the floodwaters that rushed up the Stony Creek after hitting Yoder Hill, the male residents were called on by Mr. Moxham to provide some "police" protection for the town. Over the next few days others were deputized for similar service. These temporary police became known as "tin-tag police," because a star that they cut from a tin can or any other source of metal was used to identified them. Although well intended, most of these policemen were far less capable than the task required. By numerous accounts many of them were often a hindrance, finding some sordid pleasure in wielding power that they assumed to be theirs. Others wanted a badge to avoid being called on to help clean debris or any other physical

(Left) In this view of the lower end of Main Street, the Morrell Institute can be seen on the right. It had been the home of Daniel Morrell and following his death it became home to the Morrell Institute offering courses in such subjects as art, music, commerce and language. Notice the mud encrusted streets. As the water receded, tons of silt and mud were left behind.

(Below, left) This photograph shows the intersection of Main and Franklin Streets, adjacent to Johnstown's Central Park. The tall building on the right of the picture is the opera house referred to in the description of Main Street offered in the June 3rd edition of the Chicago Tribune.

Arthur J. Moxham

This is the upper end of Main Street with Green Hill in the background.

labor. One purpose they did serve was to unmistakably demonstrate that maintaining order was a task that was far beyond current local capabilities.

If one individual best represented the misuse of policing authority in the aftermath of the flood it was former burgess and local attorney Chalmers "Chal" L. Dick. Numerous individuals who knew him would later say that in a confused and agitated state he rode through the town threatening anyone who would dare defile the dead or disturb the property of the living or the dead. Dick and numerous other self-proclaimed protectors of Johnstown directed particular attention toward Hungarians living in and around the town. Reports of atrocities carried out by the "Huns" or "Hunkies," as they were often referred to, circulated quickly. Most of these stories spoke of looting, fighting, and rioting by Johnstown's "foreign element," the score for which was quickly settled by driving them into the raging rivers or by having them hanged.

An account which appeared in the Monday, June 3, 1889 edition of the *New York Times* under the heading "Robbers of the Dead Lynched," datelined from Johnstown June 2, 1889 was typical of these stories. It provided a vivid story of an older railroad man who walked to Johnstown from Sang Hollow and on his way observed a number of men he believed to be Hungarians robbing trinkets of jewelry from the bodies of women and children along the riverbanks. Men on the railroad platform immediately headed in the direction of Sang Hollow. In short order they encountered the villains. The following is the account the *Times* provided of that encounter:

> With revolver leveled at the scoundrels the leader of the posse shouted: "Throw up your hands or I'll blow your heads off."
>
> With blanched faces and trembling forms they obeyed the order and begged for mercy. They were searched, and as their pockets were emptied of their finds the indignation of the crown intensified, and when a bloody finger of an infant encircled with two tiny gold rings, was found among the plunder in their leader's pocket, a cry went up, "Lynch them!" Without a moment's delay ropes were thrown around their necks and they were dangling to the limbs of a tree, in the branches of which an hour before were entangled the bodies of a dead father and son. After half an hour the ropes were cut and the bodies lowered and carried to a pile of rocks in the forest on the hill above.

Most of these accounts ended with a report of swift and fatal retribution. These stories were virtually all pure fabrication. In fact, Chal Dick himself later refuted them, as did most of the survivors who recorded accounts of their experiences during the days

This illustration appeared on the back cover of The Johnstown Horror, *a magazine-type publication published by Frank Touney of New York City on June 8, 1889. It depicts Hungarians being driven into the raging river, while others are hung in the background.*

and weeks following the flood. Like many stories that came out of Johnstown in the early hours and days following the flood, when information was missing imagination was used. The same was true of artists covering the flood.

Accusations against Hungarians spread so quickly and were repeated so widely, that a representative of the Hungarian residents of New York came to Johnstown to see for himself. In an article that appeared in the June 19 edition of the *Johnstown Tribune*, it was reported that Joseph Stefanko was in Johnstown to investigate the reports of the atrocities being credited to Hungarians. As reported in the article, "Local authorities have assured Mr. Stefanko that the reports are 'unfounded and entirely sensational." The writer of the article concluded with, "There is entirely too much readiness wherever there are Hungarians, to blame them for all crimes committed."

As word of the Johnstown calamity spread throughout the country, many different types of individuals began making their way to the Conemaugh Valley. Those in search of work came, as did those who thought they could simply blend in and gain some measure of the relief that was sure to be had.

Thieves, from petty pickpockets to those who felt they could mastermind profitable real estate swindles in the face of panic and fear, saw Johnstown as fruit ripe for the picking. Salesmen converged on the area in droves offering everything from buttons to livestock. Organizations seeking to further their mission, like the Woman's Christian Temperance Union arrived as did "ladies" prepared to engage in the practice of the oldest profession. Ministers, physicians, and undertakers came to help, and in most cases they did. Sightseers, relic hunters, and scavengers came to help themselves. They became an annoyance that was difficult for the locals to tolerate. An order quickly went out that if you could not work, you had no business in town. A copy of a notice that appeared on a telegraph pole in Johnstown was carried in the June 4 edition of the *New York Times*.

> Notice—During the day men who have been idle have been begged to aid us in clearing the town and many have not refused to work. We are now so organized that employment can be found for every man who wants to work, and men offered work who refuse to take the same and who are able to work, must leave Johnstown for the present. We cannot afford to feed men who will not work. All work will be paid for the same. Strangers and idlers who refuse to work will be ejected from Johnstown.
>
> By Order of Citizens' Committee

As if the flood and fires had not been enough, a number of fears, both reasonable and unreasonable, spread throughout the Conemaugh Valley and gripped the survivors during the initial days following May 31. Rumors of armed bands of thugs pillaging and raping at will spread quickly. Diseases of all nature were said to have been brought to Johnstown by the floodwaters and would surely result in epidemics that would be beyond control in a matter of days. Starvation, particularly of the young, was a major fear. Broken natural gas pipes and electrical lines created serious misgivings among those who feared potential deadly consequences. In short, the terror brought by the rush of the floodwaters was soon replaced by other terrors as the floodwaters were receding.

Arthur Moxham and the men who headed the fifteen committees organized on June 1 put forth a noble effort and are due much credit. However, the magnitude of the task of establishing order in the flooded district was well beyond local capabilities. On June 4 Moxham resigned his position as the head of the Citizens' Committee of Johnstown. James B. Scott, a member of the Citizens' Relief Committee of Pittsburgh, succeeded him. This committee, which was organized in Pittsburgh on Saturday, June 1, was among the most benevolent raising

James B. Scott

more than $48,000 in a single day. Because of its proximity to Johnstown, Pittsburgh soon became the point to which most of the supplies from around the country were sent enroute to Johnstown.

Scott picked up where Moxham had left off. He made four additions to the committee system that had been established on June 1. He added subcommittees to care for the outside search of the dead, hospitals, valuables, and created a Department of Public Safety. The Department of Public Safety provided some manner of organization for local, special, and military police. Command of this department was given to Pennsylvania's Adjutant General, Daniel H. Hastings.

Hastings had arrived in Johnstown on Saturday morning and immediately saw the situation as one that required military intervention. His suggestion that the governor be contacted to arrange for such support was not initially well-received by Moxham, Scott, and other local leaders. They still believed that local control was best. Both Moxham and Scott asserted that maintaining local control would provide some sense of hope for the people of Johnstown and surrounding boroughs. There was also some concern voiced that the arrival of state troops might result in angry responses to their presence, creating more of a problem.

Scott retained control until June 12 when command of the local relief efforts, which included all aspects of that initiative, from distribution of supplies to maintaining order, were given to General Hastings. Once in command, Hastings brought a military-like efficiency to the emergency recovery efforts. He possessed a level of

General Hastings (at center with hands folded) is seen here with some of the members of his staff in Johnstown.

authority supported by Governor Beaver that served him well in the performance of his duties. Nearly 600 troops were called to Johnstown from several companies of the 14th Pennsylvania Infantry Regiment. By all accounts their service in the town was excellent with none of the concerns expressed by Moxham and Scott being realized. Hastings organized his troops at various outposts around the flooded district, with their main camp being established in Central Park. The state militia assisted with a number of the tasks associated with the relief and recovery efforts and the rebuilding of the town. Although their primary charge in the area was maintaining order, and protecting citizens and property, they frequently went beyond this charge to render service as needed. In the

face of a calamity the magnitude of Johnstown's, it would have been difficult to do otherwise.

The June 20 edition of the *Johnstown Tribune* reported that the Johnstown police force was once again reorganized and going about their work in Johnstown. It was reported that Chief Harris was in charge and had even put up a building on a lot that he owned so that the police would have a meeting place. The writer of the article reported that the "...familiar faces of these men, going about with their old authority, exercised with judgment and discretion, gives great satisfaction to our people."

One of the soldiers who had come to Johnstown, William B. Young, aged 28, committed suicide while in town. An investigation into the suicide revealed that he had recently been ill and was despondent over that and the conditions he witnessed while on guard duty. He reportedly left a widow and two children. He was a farmer from the Pennsylvania community of Oakdale.

On June 28 a substantial portion, approximately 450, of the state militia soldiers in Johnstown were relieved of their duties and returned to their homes, most of which were in the Pittsburgh area. Three companies, approximately 150 men, were kept in town to assist the local police as needed.

The last day in Johnstown for Hastings and the remainder of the militia was July 8. At that time control of the towns and boroughs in the flooded district was returned to civilian authority. One small detachment remained in Johnstown, to be called on only if needed. On

Central Park became the grounds upon which General Hastings established a camp for his troops in Johnstown.

the evening of July 8, a celebration was held in camp and the Grand Army of the Republic recognized Hastings for his service. Several other recognitions were also made.

The relief that poured into Johnstown was nothing short of amazing. As soon as the word went out, the flow of relief toward Johnstown and the surrounding communities began. Everything was needed and it was needed in large quantity. The sphere of concern for the sufferers in Johnstown grew steadily as the news of their plight spread throughout the country and the world.

The immediate need on the morning of June 1 was for food. The quantity of food that could be found in the town that had not been totally destroyed or contaminated beyond use was minimal. What was found was given to those in the direst need and the children. It quickly became apparent that the foodstuffs from surrounding communities and towns were never going to supply the immense needs of the flooded district. There was some discussion concerning the abandonment of the town. The survivors would be sent to other towns and cities to be cared for. This proposal never gained widespread support. There were several families of means who were able to send women and children to relatives in other places for the summer, but for the most part, the survivors remained in the flooded district. By the middle of June the supply of food coming into Johnstown was more than ample to meet the demands of the survivors and the relief workers who had come to the town by that time.

As with the newspapermen, there has long been a question as to whose relief supplies arrived in Johnstown first. According to the June 14, 1889 edition of the *Johnstown Tribune*, the first supplies to reach Johnstown came from Somerset. A train from Somerset came in along the B & O tracks on Sunday morning. Under the heading, "Who Came to Our Relief First," the *Tribune* states, "A car from that place [Somerset] reached here on Sunday morning and it was received by Father Tahaney, of the relief committee." Father Tahaney was a member of the Committee on Local Distribution of Supplies of the Citizens' Committee.

The Friday, June 7, 1889 edition of the *Cambria Freeman* of Ebensburg, Pennsylvania, claimed the distinction of having their relief supplies arrive first in Johnstown, stating "Ebensburg's contributions were the first that reached the suffering people of Johnstown, and the good work has been kept up ever since." Ebensburg claims to have sent no less than five wagonloads of supplies to Johnstown on the afternoon of Saturday, June 1. The cities of Pittsburgh and Allegheny also claimed to be the first to have supplies on hand for the sufferers in Johnstown. Numerous accounts in Pittsburgh papers credit both of these cities. There is credible evidence that indicates that a train from Pittsburgh arrived at Sang

Hollow, below Johnstown, during the night of June 1. However, because the tracks between Sang Hollow and Johnstown had been washed out in several spots, the supplies were transferred to Johnstown by handcars and on the backs of men who were up for the task. Some of these supplies arrived at the Stone Bridge before dawn on Sunday.

Who had the first supplies in Johnstown is both very difficult to prove and highly irrelevant. The fact is that the first relief to the suffers of Johnstown was provided by those living in and around Johnstown who were able to help family, friends, and neighbors. There were reports of farmers passing out tins of milk during the early morning hours of June 1. On the hills around Johnstown, the more fortunate opened their homes to those in need. Children were taken in and cared for without question by families throughout the flooded valley.

The relief supplies that came to Johnstown came from every imaginable source. The best organized of these relief efforts was the Citizens' Relief Committee of Pittsburgh. As noted previously, this Committee organized with amazing speed and continued their effort until the needs of Johnstown had been satisfied. The Committee was organized on June 1 during a meeting at the Old City Hall in Pittsburgh. Before the day was out, a train of more than twenty cars was headed for Johnstown. It carried, among other things, doctors, food, clothing, lumber, medical supplies, coffins and countless individual donations offered by the people of Pittsburgh and vicinity.

The membership of the Citizens' Relief Committee of Pittsburgh was interesting to say the least. The chairman of the Committee was William McCreery and the treasurer was W. R. Thompson. James B. Scott, who was given almost dictatorial powers in Johnstown after the resignation of Moxham, was the member of the Committee charged with the responsibility of delivering the goods to Johnstown. Seven other prominent men of the Pittsburgh region were selected to serve on the ten-man committee. Of that number, four held current memberships in the South Fork Fishing and Hunting Club. They were Reuben Miller, Henry Clay Frick, Henry Phipps, Jr., and S. S. Marvin. Both Miller and Marvin offered distinguished and tireless service to the Committee with little or no recognition. There were those who would later point to their inclusion on the Committee as a crude ploy to direct attention away from the responsibility the South Fork Fishing and Hunting Club had for the disaster in the Conemaugh Valley.

Providing relief to Johnstown began as a poorly organized effort, due in large measure to the fact that the extent of the needs had yet to be determined. As such there was a great deal of waste caused by apparent mismanagement. Even as supplies were being brought into the town, men standing in the open doors of railroad boxcars threw supplies to those standing along the tracks. Some got much while others got nothing. Without a means of monitoring the distribution of supplies, greed in its cruelest form quickly reared its head. It was not until relief stations, known as commissaries, were established that some order was brought to the distribution of supplies. Commissaries were established at numerous locations throughout Johnstown and the surrounding communities. One of the major distribution points was a large building at the corner of Stony Creek and Bedford Streets. Another was the Pennsylvania Railroad Station. The commissaries continued in operation until the end of September, when the last one, the Pennsylvania Railroad Station, was closed. Those still in need of assistance were issued credit at local stores that had been re-established after the flood.

At the time of the flooding Governor Beaver was out of the state. Upon his return to Harrisburg, he issued an appeal for help that was carried by numerous newspapers throughout the country. Mayors and governors across the country called meetings as soon as they learned of the calamity that hit Johnstown and vicinity. In short order money and supplies began pouring into Pennsylvania.

The storm system that had caused some much damage in the Conemaugh Valley had caused extensive damage in other sections of the state as well. Governor Beaver's challenge was to provide an efficient system for gathering and dispersing relief to Johnstown and other flooded areas as quickly as possible.

On June 14, shortly after command of the recovery efforts in Johnstown were placed in the hands of General Hastings, Governor James A. Beaver organized the Johnstown Flood Relief Commission to provide some systematic organization to the process of relief distribution. Like most of the relief efforts, their work was frenzied in the beginning, but became considerably more organized by the end of June. On June 27 the Commission met in Harrisburg for the purpose of defining their distribution policies and procedures. Their purpose was to provide a better accounting of the funds entrusted to them, and provide clearer guidelines to those in Johnstown as to how the funds would be distributed.

The plan developed by the Commission for the distribution of supplies was based on need. Those seeking the assistance of the Commission had to complete an Application for Relief. Once completed, all applications were returned to the local office of the Commission at the corner of Franklin and Locust Streets (see Appendix C). Claims were divided into one of six classes. The following is a brief description of the various classes established by the Commission, as offered in the book *The Story of Johnstown*. The higher the class the more money claimants would receive.

Class I—women who have lost their support and are left with a large family and no property

Class II—those who have lost some family and saved only a little of their property

Class III—families that recovered something from the flood

Class IV—small families in which one will be able to work and that either had no property saved from the flood or very little.

Class V—parties requiring immediate assistance, but in smaller amounts, generally where a man is employed and has a smaller family to care for

Class VI—all other claimants.

According to J. J. McLaurin's account in *The Story of Johnstown*, the Commission received about 6,100 applications. Of that number about 1,000 were rejected. They were rejected for a variety of reasons. "Some were

In this picture, women are lined up to receive supplies at the Relief Headquarters at the Pennsylvania Railroad Station.

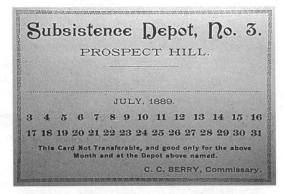

To monitor the distribution of supplies being sent to Johnstown, cards like this were issued to those in need. This facsimile relief card appeared in J. J. McLaurin's book The Story of Johnstown.

too trifling to justify the labor of an investigation, others were handed in by wealthy people who neither needed nor deserved charity, and a small number were fraudulent on their face." The amounts paid ranged from $10 to $600, with very few receiving near the latter sum.

The work of the Commission continued until the end of 1889. On January 15, 1890, a cash statement of the Commission was released. It included the following:

Total cash receipts by Commission $2,902,072.68
Total expenditures   2,683,747.11 *
Cash on Deposit in Harrisburg   218,325.57 **

Reverend David Beale offers a detailed account of the meeting of the Commission held in Philadelphia on January 16, 1890, when the Commission took several actions. The decision was made to deposit $98,900 with a trust company for the continued care of 32 orphans left by the Flood. According to arrangements made, the trust company would insure that each child received the sum of $50 each year until age sixteen. Since $16,100 had already been paid to the guardians of the orphans, the total for this purpose was $115,000. The members of the Commission also decided to allocate the sum of $40,000 for the erection of a permanent hospital in the Conemaugh Valley and $5,000 for the same purpose in Williamsport. Sundry claims in the amount of $22,442.65 were ordered to be paid from the remaining funds. As a result the commission had a balance of $70,631.40.

The members of the Johnstown Flood Relief Commission included Governor, James A. Beaver, H. H. Cummin, Edwin H. Fitler, Francis B. Reeves, James B. Scott, Robert C. Ogden, John Y. Huber, Thomas Dolan, Reubin Miller and S. S. Marvin.

---

*. Of this amount 90% was appropriations and expenditures in the Conemaugh Valley, 9% was appropriations and expenditures in other flooded areas of the state, and the final 1% was money distributed specifically as designated by donors, general and office expenses, and the money paid to guardians for care of the orphans.

** Since some of the funds that had been allocated for Johnstown and other areas of the state had yet to be distributed, the actual cash on hand for use by the Commission was $236,974.05.

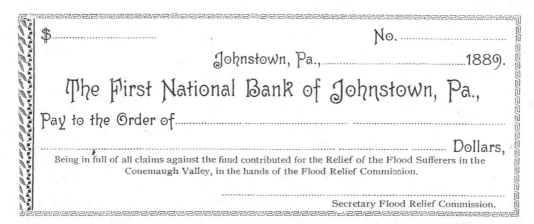

Payments from the Johnstown Flood Relief Commission were made by way of checks printed on pink paper. This facsimile of a relief check appeared in J. J. McLaurin's book The Story of Johnstown.

Governor Beaver summed up the work of the Commission in a letter to the Mayor of Concord, New Hampshire, acknowledging their contribution:

> The charity which has flowed in a constant stream almost without intermission since the second day of June toward the sufferers in our State has been a constant benediction. It has come from all parts of the civilized world. As the recipient of it, in large degree, I have been brought into very close contact with it, and have been cheered in the midst of so much that was depressing by this marvelous exhibition of the beautiful side of human nature.

The role played by Governor Beaver in the aftermath of the flooding throughout Pennsylvania did not enhance his political career or the personal regard many newspaper editors afforded him. In an article titled "Disstressing (sic) Weakness" that appeared in the June 21, 1889 edition of the Cambria Freeman from Ebensburg, Pennsylvania, the Johnstown Flood was seen as a perfect opportunity for Governor Beaver to "...gloss over a very bad record, but it served only to show his lamentable weakness." The article reported that he was "...junketing around the country..." while other governors were busy organizing relief trains to be sent to Pennsylvania. The article closed comparing Governor Beaver to the governors of Ohio and New York. It read, "Try to imagine Foraker, of Ohio, or Hill of New York, making such an exhibition of weakness."

The governor did not visit Johnstown until June 9. During this visit significant difficulties arose between him and members of the various relief organizations working in Johnstown. The governor did not feel the state should assume responsibility for the relief efforts in Johnstown. Those who had been on the job of providing that relief for more than a week at that point had a decidedly different perspective. They saw the need for immediate state control and the appropriation of emergency relief funds by the General Assembly. At the end of this heated meeting, Governor Beaver agreed that the state would assume control of the flooded district on June 12. He did, however, make it clear that there were other areas of the commonwealth that had been devastated by the spring floods of 1889, and that the General Assembly need not be called into special session for the appropriation of emergency funds. The governor contended that the relief funds coming into Pennsylvania would be sufficient to meet the needs of the flood sufferers. William McCreery, the chairman of the Citizens' Relief Committee of Pittsburgh, was possibly the most outspoken and vigorous opponent of the Governor's stand.

The resulting hostilities between the governor and those providing relief for Johnstown may well have had a detrimental effect on the relief initiatives provided by other cities. The public disagreement and a growing sense of poor management left some feeling that any aid they would provide would be mismanaged, so why bother until Pennsylvania's internal difficulties had been worked out. Fortunately, those who felt this way were few in number.

As the major news story of the day, Johnstown had gained tremendous public attention. Several benefit performances were held around the country for the sufferers of Johnstown. Edwin Booth, the brother of John Wilkes Booth and one of the most noted Shakespearean actors of his day, appeared in a special performance of *Othello*, John Philip Sousa performed a concert, and Buffalo Bill Cody offered the proceeds from one of his *Wild West shows*. The town of Altoona cancelled their annual Fourth of July fireworks program and sent the money that would have been spent for the program to Johnstown. Thomas Edison, from the Edison Laboratory in Orange, New Jersey sent $212.00. Queen Victoria offered nothing but her condolences to President Harrison, but the English people contributed in a far more royal fashion.

The members of the South Fork Fishing & Hunting Club, and the businesses and industrial interests they controlled were a high-profile source of relief funds. The following list, from the *Johnstown Flood National Memorial Elias J. Unger House Historic Structure Report*, details these contributions;

D. W. C. Bidwell	$100
Carnegie Brothers & Company	$5,000
Carnegie, Phipps & Company	$5,000
Charles J. Clarke	$1,000
W. T. Dunn	$15
Mrs. Daniel Euwer	$100
A. French Spring Company	$1,000
H. C. Frick Coke Company	$5,000
John A. Harper	$30
A. V. Holmes	$25
Joseph Horne & Company	$1,000
C. G. Hussey & Company	$1,000
Lewis Irwin	$200
Knox & Reed	$400
W. W. Lawrence & Company	$100
Jesse H. Lippincott	$1,000
T. Mellon & Sons	$1,000
Miller, Metcalf & Parkin	$1,000
Moorhead, McCleane & Company	$1,000
William Mullins	$300
Myers, Shinkle & Company	$100
O. McClintock & Company	$100
McCord & Company	$100
James McGregor	$100

S. McKee & Company	$100
D. C. Phillips	$50
Rea Brothers & Company	$100
W. B. Scaife & Sons	$200
J. M. Schoonmaker Coke Company	$1,000
Frank Semple	$50
M. B. Suydam & Company	$200
Benjamin Thaw	$50
Elias J. Unger	$500
Joseph Woodwell	$200
Joseph Woodwell & Company	$200
TOTAL	$27,320.00

President Benjamin Harrison personally offered $300 that was part of more than $30,000 that came in from Washington. In Washington, the relief effort began on Sunday with a special meeting between President Harrison and acting Secretary of War, General Schofield. They were in communication with Governor Beaver who was at Annapolis, Maryland, at the time. The governor was serving on a board of visitors to the Naval Academy. The President offered both troops and tents to be sent anywhere needed. Governor Beaver did not accept the offer. Two days later President Harrison called a meeting for the purpose of raising relief funds. Pledges of funds from this initial meeting amounted to approximately $10,000. In his speech at the meeting, President Harrison spoke of the brotherhood of man during his call for charity for the Johnstown sufferers. In part he said:

> In such meetings as we have here in the national capital, and other like gatherings that are taking place in all the cities of this land, we have the only rays of hope and light in the general gloom. When such a calamitous visitation falls upon any section of our country we can do no more than to put about the dark picture the golden border of love and charity. It is in such fires as these that the brotherhood of man is welded, and where is sympathy and help more appropriate than here in the national capital?

In New York City the relief began with a meeting called by Mayor Hugh Grant. An account carried in the June 4 edition of the *New York Times* detailed this meeting. Mayor Grant issued invitations to specific gentlemen of the city who he believed would be best suited to rise to the occasion. For example, the chairman of the meeting was General William Tecumseh Sherman. Upon accepting his position, Sherman said, "What we want to do is to take means to get money and materials to these suffering people as soon as possible. I can't give money like you millionaires but I'm willing to give my time and all the money I can spare." Before accepting money from anyone else,

Sherman pledged $100. Modern estimates as to the total amount of money that came into Johnstown are slightly more than $3.7 million.

Setting a value on the supplies and materials brought into Johnstown was impossible. However, by any and all accounts, it was an unprecedented outpouring of generosity. The material aide from Pittsburgh was overwhelming. It included, among other items, 23 boxes of lanterns and wicks from Cavitt, Pollock & Company; a boxcar load of milk from the Chartiers Creamery; 15,000 paper bags from Godfrey & Clark; 15 dozen shovels from Hussy, Binns & Company; 500 pounds of ground coffee from Singer Manufacturing Company; and 10,000 pounds of cut and dry tobacco and 15,000 pipes from Weyman & Brothers.

Aid from other cities and states, much of which came through Pittsburgh, was equally impressive. Kansas sent 400 bushels of wheat, and the Detroit House of Corrections sent 25 dozen chairs and five dozen rockers. Miss Hilts of Cincinnati, Ohio, sent an original poem. Cleveland sent 26 boxcars of lumber, doors, and windows, and Toledo added another 16 boxcar loads of lumber. Not counting individual contributions of members detailed above, the South Fork Fishing and Hunting Club contributed $3,000 and 1,200 blankets. (All of the above contributions were contained in the accounting of the *Report of the Citizens' Relief Committee of Pittsburgh*.)

Attempting to identify all of the relief organizations that sent aid to Johnstown and vicinity would be impossible. There were, however, those that provided significant and distinguished service. Various fraternal organizations, such as the Masons and the Odd Fellows displayed boundless generosity. Ethnic groups and societies respond to the cries for help with little concern for the heritage of those in need. The Yellow Cross Society came to Johnstown under the leadership of Dr. Frances S. Jerome. Organized primarily to respond to outbreaks of yellow fever, the Society performed admirably in Johnstown. Dr. Jerome and her staff reacted to the needs of the children in the flooded district. An organization with a similar mission was the Children's Aid Society, which had organized a chapter in Johnstown in 1886. The Society had more than ample work in the days and weeks after the flood. Under the headline "Notice to Destitute," the following notice appeared in the June 17 edition of the *Johnstown Tribune*: "Any person having children in charge who are not relatives will please respond, on account of friends who are inquiring for lost children, at rooms of Children's Aid Society of Western Pennsylvania, corner Jackson and Main Street."

As generous, kind and timely as the numerous relief efforts were, none compare to that offered by Clara Barton and her American National Red Cross. Upon hearing of the disaster in Johnstown, Clarissa Harlowe Barton, in Washington, D.C. at the time, initially did nothing. She felt the story simply had to be a gross exaggeration. However, as the details of the story continued to pour in, she realized that the devastation was real and began to mobilize the Red Cross for what would be their first major relief effort. Barton and the American National Red Cross had been involved in other natural disasters around the country, but nothing they ha yet faced approached the magnitude of what awaited them in the Conemaugh Valley.

Miss Barton and five Red Cross workers arrived in Johnstown on June 5. They established headquarters on Prospect Hill in a tent that they had brought with them. In her book, *The Red Cross in Peace and War*, published in 1906, Clara Barton described the initial reaction General Hastings had when she presented herself to him as the leader of a relief organization. "I could not have puzzled General Hastings more if I had addressed him in Chinese; and if ours had been truly an Oriental mission, the gallant soldier could not have been more courteous and kind." Throughout her stay in Johnstown, her headquarters was eventually moved to a railroad car in town and for the finally portion of her stay she was a guest in the home of John Ludwig at the upper end of Main Street

Prior to the flood, Johnstown did not have a public hospital. The only medical facility was the hospital of Cambria Iron of Prospect Hill. In addition to the absence of a hospital, the local medical establishment had lost members to the flood, and those who survived had lost family members, their homes and offices, and were in the same state of mental anguish and confusion as the other survivors. Even if they had all survived and not suffered at the hands of the flood, their number would have been insufficient to care for the sick and injured. To begin meeting these needs, some victims of the flood were sent to Pittsburgh for treatment. Others were taken to buildings that survived the flood, where impromptu medical facilities were set up with nothing but the barest of essentials. As rapidly as possible hospital facilities were created around Johnstown. The first such facility was established on Bedford Street on June 1. By the end of the day it was filled to capacity. A small hospital was established in Morrellville the following day in what had been a livery stable. Patients were made as comfortable as possible under the circumstances. Calls were sent out for doctors to come to Johnstown and for much needed medical supplies. The calls were answered promptly.

The Philadelphia Chapter of the Red Cross answered the pleas for medical assistance and assumed leadership in providing some degree of organized medical care. They began operating out of the Cambria Iron Hospital and two tent hospitals. One of the tent hospitals was on Yoder Hill and the other was in an orchard in the 7th ward. They also set up a small hospital facility at the corner of Wood and Cedar Streets to care for those living south of town.

As local physicians recovered from the flood, they quickly re-engaged in the practice of medicine, much to the relief of their former patients. Concerned and generous benefactors established a number of independent dispensaries in the flooded district. A notable example was the dispensary established by the Hahnemann Medical College and Hospital of Philadelphia. It opened on June 25 and was located on Adams Street. In a rather short period of time the need for these hospital facilities diminished markedly. As they were closed one by one, the Red Cross set up a central dispensary on Locust Street so as to centralize available medical care. Before leaving Johnstown a more permanent infirmary was established by the Red Cross on Walnut Street.

Interestingly the general health in Johnstown following the flood was better than normal for some time. Although difficult to explain, many observers, particularly the physicians who cared for the town's people, noted this phenomenon in their recollections of the flood.

Before leaving Johnstown, the Philadelphia Chapter of the Red Cross helped many local doctors rebuild their individual practices. They also initiated efforts that led to the creation of a public hospital. There was an unspoken yet very real rivalry between the two Red Cross chapters that came to Johnstown. Fortunately, each found their niche and thus served the Johnstown survivors well. Sensing that the Philadelphia delegation was best prepared to deal with medical needs in Johnstown, Miss Barton centered the attention of her workers on housing the homeless and providing assistance to those trying to rebuild their lives.

After the immediate needs of medical attention, food and clean water were satisfied, the most pressing concern became shelter. The number of people that crowded into the homes and buildings that were left standing after the flood quickly became a concern. The sanitary condition of Johnstown was in a deplorable state following the flood and these crowded living conditions only made the situation worse. Securing adequate accommodation for those displaced by the flood became a pressing need. This was accomplished through the construction of Red Cross Hotels, the building of permanent homes by individuals with lumber and materials sent to Johnstown by a variety of sources, and the erection of prefabricated houses purchased with relief funds.

The establishment of the Red Cross hotels was primarily the work of Clara Barton and her chapter of the Red Cross. The first of the hotels she established was erected on the site where St. Mark's Church had stood on Locust Street. This hotel was completed during the last week of July. It featured hot and cold running water, bathroom, kitchen, dining, and laundry facilities. This was a two-story frame structure managed by a landlady personally selected by Miss Barton. The immediate success of this first hotel led to the construction of a second on Somerset Street that was completed in August.

In September, a plot of land was secured in Woodvale upon which four apartment-type buildings were constructed. As the need for these structures diminished, they were eventually torn down and the lumber, much to the chagrin of area lumber dealers, was offered to locals for personal use. As a result of the protests of the lumber dealers, the remainder of the lumber was shipped to Washington, D C. It was Miss Barton's intention to use this salvaged lumber to construct a building in Washington for use by her and the Red Cross. In 1891, such a building was constructed in Glen Echo, Maryland.

The building in Glen Echo was for many years believed to have been constructed, at least in part, with lumber from the Red Cross hotels that had been built in Johnstown following the flood. Current research, offered by Ann E. Bartholomew, registrar of the American Red Cross Museum in Washington, D C., indicates that the lumber had indeed been sent from Johnstown to Washington after the flood. However, fire laws at the time prohibited the construction of strictly wooden buildings in major cities. This was due in large measure to the great Chicago fire of 1871.

In late October 1889 Miss Barton returned to Washington. At the time she was living in a boardinghouse. Her growing collection of papers and relief supplies created the need for a substantial storage facility. The Baltzley brothers of Glen Echo offered Miss Barton land on which such a structure could be built. Having been stored outside and unprotected for more than a year, most of the Johnstown lumber had deteriorated to the point where it was useless. In the papers of the construction company this sad fact was noted, along with the caution that Miss Barton should not be so informed. It then appears reasonable to assume that if any wood from the Johnstown Flood was used in the construction of the building that is now known as the Clara Barton National Historic Site in Glen Echo, Maryland, it would have been limited to a few "ceremonial" boards to at least in part carry out the wishes of Miss Barton.

Although the Red Cross hotels provided aid, comfort, and shelter to many people, the need was far greater than these hotels could meet. Tents had been sent into Johnstown from a number of sources, but they proved unpopular with those who had lost their homes. They provided no privacy and they afforded little or no stability should another storm visit the area. Early on it was suggested to the various relief committees that prefabricated housing would provide a quick and suitable solution to the housing needs in Johnstown. In 1889, there were a number of companies engaged in the prefabricated housing business. Notable among the prefabricated houses were the Oklahoma, the Hughes, and the Chicago Ready Made. Even though some of each type found their way into Johnstown, all of the prefabricated homes were most often referred to as "Oklahomas."

An article in the June 17 edition of the *Johnstown Tribune* described the ready-made houses that were being proposed for delivery to Johnstown.

> The TRIBUNE is glad to be able to say, on good authority, that plans for substantial aid are being perfected whereby a large number of portable frame houses, such as were used in building up the Oklahoma towns, will be shipped here from Chicago.
>
> The houses will be about 12 x 26 feet, substantially built, with oiled floors, and large enough to give at least half a dozen persons good accommodations. They will cost the committee about $250 each, with furniture. They are expected to begin to arrive the latter part of this week, and we see by the Pittsburgh papers that next Sunday a force of carpenters will come to Johnstown from that city to put them together.
>
> Each house will be furnished with a stove and utensils, six chairs, two beds and bed clothes, two spring mattresses, one pair pillows, two pair of sheets for each bed, woolen blanket[s], a bureau, a table and tableware to set it. In fact, a family will be given everything necessary to go to housekeeping. It is said that if the houses give satisfaction the committee will not hesitate at buying one thousand of them.

The initial popularity of the houses was great. Applications quickly poured into a local committee organized to oversee the awarding of these homes. However, this initial interest quickly declined when it was determined that anyone receiving one of the prefabricated houses would have a certain quantity of money deducted from any individual monetary flood relief they would be awarded.

Of the three types of houses that were brought to Johnstown, the Hughes house provided the best accommodations. It was a two-story structure with four rooms. The Oklahoma house came in two sizes, the larger of which was similar to the Chicago house. The smaller Oklahoma house proved to be so small that in many instances families were awarded two of them. In all approximately 700 prefabricated homes were sent to Johnstown and vicinity following the flood. Of that number an estimated 400 were Hughes, 200 were Oklahoma, and 100 were Chicago Ready Made.

Completed and opened on July 27, 1889, this was the first of the Red Cross hotels built in and around Johnstown.

This interior view from one of the Red Cross hotels shows the modest design and furnishings. The Red Cross hotels provided much needed shelter for many rendered homeless by the Flood.

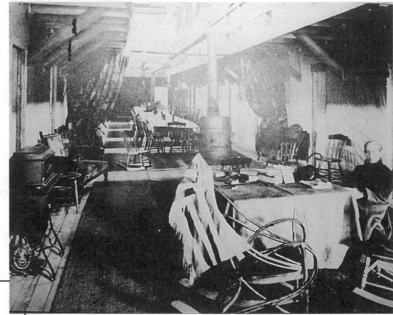

A Five O'clock Tea
is to be given
at the New Red Cross House,
Locust St., Johnstown,
Saturday, July 27, 1889
Your presence will be esteemed
a favor.

Clara Barton.
Prest. Nat. Red Cross of America.

J. B. Hubbell, M.D.
General Field Agent of the Red Cross.

To formally open her first Red Cross hotel, Miss Barton and Dr. J. B. Hubbell, the general field agent of the Red Cross, hosted a tea at the Locust Street hotel on July 27, 1889.

Possibly the last surviving prefabricated house from the aftermath of the Johnstown Flood now stands next to the Johnstown Flood Museum at the corner of Washington and Walnut Street. For many years it had stood on a lot in the Moxham section of Johnstown along with a larger structure. When ownership of the larger structure was granted to Habitat for Humanity, the organization donated the historic structure to the Johnstown Area Heritage Association. The Oklahoma was dedicated during ceremonies held on May 27, 2000.

The innocence of youth afforded no protection from the avalanche of water and debris. This photograph graphically illustrates the distressing reality of the number of children lost as a result of the flood.

This flood-era Oklahoma prefabricated house once stood in Moxham. Now it sets at the corner of Washington and Walnut Streets.

In describing the relief that was provided to Johnstown and surrounding boroughs in the aftermath of the 1889 flood, the foregoing is not a complete listing of relief organizations or relief initiatives. Instead, it is an overview of the major relief programs that helped to re-establish life in the devastated Conemaugh Valley after the 1889 flood.

The care of the dead became a sacred trust between the living and those who perished as a result of the flood. Scenes of indescribable horror were all too plentiful. Although any of the countless death scenes bespoke the tragic sorrow that gripped the Conemaugh Valley, the passing of babies and children seemed to cause a heightened sense of grief among the survivors. Their helpless nature made their plight all the more difficult to reconcile. Children who the previous day had enjoyed the celebration and merriment of Decoration Day, now laid still and silent forever. An unknown child aged six, listed as body number 373 in Morgue "C" was still wearing a "red cloth dress, a red flannel skirt, with blue and white checkered waist attached."

The reports of death stories that seemed almost unreal were plentiful in the days and weeks following the flood. An account carried in the June 20, 1889 edition

of the *Johnstown Tribune* reported that the body of a child was found in the Ohio River near Vanport, some 100 miles from Johnstown. According to the account the discovery was made during the early evening of June 1. A full physical description of the body was offered. A photograph of the body was also taken for distribution in the hopes that she might be identified. The photographs were sold with the proceeds being used for flood relief measures.

Journalists and writers who chronicled the story of the flood recounted death scenes that at times seemed to defy description. There were numerous accounts of family members who perished still clinging tightly to each other. The June 7 edition of the *New York Times*, recounted the recovery of a woman's body along Main Street near Central Park. Her body had been somewhat protected because she had come to rest in an open pocket in the field of debris. Tightly clasped in her arms was the body of a child believed to be about two years old. The two were removed from the debris and taken to the Fourth Ward Morgue. Another story that gained much attention held that a young girl trapped in the debris at the Stone Bridge was held firmly in place and could not be moved. Rescuers trying to free her got beneath the debris to see what was holding her so firmly. They found that the hands of a drowned man were tightly clenched around her ankle.

John McKee died in the town jail. He was sentenced to twenty-four hours in the town lockup for public drunkenness and disorderly conduct on Memorial Day. When the flood wave struck, he was confined in a cell.

With no possible means of escape, he drowned. In a case, which doctors reportedly could not explain, a mother was killed in the midst of giving birth to a child. She was found dead in the vicinity of the Stone Bridge with the baby only partially delivered. There were several reports of bodies found in trees. Such accounts were not at all difficult to imagine considering the terrific height of the wave that struck the town.

When bodies were discovered, they were taken as quickly as possible to the nearest morgue. Once at the morgue, they were roughly cleaned then stripped of all clothing and personal effects. To varying degrees records were kept of the physical description, clothing and personal property. The bodies were then more carefully cleaned and embalmed. Bodies not claimed in a few days were usually wrapped in a muslin shroud, placed in a coffin and removed for burial. While the bodies remained in the several morgues, family members anxiously searched for loved ones. A description provided in the June 4 edition of the *Chicago Tribune*, offers a grim yet vivid account of this process:

> Bodies have been taken from the river all day and there is a constant procession of mourners passing by to identify the bodies. Most of them pass on without a word, but now and then there would be a dreadful cry and perhaps some woman would throw herself over a body. "Another identified," would be the only comment. But it was never meant heartlessly or said heartlessly. The days have simply inured both men and women to such scenes

This illustration, from the July 1889 edition of the magazine Illustrated Home Journal, *depicts a scene from one of the morgues hastily set up in Johnstown.*

Those claimed by the flood were called to their final rest indiscriminately. Wealth, position, race, education, religion, or any other worldly standard provided no degree of immunity. Mill workers, teachers, ministers, physicians, craftsmen, and businessmen were all listed among the lost. The young, the old, and those in between were all represented on the list of victims. There was, however, one noticeable characteristic. More women and children died than men. The June 14 edition of the *Cambria Freeman* carried an article from the *Pittsburgh Dispatch* that had appeared the pervious week that described this phenomenon. Although exaggerated in its detail, the basic theme of the article was correct.

> There are so many more men than women among the living in Johnstown now because there are so many more women than men among the dead. Of the bodies recovered there are at least two women for every man, besides the fact that their natural weakness made them an easier prey to the flood. The hour at which the disaster came was one at which the women would most likely be in their homes and the men at work in the open air, or in factory yards, from which escape was easy.
>
> Children are rarely seen about the town, and for a similar reason, they are all dead. Johnstown when rebuilt will be a city of many widowers and few children.

Among the initial calls for help that went out from Johnstown was a call for undertakers. The task at hand was well beyond that which the local morticians could accomplish. The largest single group of undertakers, numbering more than fifty, came to town from Pittsburgh. They were led by Peter Flannery. In conversation with several of the Pittsburgh newspapers, Flannery estimated that approximately 125 embalmers were in the Conemaugh Valley by June 4. As the Sanitary Commission of the State Board of Health assumed greater control and responsibility in and around Johnstown, and as the number of bodies being brought to the various morgues declined, the volunteer undertakers returned to their homes.

One of the numerous volunteer morticians who came to Johnstown was Jeremiah Shull of Scalp Level, a small town east of Johnstown near Windber. Shull, the father of six children at the time of the flood, was both an undertaker and cabinetmaker in his home community. Hearing of the calamity in Johnstown, he made his way there on foot and served in several of the morgues before returning home. He later recalled the experience as one of the darkest and saddest of his life. On his way out of town he noticed a small shiny object mired in the mud along the side of the road. Upon closer inspection he found it to be a small glass creamer, which was perfectly intact. As a ray of light in what had been a most dismal experience, Schull cleaned it off. Its monetary value would have been minimal and he had no interest in it as a relic. Instead, he saw it as a reminder of what he had witnessed and how thankful he was that his family had been spared.

When the morgues were all consolidated at the Millville School, that operation was placed in the charge of a local mortician, John Henderson. Prior to the flood Henderson was a partner in the business of Henderson & Alexander located at 623 Main Street in Johnstown. Their business was undertaking and furniture. Mr. Henderson directed most of his attention to the undertaking portion of the enterprise, while Alexander, his brother-in-law, focused on the furniture business. During the flood the Henderson family suffered greatly. Henderson, his wife and two children were washed from their home but survived. Their infant son was drowned. Alexander and his wife were also both claimed by the flood. Their business establishment was totally destroyed.

Reverend David J. Beale, pastor of the Presbyterian Church on Main Street and Reverend Henry L. Chapman, pastor of the First Methodist Episcopal Church on Franklin Street, were given primary charge of the morgues that had to be set up around the town. In his book, *Through the Johnstown Flood by a Survivor*, Reverend Beale lists the following morgues and the number of bodies that were brought to each:

In this picture, taken at one of the several morgues, John Henderson is seen supervising the care of the dead. Henderson is visible here with his hand on his hip. Even though he had suffered great personal loss as a result of the flood, he rendered excellent service in its aftermath.

Morgue "A" —	Fourth Ward School-House		301
Morgue "B" —	Presbyterian Church		130
Morgue "C" —	Pennsylvania Railroad Depot		511
	Moved June 10th to Millville School-House		
Morgue "D" —	Kernville		150
Morgue "E" —	St. Columbia Church	(157)	600
Morgue "F" —	Morrellville		91
Morgue "G" —	Nineveh		194
Morgue "H" —	Old Nineveh		54
TOTAL			2031

Although the work at the numerous morgues was earnestly and honorably undertaken, the task was often mightier than the resources available to accomplish it. In the first few days following the flood, the number of bodies passing through the several morgues made precise record keeping both difficult and impractical. As a result, some of those records are incomplete. For example, the records of Morgue "E" were either not maintained in the early days following the flood or they were lost. To complicate matters, Reverend Davin, the Roman Catholic priest in Cambria Borough, died before he could turn his records over to Reverend Beale. He had assured Reverend Beale, however, that no less than 600 total bodies had passed through the Cambria Borough Morgue. The records of the Morrellville Morgue are also believed to be incomplete.

At the morgues, attempts were made to ascertain descriptions of both the physical body and any possessions found on it. These were included in the records and aided survivors in locating family members. The June 14 edition of the *Johnstown Tribune* carried a number of descriptions of property that had been taken from unknown bodies in

This simple creamer became an object of great meaning to the Schull family. It has been passed down from generation to generation. Most recently it was passed on to the author by his mother, Mrs. Peggy Gordon McGough. Jeremiah Schull was the author's maternal great-grandfather.

In this scene, a body is being passed from the window of Morgue A to be placed in a coffin.

the hope that identification would be possible. The following two descriptions were from bodies found in the vicinity of South and Napoleon Streets;

No. 69, from a young lady—A breast pin, two rings, one with inscription "F.M. to K.L."; small amount of cash, a gold watch, chain and locket, a pocket book with an address of "Mr. Voegtley, Singer Street."

No. 67, from a young man—Lot of memorandum papers, with the names of W.B. Vance and Lincoln Rhoades, a piece of chalk, one brass check, "M.J.K. No. 80."

As the work of the several morgues declined, they were all consolidated into Morgue "C" in the Millville School, which was one of the few buildings still standing on the mud flat that had been Millville. The October 26 edition of the *Johnstown Tribune* carried the following notice to the citizens of Johnstown regarding the continued search for the dead:

The Executive Committee on Search for the Dead solicit all such who have not yet succeeded in finding their lost relatives to at once communicate with the Committee by mail, advising them of the fact, and if possible, informing them where they would suggest that search be made.

The Committee cannot promise that every application will be taken up and acted on as individual cases, but where a concensus of opinion points to search in some particular locality, such search will be made. Address all communications to: Committee on Search for the Dead, Johnstown, PA.

The last body found in the immediate aftermath of the flood was taken to the Millville Morgue on December 3. It was the body of an unidentified male found on the riverbank at Coopersdale. Reports of skeletal remains being found continued for some years, with the last being reported in 1911.

Several of the church and public burial grounds in the Conemaugh Valley were disrupted by the flood and left in a condition that made interments unadvisable in the days and early weeks following the flood. As a result many bodies were hastily buried in locations other than cemeteries. These graves were intended to be nothing more than temporary resting places. This was done for sanitation purposes and to preserve human decency. These burials were accomplished in a manner so as to provide both dignity and respect. This did not, however, prevent charges of neglect being lodged against those tending to these bodies.

One of the more notable examples of such charges was lodged against those responsible for a temporary cemetery on Prospect Hill. In a letter to the editor of the *Johnstown Tribune* dated June 20, Adam Kemery, the superintendent of the Prospect Hill cemetery, boldly refuted charges contained in an article titled "Dogs Among the Graves" which had been carried by several of the Pittsburgh papers. Kemery's letter appeared in the June 21 edition of the *Tribune*.

I pronounce the whole article, which says that dogs are disturbing the bodies there, as being false in every particular, and the pure invention of some overzealous newspaper correspondent. Every corpse interred there was decently coffined, and separate graves were dug for each. There (sic) were placed at such a depth that there is no fear whatever of any animal disturbing them, and persons having friends buried there can rest assured that they have been decently interred. An accurate record has also been kept, and those wishing to lift the bodies of deceased friends will have no trouble in finding them.

In 1885, some of the leading citizens of Johnstown had organized a new cemetery just beyond the summit of Yoder Hill, on ground that had been owned by Cambria Iron and used as pasture and farmland. The 100-acre site provided a "grand view" of the town, the Conemaugh Valley, and the mountains surrounding Johnstown. As a result it was named Grandview Cemetery. A winding carriage road from Kernville led up to the cemetery. Two giant stone arches were constructed along this carriageway. One is still standing today and can be seen along the Easy Grade, which was built to replace the original carriageway. Following the flood, more bodies of flood victims were permanently interred at Grandview than in any other cemetery. Many who survived the flood such as John Hess, Victor Heiser, and Horace Rose were later buried in Grandview as well.

Not all flood victims were buried in Grandview. In any of the cemeteries of the Conemaugh Valley that date back to 1889 the graves of flood victims can be found. Numerous other bodies were released to relatives and friends and carried back to hometowns well beyond the Conemaugh Valley. As noted previously, the generally accepted figure for the death toll resulting from the Johnstown Flood of 1889 is 2,209.

Scenes of death in and around Johnstown were as numerous as they were distressing. Sketch artists and photographers recorded them. In most cases this was done with a marked degree of respect and decorum. To act otherwise would have been callous and would probably have provoked swift and harsh reproach from survivors. The beginnings of an informal code of ethics among photographers regarding what was and was not suitable for the eye of the camera was one of the byproducts of the work of Civil War photographers.

There was at least one photographer who came to Johnstown, George Barker of Niagara Falls, New York, who chose not to adhere to this informal code of professional conduct. In need of a death scene, he staged one amidst the debris. He may have arrived in Johnstown after most of the bodies had been recovered and found it difficult to find the scene he was looking for. Possibly he was weak of heart and chose not to record a real death scene. Or maybe he thought he could create a scene that would appear more realistic than those created by the flood. For whatever reason, he staged at least two death scenes.

The *Johnstown Tribune* of June 25, 1889 carried a letter written by W. Y. Boyer. In Boyer's letter, written to the *Salem* (Ohio) *Era*, he described the failure of the dam at South Fork, provided an overview of the South Fork Fishing & Hunting Club, and shared his observations of Johnstown after it was struck by the flood wave. Regarding the general state of affairs in Johnstown he said, "As far as Johnstown being a wreck, there is no such place any more."

The man in this staged picture, encircled by a chair, a table, a basket, and a barrel was obviously not a flood victim.

Chapter 6

Reclaimation and Rebirth

On the morning of June 1, the sights, sounds, and smells of the flooded district were sufficient to drive even those possessing the strongest of character and countenance from Johnstown and many of its surrounding communities. The experience of the previous day and night, and the horrible revelations of the days that followed did cause some to leave the area. Nevertheless, most of those who had called the Johnstown area home before the flood remained. In short order those who remained found themselves in the midst of one of the largest clean-up operations ever undertaken.

Certain areas of Johnstown and the other communities affected by the flood had storm and sanitary sewer systems. The magnitude of the floodwaters rendered them totally useless. Domestic waste, garbage, outhouse waste, rotten and decaying food, human and animal remains, chemicals from the mills and a variety of small businesses combined to place Johnstown in a most unsanitary condition immediately after the flood. In areas that could not be reached by those working to clean the debris, conditions worsened with each passing day. Warnings of disease and pestilence spread quickly and with them came fears of what new horrors might be visited on the valley of the Conemaugh.

The initial efforts to maintain some level of sanitation in the flooded district were accomplished by local committees. As with so much that the locals initially tried to accomplish on their own, even their best efforts were far short of that required to meet such a monumental task. Real progress in the struggle to establish and maintain an acceptable level of sanitation is credited to the state Board of Health. The Board's relief work in Johnstown was accomplished under the watchful eye of Dr. Benjamin Lee, the secretary of the Pennsylvania Board of Health.

One of the initial tasks the Board faced was evaluating the current living conditions in Johnstown, determining the most pressing needs, then developing and implementing plans to meet those needs. Sanitation was the most immediate concern facing the Board. A sanitary corps was organized and Dr. W. Edgar Matthews, a Johnstown physician, was selected to head the corps. Immediately, the flooded district was surveyed to determine the general conditions. In a report published in mid-June, it was clearly apparent that far too many people were crowded into the limited number of homes left standing after the flood. These crowded conditions added to the local health concerns. Dr. Matthews summed up the condition of homes in and around Johnstown shortly after the survey was completed.

> The homes that were not swept away were left in the most insanitatry condition imaginable. The floodwater was heavily charged with every kind of filth, and whatever this water touched it contaminated. As a result, every house in the flooded district was filled, in most cases to the second floor, with most offensive matter. There is not a place which the flood touched where a man could lay his head with safety.

Initially twenty-five latrines had been hastily built. When the Board of Health took control in Johnstown, an additional seventy-five were built. Warnings were sent throughout the Conemaugh Valley suggesting that women and children be moved as far from the flooded areas as possible. The Board of Health also published regular bulletins that offered suggestions for maintaining good health.

Most people who survived the flood stayed and reestablished themselves in Johnstown and surrounding towns and boroughs. Others who may have had little or nothing left made the decision to relocate.

This view shows Johnstown's Central Park with the home of Dr. Webster B. Lowman in the background. The filth and contamination contained within the massive piles of debris deposited throughout the flooded district was an immediate concern to locals and the state Board of Health.

This is Central Park as it appears today. The building with the stripped canopy is located where the Lowman house stood in 1889. A monument to Joseph Johns is between the two cannons.

John B. Hamilton, Surgeon-General of the United States, arrived in Johnstown on June 7 with several other federal authorities. Although Hamilton recognized the deplorable condition of the town and the surrounding communities, he did not feel that there was a serious threat to the general public from an epidemic. He communicated the same to President Harrison. Dr. Lee disagreed with this assessment and communicated his concerns directly to President Harrison. Lee requested that federal money, specifically money in the surgeon-general's contingency fund, be appropriated to work on the rivers in Johnstown. This request was denied on the basis that it was intended for relief to victims, not public works projects.

The excellent work of the Pennsylvania Board of Health in the aftermath of the flood cannot be overstated. At a time when local residents were busy helping to clear debris and, tending to their own needs and their own rehabilitation, the Board of Health provided much needed public service which benefited the community at large. The appreciation of the local residents was shown in a variety of ways. However, their confidence in Dr. Lee and the Board was never more clearly stated than when the Board announced that its work in the flooded district was done and that they would be leaving Johnstown in mid-September. The outcry for their continued support was quick and loud. Local physicians met with Dr. Lee to make their concerns known. Dr. Lee agreed to continue the work of the sanitary corps. Their primary remaining objective was the clearing and cleaning of the Stony Creek from Sandyvale Cemetery to the point. When the Board again made it known that they were ready to leave the Conemaugh Valley at the end of September, a similar request was made by the locals for

continued support. This request went to Governor Beaver. He appropriated approximately $10,000 which continued the work in Johnstown until mid-October.

The sheer magnitude of the sanitation work in Johnstown is evident in the quantity of disinfectants and cleaning agents used throughout the flooded districts. The book *Through the Johnstown Flood by a Survivor* offers the following accounting of sanitation chemicals used during the clean-up in Johnstown:

> 4,000 barrels quick-line
> 500 barrels chloride of lime
> 1,700 bottles of bromine
> 110 barrels Bullen's Disinfectant
> 100 tone copperas
> 100 gallons carbolic acid
> 3 carboys muriatic acid
> 40 gallons nitric acid
> 180 barrels rosin
> 200 barrels pine tar
> 73 barrels pitch
> 5 barrels liquid Phenyle
> 15 barrels Sanitas
> 3 barrels Phenique
> 100 kegs Utopia
> 10 carboys embalming fluid
> 720 bottles sod. hypochlorite
> 700 bottles Platt's chlorides
> 116 pounds corrosive sublimate
> 100 Werther's Disinfectant
> 50 bottles PA. R.R. Co. disinfectant
> 100 bottles Purity
> 100 bottles bromo-chloralum
> A cargo of Quibells Brother's Disinfectant

The menace of potential epidemics was initially reduced through the use of various chemical agents. However, to permanently rid the flooded district of these concerns, the debris had to be removed. Pleas were earnestly extended throughout local communities for able-bodied men and teams of horses and mules to clear the debris. The following notice was carried in the June 14 edition of the *Johnstown Tribune*:

> It is the old Macedonian cry, "Come and help us." We sadly need your aid, friends, and the aid of your sturdy teams, in cleaning up the town and removing the great masses of debris which yet remain. You can do us incalculable service, even if you can give us no more than one day's work apiece. There never can come a time when you can help us more, and you would receive the blessings of many thousands of helpless, suffering people, who, having lost their all, now stand in dread of a pestilence breeding to complete the awful work of the flood. So come in with your teams, and prove to us that we were right in feeling that we would not appeal to you in vain.

In quick order both man and beast were at work clearing the flooded district. Much of the work done in Johnstown was offered as charity, but many of those who came to labor did so for hire. Estimates of the number of men involved in the extended process of clearing the debris range between 7,000 and 10,000. The *New York Times* reported on June 7 that an estimated five thousand volunteers and locals plus an additional 2000 contracted workers were busy clearing the debris in Johnstown.

Several firms sent crews of workmen into Johnstown and vicinity. Notable among them was the firm of Booth and Flinn from Pittsburgh. Booth and Flinn did not enjoy the best of reputations as to the type of workers they hired. There were some initial concerns regarding the arrival of these workers in Johnstown. Would they be part of the solution to Johnstown's current problems, or would they add to the already chaotic environment that gripped the communities of the Conemaugh Valley? Captain Bill Jones, a noted steelman of his day, came to Johnstown with a crew of more than 300 men. Jones had been a key player in the growth and development of the Cambria Iron operations in Johnstown, as had several of the men who now returned to Johnstown in its time of great need.

The teams of men engaged in the clean-up went about their business with surprising efficiency. A description offered in the June 7 edition of the *New York Times* describes the progress that had been made up to that point:

Three thousand workmen were let loose in devastated Johnstown at 6:30 o'clock this morning [June 6] with pick, shovel, spade, saw and axe, and within a few minutes a score of bonfires were burning all over the town and the work of rehabilitation was under full sway. Gangs of workmen, from ten to a hundred in number, began operations in every pile of debris in the town. By noon a clear swath had been made though the business part of the town, and many tons of debris were consumed. Every hour, however, brought fresh details of workmen from adjacent towns and counties. The town jumped forth with fresh vigor, and the despondent business men took fresh courage.

Within the past two days the appearance of the place has changed materially. It is now comparatively easy work to get about, except at the point down toward Kernville and about the temporary station near the Baltimore and Ohio Railway. At these points the debris and wreckage are piled in places, from fifteen to fifty feet high. Street lines are obliterated and for acres it is impossible to move about with safety.

The workers that came to Johnstown were divided into a number of camps. The June 20 edition of the *Johnstown Tribune* identified six camps. These included Camp Hastings, which was named for Adjutant General Hastings, and five other camps: Flinn, Lilly, Coburn, Wilson, and McKnight, named for the contractors who brought the workers to Johnstown. These were tent camps. State militia troops were posted in each of the camps to maintain order, and although there were some reported incidents of fighting and drunken behavior, they were far fewer than some anticipated. Many who observed the work of the crews by day reasoned that their good behavior during the night was more the result of fatigue than anything else.

Horse and mule teams, and every imaginable manner of cart and wagon numbering in the hundreds were used. Steam powered winches were brought to town to accomplish some of the heavier tasks, particularly at the Stone Bridge. The two chief means of disposing of the refuse was burning and dumping it into the river. Not all of the debris could be burned, and there was great concern about dumping it anywhere in or around the flooded district. With the support of Dr. Lee of the Board of Health, the decision was made to dump the unburnable refuse in the river to allow it to be carried away. It was generally agreed that any debris dumped into the river would be quickly diluted, so as to render it no serious threat to communities down river from the Stone Bridge.

The work of removing the debris and reclaiming the town was complicated by several factors. Notable among these were an unusually high number of days of rain following the flood, a strike by the workers hired

Clean-up crews continued their work well into the fall. Although the reclamation efforts in and around Johnstown were not particularly well organized, they did accomplish a great deal and cleared the way for the rebuilding of the towns and communities that had been so seriously devastated.

by various contractors, debris that could not be budged by conventional means, and crowds of spectators. Each in its own way complicated and confounded the rehabilitation efforts in and around Johnstown.

Although nothing compared to the rains of May 30 and 31, western Pennsylvania's most significant weather feature during the month of June was rain. Numerous sources report that for every dry day there were two days of rain. The rains were not always heavy, but they were bothersome enough to complicate and hamper both clean-up and recovery. The recurring rains also frustrated sanitation efforts. Disinfectant chemicals and agents spread over the flooded district were quickly diluted by the rains, which rendered them far less effective. The June 17 edition of the *Johnstown Tribune* concluded that "A week of dry weather is a favor devoutly to be prayed for."

A severe storm visited the Conemaugh Valley on July 2. The rivers rose quickly and great fear spread throughout the valley. The local police stayed on throughout the night to watch the rivers and report if they began leaving their banks. Several temporary bridges that had been constructed in the valley were destroyed or damaged. Many basements, particularly those in Cambria City that had been cleaned, were once again flooded. Fortunately there was no loss of life, and in fact there was one positive effect of this early summer storm. The increased flow of the Stony Creek and the Little Conemaugh helped to loosen the debris field in front of the Stone Bridge, and a sizeable quantity of debris was floated off.

The laborers, both skilled and unskilled, that came to Johnstown in search of work following the flood, were at best an unorganized lot loosely tied to one of several contractors. By most accounts these workers were attracted by the promise of $2.00 a day plus board. Ex-

actly who promised these terms is not known, but these were the terms most of the workers expected and were intent on receiving.

On the evening of June 19 a mass meeting was held in Central Park. The two chief concerns of the laborers were salary and board. Their demands were simple. They wanted the $2.00 a day they were promised and decent food. During that meeting, various men addressed the crowd. For the benefit of all involved spokesmen representing Hungarians, Italians, Irishmen, African Americans, and Germans each took turns speaking to the crowd. They were unified in their desire to receive the promised wage and better board. Food, both in quality and quantity was a critical concern. It was decided that a committee would be formed to address the proper authorities the following day.

The immediate effect of the meeting was clearly evident the next morning when less than half the usual number of men showed up to work. As a result of the initial meeting, it was agreed that skilled laborers would be paid $2.00 per day, while unskilled laborers would receive $1.50. There was no agreement reached as to the food provided to the workers. Other meetings were held throughout the day, but little was accomplished to meet the demands of the workers. Sensing the futility of their efforts, most of the men returned to work. In the June 20 edition of the *Johnstown Tribune* the following summary was carried under the headline "Cause of the Trouble Among the Men:"

The food furnished, judging from the statements of the men, which are corroborated and fully endorsed by the soldiers on guard, is not only of a quality in general unfit for the use of men, but so meager in quantity as, even if of good quality, to be entirely insufficient. For instance, for supper last evening the first seven hundred men served received a small piece of beef, some musty bread, potatoes, and black coffee. No butter, milk or sugar was received. The remainder of the men—more than two-thirds of the total force—got but black coffee and bread. This meal, the reporter was informed, was a fair sample of rations furnished at each meal.

"Honest to God," said one of the guards, "I would not feed to a dog of mine the grub these men get. It is simply outrageous. Nearly all the trouble we have with the men arises from their efforts to obtain sufficient and proper food. The men are well disposed, peaceable, and orderly, and we would have no trouble with them were they treated as they should be in the matter of food."

It was estimated that no more than 500 of the workers left Johnstown because their demands were not met. Even though only a limited number of workers left, a sense of distrust arose between the workers and those in positions of authority in the Conemaugh Valley. This distrust lingered and surfaced from time to time throughout the remainder of their stay in Johnstown.

There is something in the human psyche that draws certain people to the scene of a tragedy. Johnstown was no exception. So great was the demand of people to go to the flooded district of the Conemaugh Valley that railroad excursions were quickly sold out when tickets were made available. The morbid curiosity that draws spectators to scenes of human suffering and tragedy generally does not carry with it a desire to actively engage in the relief of that suffering. This quirk of human nature was clearly evident in the tourists who came to call on the flooded Conemaugh Valley.

The June 7 edition of the *New York Times* described the spectators as the unfeeling nuisances they were:

> For days this town has been thronged with people from distant places, some of them sent here by the petty motive of curiosity, and others impelled by the purpose to steal whatever valuables they could get hold of. At a time when the attention of the honest is taken up by the work of setting things in order after an unparallel calamity, they have picnicked in the ruins, eating sandwiches and drinking liquor in the neighborhood of places where the dead are piled in cords. They have got in the way of the men working to clear the ruins, and they have, by their levity and boisterousness, been a source of disgust to all decent people who have had work to do and wanted to do it.
>
> The nuisance is now abating. Access to Johnstown is denied to all persons who have no proper business here, and the idlers and the suspicious persons are being warned to leave the town. The roads have been picketed for twenty miles around and no person without a pass from General Hastings can get by the sentries.

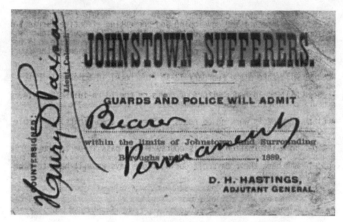

To limit the number of tourists and others with unproductive motives from coming into the flooded district, passes were issued.

One of the most troublesome problems facing the clean-up crews was breaking up the giant masses of debris. Tons of barbed wire from the Gautier plant had been thrown into the flood wave. The swirling action of the wave wrapped this wire tightly around the debris creating a mass that defied the force of horses and mules, men, and even steam-powered winches. By far the most problematic mass of debris was that lodged in front of the Stone Bridge. Picking away at the edges of the debris field seemed to produce only limited results after days of effort.

On June 4 dynamite was used for the first time to dislodge the jam at the Stone Bridge. The *Chicago Tribune* reported that the effect of the dynamite was limited. The man in charge of the dynamiting at the Stone Bridge was Arthur Kirk of the firm Arthur Kirk & Son Explosives of Pittsburgh. As they continued their work, Kirk increased the size of the charges he was using. His blasts, some utilizing as much as 500 pounds of dynamite at a time, rocked the valley, causing buildings to tremble, windows to rattle and sending debris outward for hundreds of yards. The already shattered nerves of the locals were further strained by the thunderous blasts that rocked the ground and everything that stood on it. Consternation grew toward Kirk and his work to the point where he was asked to leave. Under orders from General Hastings, Major W. M. Phillips then took up the work of blasting at the Stone Bridge.

Phillips continued the blasting at the bridge and soon generated the same consternation. So that work could continue, guards were placed with the dynamiters to protect them from enraged locals. As the debris mass was broken up, Phillips ordered 4,000 barrels of kerosene to be used as an accelerant to burn anything that could be consumed by fire that remained

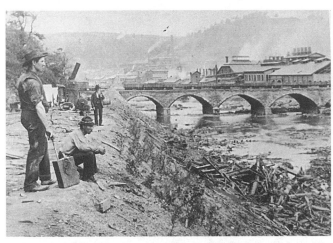

Although the work of clearing the debris was necessary, many locals objected to the means used by both Kirk and Phillips. Dynamite blasts such as the one shown above, right, sent shock waves throughout the entire town.

in the debris mass at the Stone Bridge. Phillips continued the work at the Stone Bridge until July 9 when Arthur Kirk was once again asked to come to Johnstown to finish the job.

The work of reclaiming Johnstown after the flood was an arduous task. There were many complications that frustrated these efforts, but the desire to rebuild and reestablish were stronger than any and all obstacle. As a result the reclamation of Johnstown was accomplished in remarkable time. Once accomplished the next task at hand was the rebuilding of Johnstown and the surrounding communities.

Because Johnstown was almost completely surrounded by the Stony Creek and the Little Conemaugh, bridges were an essential part of the town's road system. In the aftermath of the flood, there was scarcely a bridge in Johnstown left intact. As a result the movement of people and relief supplies was severely restricted. The first means employed for bridging the rivers around Johnstown was a system of rope bridges. Precariously strung above the still swollen rivers, crossing these temporary bridges was a challenge. They did, nonetheless, provide the first means of moving people and supplies into the flooded district.

Pontoon bridges, used extensively by army engineers during the Civil War, soon replaced the rope bridges. These floating bridges rendered valuable service, even though they provided only a single lane of traffic. In time the continuous heavy demand placed on them began to take its toll. These bridges began to show the signs of wear and fatigue. The decision was made to replace them with more substantial trestle bridges. The June 17 edition of the *Johnstown Tribune* concluded, "Along with everybody else, the people of Johnstown owe Uncle Sam a vote of thanks for so promptly coming to their aid with his floating bridges."

Work on the trestle bridges began in June and continued through July. Although more substantial than the pontoon bridges, these trestle bridges were not to be permanent structures either.

Of all the bridges in and around the flooded district, the Stone Bridge at the point in Johnstown received the most attention. It was a vital link in the east-west railroad line that passed through Johnstown. Concerns over the structural stability of the bridge immediately following the flood were considerable. These concerns were further heightened when Kirk and Phillips began using dynamite to dislodge the debris trapped in front of the bridge. The Pennsylvania Railroad Company, the owner of the bridge, inspected it for structural integrity on July 9. As a part of that inspection, a diver, who was also one of the engineers employed by the company, made several dives to inspect the piers below the water line. The

Pontoon bridges served as vital links between the various sections of the flooded district during June and much of July. This particular bridge was at Poplar Street.

work of the diver was of such great interest that a full description of his activity was carried as front-page news in the July 10 *Johnstown Tribune*:

> A hundred or more persons witnessed his first dive this morning. Since he is the first diver we have ever had in our town (we hadn't enough water for one before the flood), a sketch of his manner of operating under water and his suit will prove interesting.
>
> The air pump is placed on the large raft formerly used for transporting one of the hoisting engines. To this is attached a long hose about the size of that used on pave washers. The diving dress envelopes the whole body of the diver, the upper portion being the "helmet," to which the hose is attached, and through which the air is pumped to the diver. The helmet consists of a metal frame having glass inserted before the eyes, a place on the back of the neck for receiving the air from the pipe, and an arrangement by which the exhaled air is constantly discharged, thus preventing water from entering. The water-proof material of which the dress is made consists of sheet India-rubber, covered on both sides to protect the rubber from injury. The cuff fits tightly around the wrists, leaving the hands free. The breast-plate is made of tinned copper with an outer edge of brass, which has screws fitted to it projecting upward and passing through corresponding holes in the collar of the dress. On the top of this, and with holes in it corresponding to the screws, four pieces of a metal band are firmly screwed down, by wing nuts, nipping the soft metal of the collar between the metal of the breast-plate and band, and thus insuring a water-tight joint. The shoes are made of stout leather with leaden soles, secured by buckles and straps, each shoe weighing twenty pounds. About the diver's waist is placed a weight of lead of about forty pounds. A "life" or "signal" line tied about the diver's waist and held by a man on the boat, is used by the diver to signal a change in direction, rise, etc.
>
> Thus equipped, the diver descended this morning and examined all the piers of the stone bridge. The water in some places is ten feet, and he remained under just as long as was necessary to make a careful examination of the condition of the stone. When asked if he would not have some difficulty in seeing through such muddy water, he replied that he would be glad if he were always so fortunate in that respect as now.

At the time of the flood, three banks offered services to the people of Johnstown. They were John Dibert & Company, First National and Johnstown Savings Bank. There was great concern over the security of the banks. Judging from the general condition of the town, it was only reasonable to assume that the banks were destroyed and with them the financial records and holdings of depositors. For a time there was panic among depositors regarding accounts. The June 14 edition of the *Johnstown Tribune* reduced that panic with an announcement regarding the current state and future plans of the three banks.

The announcement declared that, "The First National Bank and the Johnstown Savings Bank are perfectly solvent and will pay every cent of their obligations." Those having business with these two banks were also told that they would re-open their doors "...as soon as they can get their papers, books, etc., that were submerged, in shape." John Dibert of the banking house of John Dibert & Company was among those killed along Main Street. John D. Roberts, the only surviving partner of the company, made it known to the *Tribune* that as soon as the time lock on the cash safe could be drilled open, all depositors would receive thirty-five cents on the dollar. Within six months, Roberts said an additional thirty-five cents would be paid on each dollar owed as loans were collected, with the balance paid to each depositor by the end of 1889. The sense of financial panic that had been just one more problem within the devastated town was thus dramatically reduced.

With personal property totally destroyed in many cases, the fate of many employers still in question, and the memory of the horrible flooding fresh in everyone's mind, concerns over the value of real estate in Johnstown became very real. With modest bank accounts being all that many of the survivors had left, a sense of financial panic was common. There were numerous reports of real estate speculators offering meager sums for property throughout the flooded district that represented pennies on the dollar. Their plan, heartless as it was, was to gather large quantities of land at panic prices, then resell it for great profit, as those in the Conemaugh Valley recovered and began the work of rebuilding their lives in and around Johnstown. The *Johnstown Tribune* in its June 14 edition offered a word of advice to the owners of local real estate.

> Our advice to real-estate owners is not to dispose of their property under pressure of the panic. It may not be worth as much for several years as it was before the flood, but it will in a very short time sell for more than it will sell for now. The Cambria Works in Millville will be in full operation within a few days; the Gautier Department will speedily be rebuilt, and the Johnson Company will continue in operation with the exception of the small portion of the works swept away in Woodvale, which will be speedily rebuilt. Beside several business men have already made arrangements for rebuilding, thus forming a nucleus for the restoring of the livest manufacturing town in the State.

Cambria Iron was the major employer in the Conemaugh Valley. Its mills and related support facilities employed an estimated 7,000 people at the time of the flood. Damages sustained by the company as a result of the flood topped the $3 million mark. For a time there was concern whether Johnstown's biggest employer would rebuild. It quickly became common knowledge that the decision made by Cambria Iron would in large measure determine the future of the Conemaugh Valley.

John Fulton, Cambria Iron's general manager in Johnstown, received word that the men should be called back to work as soon as possible. The whistles of the company and the locomotives sounded at their regular time on the morning of June 4. Undamaged portions of the plant and facilities that could be quickly repaired were to resume operations. This action by Cambria Iron provided inspiration and encouragement to many in the flooded district, even though the long-term plans of the plant were as of yet not fully determined.

On June 6, E. Y. Townsend, the president of Cambria Iron, with main offices in Philadelphia, spoke with a reporter from the *Philadelphia Record* regarding the company's future plans for their Johnstown facility. Townsend reported that there was some concern regarding the rebuilding of the plant in Johnstown. The company as of that date did not yet have an accurate estimate of their total damages and thus could not determine the feasibility of reopening on a permanent basis. Townsend shared that consideration was being given to three other sites to which the Johnstown works could be moved. He

With the most property to lose, the Cambria Iron Company suffered the greatest financial loss. As seen in this picture, much of the iron works was left in ruins.

noted that these discussions were informal and that no action of any kind had been taken. The locations discussed were Erie, Pennsylvania, the eastern shore of the Chesapeake Bay, and St. Louis, Missouri.

The decision ultimately made was to keep the plant in Johnstown and resume production there. Some of the old equipment was back in production within two weeks of the flood. New equipment was brought to Johnstown and by the end of the summer it was in operation. The first heats from the new facilities were announced in the August 28 edition of the *Johnstown Tribune*.

> The new Bessemer Steel Works of the Cambria Iron Company resumed operations to-day, after an idleness of several weeks, and the old steel works have been shut down. The first heat in the new works was made at 11:46 this fornoon , and up to 3:30 seven heats had been made, eleven tons to a heat.

The reestablishment of public utilities and services was accomplished in remarkable time. Limited gas service, which was essential to the operations of the mills, was restored by mid-June, as was partial electric service to most of the downtown area. The June 28 *Johnstown Tribune* announced that it would not be long until the Johnstown Electric Light Company would have its system totally repaired to its condition prior to the flood. Limited telegraph service had been established within twenty-four hours of the flood. As rebuilding continued, telephone service throughout the Conemaugh Valley was not only restored, but was substantially expanded.

The system of sanitary and drainage sewers was heavily damaged, but it too was reclaimed and expanded, to meet the demands of new and enlarged buildings. Postal service in Johnstown was restored on June 20. The *Johnstown Tribune* of that date declared that, "The best evidence that Johnstown is recovering itself—thanks to our generous friends the world over—and resuming its old-time condition is the reoccupation of the old office in the *Tribune* building on Franklin Street by the Postmaster and his force."

The resumption of business activities provided some sense of normalcy in what was otherwise a time of turmoil. Although some businesses did not reopen after the flood, most Johnstown businessmen did re-establish themselves as part of the local business community. Some were fortunate enough to be able to return to their old locations. Some were even able to reclaim quantities of undamaged or salvageable inventory. In either case, wholesalers were quick to respond to the needs of local merchants. Temporary buildings were erected to facilitate a quick return to some routine of regular business activity. Other businesses were housed in temporary sheds constructed wherever a suitable site could be found.

This view shows the general office of Cambria Iron on Washington Street. During the flood it sustained minimal damage since the company's store, Wood, Morrell & Company, protected it. Notice the row of coffins in the picture.

The June 8 edition of the *New York Times* credited businessman W. A. Kramer with being the first to reopen after the flood. "...W. A. Kramer, who lost nearly $12,000 worth of goods, has opened his store—the first. He raked in a small fortune yesterday by selling articles of glassware which had withstood the shock as relics. Incidentally to-day he opened a lemonade attachment to his establishment." The June 14 edition of the *Johnstown Tribune* carried a prominent ad announcing that W. A. Kramer, No. 61 Franklin Street, was indeed open for business. Some of the businessmen who operated in Johnstown following the flood sought to gather higher than usual profits. This was particularly true of out-of-towners who flocked to Johnstown in search of exaggerated profits. The last line of Kramer's ad assured his customers that this was not his intention. His good would be offered for "prices as before the flood."

The business establishments of Johnstown found themselves in a variety of circumstances. The sale of salvaged goods quickly became a local concern. This was particularly true of food and clothing. In an ad that appeared in the July 5 edition of the *Johnstown Tribune*, the business of Cohen & Marx located at 278 and 280 Main Street, announced in bold print that they were offering "NO FLOODED GOODS" to their customers.

The June 25 advertisement of Petrikin & Miller informed *Johnstown Tribune* readers that their business was "ON DECK AGAIN." In the description of the goods they would offer their customers, "S. S. Marvin's famous bread" was one of the items mentioned. S. S. Marvin was a member of the South Fork Fishing and Hunting Club, a member of the Citizens' Relief Committee of Pittsburgh and the Johnstown Flood Relief Commission. He offered tireless energy to the relief efforts for the Johnstown sufferers.

Announcements of business startups continued throughout the summer. In many instances they appeared as brief announcements rather than specific advertisements. The following is an example that appeared in the June 20 *Johnstown Tribune*:

Starting in Their Old Businesses

Kramer Bros. advertise that they have opened temporary quarters in their residence on Stonycreek street, near Levergood, and have a complete stock of wall paper, window curtains, looking-glasses, picture frames, etc.

A. G. Utecht has been able to open at his old stand, No. 119 Clinton street. Fresh bread daily.

W. A. Moses & Co., the merchant tailors are preparing to start in their old quarters on Franklin street in a few days.

Restoring electric service to the flooded district began immediately. When lighting was again available, security in and around the flooded district was greatly increased. This picture shows a workman stringing new lines. The Cambria Iron's lower works are seen in the background.

The Johnstown post office was housed on the first floor of the Tribune *building on Franklin Street. The* Tribune *building is the second building from the extreme right of the picture. Near the center of the picture is the spire of the Methodist Church also located along Franklin Street.*

Several local entrepreneurs erected temporary stands from which they conducted all manner of business. Reportedly, there was a rather brisk business in the selling of anything that could be reasonably considered a relic of the flood. Lemonade was also a popular item. These business stands were along the upper end of Main Street

These business houses were established on the corner of Main and Franklin Streets on what had been the town's central park. These were only temporary structures intended to house businesses until their proprietors could rebuild on their own.

Among the businessmen who died, was W. Lewis Clark. He was the owner and proprietor of Clark's Novelties shown here at 232 Main Street.

In the aftermath of the flood, several new businesses sprung up in and around Johnstown. Whether driven by entrepreneurship, opportunism or both, several individuals become part of Johnstown's post-flood business community. An ad placed in the June 25 edition of the *Tribune* offered the following:

> For sale—Or Exchange for Johnstown Property, a store Room at Gallitzin, Size 40 x 36 feet, with or without stock, suitable for any kind of business, having an established Cash Trade of $40,000 per year. Also, a separate BUILDING LOT 60 x 160 feet. For full particulars address BOX 112 Gallitzin, Pa., or CHAS. SIMON, Johnstown, PA.

Miss Jessie Coleman was another who sought to go into business following the flood. Her story is one of volunteer service that developed into a business opportunity. Prior to the flood, Miss Coleman was a clerk in the dry goods store of William Masterton located at 182 Main Street in Johnstown. Following the flood, she found herself unemployed. Sensing a need and having a desire to fill it, she personally called on General Hastings to request a tent in which she could establish a business. Her desire was to open a refreshment stand. She did so on Somerset Street. She offered, among other items, cakes and lemonade. Having found a marked level of success operating out of her tent, she later had a wooden building erected on Morris Street, on the site of what had been a bakery prior to the flood. Under the business name of J. D. Coleman & Company, Miss Coleman's became one of many new business enterprises to spring up in Johnstown after the flood. The July 9 edition of the *Johnstown Tribune* carried the following ad for this post-flood enterprise:

> J. D. Coleman & Company have opened a bakery and confectionery on the corner of Morris and Haynes street (on the site of the old Miller bakery) where they will be pleased to see their friends and the public. A full line of fruits, candies and cakes will be kept on hand. Ice cream will also be served. Give them a call.

Immediately following the flood, Judge R. L. Johnston, President Judge of Cambria County, ordered that all bars, saloons, and drinking establishments be closed until further notice. There was, however, still

Before the flood, Peter Carpenter operated a restaurant at 112 and 114 Franklin Street. He survived the Flood, but his business was all but a total loss.

much liquor to be had. The undamaged stock of many saloons had become part of the debris scattered around the town and was most earnestly sought by those in search of a free drink. Quantities of liquor were being brought into town as part of the relief supplies and by enterprising outside suppliers. Several local bar owners protested that they were not being permitted to engage in their legal trade, while others were capitalizing on the local market. Notwithstanding, the order of the judge stood. According to the June 14 *Johnstown Tribune*, "Immediately after the flood all the barrooms left in town were closed, some voluntarily and others under order. They are still closed and will doubtless remain so for some time yet."

At a session of court held on Monday, July 1, petitions were made to the judge for the revocation of the court's order closing drinking establishments in the flooded districts. No decision was made on the first, but the following day the judge announced that the order of the court would be revoked as of Monday, July 8. In accord with this order, saloons and bars were open for business on Monday.

In a story carried in the *Johnstown Tribune* the following day, General Hastings reported that there was considerable drunkenness in the flooded district the previous evening. He strongly objected to the rescinding of the original court order that closed the drinking establishment, and called for an immediate revocation of the order which permitted them to reopen. In support of his request, Hastings pointed out that, "At this hour, 9 o'clock, there are many drunken people upon the streets, and it is considered in some parts of Johnstown to be dangerous to travel the public thoroughfares."

The Cambria Library had been established by the Cambria Iron Company in 1879. It stood along Washington Street across from the company's general office building. The flood wave leveled the building and destroyed its contents. The librarian, Mrs. Mary E. Hurst, was also lost. Several months after the flood, Mr. & Mrs. Andrew Carnegie came to Johnstown. They came, like many others, to see firsthand what they had read and heard so much about over the past few months. During their visit, Mr. Carnegie donated the funds necessary to rebuild and re-establish a public library in Johnstown.

This donation from Andrew Carnegie was most enthusiastically received, with one notable exception. John Fulton, the head of the Cambria Library Association's Board of Directors, was not totally impressed. In his personal diary for 1889 he wrote, "Nov. 23rd, meeting of the Directors of Cambria Library Association. Andy Carnegie to pay for new building. A great bronze plate on the front to record the work of this fortunate egotist." Even though not totally appreciated by Fulton, the announcement that the library would be rebuilt boosted the spirits of locals struggling to regain some sense of normalcy. Although not absolutely essential, rebuilding the library was a definite sign that Johnstown would not only survive the flood, but that it would once again become a prosperous community offering a wide range of community services and leisure opportunities.

Addison Hutton, the well-known Philadelphia architect, designed the new library building. The Johnstown Public Library was dedicated on February 19, 1892, on the site of the former library. The new building featured more than 8,000 volumes. It had several comfortably furnished reading rooms and a large auditorium on the first floor that was frequently used for town meetings and other gatherings. The library itself on was on the second floor. The third floor was a large open room that featured exercise equipment and a running track with a padded leather surface.

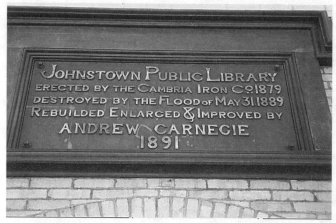

The bronze plate placed "...to record the work of this fortunate egotist [Andrew Carnegie]" remains above the main entrance of the Johnstown Flood Museum on Washington Street.

This is the building that housed the Cambria Library prior to the flood.

(Left) Following the flood, the Johnstown Public Library was established on the site of the destroyed Cambria Library. In 1973, this building became the home of the Johnstown Flood Museum.

The religious community of Johnstown and its many congregations suffered greatly as a result of the flood. Several of the church buildings were reduced to hideous plies of rubble resembling nothing of their former grace and beauty. A number of clergymen and members of their families perished, leaving several of the local congregations without a spiritual leader. Yet, impromptu worship services had been taking place at various points throughout the flooded district ever since the flood. Formal church services were not a priority of Johnstown's religious leaders. Instead, they ministered to their flocks in ways far different than they had ever done before.

The first church services were held on June 9. At the suggestion of Reverend David J. Beale, the pastor of the Presbyterian Church on Main Street, worship services were planned for several sites throughout the flooded district. Having had a week to assess the damages to local churches and learn of the fate of his fellow clergymen, Beale's purpose was to begin the process of reestablishing some order among the area congregations. In his book, *Through the Johnstown Flood by a Survivor*, Beale described the parishioners' responses to the worship services:

Those services were indeed solemn and impressive. Divine worship had never been held and the Divine truth never preached under such circumstances. Around the assembled worshipers was a scene of destruction and desolation that was fearfully sad. The homes of those worshipers were scattered fragments, and their loved ones crushed or buried in the debris at their feet, and their plans and hopes in life destroyed.

Yet the storm and flood had not shaken their faith in God or in the promise of the Redeemer. They sang the songs of Zion, lifted up their hearts in prayer and heard the assuring words of grace. They took heart from this worship to renew the struggle of life. They determined first of all to build again the "walls of Jerusalem;" to "restore its waste places."

The schools, both public and private, had long been a source of pride and a promise of hope for the future for the residents of the Conemaugh Valley. Following the flood those schools were in a state of shambles. Buildings were destroyed or so severely damaged as to be useless. The flood claimed twelve teachers from the Johnstown schools. The principal, Professor Charles F.

Gallagher, and his wife were also among the dead. Among the teachers killed was Emma K. Fisher.

Although the schools of Johnstown were the largest, the task of rebuilding was no less difficult in the surrounding towns and boroughs. Woodvale, for example had nothing left of its school but the bell that had once called its students. Since the schools were funded through taxes that were generally based on real estate within the various school districts, the loss of so much real estate left a significantly diminished base upon which to fund the schools. On July 5, the Johnstown School Board met and the decision was made that no taxes would be collected for the coming school term. Instead, a plea would be made for donations, and the state would be contacted for funds to keep the schools open. Money received from buildings and properties that had been insured would obviously be used to help fund reconstruction efforts. The state provided emergency funds of slightly more than $3,200 and insurance claims provided an additional $5,000.

During the fall of 1889 the schools in and around Johnstown opened for the 1889-1890 term. Because of the loss of several buildings there was significant overcrowding. In some instances, younger students attended one of two half-day sessions. The various school boards acted as swiftly as possible to hire teachers, set up classrooms, and reestablish some semblance of order within the local educational system. The general condition of many of the school buildings frustrated these efforts. The September 10 edition of the *Johnstown Tribune* carried a description of the Horner Street School, which had yet to be prepared for the opening of school. "One of the filthiest places in town is the yard and cellars of the public school building in the seventh ward. The yard is filled with decaying matter of all kinds, including about a barrel of old shoes, and the cellar is filled almost to the top with water that makes one gag to look at it." In spite of the conditions they faced, those responsible for the public schools had them ready to welcome students back during the fall of 1889 or the early winter of 1890. The length of the school term varied from district to district and was determined by when the schools were able to open their doors.

The Johnstown Public Schools reopened on September 30. At a meeting held on September 12 in the office of the school superintendent, T. B. Johnson, provisions were made to open twenty-four classrooms for the new term. During the previous school term there had been thirty-six classrooms. For the 1889-1890 school term the twenty-four classrooms were divided as follows: high school 1, second grammars 2, first grammars 3, second intermediates 3, first intermediates 4, third primary 3, second primary 3, first primary 5. The number of students initially enrolled was estimated at 1,100, which was approximately 300 less than the previous year. By the conclusion of the 1889-1890 school term, 1,540 pupils were registered.

The reopening of the schools in the Conemaugh Valley was yet another benchmark in the recovery of the flooded district. As positive as the sight of children returning to schools was to many, it was a stark reminder to those parents whose children did not answer the peal of the school bells. The October 1 edition of the *Johnstown Tribune* carried the following sad reminder of what the first day of school meant for numerous parents for many years to come:

"I thought my heart would break this morning when I heard the school bells ring and saw the little ones toddling off to school," said a gentleman last evening who had lost his wife and children in the flood. "I used to be so proud," he said, "when my children came to me smiling in the morning with their bright faces, to kiss me good-bye on their departure

Emma Kate Fisher, one of the Johnstown teachers claimed by the flood, was a member of the Johnstown High School class of 1885. Miss Fisher is on the far right in this picture.

for school, and now to think they are gone from me forever, " and the tears coursed down his cheeks as he spoke. Poor man! Where is there comfort for him. Who can tender him sympathy or measure the depths of his grief?

Considering the amount of death and destruction in the Conemaugh Valley, the settlements and adjustments made by insurance companies were small. A headline in the June 20 edition of the *Johnstown Tribune* read "The Travelers' Insurance Company's Remarkable Good Luck." In the story that followed, it was reported that the company lost only one of its insured as a result of the flood. That person was Mary E. Hurst, the librarian of the Cambria Library, who had a policy in the amount of $1,000. As early as June 4, insurance companies were offering estimates of their losses throughout the flooded district. The Equitable Life Assurance Society felt that their losses would not rise about $25,000. A spokesman for New York Life Insurance Company felt that $50,000 would cover all claims against them.

There were several explanations for why insurance claims were so low. In some instances entire families were lost leaving no one to file a claim. In other cases all paperwork was lost leaving the insured in a precarious position when making a claim. Even though several homes and businesses were destroyed by fire, fire insurance companies were not liable because the buildings had first been washed from their foundations by the floodwaters thus voiding the fire protection. A common superstition of the day tended to reduce the number of people who purchased life insurance. This superstition held that when a man insured himself, the time of his death was drawing near. To avoid causing fear among wives and children, many men took out policies without making anyone in the family aware that they were so protected. Regardless of the reason, the net effect of insurance payments within the flooded district was but a small portion of the total finances that went into the rebuilding of the Conemaugh Valley.

The first issue of the *Johnstown Tribune's* weekly paper was released on June 14. The first issue of the *Tribune's* daily paper was offered to readers on June 17. George T. Swank, the editor and proprietor of the *Tribune* was the toast of many newspapers for his efforts to resume publication of his paper. The *Altoona Times* edition of June 19 declared that the *Tribune* was, "On the Top Wave Again." The *Times* article stated that, "A goodly chunk of the *Johnstown Tribune* was carried away on the top wave of the late fearful flood, but the indefatigable editor, George T. Swank, and his efficient corps of assistants declined to go with it, and as a result the *TRIBUNE* is once more on the top wave of progres-

sive journalism...." The *Pittsburgh Post* offered similar praise, which appeared in the *Tribune* on June 17. "The Johnstown Weekly *TRIBUNE*, of date June 14th, has been sent to its subscribers. The first issue since the disaster, it will occupy a leaf in that great history of American journalism."

Both during and after the tragic events of May 31, 1889, a number of individuals emerged as true heroes. In one manner or another they distinguished themselves as individuals who rose to meet the difficult challenges they confronted. Undoubtedly many heroic acts went unnoticed. However, those that were noticed and are remembered speak of extraordinary courage and effort in the face of extraordinary circumstances.

If Johnstowners had been called on to select a hero of heroes following the flood, it most certainly would have been Clara Barton. Her efforts were tireless, her energy seemed to have no limits, and her desire to help was unmistakably earnest. As discussed earlier, Miss Barton played a critical role in providing both housing and provisions for those who found themselves homeless and without even the barest of essentials following the flood. Her volunteers worked as tirelessly as she did to minister to the needs of the victims. She was among the first to arrive in the Conemaugh Valley following the flood and she was one of the last to leave.

Miss Clara Barton (1821-1912).

Miss Barton left Johnstown on October 25 following a testimonial held the evening before. A large number of Johnstown residents gathered to recognize the efforts of Miss Barton and the Red Cross. The reception began at the Morrell Institute, but had to be hastily adjourned to the Red Cross Hotel on Locust Street, when the floor of the Morrell Institute began to give way. The floor sank enough to cause alarm, but not enough to cause any injuries.

After numerous testimonials were offered, Mrs. Arthur J. Moxham, president of the Woman's Branch of the Union Benevolent Association, presented Miss Barton with a gold and silver brooch, which features two diamonds and a sapphire. The inscription of the back of the brooch reads:

TO OUR FRIEND IN NEED
MISS CLARA BARTON
FROM THE
LADIES OF JOHNSTOWN
OCT. 24, 1889.

A farewell statement was published in the October 25 edition of the *Johnstown Tribune* that summarized the motives behind the generous work accomplished by Miss Barton:

How shall we thank Miss Clara Barton and the Red Cross for the help they have given us? It cannot be done, and if it could, Miss Barton does not want our thanks. She has simply done her duty as she saw it and received her pay—the consciousness of a duty performed to the best of her ability. To see us upon our feet, struggling forward, helping ourselves, caring for the sick and infirm (sic) and impoverished—that is enough for Miss Barton. Her idea has been fully worked out, all her plans accomplished. What more could such a woman wish?

The relationship between Miss Barton and Johnstown did not end with her departure. The residents of Johnstown would not soon forget the kindness and generosity shown by the Red Cross in their time of great need. In 1891-1892 a great famine struck Russia. One of the relief organizations that went to their aid was the American National Red Cross. Hearing of the extreme needs of the Russian people and the work of the Red Cross, the people of Johnstown responded. In a letter dated March 5, 1892, Miss Barton recognized the contributions of the city of Johnstown since the time of its own calamity. (See Appendix D.)

Charles William "Bill" Heppenstall was a passenger on the same train that brought Robert Pitcairn as far as Sang Hollow on May 31. The train was held up at Sang Hollow unable to move any closer to Johnstown. Shortly after the train had arrived, debris, then people, soon appeared in the flooded Conemaugh River. Many of the men on board the train did what they could to rescue those in the river.

Heppenstall, just two weeks shy of his seventeenth birthday, had been home in Pittsburgh as a result of a recent illness. He was on his way back to school, the Preparatory Department of Penn State University, where he was a student in the general science program. Seeing that a young child and mother were trapped in a house that had been washed down the river and was temporally lodged

(Modern photo courtesy Tim Skertich)

This is the brooch presented to Miss Barton on October 24, 1889.

(Library of Congress)

The train carrying Robert Pitcairn, Bill Heppenstall and others stopped near this railroad tower in Sang Hollow, along the Conemaugh River below Johnstown. Railroad ties, twisted track and other debris can be seen in this view taken shortly after the flood. This stone foundation, inset, is all that remains of the railroad tower shown in the old photo.

against a tree, Heppenstall ripped a bell cord from one of the train cars, tied it around his waist and swam out into the river. With great effort he was able to reach the mother and child. He first took the child to shore. Then, against the strong advice of those looking on, he again swam out into the torrent. He took a large piece of wood with him that he used to help bring the mother to shore.

Maxwell McAchren was a local painter who lived at Peelorville. Peelorville was part of the first ward of Millville adjacent to the Pennsylvania Railroad passenger station. At the time of the flood, there were five people living in the McAchren household and all five survived. Thanks to the strength and selfless courage of McAchren, six-year-old Gertrude Quinn also survived.

As previously noted in chapter four, Quinn was rescued after a lengthy ride on the flood wave. Finding herself all but helpless to resist the force of the waters that carried her along, Gertie, as her family knew her, saw hope in the eyes of the massive figure of McAchren. In her 1936 book, *Johnstown and Its Flood*, Gertrude Quinn Slattery recalled the details of her rescue by McAchren:

I put both arms around his neck and held on to him like grim death. Together we went downstream with the ebb and flow of the reflux to the accompaniment of crunching, grinding, gurgling, splashing and crying and moaning of many. After drifting about we saw a little white building, standing at the edge of the water, apparently where the hill began. At the window were two men with poles helping to rescue people floating by. I was too far out for the poles, so the men called:

"Throw the baby over here to us."

My hero said, "Do you think you can catch her?"

They said, "We can try."

So Maxwell McAchren threw me across the water (some said twenty feet, others fifteen. I could never find out, so I leave it to your imagination. It was considered a great feat in the town, I know).

Edwin C. Will, a moulder in a local foundry who lived with his family on Grant Street on Coopersdale, reportedly saved the lives of twenty-two people. In the midst of the flood, Will used his small boat to go out into the current and rescue those trapped in its fury. In a story carried in the June 4 edition of the *New York Times*, Will, who was twenty-seven at the time, was described as a

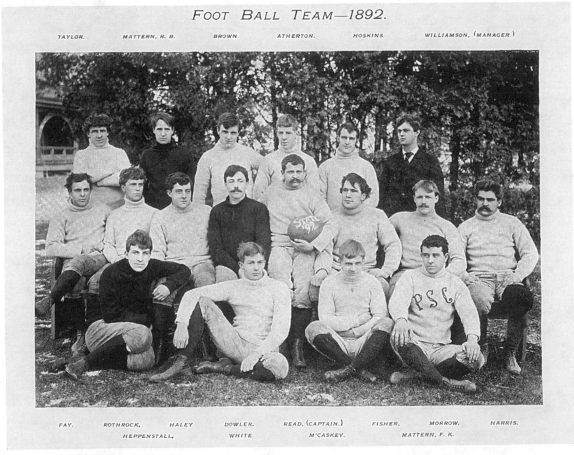

Heppenstall continued his studies at Penn State. The 1893 college yearbook, LaVie, *shows Heppenstall as a member of the 1892 Penn State "foot ball" team. At the time he also held the school record for the two-mile bicycle race with a time of 6 minutes and 16 seconds.*

Maxwell McAchren.

In this view, Romey, one of the supposed K-9 heroes of the Johnstown Flood is featured along with the owner and the small child supposedly saved. It is currently believed that this photograph was staged and has no more credibility than the imaginative, yet factious, story that prompted it.

man, "...whom no one ever suspected of possessing more than ordinary courage." Will, like many other known and unknown heroes, acted extraordinarily when faced with the extraordinary circumstances that confronted him on May 31, 1889.

In addition to the human heroes, acts of great heroism were attributed to both horses and dogs. Details regarding these animal heroes are very limited and they may well be nothing more than stories generated by vivid and creative imaginations rather than accounts of actual events. One story reported that a horse that had been washed down the river from the security of its stable, managed to pull two people out of the flood wave and carry them to safety in the vicinity of Woodvale. There were also several stories that recounted the efforts of dogs that saved lives. Most notable among these was the story of Romey. There is no credible evidence to support this story, but nonetheless it became a very popular tale when events of the flood were told. With no fear for the raging floodwaters, Romey swam out into the current and rescued a small child. The owner of the dog, the name of the child rescued, and the location of the incident are unknown.

Many heroes of the Johnstown Flood were named and their stories are known. Millions of others were part of the great mass that came to the aid of Johnstown. Financial support, clothing and other articles, and days and weeks of labor were but a few of the countless contributions that brought Johnstown out of the hopeless despair that followed the flood. Everyone who contributed to the recovery and rebuilding of Johnstown was in a small way a hero to those who called Johnstown and surrounding communities in the Conemaugh Valley home.

By any standard, the magnitude of the generosity that flowed into Johnstown was nothing short of astounding. As the recovery efforts continued, the quantity of money and supplies being shipped to Johnstown

diminished, as did the need for them. However, Johnstown remained on the minds of many for months after the flood. The November 19 edition of the *Johnstown Tribune* carried a brief story under the headline "Burgess Horrell in the Clothing Business."

Burgess Horrell continues to occasionally receive bundles of second-hand clothing and other articles of no particular value "for the flood sufferers." Generally the clothing is well worn and seedy. The other day he received a bundle from New York containing a couple of overcoats, vests, pants and under coats.

In the midst of something as colossal as the Johnstown Flood, certain events and incidents seem to defy common sense and what one would routinely expect to happen. These incidents were of particular interest to the newspaper reporters who came to the Conemaugh Valley. Under such headlines as "Fantastic Freaks of the Flood" or "Strange But True Tales From the Conemaugh Valley" countless incidents were recounted for anxious readers.

Mrs. Hettie Ogle served as both the local Western Union Telegraph operator and the operator of Johnstown's telephone system. She worked out of her home and office along Washington Street, adjacent to the Cambria Library. Realizing that she controlled the communication links between Johnstown and the rest of the world, she stayed at her telegraph key and switchboard until the last minute. As a result of her selfless efforts to duty, Hettie and her daughter Minnie both became victims of the flood. If they were even found, their bodies were never identified. However, in the field of debris lodged before the great Stone Bridge, Mrs. Ogle's ring of keys was found and identified.

The remains identified as body number 50 in the personal records kept by John Henderson, was described as follows: "Burned beyond recognition. Head, arms & legs burnt off. Telegraph instruments and chain found with body. Handkerchief in coffin." Although never positively identified, there were many who believed that this was the body of Hettie Ogle.

Some of the heaviest damage inflicted by the flood befell the churches of Johnstown. St. Mary's Church (aka, Immaculate Conception Church, or the Cambria German Catholic Church) suffered extensive damage both to its interior and exterior. The congregation of Saint Mary's had just left their sanctuary when the floodwaters struck. Having been a service for the worship of the Virgin Mary, parishioners adorned a statue of the Blessed Virgin with flowers, wreaths, and a lace veil.

Following the flood, when access to the church was finally gained, the statue of the Virgin Mary was found, just as it had been left, perfectly clean and absolutely undisturbed. The lace veil, the flowers, and the wreaths were found in the same pristine state as the statue. Water marks on the surrounding walls clearly showed that the level of the water in the church was well above the height of the pedestal upon which the figure of the Virgin Mary had rested. To those who saw the statue in the mud-filled sanctuary, its preservation was miraculous to say the least. In the midst of such total destruction, the statue had been spared. Explaining this as anything short of a divine intervention was impossible for some. Newspapers quickly picked up on the story.

The appeal of the miracle of the Virgin Mary statue was great. In the midst of so much calamity and despair, it was a bright spot, a sign to the faithful and a tangible message of hope. Inquiries and requests for verification were numerous and came from wherever the story was shared. Reverend Beale, who referred to the story as "One of the most preposterous stories that were perpetrated upon the wondering world..." provided an expla-

Hettie Ogle.

Although her body was never identified, Mrs. Hettie Ogle's keys were found and identified. They are currently part of the collection of the Johnstown Flood Museum.

This figure survived the Johnstown Flood unscathed, and is still located in the sanctuary of Immaculate Conception Church in Johnstown.

nation of what he termed a "...phenomenon [which] explained itself." In his book *Through the Johnstown Flood by a Survivor*, Beale explained that both the statue frame and the pedestal were made of wood and as such would float. He pointed out that the pedestal was heavier than the statue, which kept the statue in a perpendicular posture above the level of the water.

Regardless of Beale's logical and somewhat scientific explanation, there were those who still chose to see this incident as a miracle or at least strong evidence of some divine intervention. The Collins-Campbell Company quickly realized that this was a flood story upon which they could capitalize. They produced what they called the SHRINE TO THE BLESSED VIRGIN. Produced in 1889, the shrine was a shadow-box wall hanging that featured a likeness of the Virgin Mary, artificial flowers and a prayer composed by Saint Bernard. What follows is the description that appeared on the reverse of the shrine:

> This shrine has been issued to commemorate one of the most touching and beautiful incidents of that most fearful and disastrous flood which swept Johnstown from amongst the cities of the country. The small, but beautiful image of this Shrine is a copy of the famous, we may almost say miraculous Statue, which adorned one of the Johnstown Churches, and which, amid the crashing of walls and towers of the sacred edifice and the angry roar of the devouring waters, alone remained uninjured, as though she, the Immaculate Mother of God and Star of the Sea, was unwilling to leave Her children in the fearful hour of their peril.
>
> The prayer attached to the Shrine was composed by the great St. Bernard, and those who recite it devoutly receive three hundred days' Indulgence.
>
> There can be no more welcome faces in our homes than those of Jesus and His Blessed Mother, and this, Her Image, will serve to remind us that, in the midst of the mortal perils of our lives, Mary never deserts Her faithful children. If we wish to honor Her and secure Her protection in life and death; if we desire to instill the love of Her into the hearts of our children, let us raise an Altar to Her in our dwellings where we can kneel and implore Her protection. To the sick and suffering the sight of this Image of Mary will bring patience, to the dying Hope.

Another story regarding a possible divine intervention was recounted in the May 29, 1964 edition of the *Johnstown Tribune-Democrat*. George Walker Williams, who was 86 at the time of the 75th anniversary of the flood in 1964, shared a family story. As recounted by Williams, his mother had been given a small gold cross as a Sunday school award of merit. Her initials, M.W., for Mary Walker her maiden name, were engraved on the back of the cross.

The prayer composed by Saint Bernard, shown in this illustration at the feet of the Blessed Virgin, reads as follows: "Remember Mary, tender-hearted-virgin, how from of old the ear hath never heard that he who ran to thee for refuge, implored they help, and sought thy prayers, was forsaken by God. Virgin of virgins, Mother, emboldened by this confidence I fly to thee, to thee I come, and in they presence, I a weeping sinner stand. Mother of the World Incarnate, O cast not away my prayer: (HERE MENTION YOUR REQUEST,) but in thy pity hear and answer. Amen.   [Indulgence 300 days]"

Shortly before the flood of 1889, Williams and his sister were playing in the attic of their home on Walnut Street. As they went through some boxes of old clothing and old jewelry, they found a small wooden box that contained the gold cross that had been given to their mother. During the flood of 1889, their home was destroyed and virtually nothing was recovered. Two years later they rebuilt on the same foundation.

By the time of the 1936 flood, the Walker family had moved, and tenants were living in the house. About two months after the 1936 flood, while one of the tenants was cleaning, a small gold cross was found. It was given to George Walker Williams' uncle, his mother's brother, who in turn showed it to George. Williams immediately recognized it as the cross he had seen 47 years earlier in the small wooden box he and his sister had found in their attic. The initials M. W. were still visible on the back of the cross.

The following quote from Williams was the final paragraph of the 1964 *Tribune-Democrat* story:

> From the Flood of May 1889 until the Flood of March 17, 1936, that cross had lain in the cellar of our house, hidden perhaps, but waiting nevertheless to be discovered and redeemed from the dirt and grime. Then it was that the sentiment, expressed by my mother so many years before, came back to me—the sentiment that conveys the fact that "no matter how deeply the cross, or the things the cross represents, may be buried under the debris of time, it will rise again and shine on as a beacon of the best things in life."

On May 16, 1952, readers of the *Johnstown Tribune*, learned that a story about their town that had been featured the previous month in Ripley's "Believe It Or Not" was indeed true. According to the story, a twelve-room house was washed from its foundation on Walnut Street and carried across town to Kernville and set down by the floodwaters on a foundation that had been prepared for an identical house. Having had letters of inquiry from several readers of the column asking for verification of the amazing story, Johnstown's Mayor Walter E. Rose contacted King Features Syndicate, which distributed "Believe It Or Not." On May 15, 1952, he received a reply from Douglas Ripley the editor of the feature. In that reply, Mr. Ripley included the following resume of the account provided by Mrs. Flora B. Wood, who was eleven in 1889 and lived in half of the double house with her family:

> On Friday, May 31st, 1889 when the waters from the broken South Fork Dam roared down upon the already inundated town of Johnstown, Pa., it swept our house away and headed it towards the Arch Bridge [the Stone Bridge], where the debris was packing up and making a backwash which pushed it still further until, as the waters receded, it finally settled in what was called Kernville—or the South Side.
>
> Now comes the strange part—it was dropped directly on the cellar of a house being built from the same plans by the same contractor who built our house! He bought it; it was really only slightly damaged in one corner besides the plastering and repainting.
>
> Twenty-six years afterwards when my son was 16 we visited the home town and I showed him both sites.
>
> After the flood we recovered practically all our possessions, and today I still have some of them in my apartment here in Washington, D.C.

By 1889, both the science and the art of photography were well developed. The Civil War, as much as any other single event, had given photographers experience beyond the confines of the studio walls. The Johnstown Flood provided a similar experience for the photographers of the Victorian era. As soon as word of the flood

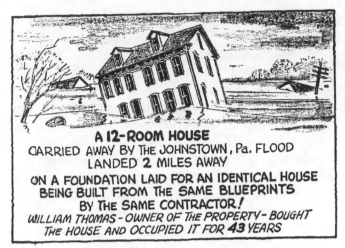

This is the artist's view that accompanied the "Believe It Or Not" story.

Guy and Steve Krisay currently own the twelve-room house carried from Walnut Street to Kernville by the 1889 flood. It is located at 521-523 Franklin Street where the Krisay's operate an appliance business. Guy Krisay is standing in front of the family business.

had spread, photographers were among the first to head for the flood-stricken valley of the Conemaugh. Many of the images they captured have left an indelible mark on the story of the flood. None, however, has done so to a greater extent than the photographs of the John Shultz house.

John Shultz was a pattern maker who lived with his family at 87 Union Street. Nine people lived in the Shultz house and all nine survived the flood. At the time the floodwaters struck, only six people were in the house. The house and its contents were a total loss. The enormous force of the flood wave pushed a giant tree through the second-floor window of the house, creating one of the more unique spectacles to be found in Johnstown.

Reports of debris being washed from Johnstown were many. The June 3 *Chicago Tribune* described the scene on the rivers west of Johnstown:

Many people crawled out along the log protruding from the overturned Shultz house to have their picture taken.

Some idea of the terrible nature of the disaster may be gleaned from this fact: Johnstown is seventy-eight miles from Pittsburg, and yet for miles the Ohio thirty miles west of Pittsburg was covered with boards, shingles, pieces of flooring, roofs household furniture, and similar things. Some bodies were swept through Pittsburg with the debris, and are probably lost forever in the Ohio.

A report from Cincinnati, Ohio on June 6, which was carried in the same day's issue of the *Lebanon Daily News*, reported that debris had already floated past Maysville, Kentucky. It was further reported that at least three bodies had been pulled from the river near that point. Police all along the rivers west of Johnstown patrolled for days in the hopes of finding survivors or "floaters," which was the name given to dead bodies found in the rivers.

A report that stimulated a great deal of interest told of a five-month-old baby boy pulled from the floodwaters near Pittsburgh. The baby was found very much alive in his cradle, which was perched above the water line on a mound of debris along the Allegheny River. This story was initially reported in the June 2 edition of

the *New York Times*. It was later carried by a number of other papers and included in several of the books written about the flood. Even though the details of the story were minimal, which cast some doubt on its reliability, it remains one of the more frequently told stories of the flood.

The July 10 edition of the *Johnstown Tribune* carried a brief story regarding another Johnstown flood. The previous day, heavy rains had washed away three big dams above the town of Johnstown located in Fulton County, New York. Several people drowned when a bridge on which they had gathered washed out. There was some property damage in the town but nothing on the scale of the damage in the Conemaugh Valley. The town's electric light house and nine bridges were washed away. As in Johnstown, Pennsylvania's flood, the tragedy in Johnstown, New York, was a combination of natural events and man-made circumstances.

Countless efforts to affix blame and establish responsibility for the flood in the Conemaugh Valley have to date been futile. They have neither affixed blame nor established responsibility, and it is now highly doubtful if either will ever truly be known. A careful study of the disaster provides a great deal of information, much of which is beyond question. However, even when viewed collectively, these facts do not provide sufficient evidence beyond a reasonable doubt to render a guilty verdict against any individual or group of individuals. If tried in the court of public opinion and popular sentiment during the months following the flood, the South Fork Fishing and Hunting Club was irrefutably, unmistakably, and positively liable. In like manner, the Club was totally, completely and absolutely responsible for the loss of life, property and prosperity throughout the Conemaugh Valley. Sentiments against the Club and its members ran high. The statement "I told you so" was on the lips of many. The opinion that the Club had a responsibility to pay for the damages it had caused was widely and openly expressed.

Numerous newspapers published stories and editorials of stern condemnation against the South Fork Fishing and Hunting Club. None, however, was more direct than the *Johnstown Tribune*. At the same time, the *Tribune* was one of the first papers to site multiple factors that contributed to the destruction throughout the Conemaugh Valley. In a story that appeared under the heading "THE CAUSE," in its June 14 edition, the *Tribune* concluded, "We think we know what struck us, and it was not the hand of Providence. Our misery is the work of man." The article went on to offer a brief history and description of Lake Conemaugh, as established by "...the Pittsburgh Club men, who wanted an exclusive resort where, in all their spotlessness and glory, they might idle away the summer days." In describing the wrath that came upon the Conemaugh Valley, either Swank, the editor, or one of his able writers concluded that, "A rat caught in a trap and placed in a bucket of water would not be more helpless than we were."

Swank and his writers clearly summarized what they felt were the three main unnatural causes of the disaster that had befallen their readers. "First, and seriously enough, though only slight in comparison, from the narrowing of the streams; second, from the building of the big stone bridge, with its ponderous arches taking up room that should have been free for the rush of water; and third from the Reservoir which dealt the final blow."

On Saturday, June 1, there was a meeting of some of the members of the South Fork Fishing and Hunting Club in Pittsburgh. That meeting, according to several accounts, took place at the home of Charles J. Clarke. The consensus of opinion within this group was that no formal statement would be made on the part of the Club or its individual members. For the time being, it was agreed that the less said the better. Although there was no formal response from the Club, several members did offer comments and opinions. On June 2 in Pittsburgh,

club member Charles J. Clarke released information that he had received from Colonel Unger that the catastrophe in the Conemaugh Valley was the result of the breaking of the dam that held Lake Conemaugh in check. This information was reported on the front page of the June 3 *New York Times*:

> The cause of the calamity, it is admitted by the President of the South Fork Fishing Club, the proprietor of the artificial Conemaugh Lake, was the weakness of the dam alone. No cloudburst or waterspout occurred to compel it—the frailty of the dam and the tremendous pressure of water behind it was the only cause of the catastrophe.

Louis Semple Clarke, the son of Charles, told reporters that there was serious doubt if it was the South Fork Dam that had broken. James McGregor, another Club member, joined him in this opinion. McGregor shared that he was going to the Club later in the month to fish, and that he expected to find the lake just as he had seen it during his last visit. Club member James Reed, of the law firm Knox and Reed of Pittsburgh, which was the legal council of the Club, also questioned reports that the dam at South Fork was in fact the one that had burst.

Numerous individuals voiced their opinions and strong sentiments against the Club. None, however, did so in more graphic detail and with more sorrowful eloquence than Neff J. Swank. Swank, a painter who rented a house at 84 Napoleon Street, lost his wife and four children as a result of the flood. On the site where they were buried on June 7, 1889 in Grandview Cemetery, Swank placed a sign that left little doubt as to how his family perished and who he felt was responsible.

Inquests conducted by two different coroners came to a similar conclusion, even though each was indepen-

The sign reads, "Family of N. J. Swank wife and four children drowned by the South Fork Fishing and Hunting Club. May 31st 1889." From left to right are the graves of Jennie (Swank's wife), Maude age 10, Susie age 8, Edna age 2, and Samuel age 5.

dently conducted. The cause of the deaths investigated through these inquests was found to be death by violence caused by the flood and drowning. The flooding was brought on by the failure of the dam of the South Fork Fishing and Hunting Club.

Coroner Hammer of Westmoreland County released the findings of his inquests on June 7, 1889. Through June 7, Hammer's jury had viewed a total of 218 bodies found in Westmoreland County. The following is the verdict of the Westmoreland County coroner's inquests.

Inquisition taken and indented at Nineveh [Seward], in the county of Westmoreland, on the 7th day of June, A.D., 1889, before me, R. B. Hammer, coroner of the county aforesaid, upon the view of the body then and there lying dead, upon the oaths of E. E. Wible, A. L. Bethune, H. M. Guy, R. B. Rogers, W. H. Work and James McCarthy, good and lawful men of the county aforesaid, who, being sworn and affirmed diligently to inquire and true presentment make, on behalf of the Commonwealth, how and in what manner the said came to its death, having viewed the body of said deceased and having heard the testimony of witnesses, do say, upon their oaths and affirmations aforesaid, that the aforesaid deceased came to its death by violence due to flood caused by the breaking of the dam of the South-Fork Reservoir, and, as well the aforesaid coroner as the jurors aforesaid, do certify under their oaths that the said deed of violence caused by the action of the flood, or there is such strong suspicion of such violence or unlawful acts as to make an inquest necessary.

In witness whereof as well the aforesaid coroner and the jurors aforesaid have to this inquisition set their hands and seals on the day and year of that place first above written.

R. B. Hammer,   H. M. Guy,
E. E. Wible,   R. B. Rogers,
A. L. Bethune,   James McCarthy,
W. H. Work.

As a result of the coroner's inquest held in Cambria County, only one body was viewed. That was the body of Mrs. Ellen Hite. According to information received by Reverend Beale, "Mrs. Ellen Hite, of Kernville, on the south side, was caught on the street and drowned while trying to climb an electric-light pole at the corner of Morris and Dibert Streets." Coroner Evans of Cambria County conducted the inquest, which closed on the night of July 6 with the following verdict:

We, the undersigned, the jury empanelled to investigate the cause of death of Ellen Hite on May 31st, after hearing the testimony, find that Ellen Hite came to her death by drowning; that the drowning was caused by the breaking of the South-Fork dam. We further find from the testimony and what we saw on

the ground, that there was not sufficient water weir, nor was the dam constructed sufficiently strong nor of the proper material to withstand the overflow; and hence we find that the owners of said dam were culpable in not making it as secure as it should have been, especially in view of the fact that a population of many thousands were in the valley below; and we hold that the owners are responsible for the fearful loss of life and property resulting from the breaking of the dam.

John Coho,   John H. Devine,
Abraham Ferner,   John A. Wissinger
H. B. Blair,   F. W. Cohick.

Although the South Fork Fishing and Hunting Club emerged as the villain, the public condemnation of the Club was not unanimous. There were those who spoke in favor of the Club, while others at least endeavored to disperse the responsibility. A notable local who did not place the blame squarely on the Club was Cyrus Elder. Elder, the solicitor and general agent for the Cambria Iron Company in Johnstown, had lost both his wife and daughter Nan in the flood. Following the death of Morrell, Cambria Iron Company's membership in the South Fork Fishing and Hunting Club went to Elder. He was the only local who was a member of the Club at the time of the flood, and the only member of the Club who lost immediate family as a direct result of it. Elder, contrary to the opinions and recollections of John Fulton and many others at Cambria Iron, was not aware of any serious concerns the Company had about the condition of the dam.

Elder recalled that there had been some initial concerns in 1881, but that changes were made in the plans for the reconstruction of the dam that relieved these concerns. Elder also shared that at about that same time his son, George R. Elder, was a student at Troy Polytechnic Institute. A problem was submitted to his class by a professor that was supposed to be hypothetical in nature, but was clearly based on the original specifications of the dam at South Fork, Pennsylvania. After completing their study of the case, the class concluded that the dam was safe.

Arthur Moxham blamed the residents of Johnstown and vicinity, at least in part, for the calamity they suffered. He felt that the fears regarding the dam at South Fork were common and real, but that nothing was ever done about them. This lack of action to address these concerns was the result of there being no unified governing body that represented the entire community. Moxham reminded the residents of the flood-ravaged district of their responsibility. "Well, we have paid for our criminal carelessness—paid for it with the lives of those dear to us—paid for it with our homes, and with our savings." Moxham reminded the residents of

Johnstown and surrounding municipalities of this as he sought to present a rationale for the consolidation of those municipalities into a city.

There were also those who felt that Johnstown and its neighbors were at least partially to blame for their tragedy because of their our lack of attention and their failure to act responsibly in the face of the warning provided on May 31 from South Fork.

John Parke agreed with the sentiment that some of the blame had to be shared with residents of the valley who ignored warnings offered early in the day. From his vantage point, Parke concluded that no one could be found guilty of neglect. He felt that the tremendous rains dumped by the several storms that had visited the area, were beyond anyone's control and more than any dam could reasonably be expected to withstand. Colonel Unger, the president of the Club, agreed with these sentiments. Parke and Unger came to Johnstown on Monday, June 3 to view the flooded district.

For his part in the controversy over who was responsible for the disaster, Colonel Unger gave two conflicting reports about events at the dam on May 31. His reports included details that were incorrect. On June 3, while in Johnstown, Unger offered a summary of what had happened in South Fork to a reporter from the *Pittsburgh Post*. His comments were carried in the June 4 edition of the paper. He spoke of the frantic efforts to establish another spillway and raise the level of the dam with a plow. He reported that the dam gave way at 1:45 p.m., instead of shortly after 3:00 p.m. He also reported that, "...George Fisher's house and stable were rolling and tumbling down the river." The Fisher house survived the flood undamaged. This initial interview given by Unger appears to be an unfaithful reporting of events based on poor recollections, rather than a willful attempt to lie. This is a reasonable assumption since there does not appear to be any reasonable explanation for willfully providing incorrect information regarding such inconsequential details.

In his second interview, carried by the *Pittsburgh Press* on Wednesday June 5, it was evident that Unger was defending his actions and the actions of others at the dam during its final hours. He hinted that the state of Pennsylvania was responsible for some long-standing structural difficulties with the dam, and he openly denied that the spillway was clogged. He also pointed out that the warnings sent down the valley, long before the dam gave way, were ignored. There is no evidence whether Unger was directed to speak for the Club or not. He was not the only Club member to be in South Fork at the time the dam burst. Others included Louis Irwin and his son H. L. Irwin, James Clarke, the son of Charles J. Clarke, Joseph and George Shea, sons of C. B. Shea,

D. W. C. Bidwell, and J. J. Lawrence. Immediately following the bursting of their dam, the members of the Club departed South Fork, without venturing down the valley to see if they could lend aid or offer support. For this they were severely censored by many of the locals who felt that they had acted in a cowardly, irresponsible, and dispassionate manner in the face of a tragedy that was of their making.

Herbert Webber, an employee of the Club who served as a guard, caretaker, handyman and coachman from time to time, made his way to Johnstown after the flood and shared his long-held concerns over the general condition of the dam at South Fork. Webber recalled that he had brought his concerns regarding the condition of the dam to the attention of the Club and its management several times in recent years. He shared with reporters and anyone else who would listen that he had been repeatedly told that the dam was strong, safe, and would stand for centuries. For his persistence Webber finally was told that he either keep his concerns to himself or his services would no longer be needed by the South Fork Fishing and Hunting Club. Still convinced that his fears were legitimate, Webber carried them to the Burgess of Johnstown during the early spring of 1889. He was told that the matter would be referred to an engineer for review and that the state would be contacted if there were indeed structural deficiencies. There is no account that anything was done to follow up on the issues raised by Webber.

The failure of the dam that impounded Lake Conemaugh created a great deal of interest among the engineering community. Shortly before going to press with their June 8 edition, the *New York Times* received a dispatch from Mr. H. W. Brinkerhoff, a civil engineer. Brinkerhoff was associated with both the *Times* and the *Engineering and Building Record*, a professional journal for engineers published in New York. He had been dispatched to Johnstown to inspect the dam and report his findings. According to Brinkerhoff, the failure of the dam was due to inadequate spillway capacity and the fact that the dam was lower at its center than at its ends. Both of these conditions, by Brinkerhoff's assessment, were the result of the reconstruction of the dam, not its original construction. In the June 9 edition of the *Times*, Brinkerhoff was quoted as saying, "To sum up, it may be said that the dam as originally designed seems to have had sufficient stability, and to have been well built." Although numerous other studies were made of the dam for the purpose of determining what led to its collapse, Brinkerhoff's assertions were among those consistently upheld as major reasons why the water of Lake Conemaugh overtopped and finally destroyed the South Fork Dam.

The American Society of Civil Engineers, which had been instituted in 1852, appointed a committee of four to travel to South Fork to investigate the failure of the dam. Members of the committee included three engineers from the Society. They were James B. Francis, W. E. Worthen, and M. J. Becker. The fourth member of the committee, A. Fteley, was the chief engineer of the Croton Aqueduct. The Croton project was in progress at the time of the failure of the dam in South Fork. On January 15 of 1890 they finished their report, and it was published in June 1891. The report offered the following conclusion:

> In concluding, we must state that, while our deductions are based on the results of observations of rain-fall and of flow which are necessarily approximate, we feel satisfied that they are not far from the truth. There can be no questions that such a rain-fall had not taken place since the construction of the dam. But the surface of the water-shed is quite steep, and the consequent rapid discharge of a large percentage of the rain-fall into the reservoir would require a very large outlet to prevent a dangerous accumulation. The spillway, however, had not a sufficient discharge capacity; contrary to the original specifications of Mr. W. E. Morris, requiring a width of overflow of 150 feet and a depth of 10 feet below crest, which would have been a sufficient size for the flood in the present case, it had only an effective width of 70 feet, and a depth of about eight feet; the accumulated water rose to such a height as to overflow the crest of the dam and caused it to collapse by washing it down from the top.

> The dam itself, or the parts of it which were left standing, showed undoubtedly that it was well and thoroughly built, and that it would have successfully resisted the pressure of the water. The exposed sides of the breaks show distinctly that the compact layers of which the structure was formed were not obliterated by the wearing action of the flood, and they stand conspicuous witness of the value of an earth embankment when well built of good materials, to impound large bodies of water.

> There are to-day in existence many such dams which are not better, nor even as well provided with wasting channels as was the Conemaugh Dam, and which would be destroyed if placed under similar conditions.

> The fate of the latter shows that, however remote the chance of an excessive flood may be, the only consistent policy, when human lives, or even when large interests are at stake, is to provide wasting channels of sufficient proportion and to build the embankment of ample height.

The prestigious *Engineering News* also conducted a thorough inspection of the dam at South Fork. Under the headline "An Engineering Crime," which appeared in the June 9 edition of the *New York Times*, A. M. Wellington and F. B. Burt of the *News* reported on the inspection they conducted of the South Fork Dam and their related research into its failure. According to the June 9 story, "Mr Wellington states that the dam was in every respect of very inferior construction and of a kind wholly unwarranted by good engineering practices of thirty years ago." He was no less kind in his assessment of the reconstructed dam.

> The reconstructed dam also bears the mark of great ignorance or carelessness, having been made nearly two feet lower in the middle than at the ends. It should rather have been crowned in the middle, which would have concentrated the overflow, if it should occur, at the ends instead of in the centre . Had the break been at the ends the cut of the water would have been so gradual that little or no harm might have resulted.

He reported that both the original earthwork and the repaired portion of the dam lacked a heart wall of stone or masonry, and that the earthen embankment was protected only by riprap on both its interior and exterior slopes.

Reverend Beale's book *Through the Johnstown Flood by a Survivor* includes extracts from flood-related articles offered by the *Engineering News* in four of its issues. In addition to providing a history of the dam from its original construction through to its destruction, the extracts cited by Beale indicate that the work of reconstruction, when the Club assumed ownership of the dam, was not supervised by anyone with engineering credentials or experience. *Engineering News* asserted that their "...information is positive, direct and unimpeachable that *at no time during the process of rebuilding the dam was* ANY ENGINEER WHATEVER, young or old, good or bad, known or unknown, engaged on or consulted as to the work."

Statements in these later articles were far less negative concerning the original construction of the dam than Wellington had been on June 8. In fact, these articles concluded that the original dam, even though it lacked a central core of masonry, was nonetheless "...thoroughly well built by the late General James N. Morehead [Moorhead]." Regarding the failure of the dam, the *Engineering News* focused on the reconstructed dam, not the original structure:

> The dam was finally made fairly tight, but there has always been some leakage at the bottom, and of late years this has been increasing. The truth as to the exact amount of leakage is very difficult to ascertain. The original crest height of the dam was decreased from one to three feet, and the spill-way was shortly after obstructed with gratings to retain fish, and a trestle bridge was built across the opening.

Negligence in the mere execution of the earthwork, however, if it existed, is of minor importance, since there is no doubt that it was not a primary cause of the disaster; at worst, it merely aggravated it. The primary causes of the disaster were the lowering of the crest, the dishing, or central sag in the crest, the closing of the bottom culvert, and the obstruction of the spill-way."

Modern research has supported this line of thinking. The May 1988 edition of *Civil Engineering* carried an article by Walter Frank titled "The Cause of the Johnstown Flood." Frank, a civil engineer who had worked for Bethlehem Steel until 1979, concluded:

If the reconstruction of the South Fork Dam had been rebuilt to the original specifications and construction, the disaster of May 31, 1889, would never have occurred. Granted a break like the one in 1862, when the culvert collapsed, could have caused great damage. However, the South Fork Dam as originally designed by Morris and constructed by Morehead and Packer would not have had water pass over it—the worst possible thing that can befall an earth and rock dam—the unquestionable cause of the 1889 Johnstown Disaster.

Resentment and sentiments against the Club continued for many years. In February 1904, an auction was held at the clubhouse to dispose of some remaining property of the Club. The February 19, 1904 edition of the *Johnstown Tribune* carried a story that announced the auction. The final paragraph of this story clearly indicates that almost fifteen years later, the Club was still viewed, at least by the *Tribune*, as the culprit responsible for Johnstown's worst flood:

Persons who attend the sale will be served with hot lunch and coffee, and the South Fork Branch trains will stop at the clubhouse. Doubtless many persons will be attracted to the sale by the possibility of securing mementoes of the famous reservoir and the organization, which, while building for the purpose of pleasure, wrought the destruction of Johnstown.

Regardless of why the South Fork Dam failed in 1889, its collapse led to the failure of the South Fork Fishing and Hunting Club. Some of the members of the Club, particularly those who owned individual cottages, periodically returned for brief vacations, but interest in the Club quickly faded. The lake, which had been the feature of the private resort which supported the most popular pastimes of members, was now gone. The empty lakebed and the broken dam stood as vivid and stark reminders of the tragic flood. The clubhouse was closed, the roads and pathways were no longer cared for, and negative sentiments against the Club lingered.

Most of the residents of the Conemaugh Valley would never miss the club members, their families and their guests. The lines of distinction between them had kept them worlds apart, and the current local sentiment against the Club further widened that gap. There was, however, a notable exception. The farmers who lived in the vicinity of Lake Conemaugh had enjoyed a pleasant period of prosperity since the Club opened. Farmers had become accustomed to healthy profits selling their produce and other goods to the Club at premium prices. With the demise of the Club, a solid portion of their income, at least for the summer months, was gone. The land of these farmers had also increased in value because of its proximity to the Club, but in June 1889, all that was over.

During the summer of 1889, the South Fork Fishing and Hunting Club found itself situated in a strange limbo. The Club still existed and it had substantial holdings of property, buildings, and equipment. There were numerous reports that angry men from the valley below went to the Club shortly after the flood looking to see if any of the members were there. Finding no one, not even Colonel Unger who was then in Pittsburgh, they reportedly broke into some of the buildings, did some damage, and pilfered some small items.

The substantial and elegant cottages along with the clubhouse and annex became temporary residences for some families displaced by the flood. In late July several families from the flooded district made the Club their temporary home. There were reports that some of these families were planning to stay on throughout the winter. Articles appeared in the *Johnstown Tribune* on July 29 and again on August 28 that referred to the families living at the Club as the "Johnstown Colony at South Fork." The July 29 article offered the following description of the Johnstown Colony:

The cottages are elegantly furnished—just as the owners left them—and the occupants are given the free range of the premises and the use of everything. A glimpse at the interior of one of these luxurious summer homes gives one an idea of the regal style in which the occupants lived. There, too, in their pretty houses on the brink of the lake are the boats of various kinds that so often bore out upon the smooth waters the dainty ladies and their escorts and the happy children. Electric boats, steam boats, sail boats, and row boats—all are there, but grass grows where the water was, and the cattle and sheep graze there. It is a strange and bewildering web of thought one weaves, as from the wide porch of a cottage he gazes out upon the scene before him.

The description of the property offered in these articles indicates that the damage done by the men from the valley who came to the Club the week after the flood must have been minimal. Interest in what the Club would ultimately do with its property and what would become of the Club itself became matters of interest and much conjecture. In July it was reported that members of the Club met in Pittsburgh for the purpose of considering a proposal that would turn the clubhouse and adjoining property into an orphanage. This proposal was not given any serous consideration because the location was entirely too remote for such a purpose.

The August 20 edition of the *Johnstown Tribune*, citing a story that had appeared earlier in the *Pittsburgh Commercial Gazette*, reported that there were indeed plans among the club members to rebuild their dam and resume occupancy of their pleasure resort. A person reportedly speaking for the Club was to have remarked that the Club had put too much money into its holdings to simply abandon them.

The August 20 edition of the *Pittsburgh Leader*, reported that at least a half dozen prominent members of the Club, who were not individually named, denied that there were plans for rebuilding the dam. One of the members said, "It has never even been hinted by the members of the South Fork Club that the dam would be rebuilt. It is true the members still own the property at South Fork, but you can publish as a fact that the Club will never have a lake there again, no matter what use we may make of the property."

With the rumors settled that the Club would not be rebuilding in South Fork, new rumors soon surfaced regarding plans for rebuilding at other locations. The August 27 edition of the *Johnstown Tribune* reported that a group of the club men, led by their president Colonel Unger, had ventured to Petoskey, Michigan for the purpose of locating and securing land where their Club could be reestablished:

> It is now about definitely settled that the South Fork Club will have its resort in Michigan hereafter. Colonel Unger and two other members of the Club have been at Petoskey lately, where they have obtained the refusal of eight hundred acres of ground facing on Little Traverse Bay, on Lake Michigan. This information was furnished by a citizen of Harbor Springs. It is certain that Colonel Unger was registered at the Arlington Hotel at Petoskey.

In March 2000, a search was conducted through the Petoskey Title Company for the purpose of locating any land transactions in Emmet County, Michigan between January 1, 1889 and January 1, 1891, to which Colonel Elias J. Unger, the South Fork Fishing and Hunting Club, or the South Fork Fishing and Hunting Club of Pittsburgh were a party. (Petoskey is located in Emmet County, Michigan. See Appendix E.)

In September 1889 another rumor surfaced that the Club was looking at land in Erie County, Pennsylvania near Lake Le Bouf. The story was carried in the September 9 edition of the *Johnstown Tribune*. The next day the *Commercial Gazette* of Pittsburgh refuted this story. Speaking for the Club, Philander C. Knox denied that the Club was looking at property in Erie County or anywhere else for the purpose of reestablishing their Club. By all accounts, this ended the rumors regarding the Club's intentions to rebuild.

Following the failure of the South Fork Fishing and Hunting Club, the only matter left to close this chapter in the history of the Conemaugh Valley was the disposition of the Club's holdings. There appears to have been little or no resistance among the Club members to the decision to dissolve the Club and dispose of its property and assets. This was true for numerous and obvious reasons. Most notable were strong sentiments against the Club, fear of both criminal and civil action, and a desire to simply put the whole terrible situation behind them.

In 1900, the *Johnstown Tribune* carried a story in its December 7 edition that the clubhouse and about a dozen of the cottages had been purchased and were to be turned into a sanitarium. Dr. S. S. Kring of Allegheny was reportedly the purchaser. According to the article, repairs were to begin on the buildings immediately, with plans set to open the facility to patients the following spring. It is doubtful if this story was ever more than a rumor, since there are no records of related land transactions.

Records related to the final dissolution of the Club and the disposition of their property are sketchy. Not surprisingly, the club continued to keep its business as far from the public eye as possible, straight through to the bitter end of the Club's existence. It had started as a strictly private venture and it would end just as privately. Court records in Cambria County, although incomplete, do indicate that the Club in 1889 had nine parcels of ground. On May 1, 1889, a mortgage for the South Fork Fishing and Hunting Club in the amount of $36,000 was recorded for Henry Holdship and Benjamin Thaw, both club members. It was reported that an action for foreclosure was started in 1891 by Holdship and Thaw on this mortgage, but no paper work can be located to support this action.

On June 26, 1901, the sheriff transferred all of the Club property to a trustee, E. B. Alsop. Alsop, an attorney, is believed to have been a friend of one or more of the Club members. The details of this transfer are not precisely known. However, during the next several months, a number of Club members transferred ownership of their interests in the Club to Alsop as well, indicating that those holdings were being organized and readied for sale.

In December 1993, Landmarks Design Associates and Wallace, Roberts & Todd released a *Historic Structures Report* prepared for the National Park Service. That report covered the clubhouse, the Brown cottage, the Moorhead cottage and clubhouse annex of the South Fork Fishing and Hunting Club. Within that report, the following account is offered regarding the sale of the Club's property:

> Indeed, a sale did occur on 17 February 1903. The nine parcels were deeded to George M. Harshberger. In a separate deed of the same day, Alsop transferred 49 acres plus "a number of cottages, houses, etc.," "saving excepting and reserving therefrom all right, title, and interest which may inhere to any and all lots upon which cottages or other buildings have been erected by virtue of leases or permits to build given by the South Fork Fishing and Hunting Club to members thereof."

As noted previously, a public auction was held at the site of the former South Fork Fishing and Hunting Club in February 1904. The February 19 edition of the *Johnstown Tribune* announced the auction that was to dispose of remaining Club property. Following this auction, the Club no longer had any holdings in Cambria County, and thus ceased to exist:

> The South Fork Hunting and Fishing Club, owners of the Conemaugh Reservoir at the time of the Great Flood in 1889, will pass out of history as an organization with the sale of all personal effects remaining in the clubhouse at the reservoir site. Auctioneer George M. Harshberger has announced that the sale will take place on Thursday, the 25th inst. [February of 1904], at the clubhouse when the entire furnishings of the house will be disposed of at auction.
>
> In the list to be disposed of are fifty bedroom suites, many yards of carpet, silverware and tableware with the club monogram engraved there on, many odd pieces of furniture and bric-a-brac. At the time of the Great Flood, the clubhouse remained open, but has been since occupied only by a caretaker, and now the real estate and clubhouse, together with a number of cottages, having been sold to a syndicate of Cambria County persons, the club's Trustee, E. B. Alsop, of Pittsburg (sic) has ordered all the personal effects disposed of. The present owners have not determined what disposition will be made of the surface and buildings, the coal rights having been disposed of some time since to the Stineman coal interests.

The venture of Benjamin Ruff and those who had joined him lasted just a quarter of a century (1879-1904). The South Fork Fishing and Hunting Club's active years were far fewer in number. The Club opened for the season of 1881 and provided members, family, and guests with vacation opportunities through the 1888 season. Following the collapse of the once great South Fork Dam, the locals, previously unwelcome on the grounds of the private resort of the "Pittsburgh Clubmen," had picnics on the slopes of the ruined earthen embankment. Men and boys fished the feeder streams well into what had once been the lakebed. Travelers and visitors from out of town went to South Fork to look at what was left of the great South Fork Dam that had unleashed a destructive force of unparallelled magnitude on the Conemaugh Valley in 1889.

Chapter 7

A Triumph of the Human Spirit

Countless attempts have been made to explain why there was such a devastating flood in Johnstown, Pennsylvania on May 31, 1889. Many of these explanations are based on a seemingly endless quantity of scientific and engineering evidence generated by investigators after the flood. These fact-based explanations have satisfied many of the curious, but to others, they are nothing more than the facts of the flood. There are many who believe that the true explanation can only be found in more ethereal or spiritual ponderings. As a result, biblical predictions, the wrath of God, dreams, punishment for man's pleasurable pursuits, visions and superstitions have all been applied. Although not fully appreciated by the scientific or engineering community, either in 1889 or now, these postulations do provide a rich sampling of how some people attempted to answer the great and perplexing question of why there was a flood in Johnstown in 1889.

In their search to understand why Johnstown and the surrounding communities were subjected to what has been identified as the worst natural disaster of the nineteenth century, many turned to the Bible. In the scriptures they found comfort in God's promise of an abiding presence for those spared and the hope of eternal life for the more than 2200 departed souls. In the scriptures they also found evidence of foretellings and predictions that were easily applied to their present situation.

Holy writ was applied to the Johnstown Flood according to the purpose of the person or persons making the application. For example, the June 20 edition of the *Johnstown Tribune* carried a small passage from the 24th chapter of the Gospel of Matthew that predicted the flood. The person who brought this particular passage to the attention of the *Tribune*, if no one else, thought it foretold the awesome destruction that struck the Conemaugh Valley, the unexpected nature of the flood, and the random pattern of death and destruction it produced.

> For as in the days that were before the flood they were eating and drinking, marrying and giving in marriage, [until the day when Noah entered the ark,] and they knew not until the flood came and took them all away.

> Then shall two be in the field; the one shall be taken, and the other left. Two women shall be grinding at the mill; the one shall be taken, and the other left. Watch, therefore; for ye know not what hour your Lord doth come, but know this, that *if the good man of the house had known in what watch the thief would come, he would have watched, and would not have suffered his house to be broken up.*

Others, even without the benefit of specific scriptural references, believed that the Conemaugh Valley disaster was a clear and present demonstration of the wrath of God. They were clear in their thinking that the failure of the valley's residents to live in a godly and holy manner had brought the ravages of a vengeful God upon them. Many accepted this explanation, because it at least provided some understandable reason for the most colossal event of their lifetime. From the numerous bars and saloons that dotted the valley to the houses of ill fame on Green and other local hillsides, one could find in the Conemaugh Valley numerous examples of wanton misconduct to support a wrath-of-God theory. However, by all accounts, such conduct was neither more nor less prevalent in Johnstown than anywhere else in the late Victorian era. In the aftermath of the flood, bars, saloons and houses of ill fame were among some of the first businesses to recover and reopen their doors to the public. The churches of Johnstown and vicinity, which in many cases suffered some of the heaviest losses as a result of the flood, required substantial time and effort to recover and rebuild. This difference in the recovery rate of the seemingly holy and the unholy caused one survivor to concluded that if the flood was in fact God's way of punishing the unholy of the Conemaugh Valley, his aim was less than perfect.

Preachers in churches around the world used the events in Johnstown as an example for their congregations. The story of the great flood from which Noah and his family were spared was among the most common themes of sermons during the summer of 1889. In an article originally carried in the *Boston Herald* and later carried by the *Johnstown Tribune* in its July 6, 1889 edition, the residents of the flooded district were complimented for their lack of superstitious pondering, which the writer believed hindered the victims of the great biblical flood.

> The splendid energy with which the surviving population of Johnstown has risen to the height of the awful occasion, the marvelous self-control exhibited, the devotion of those who lost their all in family and property to the needs of others, the lightening rapidity with which the humanity of the whole land has organized relief—all this is the grand modern interpretation of the story of the flood and ark of refuge, an

interpretation which rises mountains high above all that was possible to the superstitious generations who lived thousands and thousands of years ago.

Comparisons with the ancient disasters did not stop with the great flood. At least one writer for the *National Tribune* of Washington, D. C. placed the flood in some historical perspective declaring that it was far greater in all respects than the destruction of Pompeii 1,810 years earlier on August 24. The following passage is from an article that appeared in the June 6, 1889 edition of the *National Tribune*.

> To-day we shudder at a greater calamity than befell Pompeii. Vastly more human lives, and inconceivably more wealth than were destroyed by the Vesuvian eruption of 79 have been swept out of existence by the bursting of a dam which confined the waters of an artificial lake in the mountains of Pennsylvania. The flood has been more cruel than the wildest work of the pent-up fires which rage in the bowels of the earth. The awful spectacle, at which the world has shuddered for nearly 19 centuries, of a torrent of fire sweeping down a mountain-side, upon populous cities at its base, has at last been outdone by that of a deluge of mad waters rolling through a narrow gorge filled with people busy in all the vocations of life, hurling them by thousands into eternity in the twinkling of an eye, and spreading destruction over their smiling land.

Whether they actually did or not is anyone's guess, but there were numerous accounts of people who had dreams that foretold the events of May 31, 1889. By one account, a woman who lived with her husband in Johnstown's Kernville section had a dream that her husband was drowned by a great flood that came to Johnstown. Sharing her dream with a neighbor early on Friday, May 31, 1889, they both enjoyed a good laugh, at the expense of the abusive and demanding husband. By the end of the day, the dream had come true in all its tragic detail. The husband was claimed as one of the flood's victims, while the then-unburdened wife was spared.

The June 1 edition of the *Chicago Tribune* carried an account of the dream of a Richmond, Virginia minister that foretold the storms associated with the flooding through much of the middle Atlantic states in late May and early June 1889:

> The Rev. John Jasper, the famous colored preacher and author of the Jasperian theory that "the sun do move" is by today's events the greatest man in the world. According to the opinion of his followers he had a dream which, when he related it to the members of his congregation caused consternation among them. He said that he dreamed that seven terrible

storms would pass over the earth, that the lightening would flash, mutterings of thunder would be heard accompanied by storms of wind, rain, and hail, producing destruction in the land, that on the last day of May would be the final winding up with thunder, lightening, and a great fall of water, causing the waters in the rivers to overflow their banks and ships and steamers would go down in the mighty deep, carrying with them hundreds of souls.

While some were busy trying to explain why there was a flood, others focused their attention on seeking damages for the losses they suffered. Although they were at best minimally successful, several lawsuits were brought against the Club and its members, and the Pennsylvania Railroad. The destruction of the Conemaugh Valley was unprecedented, the Club's members were among the wealthiest men in the world, and almost everyone agreed that the waters of Lake Conemaugh caused most of the damage and destruction wrought on the Conemaugh Valley. It came as no great surprise that lawsuits were filed. However, the ease with which these suits were dispensed, producing very limited settlements, was not much of a shock either. The total holdings of the Club were purposefully limited and they were encumbered with debt that reduced them even further. In the face of the tragic loss of life and property, the holdings and assets of the South Fork Fishing and Hunting Club were a pitiful trifling by comparison. Efforts to seek reimbursement and damages from the Club and its members were further complicated by the fact that the responsibility of individual members was so remote that individual suits were quite obviously a waste of time and legal fees.

The following is a brief sampling of information found regarding legal efforts to secure damages as a result of the Johnstown Flood. This summary is a conglomeration of information drawn from numerous sources. It is certain that this is not a complete listing of legal actions taken against the Club, its members and the Pennsylvania Railroad. It is equally certain that this information is neither complete nor irrefutable in all details. No single source included all of the cases mentioned and various sources provided conflicting information about the individual cases. In addition to the legal actions outlined below, there were numerous rumors and reports of suits that either were or were going to be filed.

Unlike today, court records and accounts of legal proceedings from this era were not well kept and many that were have either been destroyed or lost. For example the records of the firm of Knox and Reed, the legal council for the failed South Fork Fishing and Hunting Club, were lost when their offices were moved to a new complex in Pittsburgh in 1917. As a result court proceedings and court records are at best sketchy. The value of the following summary is that it offers an overview of the types of cases filed against the Club, its members and the Pennsylvania Railroad, and the very limited settlements produced.

In 1889, Nancy W. Little, on behalf of herself and her eight children, sued the South Fork Fishing and Hunting Club for $50,000 for the loss of her husband, John A. Little. Mrs. Little charged the Club with negligence. A Pittsburgh court found in favor of the Club, which had entered a plea of not guilty based on the presumption that the flood had been an act of God. Little was a traveling salesman who was killed in the collapse of the Hulbert House.

In that same year, a group of Johnstown businessmen decided to file suit against the Club for damages and loss of property. John P. Linton and W. Horace Rose were retained to investigate the prospects of a successful case. Nearly two years later the case was dropped since the lawyers had determined that any case against the Club would be unsuccessful. Linton and Rose received $1,000 for their services. This suit was opened again in 1891 and some additional funds were raised to finance its prosecution. The businessmen also selected new legal council. A suit then being brought by Jacob Strayer, another local businessman, prompted this second action. Three years later the suit was again dropped and the remainder of the money the participants had gathered for both of their legal efforts, which was by then less than $300, was donated to the fund for the Conemaugh Valley Memorial Hospital.

Farney S. Tarbell brought suit against the Pennsylvania Railroad in 1889 for the deaths of his wife and three children, all passengers on the *Day Express*. They included his wife, a seven-year old daughter named Grave, a daughter named Bertie who was five, and a two-year-old son named Howard. Tarbell charged the railroad with negligence in the deaths of his family members. The railroad was acquitted of any wrongdoing. The following year, J. L. (or J. J.) Long of Philadelphia filed suit against the Pennsylvania Railroad for the loss of his luggage on the *Day Express*. In April 1891, the court returned a verdict of not guilty since the flood had been an act of God.

Two years after the flood, Jacob Strayer, a local lumber dealer initially filed suit for $80,000, which he reportedly later raised to $200,000, against the Club for damages he suffered. The Strayer case was moved first to Armstrong County and finally to Lycoming County. Colonel W. D. Moore of Pittsburgh, who died in the midst of the action, represented Strayer. Hearing nothing of his case for some years, Strayer himself investigated only to learn that the case had been settled out of court for $500, which Moore kept for himself, having never reported the settlement to his client. The source of the $500 payment, if in fact it ever was made, is not known. Strayer was successful in having the case reopened, but his own bankruptcy and the insolvency of the Club precluded any further actions on the part of the court. Along with his suit against the Club, Strayer had also filed suit against Colonel Unger individually. Unger's residency in Cambria County may well explain why he was singled out for this individual suit. The suit against Unger produced no results for Strayer. At the same time the Strayer suit was reportedly filed, Mr. Leakey, another flood victim of Johnstown, filed suit through W. D. Moore against the Club. No damages were recovered in this suit.

In 1892, Lang, Bernheimer and Company of Philadelphia sued the Pennsylvania Railroad for the loss of ten barrels of whiskey that the railroad was transporting on May 31, 1889. According to the charges filed, the conductor simply turned his back when locals broke into the car where the whiskey was being stored. A court found in favor of Lang, Bernheimer and Company. In 1894, the Club was found not guilty in a suit brought by James and Ann Jenkins for $25,000 as a result of the drowning of Mrs. Jenkins's father, mother and brother. The Jenkins were backed by a group of businessmen from Youngstown, Ohio. The decision of the federal district court of Pittsburgh was in favor of the Club, which had pleaded not guilty to the charges.

In 1896, the supreme court of Illinois found in favor of a plaintiff who argued that the Pennsylvania Railroad was negligent in the loss of his luggage, even though the flood was an act of God. The court found in favor of the plaintiff based on the assertion that they had placed the passenger's baggage in a position where it was ultimately destroyed.

For all of the legal efforts against the Club, no damages, other than possibly the $500 reportedly paid to Strayer's attorney, were ever paid by the Club or any of its members. From the above summary, the only successful lawsuits were those brought against the Pennsylvania Railroad for the loss of some luggage and the loss of ten barrels of whiskey.

By today's standards of legal practice and mountains of established past legal precedent, it is difficult to imagine that no successful legal actions were brought against the Club or its individual members. For the Club members, it appears as though when the dam failed their relationship to the Club basically ended, as did their responsibility for what had happened. Not totally unlike the survivors of the flood, the typical Club member simply put the incident behind and got on with life. When the lack of successful legal action is today questioned, it is essential to consider that the flood took place in an entirely different time. Attitudes toward basic human relations, individual rights, legal practice, and individual and group liability were not like they are today.

Martha Frick Symington Sanger, a great-granddaughter of Henry Clay Frick, is typical of many descendents of Club members. It was not until 1990, while deeply involved in research for a book on her famous great-grandfather that she first became aware of his membership in the South Fork Fishing and Hunting Club and thus his relationship to the failure of its dam. As she pointed out in an interview in 2001, "I had never before even known that he had any relationship to the Johnstown Flood. This was not something ever discussed in my family."

In speaking of the relationship between the Club members and the disaster that struck Johnstown, Mrs. Sanger does not believe that the Club or its members would today be able to avoid at least some share of responsibility for the death and destruction that the waters of Lake Conemaugh brought to the Conemaugh Valley. "Things are different now and they would simply have had to assume some level of responsibility. However, when you look at an historic event you must look at it through the eyes of that time, this is indeed the case with responsibility for the Johnstown Flood. They were living at a time when such responsibility was at best remote."

Even before the mud had been cleared from Main Street, the great Johnstown Flood of 1889 had become a major attraction. Newspaper accounts provided daily coverage of the greatest story of the day, but there was so much more to the story than the newspapers could even begin to offer. The public's interest had been piqued and they wanted more. Artist conceptions illustrated many of the initial stories that were filed. Hundreds and hundreds of photographs were taken throughout the flooded district, as soon as photographers with their cumbersome cameras and gangly tripods could make their way into Johnstown. The images of Johnstown were captivatingly real and many promoters were more than willing to use them to turn public interest and curiosity into cash. Photographic images from the flooded district were used to illustrate numerous books written about the flood, to produce stereoscopic (double-image) cards for stereoscope viewers, to create glass slides for stereopticons (also known as magic lanterns), to produce framable prints and to create an endless array of postal cards.

The rush to retell the story of Johnstown's great flood generated a flurry of book publications. Many of the early chronicles of the flood were quickly seen for what they were, a care-less rush to get a book in print before public interest faded. Many of the early books written about the flood carry stories and retell accounts that are based on rumor, conjecture and pure imagination rather than documented fact. Those who avoided the mad rush to get to press in favor of careful research and accurate retelling of events generated some excellent works that today form the basis of what is known and believed to be true about the Johnstown Flood. Two examples of these benchmark publications are *The Story of Johnstown* by J. J. McLaurin, which was first published in 1889, and Reverend David J. Beale's *Through the Johnstown Flood by A Survivor*, which was published in 1890.

Many companies, including Strohmeyer & Wyman Publishers, The New York View Company, George Barker of Niagara Falls, Kilburn Brothers, R. K. Bonine, and Webster & Albee produced cards for stereoscopes by the thousands. Underwood and Underwood of New York was an early leader in the development, production, and marketing of stereoscopes for home and school use. They also marketed a wide variety of individual and series views for their scopes. Scenes from Johnstown helped to popularize the stereoscope and are yet today part of many stereoscopic view collections.

The magic lantern was an early slide projector that permitted images to be projected on a wall or screen by passing a source of light through a glass slide which held an image. The story of the Johnstown Flood quickly became the topic of both traveling and permanent magic lantern shows. Dr. Poland, the Johnstown dentist who lost both of his sons in the flood, was one of many individuals who took to the road promoting such a slide show. The July 9, 1889 edition of the *Johnstown Tribune* carried a brief notice about the show with which Dr. Poland was associated:

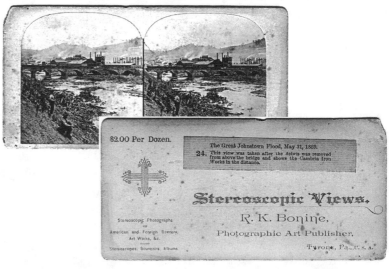

This stereoscopic card was produced by R. K. Bonine and shows a view of the Stone Bridge.

Messrs. Reuben M. Linton, S. C. Poland, and Otto Kopelin have started on the road with a stereopticon exhibition of the Johnstown flood. They gave a couple of entertainments at the P. R. R. station before leaving. The views are said to be good. Mr. Linton will do the talking and Messrs. Poland and Kopelin will run the machine. They will likely have a rich harvest.

Well into the 20th century, many amusement parks featured Johnstown Flood attractions. Generally, these were collections of still photographs, magic lantern images, hand-held stereoscope booths, collections of artifacts, and scale model demonstrations of the terrible wave. In her 1936 book, Gertrude Quinn Slattery described a visit she had made to such an attraction at Coney Island:

> At Coney Island more than twenty-five years ago, I saw a reproduction of the flood in miniature, which was at that time the best paying attraction at that resort. Many friends have told me of their seeing it, and how they sat enthralled as the barker led them word by word to the rush of gallons of water, and then capped the climax of his speech with the now famous line: "My God! The dam has burst."

Another use of the many photographic images of the flooded district was the production of prints suitable for framing. Such prints were available for sale, while others were given as advertising or as promotional items. At a time when cameras were not common household items, such frame-ready prints allowed private individuals to have permanent reminders of the scenes in and around Johnstown.

Songs and poems about the flood were numerous. P. R. McCargo & Company of Boston, Massachusetts copyrighted and published a song entitled "The Johnstown Flood" in 1889. Alberto Rivieri wrote the sheet music for this song, which was illustrated for piano. Rivieri's work was "respectfully dedicated to the sufferers." Another example of music inspired by the flood was a work by William Thomas entitled "That Valley of Tears." Copyrighted in 1890, the piece was arranged for piano and orchestra. Thomas dedicated his work to posterity.

The number of poems written with the flood as the main topic was seemingly endless. Virtually anyone who fancied him or herself a poet and could rhyme some lines seized the opportunity to chronicle and recount the main events of Johnstown's disaster. Far too numerous to mention individually, one poem does seem to stand above the rest as far as initial impact, popularity, and ultimate longevity. The poem, entitled *The Price of South Fork Fish*, written by Isaac G. Reed in 1889, left no doubt in the mind of the reader who Reed blamed for the calamity that befell the Conemaugh Valley:

(A)

(B)

(C)
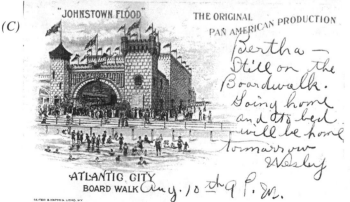

(D)

These are postcards featuring four prominent Johnstown Flood amusement park attractions. They are (A) Paragon Park at Nantasket Beach, Massachusetts, (B) White City in Chicago, (C) Atlantic City in New Jersey, and (D) Coney Island, New York.

JOHNSTOWN—VIEW OF MAIN STREET, FROM CORNER OF CLINTON, LOOKING SOUTH.

This view is taken from the roof of the building on southwest corner of Main and Clinton streets. Next to that building on the north stood the Hurlburt House, of which only the debris remains; but from that point south was a block or more of brick buildings, which stemmed the flood, and here the debris of the wooden structures carried down from above is piled to the second story, as shown in the picture.

The People's Tea Company of Allentown, Pennsylvania gave this print, which originally measured slightly more than 10 x 12 inches. The inscription on the back of the print reads, "From the People's Tea Co., 808 Hamilton Street, Allentown, PA. Beautiful Presents given away, we have our own hot air steam coffee roaster." A signature below the inscription reads, "M. F. Schrieber."

Many thousand human lives—
Butchered husbands, slaughtered wives.
    Mangled daughters, bleeding sons,
    Hosts of martyred little ones
(Worse than Herod's awful crime.)
Sent to heaven before their time;
    Lovers burnt and sweethearts drowned,
    Darlings lost but never found!
All the horrors that hell could wish,
    Such was the price that was paid for—fish!
    A dam which vomited a flood
Of water turning into blood;
    A deafening, rumbling groaning roar
    That ne'er was heard on earth before;
A maddening whirl, a leap a dash—
    And then a crash—and then a crash—
    A wave that carried off a town—
    A blow that knocked a city down.
All the horrors that hell could wish,
Such was the price that was paid for—fish!
An hour of flood, a night of flame,
A week of woe without a name—
    A week when sleep, with hope had fled,
    While misery hunted for its dead;
A week of corpses by the mile,
One-long, long week without a smile,
    A week whose tale no tongue can tell,
    A week without a parallel!
All the horrors that hell could wish,
Such was the price that was paid for—fish!

Thomas D. Reindollar of Taneytown, Maryland penned a poem that he titled *The Famous Flood of 1889.* Published on the front page of the *Gettysburg Star and Sentinel* on Tuesday, May 27, 1890, it focused more on the pathetic nature of the human tragedy of the event rather than affixing blame. Like many others who tried to tell the story of Johnstown's flood in poetic verse, Reindollar employed graphic detail at the expense of historical accuracy. The following passages from Reindollar's poem illustrate this approach:

Shortly after this was spoken and the waters died
    away,
Stout ruffians from the mountains came; but had not
    long to stay.
They tore the rings and jewels from the corpses lying
    there;
And even amputated hands and flung them in the air.
On seeing this the gallant men uninjured by the
    wave—
Perchance to do this labor—laid each tyrant in his
    grave.
They hanged them on the trees that shade the narrow
    Conemaugh,
And pierced their frames with leaden balls from sole
    of foot to jaw.

The Johnstown Flood has been mentioned in countless feature movies and has been the topic of a number of historical shorts or summaries of natural disasters. In 1946 a Mighty Mouse cartoon feature entitled *The*

Johnstown Flood pitted Mighty Mouse against the ravages of the flood wave that struck Johnstown. The flood has been used as a poignant reference to great natural tragedies, as a comparison or known point of reference when referring to great amounts of water, and even as a comedic response or as part of humorous one-liners. One of the better known one-liners also appeared for many years as a sign in bars and saloons when chewing tobacco was popular. It read, "Don't spit on the floor. Remember the Johnstown Flood!"

One of the earliest attempts to make a feature-length movie about the flood produced the film *The Johnstown Flood*. Billed as "a thrilling epic drama" the film was just that—a drama. Historically inaccurate in most of its storyline and detail, the silent film nonetheless captured considerable attention when it was released in 1924.

The setting of the movie is Johnstown. Ward Peyton is the general manager of the Hamilton Lumber Company and John Hamilton is the owner. The lumber company is located in Conemaugh. Gloria, played by Florence Gilbert, is the niece of the owner and is engaged to be married to Tom O'Day. O'Day, played by George O'Brien, is employed by Hamilton as an engineer. O'Day recognizes that the dam of the lumber company, high above Johnstown, is unsafe. He warns Peyton, his fiancée's uncle, in no uncertain terms. "Peyton, one real downpour will rip out this mass of mud—and everybody knows it!" Even though he shares his concerns with both Peyton and Hamilton, nothing is done.

Anna, the daughter of one of the other workers at the mill, is secretly in love with O'Day. On the day that O'Day and Gloria are to be married, Anna recognizes

During the era of silent films and even after sound was added to movies, black and white stills that depicted specific movie scenes were often featured in movie lobbies. In this scene, Florence Gilbert is seen kissing her soon-to-be husband, George O'Brien.

that the dam is about to break because of a sudden rainstorm. She rides toward Johnstown warning everyone she encounters. She arrives at the church just in time to tell those in attendance and proverbially "saves the day" before the flood claims her as one of its victims. Hamilton, returning by train from out of town is drowned as his train passes in front of the dam just as it fails. The final subtitle of the movie recognizes the fortitude of the survivors of the real Johnstown Flood. "Time softens tragedy—toil overcame desolation—Johnstown was built anew—a lasting tribute to the dauntless courage of its citizens."

Why this movie was so historically remote from the real events of the Johnstown Flood has never been fully explained. One theory holds that the producers of the film were not as concerned with accuracy as they were capitalizing on public interest in the actual event. Another theory is that the production company did not wish to place themselves in a situation where high-profile, former members of the Club could bring charges of libel against them. For example, at the time the movie was released, Andrew William Mellon, a former member of the South Fork Fishing and Hunting Club, was the United States Secretary of the Treasury, under president Calvin Coolidge.

In 1989, The Academy of Motion Picture Arts and Sciences presented the Academy Award for "Best Documentary Short Subject" to the film *The Johnstown Flood*, produced by Charles Guggenheim. The film, which draws on a wide variety of reliable accounts of the events on and following May 31, 1889, presents an authentic and historically articulate picture of the story

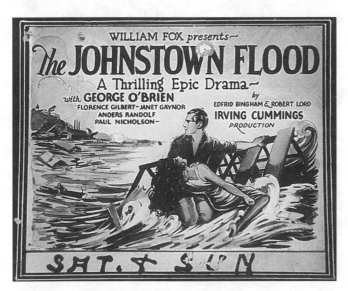

In the days of silent films, glass slides were used to announce coming attractions. This slide announced the coming of the movie The Johnstown Flood *to moviegoers in 1924.*

of the Johnstown Flood. It also provides a glimpse into life in Johnstown during the Victorian era and at the South Fork Fishing and Hunting Club. Using the resources of numerous collections, the film stands as the best filmed portrayal of the story.

Penny postal cards had become very popular during the late 19th century. They provided a quick means of communicating a message, while sending along a particular picture or view. Postal cards featuring scenes related to the Johnstown Flood became very common. Cards could be purchased individually or as a series. The first cards produced following the flood were in black and white, but in time color was added to the scenes.

❖   ❖   ❖   ❖

As Johnstown recovered, the need for outside relief diminished. In some cases, determining exactly when to pull out became difficult for certain relief groups, even though they had been most earnestly needed when they first arrived in the flooded district. The work of the Red Cross, for example, was invaluable and received the utmost praise and appreciation from the sufferers of Johnstown. Among the most appreciated, tangible, and visible of their initiatives were the Red Cross hotels. As the recovery efforts continued during the late summer

and fall of 1889, the Red Cross hotels provided accommodations and a sense of stability in what would have otherwise been utter turmoil for many families. However, as winter approached, the once welcome Red Cross hotel on Locust Street was no longer serving the purpose for which it was built. Many of those who had earlier called it home, had relocated to more permanent quarters. Miss Barton had in most cases hand selected those who were accommodated at the Red Cross hotels, and after she left Johnstown there was no well-defined plan to fill the vacancies created when the original guests moved on. The building quickly began showing signs of rapid deterioration and the clientele was causing their own special concerns among the locals.

Since the rector, Rev. Alonzo P. Diller, his wife, Marion, their son, Isaac, and their daughter Lola had all perished in the flood, Bishop Cortland Whitehead assumed responsibility for the property where Saint Mark's Episcopal Church had stood on Locust Street and where the first of the Red Cross hotels was built. In a letter to Miss Barton dated December 11, 1889, the Bishop agreed with the decision that the Red Cross hotel should be removed. He had written to Miss Barton earlier and she had returned a reply to his first letter on December 5. In his second letter, the Bishop explained why he thought the removal of the hotel was indeed

These four postal card views are representative of the type of cards that were produced following the flood.

appropriate at that time, and he offered to either purchase the lumber used in the hotel or purchase the hotel and reclaim the lumber when the church had it tore down. The following is a passage from the second letter from Bishop Whitehead to Miss Barton:

Shady Side Pittsburg Penn.
Dec. 11, 1889

My Dear Miss Barton:

Thank you very much for your letter of Dec. 5. It answers most of my questions very clearly, but not all. However, your determination to remove the building shortly meets the case, I think very well. Since I wrote you I have heard more with regard to the condition of affairs, and I believe that it would be much better to have the building come down. It has much degenerated from its first purpose. There have been several disturbances within and about it at night. It has been the stopping place for strolling bands of players and minstrels who have lately come to Johnstown, and I hear that the popular name for it is "The bummers retreat." Altogether I have felt considerable anxiety about it as being identified so closely with our property, and especially since we have put up a little chapel in close proximity to it. So I am quite sure that its demolition will be no detriment to the good work of the Red Cross Association amongst the people.

The massive debris field left behind after the floodwaters subsided was a filthy, bothersome impediment in the eyes of most. To others it was a treasure field laden with trinkets and relics ripe for the picking. Buttons, tableware, household knickknacks and coins were but a few of the items relic hunters collected from among the mud-packed mounds of debris that were everywhere in and around the flooded district. The incentive for collecting such relics went far beyond personal interest. There was a quick and strong demand for such items, which created a lively market. Some of the first businesses to spring up were small booths for the selling of flood relics. The simple desire to have something from the area to serve as a reminder of the colossal event, or something to carry away by which to remember one's visit and later share with others, supported such trade for many months. To this very day, there remains an active interest in the buying and selling of Johnstown Flood trinkets and flood-related items.

Many Johnstown families did not have to search for relics or mementos to serve as reminders of the flood. Instead, what little they had left served as a vivid reminder of what they had lost and the peril they had been through. In many families these flood relics have been cherished heirlooms for generations. An example of such a family heirloom is the pair of shoes worn by two-year-old Julia Ruth Haselbauer on May 31, 1889.

Dated 1812, this one penny coin carries the inscription "Rolling Mills At Walthamstow." It was probably a piece of company currency. The back of the coin, which had obviously been ground smooth carries the inscription "Relic Johnstown Flood May 31st 1889."

The Haselbauers lived in Woodvale at the time of the flood. Joseph Haselbauer was a laborer for Cambria Iron. He lived with his wife, Lucinda, and four daughters. Julia had a twin sister named Rosie and two older sisters, Clara and Mary. As the floodwaters approached Woodvale, Julia was among many who scampered up the hillside to escape the rising tide. She was wearing a long print dress, a light blue bonnet, and a pair of black shoes. Her outfit was kept and later handed down to her children. It was recently donated to the Johnstown Flood Museum, where it is a valued part of their permanent collection.

The numerous books, articles, newspaper accounts, reports and summaries written about the Johnstown Flood of 1889 tell the stories of many of those who were directly affected by the great flood. However, because

These are the shoes worn by two-year-old Julia Ruth Haselbauer on May 31, 1889. Her son, John H. Hershiser of Johnstown, donated them and the clothes his mother was wearing to the Johnstown Flood Museum in 2000.

of the overwhelming number of stories it was not possible to record them all. As a result many accounts of flood experiences have survived as family stories, passed from one generation to the next as oral histories or brief accounts recorded in family Bibles.

One such verbal account was that provided by Russell Croyle. Born in 1880, he was nine years old at the time of the flood. He lived with his parents in Yoder Township. Their home was beyond the reach of the floodwaters on May 31. Members of their extended family were not nearly so fortunate. In a taped discussion with his son, Paul, in 1972, Mr Croyle recalled, "I had some relatives who went through it." He spoke of two uncles and their families who lived in the flooded district. They were George Palmer and Robert Potter.

The Palmers and the Potters shared a double house on Somerset Street. Mr. Croyle's most vivid recollection was of the heroic efforts of his Uncle George to save himself and his family. "George Palmer was hurt in the flood. He was trying to save them [his wife and children], when they got away from him. He got hurt some way or another. He never did get straighten up after it." *The Johnstown Directory*, published by C. B. Clark shortly after the flood indicated that there were six people living in the Palmer house at the time of the flood, five of whom survived. Three people lived in the Potter home, and they all survived.

One of the most notable and recognizable flood relics of Johnstown is Morley's Dog. The 700-pound figure of a French bloodhound has for years been believed by many to be a statue placed to honor heroic dogs credited with saving lives during the flood. Such is not the case. The dog was a lawn ornament that stood on the front lawn of the James Morley residence located on the lower end of Main Street. The flood wave carried the K-9 statue to a pile of debris downstream. The Morley mansion survived the flood, so the figure of the dog was later retrieved and returned to the front lawn where it remained for several years. Years later it was moved to a new home built by Mr. Morley in Westmont Borough. When Mr. Morley died, the statue was again moved to Mrs. Morley's daughter's home on Palliser Street in Upper Yoder Township. In 1944 the statue was donated to the City of Johnstown for permanent display in a city park.

Morley's Dog was one of several items pulled from the debris of the flood only to become relics of conspicuous public interest. Another of these flood relics was the first steel converter vessel used in Johnstown. William Kelly reportedly built the vessel. Kelly claimed to be the inventor of the Bessemer process for the production of steel. According to those who could still recall the early days of steel-making experimentation at the

Contrary to popular belief, Morley's dog was not created to honor heroic dogs of the Johnstown Flood. It is however, a relic of the flood that was reclaimed from amidst the field of debris below Main Street. Currently it stands along Main Street adjacent to City Hall.

Cambria Works, this vessel was used in tests conducted by Kelly in Johnstown, during the early days of the Civil War. From then until 1889 it had been just another piece of outdated equipment lying about the mills.

After the flood it was heaped on one of the many piles of scrap to be removed. However, recognizing its local historical significance, the management of the plant ordered that it be kept. The May 31, 1892 edition of the *Johnstown Tribune* reported that it had been "...mounted on a nicely-dressed base of stone and attracts much attention." The monument to early steel experimentation conducted by the Cambria Iron Company at their Johnstown plant was located in a small lawn near the Cambria Iron Company's general office.

At the time of the Johnstown Flood, Johnstown was a borough surrounded by several other boroughs. Each of the municipalities had its own government, its own taxing structure, provided its own services, had its own unique heritage and thus its own identity. There had long been a strong sense of local pride that thwarted periodic efforts to consolidate the boroughs into a single unified city. Following the flood there was a renewed effort to consolidate Johnstown and its surrounding boroughs. The whole area had faced a common disaster, shared common needs, and held common goals. As such, the relief efforts were directed at the community as a whole instead of the individual municipalities they had been prior to the flood. The flood had bound them together as they had never been before.

Authur J. Moxham was one of the community leaders who strongly backed efforts to consolidate and form a unified Johnstown. Moxham suggested that the old be put solidly in the past with a new, shared vision of the future. Moxham believed that part of the reason why the dangerous South Fork Dam had been allowed to loom so long as a threat to the Conemaugh Valley was because there was no single government body strong enough or sufficiently representative to force needed inspections and repairs. In his calls for consolidation, Moxham said that even the name Johnstown should be set aside. He suggested that the new city should be known as Conemaugh Valley.

During the fall of 1889, several meetings were held to bring the question of consolidation to the citizens in preparation for the fall elections. An announcement for one of the meetings was carried in the October 25, 1889 edition of the *Johnstown Tribune*. It was typical of the announcements for meetings throughout the flooded district on the question of consolidation.

ATTENTION CITIZENS!

The Citizens of Minersville and the
Public Generally

Are requested to meet at HOSE HOUSE,
Iron street, Millville Borough, on

MONDAY, OCT. 28th,
AT 7:30 O'CLOCK P.M.

For the purpose of listening to addresses from
A. J. MOXHAM, Esq., Col., J. P. LIN-
TON, and perhaps other distin-
guished citizens, on the

Question of Consolidation
And the Advantages which Would Result Therefrom.

MANY CITIZENS.

In the public elections held on November 6, 1889, the question of consolidation was put to the voters in Cambria City, Conemaugh, Coopersdale, East Conemaugh, Franklin, Grubbtown, Johnstown, Millville, Prospect, and Woodvale. Of the almost 3200 votes cast, more than 2500 favored consolidation. As a result of the vote, Cambria City, Conemaugh, Coopersdale, Grubbtown, Johnstown, Millville, Prospect, and Woodvale were to become the City of Johnstown. As a result of a later court decision, Coopersdale was denied admission because its boundaries did not adjoin those of the new city. The voters in East Conemaugh and Franklin did not support their consolidation with their municipal neighbors in 1889. The barriers that had long held the several boroughs apart had successfully been broken down.

Moxham's effort to consolidate the boroughs was successful, but his suggestion to change the name was not adopted. There was an identity and pride in the name Johnstown, with which the locals did not wish to part. The population of the new city was just under 23,000. W. Horace Rose and Henry Wilson Storey prepared the charter for Johnstown. On December 16, 1889 they went to Harrisburg, where Governor Beaver signed the charter on December 18, 1889. The city elected its first mayor and municipal officials on February 18, 1890. W. Horace Rose, a flood survivor, became Johnstown's first mayor. In a show of support for the town he would lead, Rose announced that he would rebuild his home along the lower end of Main Street, near where it had stood before the flood.

At the same time that the seven boroughs were working toward consolidation, several new communities were developing above the floodplain. Examples of these new communities were Daisytown at the upper end of the Frankstown Road, Moxham out along the Stony Creek, Ferndale perched on a hillside on the other side of the Stony Creek just beyond Moxham, Brownstown situated above Cambria City and Westmont atop Yoder Hill. Land was offered for sale in these new communities and there were many who welcomed the opportunity to get to locations that they felt would put them beyond the reach of future flooding and away from the noise and bustle of the downtown area.

W. Horace Rose was the first mayor of the city of Johnstown.

W. Horace Rose, the first mayor of the City of Johnstown, rebuilt his home along the lower end of Main Street in 1894. By rebuilding along Main Street, Rose clearly demonstrated his belief that the flood of 1889 was a most unusual occurrence and should not deter the rebuilding of homes and businesses in Johnstown. Many others believed as Rose did.

Of all of the suburbs that developed after the 1889 flood, Westmont was the one to attract the most interest and draw the most attention. Previously agricultural lands of the Cambria Iron Company, Westmont provided a beautiful setting, high above the floodplain and well beyond the smoke and noise of the valley below. Provisions were made to offer housing for both the working class and management. Charles Miller of Philadelphia developed the basic design of the new community. Miller was familiar with the area as he had been the designer of the Grandview Cemetery, part of which was located in Westmont. Lots in Westmont were offered for sale to the public beginning in October 1889. The following announcement appeared in the October 25, 1889 edition of the *Johnstown Tribune*:

WESTMONT !

Lots in the Village of Westmont
ARE NOW

FOR SALE

At Prices and upon Terms to suit every class of purchasers. The Map can be seen at the OFFICE OF WOOD, MORRELL & CO., LIMITED, every Forenoon, and at GRANDVIEW every Afternoon.

CAMBRIA IRON COMPANY

Johnstown, Pa., Oct. 25, 1889

One of the initial complications or barriers to the settlement of Westmont was getting there. A reliable system of transportation was essential. Roads that wound up to the new mountain top community, which was originally called Tip Top, were steep, dangerous, and frequently impassable in bad weather. Sales of lots in Westmont were very slow at first. To make their new model community more readily accessible, Cambria Iron created the Cambria Inclined Plane Company, with a charter of incorporation signed by the Secretary of the Commonwealth on September 6, 1889. Samuel Diescher of Pittsburgh, a well-known designer of inclined railways was retained to develop the design. He had been involved in the development of an inclined plane in Cincinnati, Ohio, and three such railways in Pittsburgh. Diescher was also responsible for the design of many of the mechanical parts of the giant wheel ride created by G. W. G. Ferris for the Chicago World's Fair held in 1892-1893.

The work of building the inclined plane up the side of Yoder Hill began on May 1, 1890. By the time the inclined plane opened for business on June 1, 1891, it had cost an estimated $133,000. Situated 502 feet above Johnstown, the top of the inclined plane stands 1,693.5 feet above sea level. The inclined plane has two sets of tracks that permit both of the cars to run simultaneously. One car makes the trip from Westmont to Johnstown, while the other car makes the trip from Johnstown to Westmont.

With the inclined plane in operation, sales of lots in Westmont grew rapidly. By 1892, the decision was made to formally separate the new community from Upper Yoder Township of which it had formerly been a part. On June 13, 1892, the community of Westmont was granted a borough charter. In 1890 the residents of Westmont numbered less than 50, but by the close of 1892 that number was approaching 500. Westmont was one of the earlier successful suburban developments in the United States and quickly became a model for future suburban developments throughout the country.

Johnstown's first public hospital was yet another of the positive developments that followed the great flood of 1889. The hospital of the Cambria Iron Company on Prospect Hill had been the only such facility in the area up to that time. The medical needs in the several boroughs were met by a number of local doctors and surgeons engaged in the private practice of medicine. Following the flood, the need for a public hospital was recognized and steps were taken to fulfill the need.

One of the key leaders in the movement to establish a public hospital in Johnstown was Dr. Pancoast of the Philadelphia chapter of the Red Cross. Gaining the support of Mayor Fitler of Philadelphia, Pancoast brought

One of the initial areas of the village of Westmont to be developed was in the vicinity of Tioga Street and Bucknell Avenue. This view, taken in 1894, shows some of the earlier development of the area.

At the time of the 1889 flood, the only hospital in Johnstown was the Cambria Iron hospital on Prospect Hill.

The inclined plane was originally powered by a giant steam engine. The smokestack can be seen rising above the power plant of the inclined plane to the left of the top terminal. The length of the track is slightly more than 867 feet.

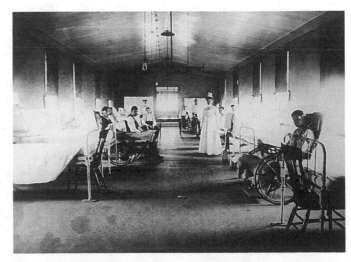

This is an interior view of the Cambria Iron hospital on Prospect Hill. When the Red Cross arrived in Johnstown, this was the facility where they first established themselves.

a $10,000 allocation from Philadelphia for such a hospital in Johnstown. The Cambria County Medical Society appointed a committee of its members to assist with the development of a hospital in Johnstown. Land was secured on what was known as Toss' Meadow, and during the late fall of 1889 a charter of incorporation was created for the Conemaugh Valley Memorial Hospital. In 1890, the Johnstown Flood Relief Commission provided $40,000 in support of the project. With that money a contract to build the hospital was granted to Jacob J. Strayer in February 1891.

Almost exactly a year later, on February 4, 1892, the hospital was dedicated. The property was transferred by James B. Scott, a key leader in Johnstown's initial recovery efforts, to Dr. George W. Wagoner, representing the Conemaugh Valley Memorial Hospital. At the ceremonies, future governor Hastings represented the commonwealth, and Mayor Rose represented the city of Johnstown. Hastings said as part of his remarks, "The dedication of this great hospital, I presume, is the last official act in the drama of death and resurrection." In its first year of operations, the Conemaugh Valley Memorial Hospital, a sixty-bed facility cared for 154 patients whose average stay was 34 days.

A bronze tablet that is still on the front of the hospital reads:

FEBRUARY 4, 1892
THIS HOSPITAL ERECTED BY
THE FLOOD COMMISSION
FROM THE RELIEF FUND
IS A MEMORIAL OF THE
SPONTANEOUS BENEFICENCE
EXTENDED BY THE CIVILIZED
WORLD TO THE PEOPLE OF THE
CONEMAUGH VALLEY IN THEIR
TIME OF TERRIBLE CALAMITY.

Following the flood, the bodies of the victims were interred in several local cemeteries, while others were carried back to many hometowns for burial. Of all of the local cemeteries, the relatively new Grandview Cemetery located high above Johnstown on Yoder Hill, was the final resting place of the largest number of the 2,209 victims. There are many individual and family plots identified with names that would forever be linked to the story of Johnstown and its great flood. However, most notable among the burial plots in Grandview is the massive section that was set aside as a final resting place for the unknown dead.

The unknown plot, which measures approximately 20,000 square feet, was purchased with funds from the Johnstown Flood Relief Commission. Many of the unknown bodies had been temporarily interred in the days and weeks following the flood in make shift gravesites. The decision to exhume and remove these bodies to a single location was prompted by the desire to provide more fitting and permanent burials. It was also felt that by exhuming and relocating the bodies that had been hastily buried, there was a chance that more would be identified. As noted in the May 31, 1892 edition of the *Johnstown Tribune* "...thirty-six bodies were thus identified and now repose in their own family plots—...." The majority of the reburials in Grandview were accomplished during late summer and early fall of 1889.

Efforts to identify bodies were earnestly carried out by the morticians who had answered the call for help in Johnstown, the clergy of the area, and family members in search of loved ones. These efforts continued during the reburial process. However, to one man, John Murtha of Pittsburgh, fell the gruesome responsibility of viewing the unknown dead and creating a careful record of the unidentified bodies. Entries were made into a journal providing as much information as was available for each of the numbered bodies. His giant journal, which is still part of the archival collection at the Grandview Cemetery, provided information that permitted several bodies to be identified. The records kept by Murtha indicate that he viewed 747 bodies or portions of bodies.

Under the handwritten heading "Description of the Unidentified Dead buried at Grand View," the following are the first and last entries made during Murtha's survey of the unidentified dead moved to Grandview Cemetery:

The original Conemaugh Valley Memorial Hospital was established as a living memorial to all who went through the terrible calamity of the Great Johnstown Flood of 1889.

1. Boy, about 12 years old, height 4 ft. light brown hair, rather long, one back tooth missing in lower left jaw.
      Wore a blue calico waist [shirt], black knee pants, & black coat, well worn button shoes

747. Children, Remains of 2 children, no descriptions possible—cotton undershirt, black & blue barred flannell skirt, black ribbed cotton hose, Elastic garters, & childs Spring heel button Shoes

Entries in the book also indicate those who were later identified. For example, body number 717 was later identified at that of John R. Day, one of the passengers killed on the *Day Express*. His body was exhumed and returned to his home in Prospect, Maryland to be buried alongside his daughter, who also perished on board the *Day Express*. (See story in Chapter 4.) The following is the description provided for body 717:

717. Man, large, height about 5 ft 11 inches, Sandy hair mixed with gray, moustache & Beard the Same, Wore corkscrew vets, & black cloth pants, white cauton [cotton] flannell underwear, Lay down collar, cuff Buttons in Shirt Sleeves, found in Conemaugh River near Company Store, Nov 24,
      (Below this entry written in red ink was the notation)
      Identified as John R. Day, (Removed)

On May 31, 1892, the unidentified plot and the Monument of Tranquility that stands before it were formally dedicated. With ceremonies that attracted a crowd estimated anywhere between five and twelve thousand, the silent sufferers of the 1889 horror were remembered and memorialized. A total of 777 white stone markers had initially been placed in the plot of the unknown. In the book *Grandview Cemetery Johnstown Pennsylvania An Historical Overview from 1885*, published by the Citizens' Cemetery Association in 1995, it is noted that "...there were not quite a full 777 bodies buried in the plot; someone had decided to set out a few extra stones just to make an even pattern." In the *Johnstown Tribune's* account of the activities on May 31, 1892, it was noted that, "The number of unknown including the one found last week, is 770." Up to the Saturday prior to the dedication ceremony, 1,965 interments, exclusive of the unknown dead, had been made at Grandview. The first was that of the remains of Mrs. Calvin (Lucretia) Hammond of Kernville, buried on April 30, 1887.

Those responsible for the creation of the unknown plot determined that this "City of the Dead" should be appropriately marked. Funds were provided by several of the flood committees that had a remaining balance. Money raised from the sale of articles of value recovered from the debris that were unclaimed for a year or more and money from the Johnstown Flood Relief Commission was also used to help fund a monument to the unidentified dead of the flood. The Monument of Tranquility, made of Vermont and Rhode Island granite, stands 21 feet high and weighs approximately 35 tons. The basic design of the monument is a sarcophagus. Three life-size figures on the monument portray Faith, Hope and Charity. The inscription on the monument reads: TO THE MEMORY OF THE UNIDENTIFIED DEAD LOST BY THE FLOOD OF MAY 31, 1889. Mr. J. L. Smith of Johnstown designed and erected the monument.

Regardless of the exact number, the unidentified dead at Grandview may well be the most unfortunate of the flood's victims. Theirs was a different death in that it lacked the dignity of identity. Their passing was nameless, frequently faceless, and by necessity often viewed as an impersonal, numbered loss from a collective whole rather than the intimate loss of a cherished loved one.

The ceremonies to dedicate Grandview's unidentified plot and the Monument of Tranquility were planned for the third anniversary of the disaster. To the casual visitor on May 31, 1892, Johnstown was a recovered town. However, to those who had survived the ordeal of the recent past, the day was a reminder of what was for most the worst day in their lives. The lead story in the *Johnstown Tribune* for the Tuesday, May 31, 1892 edition described the perceptual difference between the visitors and the survivors in vivid terms:

To the eye of the casual onlooker there is little on the surface in the Johnstown of to-day to recall the ruin of the Johnstown of three years ago. Some of the flags that were hung out yesterday still float to-day, but they have no meaning in connection with this anniversary, except when at half-mast. Here and there mourning decorations are visible. Some business places are closed. In a few of the churches special requiem services attracted large congregations. Great crowds of people came in from the country adjacent to the city and from remoter points on the morning trains on the P. R. R. and B. & O., and many residents of the city were on the streets.

These unusual considerations would doubtless cause inquiry as to their meaning from an uninformed or unthinking visitor. One familiar with the circumstances would simply answer: "This is the third anniversary of the Great Conemaugh Valley Flood." That would tell the whole story, and the visitor would doubtless ejaculate "what a marvelous transformation," and the transformation, in a material point of view, is indeed marvelous, but there is no change in the hearts of the people. The whole picture of deso-

The Monument of Tranquility features two sitting figures representing Faith and Charity, and one standing figure representing Hope.

The Unidentified plot at Grandview Cemetery contains the remains of an estimated 771 individuals who perished in the flood of 1889. There were initially 777 stones in the plot, which was later increased to 816 to complete the last of the 16 rows of 51 stones per row.

lation is as vividly before them as it was the moment after the hand of fate had so mercilessly fashioned it. In every ear the flood is still roaring, and in every heart and every home there is the weight of a great sorrow, and so it will be while those live who were involved in the calamity on that dreadful day.

Some of the notables in attendance at the ceremonies at Grandview included the following:
- Pennsylvania Governor Robert Pattison,
- former Pennsylvania Governor James Beaver,
- Cambria County President Judge A. V. Barker of Ebensburg,
- Robert Pitcairn of the Pennsylvania Railroad,
- James B. Scott, of Pittsburgh, who had lead the Citizens' Relief Committee of Pittsburgh in Johnstown,
- S. S. Marvin and Reuben Miller, both members of the South Fork Fishing and Hunting Club who had contributed liberally of their time, talents and resources to the Johnstown relief efforts,

- Resident-Director McMillen of the Cambria Iron Company,
- W. Horace Rose, the Mayor of the City of Johnstown,
- Robert C. Ogden, one of the flood commissioners, led the Philadelphia delegation,
- and Dr. George W. Wagoner, the local physician designated as the Chief Marshall of the parade for that day.

Earlier in the day, several of the dignitaries who came to Johnstown were taken by carriage to inspect the new Memorial Hospital. After lunch, the parade formed along Main Street about 2:00 p.m. The line of march moved along Main to Franklin, to Morris, to South, to Grant, to the Cemetery Road and on to the cemetery. The march took approximately an hour. As the sun was bright with seasonally warm temperatures, many umbrellas were visible as shields from the sun.

Once at Grandview, the honored guests took their place on a grandstand at the western corner of the unidentified plot. Father Field of Boston offered the invocation, in the absence of Father Boyle of St. John's who was unable to attend. Mayor Rose had the honor of introducing Governor Pattison, who delivered the keynote address of the ceremonies. In his remarks, the governor recounted the vast relief efforts that came to Johnstown and vicinity from around the world. He complimented those who had worked so hard toward the goal of Johnstown's recovery. He said, "The City of Johnstown, the old City of Johnstown, fell before the flood; but the visitor to-day admires another and more beautiful city."

Regarding those whose lives were claimed by the flood, Pattison likened them to the woman mentioned in the Bible who brought a pot of alabaster ointment to Christ. He said:

> All local associations of that good woman have passed away. It would now be utterly impossible to find the place where this good deed was done. It is an "unknown" as are these dead who lie here before me; but the memory of her is as fresh and vigorous to-day in the hearts of the people who are in love with her humanity as though the most towering monument had been erected on the spot at the time she performed the act.

Following Pattison's remarks, Mayor Rose than introduced Mr. Ogden who addressed the audience. At the conclusion of Ogden's comments, the dignitaries gathered around the Monument of Tranquility. With the Mineral City Band playing in the background, the unveiling ceremony took place. Following the unveiling the program continued until shortly before 5:00 p.m.,

when the crowd dispersed and headed back down into town. In the eyes of Editor Swank of the *Johnstown Tribune* "the last public act in the tragedy," had finally been performed.

Reminders of the flood and the massive devastation left in its wake were found for years. The *Johnstown Tribune* periodically would report the discovery of skeletal remains in and around Johnstown. Two such incidents were reported in 1899. The remains of one body was discovered in late May during an excavation project on Napoleon Street, and in early June another set of remains were uncovered along the Conemaugh River by a Lower Yoder Township man digging for fishing worms. In 1911, skeletal remains were found on the Lempke property west of Seward. Although no one was absolutely certain, it was widely assumed that it was the body of a flood victim. By all accounts, it was the last body found. The remains found in 1911 were returned to Johnstown and buried in the unidentified plot at Grandview, bringing the total bodies buried there to 771.

In July 1998, during some construction excavation behind the former Glosser Brothers' Department Store across from Central Park, a deposit of bones and artifacts was uncovered. It was initially assumed that the remains were human and that the artifacts and bones were remnants of the 1889 flood. The story quickly attracted national attention. However, following forensic examination, the bones were determined to be animal remains not human.

Numerous efforts have been made to try and quantify the losses brought about by the Johnstown Flood. Numbers of bodies, destroyed businesses, shattered homes, huge investment losses, and even personal property damage were all reducible to statistical calculations. What has never been and will never be calculated, estimated, or even fathomed is the regrettable loss of human potential. It is not now and never will be possible to do more than consider what contributions those who died may have made. The potential that rested in each of those lost souls is most definitely the greatest of all losses. An example of that late nineteenth century potential can clearly be seen in the life of Victor George Heiser. (See story in Chapter 4.)

Born on February 5, 1873, Heiser survived the flood by clinging to a rooftop. His parents, who ran a store on Washington Street, both drowned. Having received his early education in Johnstown, Heiser went on to Jefferson Medical College in Philadelphia where he earned his medical degree in 1897. Following graduation he entered the Marine Hospital Service, which was the forerunner of the United States Public Health Service. In 1903 he went to the Philippines where he stayed until 1915. Following his time in the Philippines, he was

Dr. Victor George Heiser.

Following his death in New York City at the age of 99, the remains of Dr. Victor Heiser were returned to Johnstown's Grandview Cemetery for burial, near the gravesite of his parents, George and Mathilda. The epitaph on Dr. Heiser's gravestone defines his life in simple terms.

a member of the staff of the Rockefeller Foundation, he worked with the World Health Organization, he became the research director for the National Association of Manufacturers, and he organized the Leonard Wood Memorial for the Eradication of Leprosy. He also served as the first president of the International Leprosy Association between 1931 and 1938. Toward the end of his active career, he was one of the sponsors of the World Leprosy Day, February 16, 1969. In that same year he was given the Damien-Dutton Award in recognition of his life long work toward the eradication of leprosy.

In his obituary, which was reported in the February 28, 1972 edition of the *Johnstown Tribune-Democrat*, the magnitude of this one man's contribution and what the world would have missed had he not survived on May 31, 1889, were clearly evident:

> In his work with the Public Health Service, the World Health Organization and the Wood Memorial, Dr. Heiser pushed for the worldwide vaccination against leprosy and tuberculosis.
>
> When he left the Philippines, he was credited with reducing the death rate by 50,000 persons a year.

The last survivor of the Johnstown Flood of 1889, Frank Shomo, died on March 20, 1997. Shomo, who was born on February 20, 1889 in Indiana County, Pennsylvania, was just 100 days old on May 31, 1889. At the time of the flood, Shomo lived with his family in the small Indiana County community of Lockport in a house

that had been part of the old Main Line Canal System. Although he had no personal memories of the flood, he often recalled family stories about how his father pulled survivors from the river and how his mother took in homeless survivors to provide what comfort she could. Following the death of Elsie Frum in January 1991, Mr. Shomo became the lone flood survivor.

In a 2001 interview with Adda Lee Hoskinson, Mr. Shomo's only granddaughter, she shared many observations of her grandfather. As a part of this interview, she shared the eulogy from his funeral service held on March 23, 1997. As part of that eulogy, which Adda Lee prepared for her grandfather, she included his advice for living a long life. "He attributed a long life to three things. He said you must lay a firm foundation, don't drink, and above all believe in the Almighty."

Although local flooding continued to be a periodic problem for Johnstown and other points throughout the Conemaugh Valley, Johnstown did not have another serious incident of flooding until March 17, 1936. As was true in 1889, heavy rains and an early spring thaw of accumulated ice and snow produced far more water than the local streams could handle. As a result of the 1936 flood, an estimated 24 lives were lost, and property damage estimates ranged between $40 and $50 million. As a result of the St. Patrick's Day flood, some 9,000 people were left homeless. With two major floods in less than 50 years, and other significant yet less serious floods in 1894, 1907 and 1924, calls to develop measures to reduce the possibility of such flooding in the future were numerous and loud.

As was true in 1889, the task of recovery and rebuilding was well beyond local means. To provide much-needed funds, a special liquor tax was enacted

In this family picture, probably taken in Johnstown, Frank is the baby flanked by his brothers George and William. Their parents were Joseph H. and Harriette "Addie" (Milliken) Shomo.

At the time of his death on March 20, 1997, Frank Shomo, the last survivor of the Johnstown Flood was 108 years old. (Photograph courtesy of Adda Lee Hoskinson.)

As was true during the 1889 flood, Washington Street sustained significant damage during the flood of 1936.

throughout the Commonwealth. It was known as the Emergency Liquor Sales Tax or the Johnstown Flood Tax. An article, which appeared in the April 9, 2001 *Intelligencer Journal* of Lancaster, Pennsylvania, reported on current efforts in the Pennsylvania General Assembly to abolish this tax. "The desire to do away with this tax is not, however, unanimous among the legislators. There are those who feel that it should continue, with money so raised put aside in a special account, to be used if another Pennsylvania community should face a need like that felt by Johnstown in 1936." According to the *Journal* article, this tax produced $153.8 million in state revenue, during the 1999-2000 fiscal year.

Shortly following the 1889 flood, the City of Johnstown took steps to attempt to mitigate future flooding. Dumping into the rivers, building anything that would obstruct the flow of the rivers, and the construction of a limited number of masonry and concrete flood walls at specific locations were some of the actions

taken. Although well intended, these local measures did little to reduce the threat of future flooding in Johnstown. Following the flood of Saint Patrick's Day in 1936, a request was made for help from the federal government. In response to flooding in Johnstown and other areas of the country, the Congress of the United States passed the Flood Control Act of 1936. This act was significant in that it authorized the federal government to appropriate federal funds for flood control projects. In August 1936, President Franklin Roosevelt visited Johnstown and committed the federal government to a flood control project for Johnstown.

In 1889, when the federal government was asked to involve the Army Corps of Engineers in the recovery efforts in Johnstown, President Harrison ordered troops from the United States Engineer School at Fort Totten in New York to came to Johnstown. They assisted with the building of bridges and the reclamation of the town. However, when asked to help increase the water carrying capacity of the rivers that flow through Johnstown, the Corps had to decline the request. They had to do so because their authorization was only to provide navigation improvements, not flood control.

Under the Flood Control Act of 1936, the Pittsburgh District of the United States Army Corps of Engineers began work on the Johnstown Local Flood Protection Project (JLFPP) in 1937. The Corps planned the project to handle flows equal to that measured during the flood of 1936. It has been estimated that a flood of that magnitude would have a one-in-sixty chance of happening in any given year. The work on the project, which took from 1938 through 1943, included widening and deepening all three of Johnstown's river channels, construction of concrete-faced sideslopes, and the erection of concrete flood walls where needed.

Dedicated in November 1943, the final cost of the project was $8.87 million. An estimated 2.75 million cubic yards of material was excavated during the project, and 156,631 cubic yards of concrete were placed. If the excavated material had all been dumped in Johnstown's Central Park, which measures 240 feet square, it would have reached a height taller than the Empire State Building. If the concrete used in the project was laid as a roadbed, a twenty-foot wide road from Johnstown to Pittsburgh could have been constructed. At the dedication, Pittsburgh District Engineer, Colonel Gilbert Van B. Wilkes, said, "Today, Johnstown can boast that it has the largest and best channel improvement in the United States." Extending slightly more than nine miles along Johnstown's rivers, the Johnstown Local Flood Protection Project is today the second largest flood control project of its type in the United States.

Following the completion of the JLFPP, it was commonly agreed that Johnstown had been made "flood free," and for a period of nearly 35 years, the town lived up to that reputation. However, on July 19 and 20 of 1977 a freak storm, the likes of which was absolutely unprecedented, reminded Johnstown and the world that the city at the forks of the Stony Creek and the Little Conemaugh was not flood free. If the harshest furies of Mother Nature came to call in the Conemaugh Valley, flooding in Johnstown was inevitable. The likelihood of the storm that struck Johnstown and vicinity in July 1977 has been estimated by various sources to be between one-in-250 and one-in-500 in any given year. The town that had been established on a flood plain nearly 177 years before had never been and never would be absolutely flood free.

As a result of the 1977 flood, 85 people were killed. Of that number 77 were found. The remaining eight were never found, but later were declared dead. Although estimates vary, property damage was estimated

This is a section of the JLFPP along the Stony Creek River, at the Franklin Street Bridge.

In the aftermath of the 1977 flood, lifelong residents once again found themselves looking for familiar landmarks to get their bearings. They were shocked to learn that Johnstown was not a "flood-free city."

at between $250 and $350 million. Throughout the flooded area which touched at least seven counties, more than 50,000 people were homeless, and business and industrial losses were dramatic.

The realization that Johnstown was not a flood-free community initiated calls for a general inspection and review of the JLFPP. A thorough inspection revealed that, although the project was still in remarkably good condition for its age, there was a clear need for both repairs and improvements. In 1991, by an act of Congress, the Pittsburgh District of the Army Corps of Engineers was once again authorized to assist Johnstown in its ongoing efforts to remain as flood free as possible. In 1997, the Corps began a rehabilitation of the JLFPP with a budget of $32 million. General repairs to the existing structures, dredging of the channels, and general maintenance of the project were all part of the rehabilitation plan.

Although May 31 has long been and will undoubtedly continue to be a date to be remembered in the Conemaugh Valley each year, a number of specific anniversary dates have been marked with ceremonies, observances, and remembrances. These anniversary celebrations have paid tribute to the memory of those whose lives were lost, while honoring those who survived to build a new Johnstown and help it to prosper into a third century.

On Saturday, May 31, 1890, many of the churches in Johnstown held memorial services in recognition of events of the pervious year. Others held similar services the following day. Several local business houses were closed and many were draped in black. The business community of Johnstown and vicinity did little else to mark the somber anniversary. A parade that had formed in Johnstown made its way to the unidentified plot in Grandview where services were held. The Mineral City Band performed during the parade and at the cemetery services. One of the songs played was the familiar "Departed Comrades." Several local societies also held services of memory and remembrance. Some of those who acted to remember the day included the Knights of Pythias, the Young Men's Christian Association, the White Cross Society, and the Mystic Chain of the Conemaugh Valley.

On the front page of the May 31, 1890 edition of the *Johnstown Tribune*, there was an article that described the major events marking the first anniversary of the flood. Right next to that article was one titled "The Old Town and The New." As a sub-headline of the story indicated, the article provided "The Record of the Year." Many of the critical milestones of recovery were presented as a running account beginning with East Conemaugh and moving down the valley to Johnstown. Johnstown was given the most attention in the article with specifics provided for nearly every street in town. Mention was made of plans for a memorial hospital and an inclined-plane railroad. The need for broadening the rivers was mentioned and it was pointed out that that was one of the chief reasons why the previous February the vote for consolidation had been successful. The writer also mentioned the need for either a new opera house or a public hall for the purpose of holding public gatherings for which churches were not appropriate meeting places.

Regarding the general rehabilitation of Johnstown, the writer concluded that, "On the whole, it can be truthfully said that all the territory within the old Johnstown Borough limits has been improved very satisfactorily, and with probably as much rapidity as the circumstances would permit."

By 1914, virtually all visual reminders of the great flood that had taken place a quarter of a century earlier were gone. On Sunday, May 31, 1914, in churches throughout the valley the dearly departed were remembered, some in separate memorial services others as part of the regular worship service of the day. Doubtless there were numerous references made to a letter that was carried in the previous evening's *Johnstown Tribune* through the courtesy of John M. Bowman, Jr. of Philadelphia. The letter had been written to Bowman on June 8, 1889, by his father Colonel John M. Bowman, Sr. The senior Bowman had been an editor of the *Cambria Tribune*, the forerunner of the *Johnstown Tribune*, for a time shortly before and during the Civil War, and later became a noted newspaperman in Everett, Bedford County. Making his way to South Fork by train and on to Johnstown by foot, Bowman surveyed the flooded district and recorded what he saw for his son. The letter provides a graphic eyewitness account of conditions in the Conemaugh Valley, and Johnstown in particular, during the first week after the flood.

The same issue of the *Tribune* carried a summary of the past twenty-five years under the somber headline "Johnstown's Marvelous Advance Throughout 25 Years Sheds a Mellow Light on the Days of Terrible Disaster." The article concluded with the following passage:

> Those hundreds who sleep in graves marked or unmarked, as a result of the coming of the rush of waters, are honored by the work and doing of their survivors, and the Johnstown of 1914 is a tribute, as well as incontrovertible proof, that those who died, died not in vain or to be dishonored by the supine surrender to disaster to those left behind.

The fiftieth anniversary of the flood was celebrated in 1939, during some of the darkest days of the Great Depression and on the eve of America's entry into the Second World War. Like most industrial towns across the country, the depression and the rumors of war hit Johnstown hard. The celebration of the fiftieth anniversary of the flood was a temporary respite from the larger concerns of the day.

Advances in the reproduction of photographs in newspapers permitted the *Johnstown Tribune* to present its readers with a pictorial record of the 1889 flood on the front page of the Wednesday, May 31, 1939 paper. Tribute in the article was given to George Gibbs, a writer for the *Tribune*, credited with writing the first article that paper presented its local readers on the details of the flood. Other stories of the day related to the flood included a summary of the river control project that was at that time well underway but far from done. A spectacular aerial view of the unknown plot in Grandview showed the almost perfect pattern with which the cemetery plot had been designed and completed. A caption under the picture noted that there were in fact 816 markers for the 777 unidentified bodies. (As noted previously, current research indicates that the number of dead buried in the unknown plot at Grandview is 771.) Authorities at Grandview reported that 39 additional markers were placed to finish the last of the 16 rows, each containing 51 stones.

On May 31, 1939, at least three flood survivors were celebrating their fiftieth birthday. They were Moses Williams, Flood Charles Raymond and Flood S. Rhodes. A fourth local resident with the word flood as part of her name, had been in Johnstown the week before the 50th anniversary celebration. She was May Flood Itinger. A brief account of each of these births illustrates why the babies born were named as they were.

The home of the George Doerr family, a double house located at the corner of Vine Street and Lee Place, became the refuge for many washed from their own homes by the raging floodwaters. The John Masterton family occupied the other side of the house. Among those who took refuge there were Dr. L. H Mayer and his wife, and Mr. & Mrs. Griffith Williams, formerly of Wales. During the night of May 31, Mrs. Williams gave birth to a son who was named Moses. Dr. Mayer was in attendance to assist with the birth, which took place in the spacious attic on the Doerr side of the home. Recalling the story of Moses from the Bible, the Williams decided to name their son Moses. Moses was taken by his parents to live in Wales shortly after the flood. He remained there until 1912, when he returned to America. He fought during World War I with the 15th Engineers of Pittsburgh. In 1939, he was residing in the Y.M.C.A. building on Market Street in Johnstown.

Flood Charles Raymond was born shortly after the giant wall of water from South Fork struck Minersville where his family was living at the time of the flood. As the waters approached, Mrs. Raymond fled to a small hill behind the house with her two children. Later in the day her husband came to the hillside where they had sought safety to tell her that the waters were no longer rising. They returned to their house, where a son was born around 8:00 o'clock in the evening. That child was later christened Flood Charles Raymond. In 1939, Flood was living on Jacoby Street and was employed by a local contractor. His mother was also living with him at the time.

Mr. & Mrs. John (Nettie) Rhodes were expecting a child in late May 1889. The family lived at Delaware Avenue and B Street in Morrellville. As the floodwaters reached their house, Mrs. Rhodes was carried out of the house on a mattress and taken to a nearby hillside. During the ordeal, a son was born. He was later named Flood S. Rhodes. In 1939, Mr. Rhodes was employed by the Bethlehem Steel Company in their 18-inch mill.

Although born more than two months after the flood, May Flood Itinger's name recalls the proximity of her birth to the flood. Living in Trenton, New Jersey in 1939, May Flood, then Mrs. Christ Thomas, returned to Johnstown to visit her mother just prior to the 50th anniversary of the great flood. At the time of the flood the Itingers lived on Market Street in Johnstown.

In celebration of the 50th anniversary of the flood, a dinner was held at the Masonic Temple on Wednesday, May 31, 1939. Those attending the dinner and anyone else with an interest in relics of the flood could view numerous items on display at the Masonic Hall. One of the many items displayed was a clock, brought back to Johnstown by Mrs. Susan Slick from Glenford, Ohio. According to the story that had been shared with her, the clock, an ornate alarm clock, was stopped by the floodwaters never to run again. The hands of the clock pointed to 10 seconds after 4:10.

The Monday, June 1, 1964 edition of the *Johnstown Tribune-Democrat*, carried a summary of the 75th anniversary events under the headline "Honor Paid Flood Survivors, Symbols of City's Courage." For the anniversary in 1964, a banquet was held at the Cambria County War Memorial arena on Saturday evening, May 30. The banquet hosted approximately 300 survivors of the flood and more than 600 guests. As during the 1939 celebration, an impressive display of flood relics was gathered and displayed in the War Memorial Arena lobby. Congressman John Saylor brought greetings from President Johnson and recounted the work of the United States Army Corps of Engineers in Johnstown's recovery, rehabilitation, and flood control projects. Johnstown Mayor Kenneth O. Tompkins recalled the hard work of the survivors in the rebuilding of flood-ravaged Johnstown:

> You are truly unique citizens for without your faith, without your courage, Johnstown may never have been rebuilt. It would never have been incorporated. It would never have become known as the Friendly City where people enjoy working and living together. It may have become a vast wasteland known only by nature and the elements.

On Sunday, memorial services and services of remembrance were held in local churches. Many of the survivors took part in and were honored guests at these church services and at services held at Grandview to remember both the identified and unidentified dead. Large numbers of local citizens and out-of-town guests observed and joined in the various anniversary events around the town.

Of all of the flood anniversaries, the 100th celebration in 1989 was by far the grandest. The centennial observance got under way on Tuesday evening, May 30, with a ribbon cutting at Central Park and a parade that featured 18 units. Pennsylvania Governor Robert Casey captured the sentiments of the more than 30,000 people who had gathered in the streets of Johnstown when he said, "Johnstown refused to die that day. It's refused to die ever since. It's a new beginning, another beginning for the people of Johnstown." Later that evening a crowd estimated at more than 18,000 gathered in Johnstown's Point Stadium to listen to a number of speeches and musical selections. At one point in the program each of the 2,209 flood victims was recognized with one of 2,209 candles lit in the darkened stadium.

The 1989 festivities in and around Johnstown brought out the media in force. Once again Johnstown and its 1889 flood were national news. On Wednesday, May 31, the Johnstown Flood National Memorial visitor center of the National Park Service was dedicated in St. Michael. More than 400 people turned out for the dedication ceremony. As part of his speech, Congressman John P. Murtha said, "This is a project that was long in coming, but in my mind is the most important economic development project the park service has ever been involved in. The people in Johnstown have come back so often. The people in this area are what America is all about."

Later in the day, ceremonies were held in Johnstown to dedicate the renovated Johnstown Flood Museum. Congressman Murtha officiated at the ribbon cutting ceremony. Using an ax once used by Joseph Johns, Murtha cut a red ribbon. Lieutenant Governor Mark Singel, one of many speakers at the rededication of the Flood Museum, said, "I'm confident that we're going to prosper in this area once again. The best is yet to come."

The activities of the day also included memorial events at the Point and in Grandview Cemetery. The mayor of Johnstown, Herbert Pfuhl, and Lieutenant Governor Singel lit an eternal flame at the Point. A solitary train, a diesel engine of the Conemaugh & Black Lick Railroad, came down the valley with its whistle tied down. Although not a totally faithful recreation of the warning John Hess provided to the residents of East Conemaugh, it was symbolic of his efforts to offer a warning that the dam at South Fork had burst.

For the centennial celebration and memorial services, only two survivors were in attendance. They were Elsie Frum and Frank Shomo. They were the honored guests at the survivor's banquet held on Wednesday evening, May 31, at the Christ the Savior Education Center. At the time of the flood, Frum was 6 years old and Shomo was just 100 days old.

Frum's recollections were vivid a hundred years later. She recalled being at her mother's side when her father entered the house and announced that the South Fork Dam had broken. "He grabbed me and my sister and took us uphill. I don't like to remember a lot of it." Frum also recalled her feelings about Johnstown's future in 1889. "I never thought it (Johnstown) would survive, not the way it was destroyed so." Frank Shomo recalled the numerous accounts that had been shared with him over the years. He said, "They had the spirit and that's what it took to get out of it."

In a picture that captured the very essence of the 1989 centennial celebration of the flood, Shomo kneels to kiss the hand of fellow flood survivor Elsie Frum of Johnstown.

(*Photo courtesy of the* Johnstown Tribune-Democrat)

Epilogue

More than a century has passed since the failure of the dam in South Fork, Pennsylvania. During this time countless efforts to positively affix responsibility have failed. Definitively answering the question of why has been nearly as futile. These efforts, most of which are nothing more than postulations at best, have nonetheless generated a number of lingering questions. Collectively, these questions offer some degree of insight and perspective regarding the relationship between man and nature, and the relationship between the South Fork Fishing and Hunting Club and the flood stricken district of the Conemaugh Valley. As such, they may provide the best possible explanation of why, while providing evidence of where responsibility lies.

1. Did Joseph Johns permanently predispose his settlement to periodic flooding when he established it on a flood plain?

2. Because local flooding had been an ongoing problem in the Conemaugh Valley for many years, should local officials have acted more aggressively to reduce the impact of seasonal periods of high water?

3. Should local authorities have been more united in their concerns for and efforts to address the safety of a dam that impounded 20,000,000 tons of water over their heads?

4. Did a somewhat reckless deforestation of many regional mountainsides by resource-hungry industry predispose the entire watershed of the Conemaugh Valley to greater than normal runoff, during spring thaws and periods of heavy rain?

5. Was a decrease in the width of the rivers through Johnstown, brought on by the dumping of industrial waste and the depositing of landfill for construction, a major factor in the reduction of the carrying capacity of those streams?

6. Did the Stone Bridge at the juncture of the Stony Creek and the Little Conemaugh appreciably obstruct the flow of those streams into the Conemaugh?

7. If Ruff had accepted Morrell's offer of help during the reconstruction of the dam at South Fork, could the 1889 disaster have been avoided?

8. Had a qualified engineer been thoroughly engaged to oversee all of the repairs made to the dam when Benjamin Ruff purchased the property, would those repairs have been sufficiently accomplished so as to prevent the failure in 1889?

9. If the Commonwealth of Pennsylvania or the Pennsylvania Railroad had forced later owners of the dam to adhere to the critical attributes of its original design, would it have failed in May 1889?

10. If an experienced engineer, particularly one with earthen-dam experience, had been onsite in South Fork the morning of May 31, 1889, would different or additional steps have been taken that may have prevented the collapse of the dam later in the day?

11. Had the dam at South Fork not been lowered to widen the cart way that ran across it, would the rising waters have ever overtopped the earthen structure?

12. If the discharge pipes originally placed through the base of the dam had not been removed, could enough water have been run off to prevent the fatal overtopping of the dam?

13. If periodic, professional inspections of the dam had been conducted by independent engineers, would the Club and the public have been more aware of the general condition of the South Fork Dam?

14. If the fish grates across the breast of the South Fork Dam had been removed before they were packed with debris, could the spillway have discharged enough water to prevent overtopping?

15. If the dam had been partially cut through and allowed to release some of the waters behind it before it burst, could the flow have been a more controlled and less damaging discharge?

16. Were the warnings sent to Johnstown of a sufficient level of urgency to report the level of pending danger accurately?

17. Were the warnings sent to Johnstown ignored because of a local complacency based on years of unfounded scares sent through the valley during periods of high water?

18. Should local authorities have called for an evacuation of the several towns and villages between South Fork and Johnstown when warnings went down the valley?

19. Was the storm that called on the Conemaugh Valley in late May 1889 so dramatic in nature that the dam at South Fork was doomed to failure regardless of any of its preexisting conditions?

20. Was the Johnstown Flood a visitation of the wrath of God well beyond the control of man?

Regardless of how or why, one of the most tragic and devastating natural disasters of all times ravaged the Conemaugh Valley in May 1889. Although some decided to leave Johnstown following the flood, the majority of those who survived the onslaught of 20,000,000 tons of water and countless tons of debris, rebuilt their lives in their hometowns and by so doing rebuilt those towns. The City of Johnstown survives today as possibly the best testimonial of the fortitude, courage and resolve of the survivors of the Johnstown Flood of 1889.

Congressman John Murtha, serving in his fifteenth term in the United States House of Representatives in 2001, has had the pleasure of knowing Johnstown in its past, the honor of serving the town in the present, and the opportunity to be a key player in the shaping of its future. When asked to reflect on the impact the great flood of 1889 had on Johnstown, while projecting on the future of that city, Congressman Murtha offered the following thoughts:

> Anybody who looks at the impact of the Johnstown Flood just can't help but be impressed by the spirit of people. With over 2200 dead and many thousand homeless, widowed or orphaned, it's actually pretty amazing that we have a city here at all. I think Johnstown is a testament to the humanspirit.

> I had the opportunity recently to tour the new Frank and Sylvia Pasquerilla Heritage Discovery Center in Johnstown, which explores in depth what it was like to be an immigrant to American around 1900. When you think about how hard these immigrants worked, for such measly wages, in such deplorable conditions, you wonder why they kept coming through Ellis Island into the heartland of America. Conditions were at least as bad 11 years earlier when the great Johnstown Flood hit. Why would they stay? Not only that, but to be so dedicated that they had the local mills back in operation within a week of that devastating flood is beyond what I can fathom.

> It's not surprising, then, that the Johnstown Flood was such a vivid event on the American psyche throughout the 20th Century and continues to touch thousands of people who visit our Flood Memorial and Flood Museum. Johnstown has changed dramatically in the last twenty years. Now, these memorials to the flood are part of a new economy — a diverse economy that draws on tourism, high tech, education and services rather than the traditional heavy industry that attracted so many people here. But as this region has weathered new storms — economic storms from the collapse of those heavy industries — it's been clear to me that the human spirit remains strong here. I think it's the traditional values that have been passed down from one generation to the next in our close-knit families, who have an intense pride in their ethnic heritage and their willingness to work to overcome and triumph over whatever life throws their way.

Signs placed in recent years on most of the roads leading into the city, welcome visitors and bespeak local pride in Johnstown. Johnstown and its citizens have survived, rebuilt and have continued to prosper even after two more devastating floods during the last century. Resolve, tenacity and determination are part of the legacy of the 1889 survivors that lives on throughout the Conemaugh Valley.

Epigraph

In his book *The Johnstown Flood*, published in 1889, Herman Dieck spoke of the great difficulty anyone who tried to tell the story of the Johnstown Flood would face. In his book he wrote:

> No man, nor any corps of men, with every facility that can be devised, will ever be able to write a story that shall fully tell of the awful visitation that has made the valley one vast charnel house, twenty miles long and half a mile wide, and that has stained the bright mountain stream a color that not all the water that can flow between now and eternity can ever wash out."

Through this, my own humble attempt at retelling the story of Johnstown's greatest flood, I have discovered that he was indeed correct!

FINIS

Appendix A

Membership Lists

The following two lists identify men believed to have belonged to the South Fork Fishing and Hunting Club. The first list of sixty was handwritten in the final pages of the Guest Register (126-127), now located in the Johnstown Flood Museum Archives. The second list of sixty-one was published in the *Tnbune* after the flood. Only thirty-eight names appear on both lists. Neither list has been documented as a totally reliable source.

Guest Register list, c. 1886

B. F. Ruff	H. C. Yeager	Jos. R. Woodwell
C. C. Hussey	D. R. Ewart	A. C. Crawford
H. Hartley	C. A. Carpenter	Durbin Horne
Jno. D. Hunt	C. J. Clarke	A. V. Holmes
H. Holdship	Thos. S. Clarke	O. F. Wharton
M. B. Suydam	H. C. Frick	J. B. White
J. J. Lawrence	F. T. Bissel	Jno. A. Harper
C. B. Shea	R. C. Gray	Geo. W. Jope (?)
Jno. B. Jackson	Jno. Caldwell, Jr.	Thos. M. Carnegie
0. McClintock	Jno. W. Chalfant	Jessie Lippencott
W. L. McClintock	Jas. K. Ewing	Jas. M. Schoonmaker
F. T. McClintock	H. J. Brunot	J. E. Schwartz
Jno. F. Wilcox	Jas. McCreggor	Lewis Irwin
B. Thaw	Robt. Pitcairn	Wm. Rea
F. Semple	Wm. Mullins	A. Carnegie
F. B. Laughlin	W. A. McIntosh	Saml. Rea
W. T. Fundenberg	Geo. B. Roberts	D. J. Morrell
W. T. Dunn	W. C. Taylor	H. Sellers McKee
D. C. Phillips	E. A. Myers	Calvin Wells
E. J. Unger	W. K. Woodwell	Aaron French

Johnstown Tribune list, June 20, 1889

F. J. Allen	A. M. Harncs	William Mullens
Dr. W. C. Bidwell	Durbin Horne	F. A. Meyers
James W. Brown	George F. Huff	Frank T. McClintock
Hilary J. Brunot	Dr. D. W. Rankin	Oliver McClintock
John Caldwell	Samuel Rea	W. L. McClintock
Andrew Carnegie	James H. Reed	James McGregor
John W. Chalfant	Marvin F. Scaife	W. A. McIntosh
James A. Chambers	Jas. M. Schoonmator (sic)	H. Sellers McKee
Charles J. Clarke	J. E. Schwartz	H. P. Patton
Louis S. Clarke	Frank Semple	D. C. Phillips
A. C. Crawford	M. H. Suydam (sic)	Henry Phipps, Jr.
George Christy	Lewis Irwin	Robert Piteatril (sic)
W. T. Dun	P. C. Knox	Benjamin Thaw
Cyrus Elder	Frank B. Laughlin	F. J. Unger (sic)
J. K. Ewing	J. J. Lawrence	Calvin Wells
C. R. Shea	John G. A. Leishman	John F. Wilcox
J. S. McCord	J. H. Lippincott (sic)	Joseph R. Woodwell
A. French	S. S. Marvin	William K. Woodwell
H. C. Frick	A. W. Mellon	James H. Whitlock
John A. Harper	Reuben Miller	
Henry Holdship	Max K. Moorhead	

Appendix B

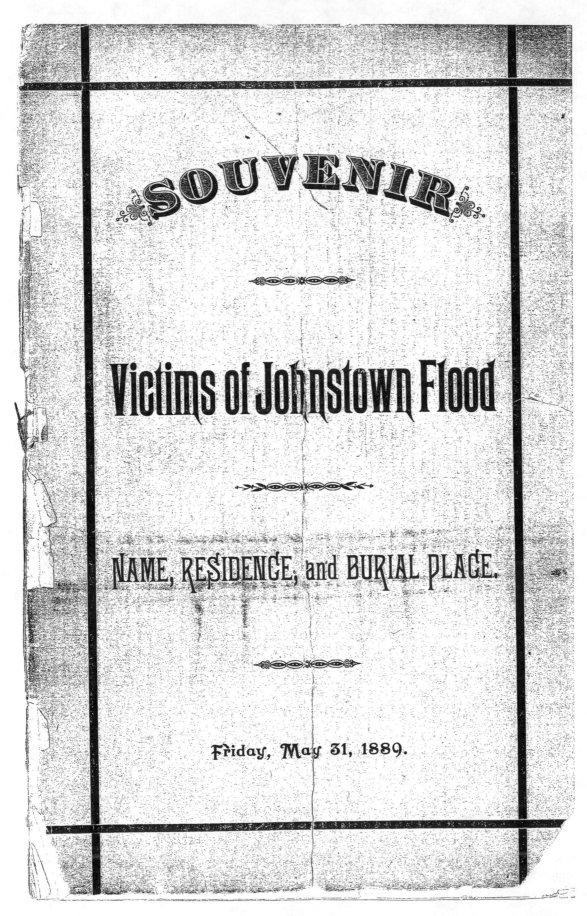

SOUVENIR

Victims of Johnstown Flood

NAME, RESIDENCE, and BURIAL PLACE.

Friday, May 31, 1889.

VICTIMS

OF THE

Johnstown Flood

DEDICATION.

THE title page has spoken. The reader sees the cemetery gate and enters in.

This little volume is intended to perpetuate, so far as ink and paper can, the memory of lost friends—victims of the Johnstown Flood, May 31, 1889. But not more to perpetuate their memory than to afford the living a ready index to the victims of Johnstown's great calamity ; and not more the people of to-day than of future days. It is the idea of usefulness, no less than sentiment, that prompts the printing.

This list is the list of July 31, 1890, as printed in the Johnstown *Tribune* fourteen months succeeding the Flood. So far as human agency can accomplish, it is complete. Here and there a name is missing ; a name or two perhaps appears whose owner was not drowned ; but the list has passed the jealous scrutiny of all survivors, and is pronounced correct.

Nothing more need be said. The Flood is history. The child of 1989 may know more of it than the child who saw it, and was in it, yet realized it not at all.

For posterity, then, this little book is meant, and to posterity it is dedicated.

The time when man's cupidity and selfishness were supreme, yet near their lowest ebb ; the time when, of all times since the Cross, God and man stood closest together—that time has been recorded. In that spirit this book is given.

Only a word in way of ready reference for the reader need be added. The figures accompanying the names indicate the age of the victims ; and to save counting, the number of victims in the different cemeteries is annexed :

Grand View	441
Sandyvale	78
Old Catholic (Conemaugh Borough)	23
Lower Yoder	128
Public Plot (Grand View)	115
St. Mary's	71
German Catholic	47
No Cemetery Record	206
Day Express	38
Miscellaneous	95
Not Known to be Found	967
Total	2,209

The list under the head of "Not Known to be Found" is the list of those who were never heard of again after they were torn from their friends ; whose remains may have been recovered and buried in the "Unknown Plot" (and doubtless were, the most of them), but who are *still missing* to those who loved them.

With this explanation the publishers—three printers who seek only to do a service to mankind—present this volume to those who loved Johnstown and its people.

List of Victims of the Johnstown Flood.

TOTAL NUMBER LOST, 2,209.

GRAND VIEW CEMETERY.

[Buried in private lots in Grand View.]

Alexander, Arailia K., Broad street.
Andrews, John, Sr., 57, John street.
Arthur, Mrs. Alice, 29, Water street.
Bantley, William G., 36, Third Ward.
Bantley, Mrs. Ella, 30, Third Ward.
Bantley, George L., 6 months, Third Ward.
Barbour, Mrs. Mary, 25, Woodvale.
Barbour, Florence, 4, Woodvale.
Barley, Mrs. Barbara, 56, Woodvale.
Barley, Nancy, 29, Woodvale.
Barley, Viola, 9, Woodvale.
Beam, Dr. Lemon T., 55, Market street.
Beam, Charles C., 4, Market street.
Beam, Dr. W. C., 35, Locust street.
Beam, Mrs Clara, 32, Locust street.
Beckley, E. E., 23, Main street.
Bending, Mrs Elizabeth, 48, Locust street.
Bending, Jessie, 24, Locust street.
Bending, Katie, 15, Locust street.
Beneigh, John C., 65, Cambria.
Benford, Mrs. E. E., 63, Hulbert House.
Benford, Maria, 34, Hulbert House.
Benford, May, 26, Hulbert House.
Benford, Louis, 30, Hulbert House.
Benshoff, J. Q. A., 62, Somerset street.
Benshoff, Arthur, 27, Somerset street.
Bowman, Nellie, 9, Haynes street.
Bowman, Charles H., 7, Haynes street.
Bowman, Frank P., 33, Woodvale.
Bowman, Emma, 28, Woodvale.
Brinkey, Dr J. C., 28, Franklin street.
Brinkey, Elmer, 26, Hulbert House.
Buchanan, John S., 69, Locust street.
Buchanan, Mrs. Kate J., 63, Locust street.
Buchanan, Robert L., 20, Locust street.
Connelly, Maud, 6, Franklin.
Constable, Philip E., 60, Broad street.
Cope, Mrs. Margaret, 65, Conemaugh.
Cope, Ella B., 28, Conemaugh.
Cooney, Mrs. Elizabeth.
Davis, Mary Ann, 40, Woodvale.
Davis, Thomas S., 59, Locust street.
Davis, Mrs. Elizabeth.
Davis, Mrs. Susan, 27, Millville.
Davis, Clara, 8, Millville.
Davis, Willie, 3, Millville.
Davis, Eliza M.
Davis, Margaret, E.
Davis, Mrs Cora B., 25, Water street.
Davis, William L.
Davis, Willard G.
Davis, Mary G.
Delaney, Mrs. Jessie, 29, Vine street.
Delaney, Mrs. Ella A.
Dibert, John, 56, Main street.
Dibert, Blanche, 9, Main street.
Dixon, David, 40, Millville.
Diller, Rev. Alonzo P., Locust street.
Diller, Mrs. Marion, Locust street.
Diller, Isaac, Locust street.
Dinant, Lola, Locust street.
Dorris, August.
Drew, Mrs. Mark, 62, Millville.
Drew, Mollie, 8, Conemaugh street.
Duncan, Mrs. Sarah A., 23, Woodvale.

Dyer, Mrs. Nathan, 64, Somerset street.
Eck, Mary Ellen.
Edwards, Mrs. Annie R.
Eldridge, Samuel B., Apple Alley.
Eldridge, Abram S., 34, Merchants' Hotel.
Etchison, John, 44, Napoleon street.
Evans, Mrs. William F., 63, Union street.
Evans, Maggie, 11, Lewis Alley.
Evans, Kate, 5, Lewis Alley.
Evans, Mrs. Josiah, 36, Vine street.
Evans, Maggie, 16, Vine street.
Evans, Lake, 6, Vine street.
Evans, Ira, 6 months, Vine street.
Evans, Mrs. Maggie, 37, Vine street.
Evans, Mrs. Ann.
Evans, Sadie, 8, Vine street.
Evans, Herbert, 3, Vine street.
Evans, Pearl, 1, Vine street.
Evans, Lizzie.
Fails, Francis.
Fenn, John, 35, Locust street.
Fenn, Genevieve, 9, Locust street.
Fenn, Bismarck S., 3, Locust street.
Findlay, Lulu, 16, Woodvale.
Fisher, John H., 55, Main street.
Fisher, Mary J., 46, Main street.
Fisher, Emma K, 23, Main street.
Fisher, Ida, 19, Main street.
Fisher, Madge, 10, Main street.
Fisher Minnie, 21, Main street.
Fisher, George, 12, Main street.
Fisher, Frank, 9 months.
Fleck, Leroy Webster.
Fox, Martin, 51, Conemaugh.
Frank, John, Sr, 58, Washington street.
Frank, Mrs. Eliza, 44, Washington street.
Frank, Katie, 19, Washington street.
Frank, Emma, 17, Washington street.
Frank, Laura, 12, Washington street.
Fredericks, Mrs. A. G., 45, Millville.
Fredericks, Mrs. Sarah A.
Frederick, Edmon.
Fritz, Maggie, 26, Conemaugh.
Fritz, Kate, 22, Conemaugh.
Fronheiser, Mrs. Kate, 33, Main street.
Fronheiser, Bessie, 8, Main street.
Fronheiser, Catherine, 3 months, Main street.
Gageby, Mrs. Rebecca, 74, Jackson street.
Gageby, Sadie, 27, Jackson street.
Gallagher, Prof. C. F., 34, Main street.
Gallagher, Lizzie, 29, Main street.
Gard, Andrew, Jr., 25, Main street.
Geddes, George, 47, Woodvale.
Geddes, Marion, 17, Woodvale.
Geddes, Paul, 15, Woodvale.
Gilmore, Mrs. Margaret, 40, Union street.
Gilmore, Anthony, 8, Union street.
Gilmore, Llewelyn, 6, Union street.
Gilmore, Willy, 4, Union street.
Gilmore, Clara, 2, Union street.
Golde, Mrs. Henry, 32, Walnut street.
Griffin, Mary, 47, Walnut street.
Hager, Mary E., 33, Washington street.
Hager, Mrs. Emma.
Hamilton, Jacob, 70, Bedford street.
Hamilton, Jessie, 30, Bedford street.
Hamilton, Laura, 24, Bedford street.
Hamilton, Alex. Jr., 35, Locust street.

Hamilton, Mrs. Alex., 30, Locust street.
Hamilton, Marion, Locust street.
Hamilton, Louther J.,
Hammer, George K., 19, Moxham.
Harris, Mrs. William T.
Harris, John, 3, Market street.
Harris, Margaret, 47, Market street.
Harris, Wm. L., 23, Market street.
Harris, Winnie, 21, Market street.
Harris, Maggie A., 19. Market street.
Harris, Sarah, 16, Market street.
Harris, Frank, 12, Market street.
Haynes, Walter B., 22, Horner street.
Haynes, Laura C., 20, Horner street.
Hennekamp, Rebecca, 24, Franklin street.
Hennekamp, Oscar E., 2. Franklin street.
Hennekamp, S. E., 27, Lincoln street.
Heidenthal, Harry R.
Heiser, George, 50, Washington street.
Heiser, Mrs. George, 48, Washington street.
Helsel, George, 16, Johns street.
Hite, Mrs. Ella, 37, Somerset street.
Hochstein, Henry, 30, Conemaugh.
Hoffman, Benjamin F., 56, Market street.
Hoffman, Mrs. Mary, 43, Market street.
Hoffman, Bertha, 19, Market street.
Hoffman, Minnie, 16, Market street.
Hoffman, Marion, 14, Market street.
Hoffman, Florence, 10, Market street.
Hoffman, Joseph, 8, Market street.
Hoffman, Helen, 4, Market street.
Hoffman, Freda, 1, Market street.
Hoffman, Mrs. Mary, 41, Washington street.
Hohnes, Mrs. Ann, 24, Conemaugh.
Hohnes, Mrs. Elizabeth, 80, Lincoln street.
Hohne-, Julia, 18, Conemaugh.
Hollen, Charles.
Howe, Thomas J., Bedford street.
Howells, William, 59, Union street.
Howells, Maggie, 23, Union street.
Howells, Mrs. Ann.
Hughes, Maggie, 22, Sugar Alley.
Hughes, Evan, 57, Sugar alley.
Humm, Geo. C., Merchants' Hotel.
Humphreys, William, 18, Levergood street.
Jacobs, Lewis, 41, Cambria City.
James, Mrs. Ellen M., 42, Main street.
James, Mollie, 13, Market street.
Jones, Mary J.
Jones, Reuben, 1, Main street.
Jones, James, 32, Conemaugh.
Jones, Ann, 9, Conemaugh.
Jones. Mrs. W. W.
Jones, Edgar R.
Jones, Mrs. Mary A., 52, Pearl street.
Jones, Eliza, 15, Pearl street.
Karns, Joseph, 50, Locust street.
Keedy, Harry C., 30, Millville.
Keedy, Mrs. Mary, 32, Millville.
Kegg, William E., 17, Locust street.
Keiper, Essie J., 24, Franklin.
Keiper, Ralph, 5 months, Franklin.
Kennedy, H. D., 32, Stonycreek street.
Keyser, Mrs. John.
Keyser, Ralph.
Keighly, Mary L., 52, Main street.
Kidd, Joshua, 65, Walnut street.
Kidd, Mrs. Sarah, 60, Walnut street.
Kirkbride, Mahlon, 33, Hager Block.
Kirkbride, Mrs. Ida, 30, Hager Block.
Kirkbride, Luida, 8, Hager Block.
Kirlin, Thomas, 40, Conemaugh street.
Kirlin, Eddie, 12, Conemaugh street.
Kirlin, Frank, 5, Conemaugh street.
Knorr, Mrs. Mary, 45, Jackson street.
Knorr, Emma, 16, Jackson street.
Knorr, Bertha, 14, Jackson street.
Knox, Mrs. Thomas, 45, Somerset street.
Koenstyl, Samuel.
Kratzer, Mrs. Mary, Market street.
Kuntz, Wade, 21, Morris street
Lambreski, Mrs. Barbara, 35, Cambria.
Lambreski, Mary, 6, Cambria.
Lambreski, John, 4, Cambria.
Layton, Mrs. Elvira.
Layton, William, 58, Broad street.
Layton, Mrs. William, 53, Broad street.
Layton, May, 22, Broad street.
Layton, David, Broad street.
Layton, Ella, Broad street.

Lee, Dr. J. K., 48, Main street.
Leitenberger, Mrs. Leah, 68, Vine street.
Leitenberger, Nancy, 48, Vine street.
Leitenberger, Ella, 35, Vine street.
Leitenberger, Eliza, 46, Vine street.
Lenhart, Samuel, 58, Clinton street.
Lenhart, Mrs. Mary, 56, Clinton street.
Lenhart, Annie E., 20, Clinton street.
Lenhart, Emma J., 17, Clinton street.
Lenhart, Katie M., 13, Clinton street.
Lewis, Mrs. Ann.
Lewis, Ananias, 41, Millville.
Levergood, Mrs. Jane, 75, Bedford street.
Levergood, Lucy, 45, Bedford street.
Lewis, Orrie P., 6, Millville.
Lewis, James.
Linton, Minnie, 20, Lincoln street.
Litz, Mrs. John, 74, Morris street.
Llewellyn, Mrs. Margaret, 37, Walnut street.
Llewellyn, Sadie, 8, Walnut street.
Llewellyn, Herbert, 3, Walnut street.
Llewellyn, Pearl, 1, Walnut street.
Luckhart, Louis, 69, Main street.
Luckhart, Mrs. Adolph, 26, Main street.
Ludwig, Charles.
Ludwig, Henry G., 34, Bedford street.
Ludwig, Mrs. Kate, 35, Bedford street.
Mangus, Martha.
Marbourg, Dr. H. W., 56, Market street.
McDowell, Geo., 29, Pearl street.
McDowell, Mrs. Agnes, 33, Pearl street.
McDowell, Lilly, 3, Pearl street.
McDowell, Georgia.
McClelland, Mrs. Jennie, 34, Sherman street.
McConaghy, Mrs. Kate, 68.
McConaughy, James P., 72, Walnut street.
McConaughy, Mrs. Caroline M., 65, Walnut.
McConaughy, Wallace, 25, Walnut street.
McConaghy, Robert W.
McKee, John, 21, Bedford street.
McKinstry, Mrs Mary C., 45, Hager Block.
McKinstry, Annie R., 14, Hager Block.
Merle, Elmer E.
Moore, Mrs. Charlotte L.
Meyers, Mrs. Elizabeth, 55, Washington street.
Meyers, Mary, 24, Washington street.
Meyers, Mrs. Catherine, 31, Millville.
Meyers, John, 3, Millville.
Miller, Jessie B., 16, Somerset street.
Morgan, Mrs. Charlotte, 49, Millville.
Morgan, Martha, 13, Millville
Morgan, Minnie, 4, Millville.
Murr, Charles, 41, Washington street.
Murr, Maggie, 14, Washington street.
Musser, Charles, 23, Main street.
Nixon, Mrs. Elizabeth, 39, Woodvale.
Nixon, Emma R., 16, Woodvale.
Nixon, Eddie, 8, Woodvale.
Noro, Kate.
Owens, Gladies, 5 months, Conemaugh street.
Owens, Thomas, 10, Conemaugh street.
Owens, William, 65, Market street.
Owens, Annie.
Owens, Mrs. Mary Ann, 31, Conemaugh street.
Owens, Mary, 8, Conemaugh street.
Oyler, Mrs. Mary R., 27, Woodvale.
Oyler John R., 6, Woodvale.
Parke, Mrs Agnes J., 56, Bedford street.
Parke, William E., Bedford street.
Parsons, Mrs. Eva M., 23, Locust street.
Penrod, William H., 59, Conemaugh.
Peyton, John W., 65, Clinton street.
Peyton, George A., 19, Clinton street.
Peyton, Marcellus K., 16, Clinton street.
Peyton, Julia F., 13, Clinton street.
Phillips, Mrs. Jane M., 63, Market street.
Pike, William W., 50, Haynes street.
Pike, William W., Jr., 15, Haynes street.
Pike, S. Bowen, 10, Haynes street.
Poland, Walter, 5, Market street.
Poland, Frederick, 3, Market street.
Potter, Joseph R., 63, Woodvale.
Potter, Mrs. Sarah, 59. Woodvale.
Potter, Nora G., 17, Woodvale.
Potts, Miss Jane E., 47, Walnut street.
Powell, Richard, 4 weeks, Vine street.
Powell, George, 1½, Vine street.
Pritchard, Henry, 62, Market street.
Prosser, Fannie, 22, Market street.
Prosser, Bessie, 19, Market street.

Prosser, Maria.
Purse, Mary L., Market street.
Raab, George, 44, Clinton street.
Raab, Mrs. George, 88, Clinton street.
Raab, Norma, 16, Clinton street.
Raab, Lizzie, 24, Washington street.
Raab, Emilia, 20, Washington street.
Raab, John C.
Raab, Ella.
Rainey, Mrs. Lizzie L., 25, Bedford street.
Rainey, Parke. 1½, Bedford street.
Randolph, George F., 26, Beaver Falls.
Reibert, Julius, Washington street.
Reese, Sarah, 10, Conemaugh street.
Reese, John, 2, Conemaugh street.
Reese, Mrs. J. W.
Reese, Samuel.
Reese, Idris, 3, Vine street.
Reese, Gertie.
Reese, Mrs. Mary D., 74, Market street.
Repp, Mrs. Catherine, 26, Sherman street.
Rhodes, Link, 26, Somerset street.
Rhodes, Ellen, 20, Somerset street.
Rhodes, Clarence, 10 months, Somerset street.
Ripple, Jackson, 34, Apple alley.
Roberts, Howard J., 59, Walnut street.
Roberts, Mrs. Howard J., 50, Walnut street.
Roberts, Otis, 23, Walnut street.
Roberts, Mrs. Lucinda H., 81, Main street.
Robinson, Thomas, 60, Woodvale.
Rodgers, Mrs. D. L.
Rodgers, Mrs. Rose, 48, Millville.
Roland, Louis, 31, Conemaugh.
Roland, Lizzie, 29, Conemaugh.
Rosensteel, James M., 50, Woodvale.
Rose, Harry G., 29, Locust street.
Roth, Mrs Kate, 27, Bedford street.
Roth, John, 38, Potts street.
Schoff, Mrs. E. T., 32, Clinton street.
Schotz, Mrs. Elizabeth, 63, Union street.
Schotz, Annie, 23, Union street.
Schotz, Jennie, 21, Union street.
Schubert, C. T., 39, Stonycreek street.
Seibert, Henry, 58, Woodvale.
Shaffer, Jacob, 47, Cambria.
Shulteis, Henry, 26, Potts street.
Shumaker, John S., 11, Locust street.
Shumaker, Edith M., 7, Locust street.
Shumaker, Irene G., 5, Locust street.
Shumaker, Walter S., 2, Locust street.
Slick, George R., 60, Stonycreek street.
Smith, Mr., 54, Cambria.
Smith, Mrs. Sarah, 72, Walnut street.
Stremel, Julius R., 21, Washington street.
Streum, John, 63, Locust street.
Stufft, J. Wesley, 37, Woodvale.
Stufft, Mrs. J. W., 39, Woodvale.
Suder, Homer, 7, Millville.
St. John, Dr. C. P., 32, Hulbert House.
Stophel, Mrs Maggie, 21, Baumer street.
Stophel, Frank Earl, 4, Baumer street.
Stophel, Bertha, Hulbert House.
Swank, Mrs. Ella, 29, Main street.
Swank, Jennie, 15, Bedford street.
Swank, Jacob, 61, Bedford street.
Swank, Mrs. Catherine, 57, Bedford street.
Swank, Maud, 11, Napoleon street.
Swank, Fred B., 10, Bedford street.
Swank, Susan, 8, Napoleon street.
Swank, Mrs. Neff, 31, Napoleon street.
Swank, Samuel, 5, Napoleon street.
Swank, Edna, 3, Napoleon street.
Statler, Mrs. Amelia, 51, Park Place.
Statler, May, 23, Park Place.
Statler, Frank E., 17, Park Place.
Teeter, Mrs. Mary, 83, Locust street.
Tittle, Cyrus P., 53, Broad street.
Tradenick, Edward, 18, Union street.
Turner, May, 15, Main street.
Tyler, Jno. T., 29, Stonycreek Township.
Thoburn, Thomas, 17, Millville.
Thoburn, Jennie, 7, Millville.
Thomas, Mrs. Mary A., 39, King street.
Thomas, Ida, 7, King street.
Unverzagt, George, Sr., 67, Main street.
Unverzagt, George, Jr., Main street.
Updegraff, Samuel, 15, Woodvale.
Viering, Mrs. Louisa, 38, Conemaugh.
Viering, Lizzie, 20, Conemaugh.
Viering, Henry, 14, Conemaugh.

Viering, Herman, 1, Conemaugh.
Vinton, Margaret, 8, Jeannette, Pa.
Von Alt, Mrs. Catherine, 80, Washington street.
Wagoner, Dr. George, 63, Market street.
Wagoner, Lizzie, 20, Market street.
Wagoner, Mrs. Mary L.
Wagoner, Frances E., 18, Market street.
Wagoner, Cora M., Market street.
Wenner, Carl, 32, Locust street.
Wenner, Mrs., Locust street.
Wenner, Mary, 1, Locust street.
Weaver, Mrs. Sue D., 27, Market street.
Weaver, Martha B., 15 months, Market street.
Weakland, John W., 30, Napoleon street.
Werry, Thomas Albert, 17, Chestnut street.
White, Mrs. Mima.
White, Mrs. Ella, 34, Union street.
White, Mrs. Margaret E.
White, Mary P., 20, Market street.
White, Maggie, 31, Union street.
Wild, Jacob, 72, Main street.
Wild, Mrs. Jacob, 58, Main street.
Wild, Bertha, 16, Main street.
Williams, Maggie 26, Lewis alley.
Williams, Joseph M., 22, Conemaugh street.
Williams, William J., Union street.
Williams, Carrie E., 20, Woodvale.
Worthington, Mrs. Richard, 28, Conemaugh st.
Worthington, Richard, Jr., 1, Conemaugh st.
Worthington, Mamie, 7, Conemaugh street.
Worthington, Annie, 4, Conemaugh street.
Young, Katie.
Young, Emil, 48, Levergood street.
Young, Frank, 16, Levergood street.
Young, August, 29, Main street.
Young, Andrew C., 36, Broad street.
Zimmerman, Emma, 16, Bedford street.
Zimmerman, Theo. F., 34, Locust street.

SANDYVALE CEMETERY.

Abler, August, 28, Conemaugh.
Abler, Mrs. Louisa, 31, Conemaugh.
Abler, George, 11, Conemaugh.
Baldwin, George, 60, Apple alley.
Bishop, Charles, 45, Woodvale.
Brindle, Mollie, 25, Conemaugh.
Clark, John.
Davis.
Davis.
Davis.
Eberle, Joseph, 63, Conemaugh.
Forbes, Mrs. Rachael, 38, Pearl street.
Forbes, Harry E., 10, Pearl street.
Fredericks, Mrs. Annie E., 78, Vine street.
Gray, S. Taylor, 37, Woodvale.
Gallagher, C. F.
Gallagher, Mrs. C. F.
Greenwood.
Greenwalt, Mrs.
Greenwalt, child.
Given, Jane, Millville.
Given, Benj. F., Millville.
Greenwood, Jennie, 17, Cambria.
Greenwood, Geo., 55, Cambria.
Hammer, Daniel, Railroad street.
Hite, Samuel, 26, Woodvale.
Hoffman, Gottfried, 40, Washington street.
Hoffman, Harry, 6, Washington street.
Hoffman, Daniel.
Hoffman, Godfrey, 41, Washington street.
Hoffman, Lizzie, 16, Washington street.
Hoffman, Mrs. Conrad, 38, Market street.
Hoffman, Charles B., 16, Market street.
Hoffman, Willie, 15, Market street.
Hoffman, Annie, 11, Market street.
Hughes, Emma, 26, Potts street.
Hesselbein, Chas., 27, Conemaugh.
Hesselbein, Lewis, 23, Conemaugh.
Jones, Thomas, 50, Woodvale.
Jones, Mary W., 21, Woodvale.
Jones, Richard, 46, Woodvale.
Jones, child of Richard, Woodvale.
Jones, Clara, 6, Woodvale.
Kimpel, Christ., 47, Clinton street.
Knee, Geo. D., 54, Conemaugh.
Meyers, Mrs. Mary, 69, Cambria.
Morgan, Job, 50, Walnut street.
McClarren, Samuel, 49, Cambria.
McClarren, Mrs. Jane, 42, Cambria.

McClarren, Smith, 22, Cambria.
McClarren, Jno. J., 19, Cambria.
McClarren, James, 4, Cambria.
Peppler, Wm., 20, Conemaugh.
Raab, Geo. C., 28, Washington street.
Reese.
Reese.
Reese.
Reese.
Recke, Alex., 35, Washington street.
Scheetz, Jacob, 61, Clinton street.
Schnable, Conrad. 38, Baumer street.
Schnable, John, 20, Main street.
Stahr, Fred.
Strayer, Mrs. Elizabeth, 47, Market street.
Strayer, Cora, 17, Market street.
Strayer. Bertha, Market street.
Teeter, Mrs.
Thomas, Mrs. Edward, Woodvale.
Thomas, Edward, 49, Woodvale.
Thomas, Lydia, 12, Woodvale.
Thomas, Frank, 8, Woodvale.
Tross, Mrs. Margaret, 39, Woodvale.
Unverzagt, Lizzie, Washington street.
Unverzagt, Minnie, 27, Washington street.
Will, Casper, 45, Bedford street.
Wier, Frank A., 18, Cambria.
Willower, Miss Bella, Somerset street.
Wehn, Mrs. Rachel, 57, Main street.

LOWER YODER CATHOLIC CEMETERY.

Blair, Mrs., 50, Woodvale.
Bopp, Jacob, 32, Broad street.
Bracken, Katie 21, Woodvale.
Bracken, Minnie, 19, Woodvale.
Bridges, Chas., 2, Cambria
Bridges, Emma, 18, Cambria.
Brown, Peter, 65, Woodvale.
Brown, Thomas, 24, Woodvale.
Brown, Emma, 20, Woodvale.
Brown, Gertrude, 17, Woodvale.
Byrne, John, 32, Hulbert House.
Byrne, Ella, 24, Hulbert House.
Carroll, Mrs. Bridget, 70, Conemaugh.
Carroll, Thomas, 30, Conemaugh.
Carroll, Rose, 20, Conemaugh.
Clark, Mrs. J. B., 39, Conemaugh.
Cronin, Daniel, 50, Vine street.
Cullen, James, 55, Cambria.
Cullen, Mrs. Ann, 50, Cambria.
Cullen, Mrs. Alice, 48, Cambria.
Cullen, Annie, 20, } Pro'bly dupl'ted { Cambria.
Cullen, Annie, 20, }   { Locust st.
Cush, Mrs. Ann, 55, Cambria.
Cush, Daniel, 33, Cambria.
Cush, Joseph, 19, Cambria.
Cush, Mrs. Tillie, 20, Cambria.
Daily, Mrs. Ann, 60, Locust street.
Daily, Frank, 30, Locust street.
Degnan, Mrs. Mary, 60, Cambria.
Downs, Mrs. Catherine, 55, Millville.
Downs, Mary, 32, Millville.
Downs, Katie, 28, Millville.
Dowling, Mrs. Catherine, 42, Market street.
Dowling, Mary E., 21, Market street.
Dunn, Mary Ann, 25, Prospect.
Early, Mary, 22, Woodvale.
Fitzpatrick, Mrs. Peter, 28, Cambria.
Fitzpatrick, Ella, 6, Cambria.
Fitzpatrick, Mary, 3, Cambria.
Fitzharris, Christ, 42, Franklin street.
Fitzharris, Mrs. Margaret, 40, Franklin street.
Fitzharris, Christ, Jr., 14, Franklin street.
Fitzharris, John, Jr., 12, Franklin street.
Fitzharris, Maggie M., 9, Franklin street.
Fitzharris, Gertie, 5, Franklin street.
Fitzharris, Katie, 7, Franklin street.
Gaffney, Catherine, 2, Cambria.
Gaffney, John, 4, Cambria.
Gallagher, Mrs. Margaret, 32, Washington st.
Gallagher, Thomas, 4, Washington street.
Garvey, Bernard. Sr., 62, Cambria.
Grady, Mrs. Abbie, 60, Cambria.
Halleron, May, 5, Washington street.
Hayes, Mrs. Jane, 32, Cambria.
Hayes, Michael, 12, Cambria.
Hayes, Mary, 8, Cambria.
Hayes, Rose, 7, Cambria.
Hayes, John, 6, Cambria.

Hart, Eliza.
Harrigan, Ella, 22, Hulbert House.
Howard, James B., 45, Conemaugh.
Howe, Mrs. Edward, 50, Railroad street.
Howe, Mrs. Bridget, 48, Cambria.
Howe, Maggie, 24, Cambria.
Howe, Lizzie, 22. Cambria.
Howe, Rose, 19, Cambria.
Howe, Gertrude, 13, Railroad street.
Kane, John, 20, Cambria.
Kane, Mary, 18, Cambria.
Kinney, Mrs. Mary, 50, Washington street.
Kinney, Mary Ellen, 12, Washington street.
Kirby, Wm., 32, Washington street.
Kirby, Mrs. Lena, 25, Washington street.
Lambert, Johanna.
Lavelle, Michael, 22, Broad street.
Lavelle, Wm. M.
Madden, Kate, 17, Cambria.
Matthews, Thos., 22, Clinton street.
McAneny, Neal, 50, Cambria.
McAneny, Mrs. Neal, 45, Cambria.
McAneny, Rose, 23, Cambria.
McAneny, Kate, 18, Cambria.
McAneny, Mary, 13, Cambria.
McAneny, Wm., 9, Cambria.
McAneny, Annie, 5, Cambria.
McAneny, Agnes, 2, Cambria.
McGee, John, 55, Market street.
McGinley, James, 34, Conemaugh.
Mullin, Peter, 50, Conemaugh.
Murphy, Michael J., 34, Brunswick Hotel.
Murphy, Mrs. Mary. 26, Millville.
Murphy, John, 17, Millville.
Murphy Rose, 14, Millville.
Murphy, Wm., 11, Millville.
Murphy, J. J., 55, Park Place.
Murphy, Lily, 9, Park Place.
Nightly, John, 30, Millville.
O'Connel, Capt. Patrick, 70, Washington street.
O'Connel, Margaret, 63, Washington street.
O'Connel, Nora, 60, Washington street.
O'Donnel, Frank, Washington street.
O'Neil, Edward, 3 months, Cambria.
O'Neil, Mrs Bridget, 28, Cambria.
O'Neil, John.
Quinn, Ellen, Franklin street.
Quinn, John, Franklin street.
Riley, Frances, 15, Cambria.
Riley, Gertrude, 13, Cambria.
Riley, Mary, 18, Cambria.
Rogers, Mary, 17, Millville.
Rogers, Tatt.
Rogers, Mrs. Susan.
Rogers, Jane, child.
Ryan, John, 55, Washington street.
Ryan, Mrs. John, 50, Washington street.
Ryan, Maggie, 14, Washington street.
Ryan, Mrs. Mary, 73, Washington street.
Sagerson, Catherine, 4, Railroad street.
Sagerson, Agnes, 2, Railroad street.
Sagerson, Thomas, 6 months, Railroad street.
Sharkey, Mary, 4, Washington street.
Sinniger, Mrs. Mary, Cambria.
Slick, Mrs. Nancy, 55, Fourth Ward.
Takacs, Mrs. Teresa, 31, Cambria.
Takacs, Mrs. John, 21, Cambria.
Tokar, Mrs. Dora, 23, Cambria.
Tokar, Mary, 4, Cambria.
Tokar, Annie, 1, Cambria.
Taylor, Frances.

ST. MARY'S CEMETERY.
(Lower Yoder.)

Banyan, Mrs. Rose, 36, Cambria.
Betzler, Mrs. Agnes, 38, Cambria.
Boyle, Charles, Sr., 45, Cambria.
Boyle, Mary, 12, Cambria.
Boyle, Charles, 8, Cambria.
Boyle, Thomas, 7, Cambria.
Brotz, Pancrotz, 55, Cambria.
Brotz, Mrs. Lena, 50, Cambria.
Brady, John, 53, Franklin street.
Brady, Mrs. Julia, 50, Franklin street.
Coby, Elizabeth, Cambria.
Culliton, Mrs. Teresa, 28, Cambria.
Deitrich, Mrs. Amelia, 23, Cambria.
Fish, Lena, 17, Cambria.
Fisher, Ignatius, 59, Cambria.

Fisher, Margaret, 14, Cambria.
Fleckenstein, Mrs. Ann, 25, Cambria.
Fleckenstein, Regina, 2, Cambria.
Gerber, Mrs. Margaret, 41, Cambria.
Gerber, John C., 45, Cambria.
Gerber, Rose, 8, Cambria.
Gerber, Vincent, 6, Cambria.
Hanki, Edward, Cambria.
Hecker, Mrs. Christ, 58, Cambria.
Heider, Mrs. Ella, 24, Cambria.
Heider, John Leo, 6 months, Cambria.
Hessler, Mrs. Fedora, 29, Cambria.
Hessler, Mary, 10, Morrellville.
Hessler, Joseph, 1½, Cambria.
Hirsch, Eddie, 3, Cambria.
Just, Magdalena, 29, Cambria.
Just, William, 9, Cambria
Just, Eddie, 4, Cambria.
Kintz, Mrs. Mary, 26, Cambria.
Kintz, Katie, 19, Cambria.
Kintz, Mrs. Mary, 25, Cambria.
Knoblespeice, Maggie.
Koebler, Mrs. George, 60, Cambria.
Kropp, Katie, 21, Cambria.
Lambert, Johanna, 19, Washington street.
Lambreski, Kate, 12, Cambria.
Macheletzky, Stanislaus, 10, Cambria.
Martinades, Mrs. Mary, Cambria.
Miller, Mrs. Annie M., 46, Cambria.
Miller, George, 65, Cambria.
Miller, Eddie, 3, Cambria.
Miller, Annie, 1, Cambria.
Nich, Mrs. Margaret, 30, Cambria.
Nich, Frank, 6 Cambria.
Nich, John, 4, Cambria.
Osterman, Joseph, 38, Cambria.
Quinn, Mrs. Terry, 26, Railroad street.
Schnell, Mrs. Fidel, 68, Cambria.
Schnell, Mrs. Margaret, 60, Cambria.
Schnell, Mrs. F., Cambria.
Schmitt, Mary, 31, Cambria.
Schmitt, George, 4, Cambria.
Schmitt, Sophia, 1½, Cambria.
Shmitt, Fredericka, Cambria.
Shmitt, Mrs. Hortena, Cambria.
Shmitt, Leo, Cambria.
Sininger, Mrs. Mary, Cambria.
Sarlouis, Mrs. Barbara, 48, Cambria.
Sarlouis, Mrs. Peter, Cambria.
Snell, Mary, 13, Cambria.
Stinely, Mrs. Mary, 35, Cambria.
Stinely, Kate, 12, Cambria.
Stinely, Joseph, 5, Cambria.
Weber, Mrs. Tresa, 43, Cambria.
Weber, John, 4, Cambria.
Weinzierl, Louis, 41, Cambria.

OLD CATHOLIC GRAVEYARD.
(Conemaugh Borough.)

Akers, Alvar, 54, Upper Yoder.
Coad, Mrs. Mary, 57, Washington street.
Coad, John, 59, Washington street.
Conrad, William, 26, Woodvale.
Halleran, Mrs. Mary C., 30, Washington street.
Hannan, Eugene, 14, Woodvale.
Howe, Abner.
Lynch, John, 27, Conemaugh.
Lynch, Mary, 16, Conemaugh.
Mayhew, Jennie, 18, Woodvale.
Mayhew, Joseph, 16, Woodvale.
Mayhew, Annie, 12, Woodvale.
Mayhew, Earnest, 9, Woodvale.
Mayhew, Harry, 6, Woodvale.
Mayhew, James, 3, Woodvale.
McKarley, Mrs. Mary.
Nugent, Mrs. Mary Jane, 50, Hager Block.
Quinn, Vincent, 14, Main street.
Wehn, Mrs Laura, 29, Conemaugh.
Wehn, Annie, 4, Main street.
Wehn, Mary, infant, Conemaugh.
Wehn, Joseph, 4, Conemaugh.
Wheat, Frank, 28, Clinton street.

GERMAN CATHOLIC CEMETERY.
(Sandyvale.)

Brindle, Mary.
Geis, Mrs. Abbey, 24, Salina, Kansas.

Geis, Richard P., 2, Salina, Kansas.
Hable, John, 29, Conemaugh.
Hoffgard, Conrad, 18, Clinton street.
Holtzman, Joseph, 35, Woodvale.
Horne, William J., 21, Conemaugh.
Horne, Emma J., 22, Stormer street.
Hornick, John P., 26, Conemaugh.
Hornick, Mrs. Amelia, 25, Conemaugh.
Horton, Joseph, Sr., 51, Woodvale.
Keifline, Mrs. Catherine, 58, Conemaugh.
Maloy, Manassas, 45, Clinton street.
Malzi, Jacob, 34, Washington street.
Murtha, James, 65, Conemaugh.
Murtha, James, 28, Main street.
Murtha, Mrs. Barbara, 24, Main street.
Murtha, Frank, 6, Main street.
Murtha, Flora May, 4, Main street.
Murtha, Lily, 1, Main street.
Oswald, Charles, 44, Third Ward.
Oswald, Mary, 19, Third Ward.
Quinn, Vincent D., 16, Main street.
Ripple, Maggie B, 27, Merchants' Hotel.
Robine, Christina, 25, Franklin street.
Sarlouis, Sophia
Schnurr, Charles, 40, Conemaugh.
Schnurr, Robert, 27, Smith alley.
Schry, Joseph, Sr., 78, Woodvale.
Schry, Mrs. Joseph, 68, Woodvale.
Shellhammer, Lorentz,
Shellhammer, Patricius.
Schaller, Joseph, 62, Woodvale.
Schaller, Mrs. Joseph, 62, Woodvale.
Schaller, Annie, 24, Woodvale.
Schaller, Rose, 21, Woodvale.
Werberger, Prof. F. P., 70, Locust street.
Voegtly, Germanus, 62, Conemaugh.

(Geistown.)

Rubritz, Peter, 65, Franklin Borough.
Rubritz, Mrs Margaret, 56, Franklin Borough.
Rubritz, Maggie, 20, Franklin Borough.
Schiffhauer, John, 62, Washington street.
Stenger, John, 12, Main street.
Stenger, Leo, 3, Main street.
Steigerwald, William, Conemaugh.
Steigerwald, Mrs. Mary, 38, Conemaugh.
Steigerwald, infant, 1 month, Conemaugh.

PUBLIC PLOT.

[Known to have been found, but bodies never recovered by friends, and buried in Public Plot in Grand View Cemetery.]

Arthur, Earl H., 8, Water street.
Baker, son of Andrew.
Bohnke, Charles.
Bopp, son of Jacob.
Bopp, Katie, 9, Broad street.
Bricker, Henry.
Burns, John.
Barbour, Harry L., 16, Locust street.
Barker, Mrs. Susan, 28, Woodvale.
Behnke, Charles.
Bloch, Louisa, 17, Conemaugh.
Boehler, Mrs. Annie, 39, Conemaugh.
Brawley, George D., 17, Cor. Union and Vine sts.
Brennan, Mrs. Martha, 36, Woodvale.
Brennan, Mary, 16, Woodvale.
Brennan, William, 12, Woodvale.
Brennan, Lewis, 10, Woodvale.
Brennan, Arthur, 7, Woodvale.
Brennan, Frank, 3, Woodvale.
Brown, Sadie, 22, Woodvale.
Bruhn, Claus, 58, Conemaugh.
Bryan, Wm. A., 45, Mansion House.
Campbell, Peter, 40, Conemaugh.
Casey, William, 48, Cambria.
Cornelison, Maggie.
Craig, Thomas A., 32, Market street.
Craig, Mrs. T. A., 30, Market street.
Craig, Christ, 45, Cambria.
Craig, Annie, 13, Walnut street.
Cunz, Lydia, 6, Napoleon street.
Cunz, Robert, 4 months, Napoleon street.
Dillon, James, 35, Napoleon street.
Downey, Mrs. Mary, 55, Pearl street.
Dudzik, Andrew, 28, Cambria.
Eager, Annie.
Eck, Mary Ann, 37, Woodvale.

Eck, Lily, 12, Conemaugh street.
Edwards, Mrs. Ann R., 70, Union street.
Elsaesser, Andrew, 16, Conemaugh.
English, Joseph, 24, Railroad street.
Fagan, Matthew, 40, Millville.
Fagan, Mrs. M., 38, Millville.
Fagan, Monica, 12, Millville.
Fagan, Daniel, 10, Millville.
Fagan, Clara, 3, Millville.
Fagan, Thomas, 1, Millville.
Faloon, Mrs. Ann E., 63, Pearl street.
Fichtner, Mrs. Tillie, 33, Main street.
Fiddler, Elmira, Bedford street.
Fiddler, Eliza J.
Fockler, Herman, 21, Franklin street.
Griffin, Miss Mary.
Hamilton, Mary, 33, Bedford street.
Hanki, Mrs. Teresa, 40, Cambria.
Hause, Mollie.
Hellriggle, Chas.
Hellrigle, Mrs. Lizzie, 30, Woodvale.
Henry, William, 34, Cumberland, Md.
Hocker, Mrs. John, 72, Somerset street.
Hop Sing, Franklin street.
Hurt, Charles, London, Eng'and.
Irwin, Maggie, 22, Hulbert House.
Johnson, David, 45, Conemaugh street.
Jones, Mary, 14, Main street.
Kast, Clara, 17, Clinton street.
Keene, Katie, 16, Union street.
Keinxstoel, Samuel, 30, Market street.
Larimer, James, 45, Somerset street.
Lee Sing, Chinaman, Franklin street.
Lucas, Maria, 50, Conemaugh.
Madden, Mrs. Mary, 47, Cambria City.
Mack, August.
McClarren, Cora, 8, Cambria City.
McCue, Mrs.
Melden, Richard.
Maley, Henry.
Mosser, Mrs. Mary, 65, Conemaugh street.
Mullen, Margaret.
Oswald, Mrs.
Owens, Mrs.
Oyler, John R.
Phillips, Mrs. Eliza, 48, Union street.
Reese, Mrs. Lizzie, 30, Conemaugh street.
Reese, Annie, 7, Vine street.
Reidel, John C., 60, Conemaugh.
Rich, Mrs. Charlotte, 45, Stonycreek street.
Roberts, Mrs. Jennie, 18, Somerset street.
Rosenfelt, Solomon, Washington street.
Saylor, Henry.
Schnable, Mrs. Conrad, 35, Baumer street
Schittenbelm, Anton, Cambria.
Schittenhelm, Anton Jr., Cambria.
Shumaker, Mrs James M., Locust street.
Skiba, Mrs. Staiuslous, 32, Cambria.
Skiba, Joseph, 4, Cambria.
Smith, Ralph, 11, Woodvale.
Smouse, Jennie, Hulbert House.
Stern, Bella.
Strauss, Moses, 77, Vine street.
Strauch, Henry, 50, Conemaugh.
Smith, Willie, 1, Cambria.
Surany, David
Thomas, John T.
Till, Arthur, 27, Market street.
Unverzagt, Daniel, 66, Washington street.
Unverzagt, Mrs. Daniel, 62, Washington street.
Viering, Mrs.
White, Mrs. John, 76, Union street.
Wagnor, Henry, Cambria.
Warsing, Jane, 24, Coopersdale.
Warkeston, Miss.
Weinzierl, Mrs. Mary, 38, Cambria.
Wearn, Willie, 6, King street.
Walford, Frank.
Will, Elizabeth, Conemaugh.

PASSENGERS ON DAY EXPRESS.

[Those marked ? bodies never found. Those found lived at the places named, to which places the remains were taken.]

Bates, Mrs. Annie, Delavin, Wis.
? Brady, Mrs. J. W., Chicago, Ill.
Bryan, Elizabeth M., 20, Philadelphia.
Christman, Mrs. A. C., Dallas, Texas.

Day, John R., 60, Prospect, Md.
Day, Miss, Prospect, Md.
Ewing, Andrew, Snow Shoe, Pa.
? Feustermaker, Victor, Egypt, Lehigh County.
Harnish, Blanche, Dayton, O.
? Hemingway, Fred. and wife, Kokomo, Ind.
King, Mrs. J. F.
? Lyon, E., New York.
? McCoy, Mrs.
? McCoy, ——
? McCoy, ——
Meisel, Christ, 32, Newark, N. J.
Minich, Kate, Fostoria, Ohio.
Paulson, Je nie, 20, Allegheny City.
? Phillips Frank (porter), Jersey City.
Rainey, Mrs. Sophia, 64, Kalamazoo, Mich.
Ross, John D.
Schrantz, George, Pleasant Gap, Pa.
? Shelly, W., Newark, N. J.
Shick, Cyrus, Reading.
? Sible, Mrs., Springtown, Bucks County, Pa.
Smith, Mrs. H. K., 25, Osborn, Ohio.
Smith, R. Wardwell, 3, Osborn, Ohio.
Stinson, Eliza, Norristown, Pa.
? Swaney, Mrs. Mary A., 67.
Swineford, Mary A., St. Louis, Mo.
Swineford, Mrs. Ed., St. Louis, Mo.
Tarbell, Mrs. Farney, 32, Cleveland, Ohio.
? Tarbell, Grace, 7, Cleveland, Ohio.
? Tarbell, Bertie, 5, Cleveland, Ohio.
? Tarbell, Howard, 2, Cleveland, Ohio.
Weaver, Beneval, Millersburg, Pa.
Woolf, Jennie, Chambersburg, Pa.

MISCELLANEOUS.

[Bodies taken to places named in sub-heads for burial. The place named in line with name of individual is where they were lost from.]

LOYSBURG, BEDFORD COUNTY, PA.
Aaron, Mrs. H. B., 29, Railroad street.
Aaron, Flora, 10, Railroad street.
BLAIRSVILLE, PA.
Alexander, John G., 45, Woodvale.
Alexander, Mrs. John G., 45, Woodvale.
Brown, Emma, 20.
McLaughlin, Mrs. Julia, 60, Cambria.
Miller, Robert, 22, Sixth Ward.
Pike, Fanny, 19, Haynes street.
WILMORE, PA.
Beiter, Mathias, 3, Clinton street.
PHILADELPHIA, PA.
Butler, Chas. T., Hulbert House.
Carlin, Jonathan, Hulbert House.
Cox, James G., Hulbert House.
Clark, W. H. L, 50, Hulbert House.
De Walt, Chas. B., 36, Hulbert House.
Dorsey, John D., Hulbert House.
Lichtenberg, Rev. John, Locust street.
Lichtenberg, Mrs.
Murray, James, 50, Hulbert House.
Nathan, Adolph, 40, Main street.
Overbeck, William H., 38, Main street.
Spitz, Walter L., Hulbert House.
Woolf, Mrs. M. L., Jackson street.
LOUISVILLE, KY.
Marshall, Chas. A., 34, Hulbert House.
BRADDOCK, PA.
Cadogan, Mrs Mary A., 46, Millville.
Cadogan, Ann, 25, Millville.
Young, Mrs. Kate, 34, Market street.
Young, Samuel, 13, Market street.
PITTSBURGH, PA.
Creed, David, 60, Washington street.
Creed, Mrs. Eliza, 55, Washington street.
Creed, Maggie, 23, Washington street.
Fisher, Moses, 24, Mansion House.
Sweeney, Mrs. Ann, 70, Conemaugh.
BENSHOFF'S, CAMBRIA COUNTY, PA.
Custer, William H., 35, Millville.
STEUBENVILLE, OHIO.
Davis, Frank B., 40, Main street.
Davis, Frank, infant.
SOMERSET, PA.
Gaither, Harry, 18, South street.
Houston, Minnie, Hulbert House.
Hurst, Nathaniel, 15, Washington street.

SHIPPENSBURG, PA.
Diehl, Carrie, 20, Hulbert House.
Wells, Jennie, 22, Hulbert House.
MERCER COUNTY, PA.
De France, Mrs. H. T., 32, Hulbert House.
NEW YORK, N. Y.
Dow, W. F., Hulbert House.
HOLLIDAYSBURG, PA.
Fitzharris, John, Sr., 97, Franklin street.
PHILIPSBURG, PA.
Eskdale, James, 42, Woodvale.
Eskdale, Mrs. James, Woodvale.
BERLIN, PA.
Garman, Grace, 21, Washington street.
PITTSTON, PA.
Groff, Nellie C., 20, Hulbert House.
LEECHBURG, PA.
Hill, Ivy, 6, Washington street.
Jack, Jennie.
COVER'S HILL, CAMBRIA COUNTY, PA.
Hinchman, Harry, 4, Woodvale.
Long, Samuel.
Shaffer, Fred, 21, Conemaugh.
DERRY, PA.
Jackson, H. A., 36.
CUMBERLAND, MD.
Katzenstein, Mrs. Ella, Hulbert House.
Katzenstein, Edwin, Hulbert House.
HARRISBURG, PA.
Keis, Charles A., 26, Conemaugh.
Weber, E. Vincent, 26, Woodvale.
Weber, Mrs. Florence, 25, Woodvale.
BUTLER, PA.
Bonner, Mrs. Ann, 24.
Kenna, Mrs. Alice B.
HUNTINGDON COUNTY, PA.
McDivitt, Mattie, 32, Water street.
HEADRICK'S, CAMBRIA COUNTY, PA.
Allison, Florence, 12, Texas.
Beck, William J., 30, Woodvale.
Beck, Mrs. Blanche, 29, Woodvale.
Wilson, Dr. J. C., 53, Franklin.
Wilson, Caroline E., 52, Franklin.
QUAKERTOWN, PA.
Smith, Mrs. J. L., 34, Hulbert House.
Smith, Florence, 9, Hulbert House.
Smith, Frank, 7, Hulbert House.
Smith, infant, 4 months, Hulbert House.
Wilson, Charles H., 45, Hulbert House.
ARMAGH, PA.
Young, Sarah C., 66, Court street.
BEAVER FALLS, PA.
Leslie, John S., 30, Levergood street.
YPSILANTI, MICH.
Richards, Carrie, Hulbert House.
Richards, Mollie, Hulbert House.
BALTIMORE, MD.
Goldenberg, Henry, 54, Lincoln street.
Hoopes, Walter E., 30, Woodvale.
Smith, Mrs. Alice M., 29, Woodvale.
GREENSBURG, PA.
Kilgore, W. Alex., 52, Washington street.
Montgomery, Alex., 55, Stonycreek street.
SEWICKLEY, PA.
Little, John A., 43, Hulbert House.
BANGOR, PA.
Llewellyn, Mrs. J. J., 27, visiting at J. T. Llewellyn's.
SOUTH FORK, PA.
Mullin, James, 24.
JERSEY HEIGHTS, N. J.
Myer, Bernhart.
ROME, N. Y.
Richards, John O., 70.
YOUNGSTOWN, OHIO.
White, Mrs. Alex., 42.
INDIANA, PA.
Ziegler, James B., 24.
READING, PA.
Fediman, W. M., 56, Main street.
BLOUGH'S, STONYCREEK TOWNSHIP, PA.
Blough, Samuel, 40, Market street.
Blough, Sophia, 38, Main street.
Blough, child, Main street.
SCALP LEVEL, PA.
Owens, William L., 11, Market street.
Owens, Daisy, 13, Market street.
NICHOLSON, PA.
Rosensteel, Mrs. J. M., 35, Woodvale.
Rosensteel, Ray Halstead, 18, Woodvale.

NO CEMETERY RECORD.

[Bodies found, but not known where buried.]

Adams, Henry Clay.
Alberter, Anna, 22, Cambria.
Amps, Nicodemus, 42, Cambria.
Amps, Mrs. Teresa, 32, Cambria.
Atkinson, John, 72, East Conemaugh.
Baer, Rosa L., 17, Grubbtown.
Bagley, William, Morrellville.
Baird, Charles.
Baker, Mrs. Nelson.
Baker, Mrs Mary, Woodvale.
Baker, Catherine, 70, Market street.
Baker, Agnes, 68, Market street.
Barley, Myrtle, 11, Woodvale.
Barley, Mamie, 7, Woodvale.
Barley, Effie, 5, Woodvale.
Barley, Laura, 6 months, Woodvale.
Barrett, Jas., 27, Franklin st, St. Charles Hotel.
Berg, Mrs. Marion, 24, Woodvale.
Berkebile, Mahlon, Morrellville.
Blough, Emanuel, 22, Bedford street.
Blough, infant, School alley.
Bowersox, Frank, 22, Market street.
Boyer, Solomon, 62, East Conemaugh.
Bradley, Thomas, 42, Conemaugh.
Bruhn, Mrs. Anna, 45, Portage street.
Bunting, Mrs. Caroline, 45, Woodvale.
Burk, Mrs. Matilda, 38, East Conemaugh.
Burkhard, Mrs. Mollie, 36, Woodvale.
Carr, Alexander, 36, East Conemaugh.
Carr, Sissie, 2, East Conemaugh.
Christie, Andrew C., 50, Woodvale.
Clark, Thomas, 42, Union street.
Clark, John B., 50, Portage st., and 7 children.
Cole, John, Cambria.
Connors, Mrs. Mary, Millville.
Cooper, Otto, 8, Kurtz alley.
Cooper, Mrs. 38, Kurtz alley.
Couthamer, Mr.
Coy, Mrs. Sarah, 46, East Conemaugh.
Coy, Newton G., 16, East Conemaugh.
Craig, Mrs. Catherine, 40, Walnut street.
Crowthers, infant, 3, Chestnut street.
Cummings, Amy, Somerset street.
Davis, Frank, 8, Woodvale.
Davis, Mrs. Philip, 60.
Davis, Mrs. Thomas S., 55, Market street.
Delaney, Mrs. C. W., 59, Conemaugh street.
Dimond, Frank, 36, Conemaugh.
Dimond, Mrs. Ann, 64, Conemaugh.
Doorocsik, Mrs. Annie, 28, Cambria.
Doorocsik, Miss, 6, Cambria.
Doorocsik, Mary, 4, Cambria.
Dorriss, August, 54, Conemaugh.
Doubt, Mrs. William, 63, Cambria.
Dougherty, Mary, 16, Cambria.
Eberle, Lena, 14, Woodvale.
Fails, Dolly F., 15, Union street.
Fers, Frank, 23, Millville.
Fink, Mary E., 17, Conemaugh street.
Fisher, Wolfgang, 33, Main street.
Fisher, Noah, East Conemaugh.
Flegle, David G.
Flegle, Miss Annie.
Flinn, Mrs. Mary, Bedford street.
Fogarty, Thomas, 50.
Forrest, Frank, 12, Locust street.
Foust, Conrad, Woodvale.
Gardner, Rose, 20, Prospect.
Gill, William, 7, Prospect.
Gillen, Laura, Bedford street.
Gordon, Susan L., 62, Hager Block.
Greenwood, Mrs. Rose, 33, Conemaugh.
Gromley, Lilly, 19, Mineral Point, Pa.
Gromley, J. A., 14, Mineral Point, Pa.
Hallen, Charles E., 33, Millville.
Harris, Mrs. Mary T., 48, Walnut street.
Hartzell, Mr., Market street.
Hecker, John, 10, Cambria.
Heckman, Francis, 25, Main street.
Heffley, Edward, 22, Somerset street.
Heine, Henry, 26, Cambria.
Heine, Mrs. Lizzie, 25, Somerset street.
Herman, Edward, Cambria.
Hess, William B., 55, Millville.
Hipp, Elizabeth P., 20, Main street.
Hitchins, Mrs. Cordelia, 35, Market street.
Hornick, Agnes, Broad street.

Hughes, Mary, 7, Che tnut street.
Hughes, Mrs., 64, Union street.
James, Lena, 26, River avenue.
James, Maggie, 1, River avenue.
Jenkins, Mrs. Susan, 40, Somerset street.
Johill, Joseph, Third Ward.
Johnson, John M., 40, Union street
Johnson, Mrs. John M., 38, Union street.
Johnson, Mrs Oliver, 22, Conemaugh street.
Jones, Maggie, 29.
Kane, John, 45, Union street.
Kane, Bridget, 20, Market street.
Keifline, Mary, 4, Conemaugh.
Kelly, Charles, Millville.
Kunkle, Lizzie, 21, Washington street.
Laban, Mrs. Teresa, 50, Cambria
Leech, Mrs. Sarah E., 60, Franklin.
Leech, Alice M, 18, Frankin.
Lingle, Mrs. Mary J., 44, Pearl street.
Long, Samuel, 60, Vine street.
Lotz, Conrad, 64, Sherman street.
Lyden, Mary, 20, Merchants' Hotel.
Maneval, Clarence, 17, Lincoln street.
Mann, Michael, 41, South Fork.
Marczi, Mrs. Mary, 42, Cambria.
Marshall, Wm. H, 23, Clinton street.
Maurer, John, 77, Morris street.
McAuliff, Laura, 16, Woodvale.
McDowell, Geo., , Pearl street
McGuire, Mrs. Mary, 45, Walnut street.
McHugh, Mrs. D. A., 45, E. Conemaugh.
McHugh, Gertrude, 16, E. Conemaugh.
McHugh, Jno. L., 14, E Conemaugh.
McNally, Patrick, 42, Prospect.
Mecke, August, 51, Cambria.
Melczer, Frederick, 28, Cambria.
Miller, Robert, 5, Napoleon street.
Miller, John A., 25, Cambria.
Miller, William, 44, Franklin.
Mingle, Sarah
Monteverde, Mary, 11, Washington street.
Monteverde, Emelia, 7, Washington street.
Morran, James A., 53, Somerset street.
Nau, Katie, 20, Bedford street.
Neary, Mrs. Kate, 34, Bedford street.
Neary, Mary Ellen, 11, Bedford street.
Noblespiece, Maggie, 14, Morrellville
Nugent, Mrs. Mary Jane, 60, Hager Block.
O'Connell, ——, Cambria.
O'Conner, Rose, 20, Locust street.
O'Neal, John, 19, Wood alley.
Oswald, Appahmarian, 12, Cambria,
Page, Emma, 11, Mineral Point.
Page, Herman, 6, Mineral Point
Palmer, Mrs. J. H., 76, Napoleon street.
Partsch, Mrs. Josephine, 59, Woodvale.
Phillips, John, 15, Union street.
Rausch, John, 44, Daisytown.
Repp, George, 5 months, Daisytown.
Robine, Eddie, 2, Franklin.
Robine, Willie, 9 months, Franklin.
Rodgers, Patrick, 52, Millville.
Rodgers, Grace, 5, Millville.
Rodgers, Mrs. Mary, 50, Millville.
Ross, Joseph, 30, Conemaugh.
Roth, Annie, 5, Cambria.
Rowland, Emma, 32, Market street.
Rowland, Ran, 16, Market street.
Samen, Mrs. Annie, 25, Cambria.
Samen, John, 4, Cambria.
Samen, Annie, 3, Cambria.
Samen, Mary, 3 months, Cambria.
Schmidt, Mrs. Frederick, Cambria.
Schmidt, Hortense.
Schmidt, Leo.
Schmitz, Gustave, 33, Clinton street.
Schittenhelm, Max, Cambria.
Snyder, Mrs. Annie, 34, Woodvale.
Spareline, John, 64, Railroad street.
Smith, Mrs. Maggie L, 38, Woodvale.
Smith, Addie, 13, Pearl street.
Smith, Philip, 16, Walnut street.
Smith, Mrs. Amelia, 32, Cambria.
Smith, Mrs. Mary, 52, Conemaugh.
Smith, Philip, 16, Conemaugh.
Slick, Josephine, 20, Woodvale.
Sutliff, George, 25, Somerset street.
Stern, Bella, 1, Washington street.
Stewart, ——, Second Ward.
Spicsak, Mrs. Annie, 27, Cambria.

Tacey, Peter L., 20, Woodvale.
Trindle, John M., 39, Nineveh.
Trawatha, Mrs. Annie, 60, Conemaugh.
Thomas, Mabel, 6, Market street.
Thomas, Edward M., 71, Woodvale.
Uhl, Mrs. Ludwig, 80, Peter street.
Valentine, George M., 42, Market street.
Weisz, Mrs. Martin, 46, Cambria.
Weisz, Jacob, 13, Cambria.
Weisz, Jacob.
Weisz, Isaac, 6, Cambria.
Weisz, Anna, 4, Cambria.
Welsh, Thomas, 60, Cambria.
Weinzierl, Louis, 41, Cambria.
Williams, Elanor, 7 months, Lewis alley.
Williams, Mrs. Margaret, 27, Conemaugh street.
Wild, Mrs. Margaret, 80, Conemaugh.
Willower, Miss Bella, Somerset street.
Willower, Bertha, Somerset street.
Wissinger, Mrs. Catherine, 47, Morris street.
Yost, Charlotte, 16, Pine street.

NOT KNOWN TO HAVE BEEN FOUND.

Abele, Katie, 21, Main street.
Abler, Lulu, Woodvale.
Alberter, Teresa, 3, Cambria.
Alexander, Mrs. Martha, Main street.
Allison, Mrs. Jane, 45, Pittsburgh.
Alt, John, 65, Conemaugh.
Alt, Teresa, 20, Conemaugh.
Alt, George, 60, Cambria.
Alt, Mrs. Ann, 75, Cambria.
Amps, Mary, 11, Cambria.
Aubrey, Thomas, 45, Conemaugh street.
Backer, George, 27, Conemaugh.
Baker, James, 22, Woodvale.
Baker, Catherine, Market street.
Baker, Lydia, 20, Woodvale.
Baker, Nancy, Market street.
Baker, Richard, 1, Woodvale.
Baker, Mellville, 11, Woodvale.
Baker, Deronda, 5, Woodvale.
Baker, Dolly, Woodvale.
Baker, Clara, 17, Woodvale.
Banyan, John, 7, Cambria.
Banyan, Albert, 4, Cambria.
Banyan, Theodore, 2, Cambria.
Barbour, Howard, 7, Woodvale.
Barbour, John F., 3 months, Woodvale.
Barbour, Mrs Sarah, 59, Woodvale.
Barker, Edward, 27, Woodvale.
Barker, Clara, 2½, Woodvale.
Barker, infant, 1 month, Woodvale.
Bartosh, Mrs. Hannah, 39, Cambria.
Bartosh, Frank, 14, Cambria.
Baumer, Mrs. Eliza, 68, Woodvale.
Beam, Roscoe, 2, Locust street.
Beecher, Mrs. Jane, 44, Woodvale.
Beecher, Mary, 23, Woodvale.
Beck, Alfred, 6.
Beck, Roy, 3.
Beckley, Mrs. Mary, 48, Woodvale.
Benson, Mrs. Bessie, 23, Cambria.
Benson, Flora, 3, Cambria.
Bare, Mrs.
Bare, Infant.
Barkley, George.
Barnes, Andrew, Conemaugh.
Barron, Anton.
Barron, Mrs.
Benson, Cora Belle, 1½, Cambria.
Berkey, Henry S., 45, Clinton street.
Beske, John, 7, Cambria.
Beske, Joseph, 5, Cambria.
Beske, Frank, 3, Cambria.
Beske, Lewis, 1, Cambria.
Betzler, Frank, 9, Cambria.
Betzler, Katie, 7, Cambria.
Bishop, Julius, 55, Cambria.
Bitner, A. B.
Blair, Alfred, 53, Woodvale.
Blair, Oliver, 25, Woodvale.
Blair, Alfred, Jr., 14, Woodvale.
Blair, Emanuel, 12, Woodvale.
Blair, Rosana, 10, Woodvale.
Bloch, Mrs. Rose, 54, Conemaugh.
Bloch, Annie, 16, Conemaugh.
Bloch, Minnie, 15, Conemaugh.
Bloch, Emma, 13, Conemaugh.

Boehler, Barbara, 7, Conemaugh.
Boehler, Annie, 9, Conemaugh.
Bogus, William
Blough, Mrs., First Ward.
Bopp, Naomie, 7, Broad street.
Bonson, Charles R.
Boeser, Eddie, 14, Market street.
Bowers, George, Woodvale.
Bowersox, Mrs. Ella, 16, Market street.
Bowersox, Cordelia, 3, Market street.
Bowman, Jessie, 4, Woodvale.
Bowman, Blanche, 2, Woodvale.
Boyer, Emma, 17, Woodvale.
Boyle, Rose, 6, Cambria.
Boyle, Bridget, 4, Cambria.
Boyle, William, 2, Cambria.
Boyle, Joseph, 8 months, Cambria.
Braden, Patrick, Millville.
Bradley, Mrs. Elvira, 39, Conemaugh.
Brawley, Mrs. Maggie, 42, Union street.
Brawley, Robert J., 4, Union street.
Brawley, John.
Brennan, Mrs. Mary Ann, 46, Woodvale.
Brennan, Mary Ann, 23, Woodvale.
Brennan, Ellen, 19, Woodvale.
Brennan, Jane, 16, Woodvale.
Brennan, Agnes, 13, Woodvale.
Bridges, Mrs. Jane, 64, Market street.
Brindle, Vincent.
Brindle, Frank.
Brindle, Rose.
Brinker, Henry.
Briney, Matilda, 25, Woodvale.
Brockner, Samuel, 28, Conemaugh.
Brown, Mrs. Magdalena, 58, Cambria.
Brown, Lizzie, 15, Woodvale.
Brown, Mrs., Conemaugh.
Buckhard, Mrs. Elizabeth, 50, Woodvale.
Buckhard, Charles, 19, Woodvale.
Buckhard, Mrs., 63, Woodvale.
Buckley, Mrs. Mary, 48, Woodvale.
Burket, Frank, 14, Washington street.
Burket, Blair, 8.
Burkhard, Howard, 12, Woodvale.
Burkhard, Gussie J., 5, Woodvale.
Burkhard, Charles C., 2, Woodvale.
Burkhard, Mrs. Catherine, 85, Mineral Point.
Burns, Peter, Woodvale.
Butler, John, 51, 84 John street.
Butler, Robert, 40, Millville.
Butler, Mrs., 70, Millville.
Butler, Annie, 17, Millville.
Butler, Fannie, 14, Millville.
Butler, George, 11, Millville.
Butler, Mrs. Sarah.
Byers, Mrs. Catherine, 46, Mineral Point.
Callahan, Mary, 22, Locust street.
Callahan, Mrs Frank, Locust street.
Carr, Mrs. Mary, 42, Woodvale.
Carr, William, 7, Woodvale.
Carr, Patrick, 22, Cambria.
Carr, Mrs. Sarah, 20, Cambria.
Cartin, Mrs. Thomas, 46, Woodvale.
Cartin, Frank, 5, Woodvale
Christie, Mrs. Lizzie, 46, Woodvale.
Christie, Daisy, 19, Woodvale.
Clark, Thomas, Jr., 9, Union street.
Clark, Annie, 5, Union street.
Clark, Hamilton.
Coad, William, 12, cor. Market and Washington.
Cleary, Alice, Cambria.
Conrad, John, 21, Woodvale.
Constable, Mrs. Sarah E., 48, Broad street.
Constable, Clara, 16, Broad street.
Constable, George, 39, Franklin.
Cope, Ahlum, 70, Conemaugh.
Costlow, Michael, 70, Locust and Union streets.
Costlow, Zita, 6, Woodvale.
Costlow, Juniata, 2½, Woodvale.
Costlow, Regina 1, Woodvale.
Craig, William, 8, 314½ Walnut street.
Creed, Kate 26, 200 Washington street.
Creed, Mary, 16 Washington street.
Crown, Thomas, 51, Conemaugh.
Crowthers, Samuel, 30, Cambria
Crowthers, Mrs. Verna, 27, Cambria.
Culleton, George F., 1, Chestnut street.
Culleton, John F., 2, Chestnut street.
Cummings, Mrs., Somerset street.
Cummings, ——, Somerset street.

Cunz, Mrs. Catherine, 37, Napoleon street.
Cunz, Edward, 12, Napoleon street.
Cunz, Gussie, 3, Napoleon street.
Curtin, Johanna.
Cush, Annie, 17, 112 Railroad street.
Cush, Thomas, 1½, 116 Railroad street.
Custer, Mrs. Emma J., 27, Bedford street.
Curry, Robert.
Darr, George F., 28, Millville.
Davis, Martha, 18, Woodvale.
Davis, Ada, 15, Woodvale.
Davis, Mrs. Ann, 60, Locust street.
Davis, Mrs. Mary, 54, Locust street.
Davis, Della, 22, Locust street.
Davis, Evan, 16, Locust street.
Davis, Reese, 13, Locust street.
Davis, Mrs. Mary D., 55, Millville.
Deible, Harry, Woodvale.
Deihl, Mrs. Mary, 40, Conemaugh.
Delaney, Charles, 18, 51 Conemaugh street.
Devlin, Melissa, 12, East Conemaugh.
Dick, Cornell, 17, Cor. Locust and John streets.
Dill, Robert, 26, Woodvale.
Dill, Mrs. Robert, 26, Woodvale.
Dill, William, 7, Woodvale.
Dill, Harry, 3, Woodvale.
Dinkel, Adam, 50, Conemaugh.
Dishong, Lizzie, 22, Union street.
Dluhos, Jacob, 3, Cambria.
Dluhos, Mary, 3 months, Cambria.
Dolny, Mike, Cambria.
Dorillia, Mrs., 30, Cambria.
Do illia, ——, Cambria.
Dorillia, ——, Cambria.
Downs, Willie, Millville.
Dudzik, Mike, 21, Cambria.
Dudzik, Albert, 21, Cambria.
Early, Mrs. Ella, 59, Woodvale.
Eck, Ellen C., 6, Woodvale.
Eck, Edna Marie, 1½, Woodvale.
Eck, John B., 38, Conemaugh street.
Eck, Cora, 7, Conemaugh street.
Eck, Maoon, 2, Conemaugh street.
Edmonds, Nancy.
Edwards, Roger, 55, Millville.
Edinger, Annie, 19, Millville.
Elder, Mrs. Cyrus, 49, Walnut street.
Elder, Nannie M., 23, Walnut street.
Eldridge, Pennell, 39, Morrellville.
Eldridge, Mrs. Sarah T., 71, Woodvale.
Eldridge, Mrs. Sallie, 27, Woodvale.
Eldridge, Clara, 3, Woodvale.
Eldridge, Annie, 1, Woodvale.
Elsaesser, Constantine, 44, Railroad street.
Elsaesser, Mrs. Frances, 41, Railroad street.
Elsaesser, Charles, 13, Railroad street.
Elsaesser, Adolph, 11, Railroad street.
Elsaesser, Maggie, 10, Railroad street.
Elsaesser, Rose, 4, Railroad street.
Elsaesser, Mary, 1, Railroad street.
English, John.
Etchison, Samuel, 37, Hulbert House.
Evans, Evan B., 50, Woodvale.
Evans, Susannah, 16, Woodvale.
Evans, Mrs. Mary, 55, Main street.
Evans, Annie, 26, Millville.
Evans, Jennie, 13, Millville.
Evans, Susannah, 9, Millville.
Evans, Idris, 3, Millville.
Evans, Walter, 8, Vine street.
Evans, Albert, 12, Conemaugh.
Evans, Elizabeth.
Fairfax, Mrs. Susan, 94, Somerset street.
Fairfax, Mrs. G. W., 38, Somerset street.
Fedorizen, Miklosz, Cambria.
Fenlon, Patrick, 70, Conemaugh.
Fendra, E. H.
Fenn, John Fulton, 12, Locust street.
Fenn, Daisy, 10, Locust street.
Fenn, George Washington, 8, Locust street.
Fenn, Virginia, 5, Locust street.
Fenn, Esther, 1½, Locust street.
Fentiman, Edwin F., 19, Main street.
Fees, Frank, 23, Millville.
Fichtner, Carrie, Stonycreek street.
Fichtner, Annie, 21, Main street.
Fiddler, son of Jacob, Cambria.
Findlay, Mrs. Phœbe, 58, Woodvale.
Findlay, Robert B., 17, Conemaugh.
Fingerhute, Mary, 18, Conemaugh street.

Fingle, Mrs. Mary.
Fink, Samuel P., 54, Conemaugh street.
Fink, Mrs. Mary, 47, Conemaugh street.
Fisher, John, 60, Cambria.
Fisher, Johanna, 19, Cambria.
Fisher, Kate, 9, Cambria.
Fisher, Eddie, 7, Cambria.
Fisher, George, 3, Cambria.
Fisher, August.
Fisher, William.
Fitzgerald, Mrs. Catherine, 40, Millville.
Fitzpatrick, Eliza, 15 months, Cambria.
Fitzharris, Mary J., 16, Franklin street.
Fitzharris, Sarah A., 15, Franklin street.
Foling, August, Cambria.
Foster, Mrs. Margaret, 64, Woodvale.
Foster, Maggie, 29, Woodvale.
Frank, August, 26, Washington street.
Frank, Lena, 15, Washington street.
Fritz, Mrs. Matilda, 26, Horner street.
Fritz, Jane, 2, Horner street.
Fritz, Lily, 1, Horner street.
Gaffney, Mrs. Ellen, 26, Cambria.
Gaither, Willie, 15, South St.
Gardner, John.
Geczie, John, 47, Cambria.
Geczie, Veronca, 37, Cambria.
Geczie, Stephen, 8, Cambria.
Geczie, Annie, 4, Cambria.
Geczie, August, 2, Cambria.
Geczie, Belle, 3 months, Cambria.
Geddes, Mrs. George, 40, Woodvale.
Geisel, Julia, 9. Cambria.
Geisel, Rolla, 9, Cambria
Geraldan, Mrs., 17, Conemaugh street.
Gillas, David, 66, Cambria.
Given, Cora, Millville.
Glass, James, 45, School Alley.
Golde, Harry, 5, Walnut street.
Gouchenour, Frank, 31, Conemaugh.
Grant, Mrs. Kate, 24, Cambria.
Grant, Bernard, 5, Cambria.
Grant, John, 3, Cambria.
Gray, Mrs. Frances, 36, Woodvale.
Gray, Gerald, 5, Woodvale.
Gray, Inez, 3, Woodvale.
Greenwood, Mary A., 8, Cambria.
Greitzer, George, 27, Cambria.
Greger, Ann.
Griffith, Mr.
Gromley, Mrs. Magdalena, 48, Mineral Point.
Gromley, Mary, M., 16, Mineral Point.
Gromley, Daniel J., 13, Mineral Point.
Gromley, Emanuel L., 9, Mineral Point.
Gromley, Emma B, Mineral Point.
Hager, Mrs. Mary, 62, Washington street.
Hagerty, Mrs. Mary J., 36, School alley.
Hagerty Kate, 12, School alley.
Hagerty, Stella, 8, School alley.
Haight, Annie, First Ward.
Haltie, Miss.
Haldiman, Hy, Woodvale.
Hammers, George.
Hammill, Mrs. Catherine, 70, Cambria.
Hamilton, Lou.
Hannan, Mamie, 22, Woodvale.
Hanekamp, Mrs. Louise, 28, Lincoln street.
Hanekamp, child.
Harrigan, Mary L., Millville.
Harris.
Hart, May, 9, Market street.
Harkey, William G.
Hess, Mrs.
Haugh, John, Conemaugh.
Hayes, Thos., 10, Cambria.
Hayes, Annie, 5, Cambria.
Hayes, Agnes Gertrude, 3 weeks, Cambria.
Heckman, Miss, 18, Cambria.
Heidenthal, Mrs. Mary, 38, Woodvale.
Heidenthal, Joseph, 14, Woodvale.
Heidenthal, Annie, 12, Woodvale.
Heidenthal, Phœbe, 10, Woodvale.
Heidenthal, Bertha, 6, Woodvale.
Heidenthal, Alfred, 2, Woodvale.
Heingard, Annie, 22, Woodvale.
Heine, Joseph, 1, Cambria.
Heine, Amelia, 8 months, Cambria.
Hellenberger, Miss E.
Hellreigle, Chas. J., 28, Woodvale.
Henahan, John, 40, Cambria.

Henahan, Mrs. Mary, 24, Cambria.
Henahan, Mary, 7, Cambria.
Henahan, Catherene, 4, Cambria.
Henahan, Frances, 1, Cambria.
Henderson, Thomas, South Fork.
Henderson, Robert, 6 months, Main street.
Henning, John
Henning, Mary
Hickey, Stephen, 9, Conemaugh.
Hicks, Miss Ella, Woodvale.
Himes, Charles C., Conemaugh street.
Himes Mrs. C. C., Conemaugh street.
Himes, } children.
Himes, }
Hinchman, Franklin, 2, Woodvale.
Hirsch, Henry, 10, Cambria.
Hockenberger, Ann, Napoleon street.
Hoffman, Mrs., Mary, 69, Conemaugh.
Hoffman, Joseph, 10, Conemaugh.
Hoffman, Mary, 8, Conemaugh.
Hoffman, Peter, 78, Market street.
Hoffman, Frank C., 11, Market street.
Hoffman, Selma, 3, Market street.
Hoffman, Lena, 19, Washington street.
Hoffman, George, 12, Washington street.
Hoffman, Crisse, 9, Washington street.
Hoffman, Albert, 4, Washington street.
Hoffman, Walter, 2, Wasington street.
Hoffman, Stella, 6 months, Washington street.
Hoffman, Fred. W., 42, Conemaugh.
Hoffman, Mrs. Jennie, 40, Conemaugh.
Hoffman, Lena, 19, Conemaugh.
Hoffman, Henry, 65, Conemaugh.
Hoffman, Mrs. Mary Ellen, 55, Conemaugh.
Hoffman, Stewart, 24, Conemaugh.
Hoffman, Mrs., Conemaugh.
Hoffman.
Hoffman.
Hoffman.
Hoopes, Mrs. Maria, 25, Woodvale.
Hoopes, Ernest, 5, Woodvale
Hoopes, Allen C., 6 months, Woodvale.
Hopkins, Hannah, 40, Locust street.
Hopkins, Elizabeth, 4, Conemaugh.
Hopkins, Geo., 8. Conemaugh.
Hopp, Mary E., 7 months, Vine street.
Horner, Miss, Hulbert House
Horner, Elwood, 15, Levergood street.
Hornick, Wm., 23, Conemaugh.
Hough, Mrs. Louisa, 48, Conemaugh.
Hough, Patrick, 5, Conemaugh.
Houghton Mrs. Lizzie, J., 24, Walnut street.
Howe, Mary, E., Washington street.
Howe, Mrs Nancy, 50, Bedford street.
Howe, Robert, G., 8, Bedford street.
Howe, Mrs. W. J.,
Howells, Maggie, 15, Union street.
Howells, John, 25, Union street.
Howells, Wm., 4 days, Union street.
Hughes, Lizzie, A., 1, Chestnut street.
Hurst, Mrs. Minnie, 60, Washington street.
Hurst, Emily, 10, Washington street.
Hammell, Margaret, 14, Washington street.
Illis, Daniel, Cambria.
James, John K., 8, Main street.
James, William, 10, Market street.
James, Mrs. John.
James, Benjamin, Third Ward.
Janosky, Mrs. Lena, 27, Market street.
Jenkins, John, 20, Upper Yoder.
Jenkins, Harvey, 6, Vine street.
Jenkins, Thomas, Third Ward.
Jenkins, Mrs. Thomas, Third Ward.
Jenkins, ——.
Johns, Mrs. Josephine, 32, Woodvale.
Johns, Richard, 14, Woodvale.
Johns, Silvie, 11, Woodvale.
Johns, Stephen, 5, Woodvale.
Johnson, Mrs. David, 40, Conemaugh.
Johnson, Geraldine, 17, Conemaugh.
Johnson, George, 17, Union street.
Johnson, William, 15, Union street.
Johnson, Gertrude, 13, Union street.
Johnson, Lottie, 11, Union street.
Johnson, Dollie, 7, Union street.
Johnson, Frederick, 4, Union street.
Johnson, Lulu, 3, Union street.
Johnson, Ellen, Hulbert House.
Jones, Mrs. Alice, 65, Millville.

Jones, Mrs. Rachael, 41, Main street.
Jones, Ella, 11, Main street.
Jones, Sarah, 8, Main street.
Jones, Abner, 6, Main street.
Jones, Ida, 3, Main street.
Jones, Thomas, 6, Conemaugh street.
Jones, Elmer, 2, Conemaugh street.
Jones, Mrs. Jennie, 50, Woodvale.
Jones, Williams, 17, Woodvale.
Jones, Amanda, 40, Woodvale.
Jones, Pearl, 9, Woodvale.
Jones, William, 4 months, Woodvale.
Jones, James, 19, Pearl street.
Jones, Charles, 16, Pearl street.
Jones, Emma, Second Ward.
Jones, Walter B., 7, Main street.
Jones, Mrs. Margaret, 65, Llewellyn street.
Jones, Rev. E. W., 56, Vine street.
Jones, Mrs. Rev. E. W., 55, Vine street.
Kane, Mrs. Lidia, 44, Union street.
Kane, Ellsworth, 18, Union street.
Kane, Laura, 15, Union street.
Kane, Willie, 12, Union street.
Kane, Dollie, 10, Union street.
Kane, Lester, 2, Union street.
Kane, Emma, 21, Prospect.
Kane, Mrs. Ann, 60, Cambria City.
Kast, Mrs Charlotte, 43, Clinton street.
Kalor, Mrs. Philapena, 67, Conemaugh.
Kalor, Jamanes.
Kalor, Jane.
Kaylor.
Kaylor.
Kaylor.
Kaylor.
Keedy, Clay, 5, Millville.
Keelan, Mrs. Catherine, 55, Cambria.
Keelan, Daphne, 13, Cambria.
Keelan, Edward.
Keelan, Frank.
Keene, Mrs. Elizabeth, 60, Union street.
Keenan, Mrs. Jane, 26, Washington street.
Keiflein, Philamena, Conemaugh.
Keis, Mrs. Caroline, 24, Railroad street.
Keis, infant, Railroad street.
Kehoe, Thomas, 24 South Fork.
Kelly, Mary M., 30, Millville.
Kelly, Mary C., 1½, Millville.
Kelly, Maggie, 17 days, Millville.
Kelly, Mrs. Ann, 45, Cambria.
Kelly, John W., 24, Cambria.
Kidd, Mrs. Jenny, 35, Walnut street.
Kidd, Laura, 5, Walnut street.
Kilgore, Mrs. W. A., 48, Washington street.
Kilgore, Jessie, 15, Washington street.
Kilgore, Fred, 12, Washington street.
Kilgore, Alex., 9, Washington street.
Kimpel, Mrs. Christ, 43, Clinton street.
Kinder, Thomas, 40, Moxham.
King, Mrs. James, 48, Broad street.
King, Katie M., 24, Broad street.
King, James, 5, Broad street.
Kinney, Mrs. Margaret, 31, Washington street.
Kinney, ——, 4, Washinging street.
Kinney, Agnes, 10, Washington street.
Kintz, Teresa, 24, Cambria.
Kinley, Jane, Bausman alley.
Kirkbride, Fannie, 11, Hager Block.
Kirkbride, infant, Hager Block.
Kirkwood, Finley, 19, Conemaugh.
Kirlin, Mrs. Thomas, 32, Conemaugh street.
Kirlin, Willie, 2, Conemaugh street.
Knable, John.
Knable, Leonard.
Knox, Thomas, 54, Somerset.
Keohler, Mrs. Philomen, 87, Conemaugh.
Keohler, Wm., 16, Conemaugh.
Kraft, Mrs. Maggie, 37, Walnut street.
Kraft, Herman, 12, Walnut street.
Kraft, Frederick, 10, Walnut street.
Krieger, Katie.
Kunkle, Katie, 19, Washington street.
Lambreski, Willie, 2, Cambria.
Lavelle, Miss Mary, 31, Broad street.
Lavelle, Kate, 24, Broad street.
Lavelle, Sallie, 18, Broad street.
Lavelle, Mrs. Mary, 58, Broad street.
Lavelle, John F., 8, Conemaugh street.
Lavelle, Edgar R., 4, Conemaugh street.
Lavelle, Frances A., 6, Conemaugh street.

Laystrom, Mrs., 30, Union street.
Layton, infant, Broad street.
Lewis, Mrs. Lizzie, 28, Lewis alley.
Lichtenberg.
Lichtenberg.
Lichtenberg.
Lightner, James, 23, Cambria.
Lightner, Mrs. Mary, 21, Cambria.
Lightner, Eddie, 1, Cambria.
Llewelyn, Ann, 5, Walnut street.
Lohr, Julia, 17, Bedford street.
Lonaenstein, Mrs. Ida, 27, Franklin.
Ludwig, Charles E., 30, Railroad street.
Luther, Michael, 40, Cambria.
Madden, Willie, 12, Cambria.
Maloy, Mrs. Ann, 35, Millville.
Maloy, Jane, Hulbert House.
Marks, William.
Martin, Edward, 48, River avenue.
Martin, Mrs. Catherine, 40, Millville.
Martin, Mary, 18, Millville.
Martin, Ann, 7, Millville.
Martin, Celia, 7, Millville.
Masters, Margaret.
Masterton, Miss.
Mayhew, Annie, 12, Woodvale.
Mayhew, Earnest, 9, Woodvale.
Mayhew, Harry, 6, Woodvale.
McAteer, Mrs. Jane, 38, Cambria.
McAneny, Sarah, 7, Cambria.
McAley, P.
McCann, Mrs. John, 30, Railroad street.
McCann, John, 31, Railroad street.
McCann, infant, Railroad street.
McClarren, Mary, 13, Cambria.
McClarren, Philip, 1½, Cambria.
McConaghy, Harry M., 6, Main street.
McConaghy, Frank A., 2, Main street.
McCoy, Mr., Railroad street.
McGrew, Oscar, Conemaugh.
McGuire, Constantine, 48, Woodvale.
McGuire, Ann, 19, Woodvale.
McGuire, Christian, 17, Woodvale.
McHugh, Kate, 19, Cambria.
McKeever, Mrs. Mary.
McKim, Mrs. Polly, 65, East Conemaugh.
McMeans, William, 33, Conemaugh street.
McPike, Rosie, 4, Cambria.
McVey, Lizzie, 24, Franklin.
McWilliams, Susie, 13, Pittsburgh, E. E.
Melczer, Robert, 35, Cambria
Melczer, Mrs. Johanna, 30, Cambria.
Melczer, Albert, three weeks, Cambria.
Melczer, Mary, 4, Cambria.
Melczer, John, 2, Cambria.
Merle, Mrs. George, Washington street.
Merle, Mrs. Ida, 29, Washington street.
Merle, Nettie, 5, Washington street.
Merle, Elmer, 2, Washington street.
Meredith, Mr. (probably duplicate).
Meyers, Joseph, 70, Cambria.
Meyers, Lizzie, 11, Millville.
Meyers, Annie, 9, Millville.
Meyers, Stella, 7, Millville.
Meyers, Charlie, 5, Millville.
Meyers, Philip, 1, Millville.
Michalitch, Mrs. Mary, 38, Cambria.
Michalitch, Martin, 6, Cambria.
Michalitch, Mary, 3, Cambria.
Michalitch, John, 1, Cambria.
Miller, Lizzie, 11, Woodvale.
Miller, John, 1, Cambria.
Miller, Mrs. Sophia, 45, Cambria.
Miller, John, 8, Cambria.
Miller, Mary, 12, Horner street.
Monteverde, Mrs. Maria, 40, Washington street
Monteverde, Joseph, 5, Washington street.
Monteverde, Eleanora, 1½, Washington street.
Moore, Melda, 20, Main street.
Moreland, Mrs. Margaret, 48, Quarry street.
Morgan, Gertie, 11, Millville.
Morgan, Mrs. Mary R., 66, Conemaugh street.
Morgan, Miss, Conemaugh.
Moser, Heinrich, Cambria.
Moschgat, Amelia, 22, Bedford street.
Mullen, Mrs Mary, 65, Conemaugh street.
Mullen, Mrs Margaret, 47, Prospect.
Mumma, Mrs. Eliza, 26, Washington street.
Murphy, Mrs. Kate H., 48, Park Place.
Murphy, Mrs. Maggie, 34, Brunswick Hotel.

Murphy, John, 10, Brunswick Hotel.
Murphy, Clara, 8, Brunswick Hotel.
Murphy, Genevieve, 6, Brunswick Hotel.
Murphy, Martin F., 4, Brunswick Hotel.
Murphy, Maggie, 2, Brunswick Hotel.
Murr, Stella, 16, Washington street.
Murr, Frederick, 11, Washington street.
Murr, Nellie, 6, Washington street.
Murr, Frida, 3 months, Washington street.
Nadi, Frank.
Nainoaugh, Henry.
Nayuska, Mrs. Hannah, 65, Market street.
New, Frank.
Newell, August.
Newman, Banheim, 68, Washington street.
Nich, Peter, 30, Cambria.
Nich, William, 2, Cambria.
Nich, Lena, 23, Cambria.
Nich (infant), Cambria.
Nix, Frank, Cambria.
Nixon, Fannie, 5, Woodvale.
Neice, Conrad.
O'Brien, Mrs. Sarah, 60, Millville.
O'Brien, Mrs. Ellen, 31, Millville.
O'Brien, Mrs. Catherine, 55, Millville.
O'Callahan, James, 70, Millville.
O'Callahan, Mrs. Bridget, 68, Millville.
O'Callahan, Miss Ella, 25, Millville.
O'Connell, Edward, Cambria.
O'Donnell, Mrs. Julia, 26, Washington street.
O'Donnell, John, 2, Washington street.
Ogle, Mrs. Hettie M., 52, Washington street.
Ogle, Minnie T., 32, Washington street.
Oberlander, Robert, 35, Locust street.
Oberlander, Mrs. Robert, 30, Locust street.
Oberlander, Mary, 2, Locust street.
O'Lily, Catherine, 20, Cambria.
O'Neill, James, 2, Cambria.
Oswald, Eulaliah, 9, Third Ward.
Osterman, Mrs. Victoria, 31, Cambria.
Osterman, Conrad, 4, Cambria.
Osterman, Joseph Jr., 6, Cambria.
Osterman, Mary Ann, 1½, Cambria.
O'Shea, Mary, Second Ward.
Owens, Mrs. Mary, 62, Market street.
Owens, John, 12, Conemaugh street.
Owens, Amelia, 6, Conemaugh street.
Owens, Willie, 4, Conemaugh street.
Owens, Mrs. Elizabeth, 37.
Pfeifer, Charles, 30, Woodvale.
Pfeifer, Ella, 21, Woodvale.
Pheng, John, Conemaugh.
Phillips, Mary, 16, Union street.
Phillips, Grace, 12, Union street.
Phillips, John, J., 14, Market street.
Phillips, David, 12, Market street.
Phillips, Richard, 10, Market street.
Phillips, Mary, 8, Market street.
Phillips, Evan, 6, Market street.
Pipple, Mrs., Fourth Ward.
Plummer Alvin.
Pollocks, Louis, 19, Cambria.
Polk, John.
Potts, Mrs. Mary, 29, Market street.
Powell, Mrs. Reese, 74, Main street.
Pratt, —— Cambria.
Pratt, —— Cambria.
Pritchard, Mrs. Henry, 48, Market street.
Pritchard, Howell, 9, Market street.
Pritchard, Alice, 5, Market street.
Pritchard, Rachael, 3, Market street.
Price, Mrs. Abe, 29, Millville.
Progner, Samuel, 28, Conemaugh.
Prosser, Mrs. David, 68, Union street.
Pukey, Julius, 23, Cambria.
Pukey, Matilda, 1, Cambria.
Raab, Mollie, 18, Clinton street.
Raab, Bertha, 13, Clinton street.
Raab, Katie, 3, Clinton street.
Raab, Mrs. Minnie, 24, Washington street.
Rawn, Mrs. Henrietta, 78, Conemaugh.
Ream, Mrs. Mary, 34, Woodvale.
Ream, Joseph, 10, Woodvale.
Ream, Effie May, 6, Woodvale.
Ream, Cora, 1, Woodvale.
Reamus, Gussie, 17, Woodvale.
Ream, Frederick E., 23, Third Ward.
Ream, Amelia, 20, Third Ward.
Recke, Mrs. Alex., 29, Washington street.
Reed, Charles.

Reese, Susie, 14, Millville.
Reese, Sarah, Woodvale.
Reese, Mrs., 70.
Reidel, Mrs. Teresa, 56, Conemaugh.
Reilly, Timothy, 27, Millville.
Reynolds, Mrs. Elizabeth, 40, Woodvale.
Reynolds, Idella, 14, Woodvale.
Ressler, John.
Reynolds, Columbia, Conemaugh.
Rhodes, Frank, 2, Somerset street.
Rich, Harry, 16, Stonycreek street.
Richards, Mrs. Margaret, 40, Union street.
Riffle, Mary C., Cambria.
Riley, Mrs. Bridget, 40, Cambria.
Riley, Annie, 8, Cambria.
Riley, Katie, 6, Cambria.
Ripple, Emma, 24, Bedford street.
Ritter, Katie, 20, Cambria.
Ritter, Sophia, 12, Cambria.
Rodgers, Mary, Hulbert House.
Rodgers, Mary G., 19, Woodvale.
Rodgers, Mrs. Mary, Water street.
Roland, Lizzie, 5 months, Conemaugh.
Roose, John, 31, Haynes street.
Rosenfelt, ——
Rosenfelt, ——
Rosenfelt, ——
Rosenfelt, ——
Rosenfelt, ——
Rosensteel, Matilda V., 19, Woodvale.
Roth, Albert, 8, Cambria.
Roth, Mary, 6, Cambria.
Roth, Sebastian, First Ward.
Ruth, John.
Rowland, Mrs. E. J., 64, Market street.
Ryan, Sadie, 16, Washington street.
Ryan, Gertie, 3, Washington street.
Ryan, Mary, Third Ward.
Sagerson, Mrs., 96, Millville.
Salenty, E.
Sample, Mrs. Catherine, 63, East Conemaugh.
Sarlous, Grace, 16, Cambria.
Savage, Mrs. Bridget, 76, Woodvale.
Salev, Joseph, 50, Millville.
Shaffer, Mrs. Mary, 43, Cambria.
Shaffer, Carl, 19, Cambria.
Schanvisky, August, 10, Cambria.
Sherer, Mrs. Kate, 49, Conemaugh.
Sherer, Emma, 24, Conemaugh.
Sherer, Mary, 11, Conemaugh.
Schiffhauer, Frances, 19, Washington street.
Schittenhelm, Wilmena.
Schmitt, William J., 7, Cambria.
Schmitt, Mrs. Augustina, 38, Cambria.
Schmitt, August, 8, Cambria.
Schmitt, Anton, 2, Cambria.
Schmitt, Annie, 1, Cambria.
Schmitz, Ferdinand, Cambria.
Schmitz, Gabriel, 50, Conemaugh.
Schmidt, John L., Cambria.
Schonhardt, Victoria, 56, Conemaugh.
Schultz, Mrs. William, Clinton street.
Schultz, Clinton street.
Schultz, Clinton street.
Schultz, Clinton street.
Schultz, Clinton street.
Schultz, Joseph, First Ward.
Schweitzer, William, Conemaugh.
Schweitzer, Catherine E., Conemaugh.
Schurtz, Peter, 38, Conemaugh.
Seibert, Mrs. Elizabeth, 56, Woodvale.
Schaffer, Howard, 21, South Fork.
Shea, Mrs. Mary, 30, Locust street.
Sheldon, H.
Sherman, Mrs. Ann, 35, Market street.
Shinkey, Mrs., Second Ward.
Shorper, Jacob.
Shorper, Jacob, Jr.
Silverman, Moses, Second Ward.
Seigmund, Mrs. Matilda, 52 Woodvale.
Seigmund, Mrs. Carolina, 28, Woodvale.
Seigmund, John, 20, Woodvale.
Singer, Mrs. E. H., Unionport, Ohio.
Siroczki, Mrs. Mary, 30, Cambria.
Siroczki, Mary, 7, Cambria.
Siroczki, Annie, 4, Cambria.
Siroczki, Lizzie, 2, Cambria.
Skiba, Annie, 6, Cambria.
Skiba, Sophia, 1½, Cambria.
Smith, Harry, 5, Woodvale.

Smith, Hattie, 4, Woodvale.
Smith, infant, 3, Woodvale.
Smith, Alice, J., 2, Woodvale.
Smith, Clarence, 6 months, Woodvale.
Smith, George A., 38, Pearl street.
Smith, Mrs. Jennie, 36, Pearl street.
Smith, Charles, 7, Pearl street.
Smith, Alum, 4, Pearl street.
Smith, Effie, 9 months, Pearl street.
Smith, Mrs. Mary, 21, Cambria.
Smith, Mollie, 22, Cambria.
Smith, Mrs. Ann, 55, Cambria.
Smith, Francis, 3, Cambria.
Smith, Charles, 1, Cambria.
Smith, John M., 38, Millville.
Smith, William, 9, Millville.
Smith, Mrs. Mary, Third Ward.
Smith, William, Third Ward.
Smith, Esther, Third Ward.
Smith, Charles, First Ward.
Smith, Richard, First Ward.
Smith, Frank, First Ward.
Snyder, Polly, 14, Woodvale.
Snyder, William, 8, Woodvale.
Snyder, Annie, 6, Woodvale.
Snyder, John, 3, Woodvale.
Snyder, Patrick V., 5 months, Woodvale.
Snyder, Hollis, Woodvale.
Snyder, Mary.
Snyder, Annie.
Snyder, John.
Snyder, Mary E.
Snyder, Harrison V.
Speers, Mrs. L. E.
Spenger, Mrs. Catherine, 56, Stonycreek street.
Spenger, Edward, 16, Stonycreek street.
Spoller, Mrs.
Spoller, Lee.
Stansfield, James C., 30, Woodvale.
Stansfield, Mrs. J. C., 25, Woodvale.
Stansfield, Ralph, 9 weeks, Woodvale.
Steckman, Fred, 42, Cambria.
Stewart, Watson, 60, Pearl street.
Stewart, Mrs., 70, Walnut street.
Stews, Louis, Walnut street.
Stinely Annie, 4, Cambria.
Stinely, infant 4 months, Cambria.
Stork, Casper, 43, Walnut street.
Stork, Mary, 38, Walnut street.
Stork, John, 20, Walnut street.
Stork, Lizzie, 14, Walnut street.
Strauss, Charles ., Conemaugh.
Strayer, Katie, 22, Market street.
Strayer, Bertha, 14, Market street.
Stroup, Henry, Conemaugh.
Stufft, Vera, 10, Woodvale.
Stufft, Earl B, 8, Woodvale.
Stufft, Lula B., 6, Woodvale.
Stufft, Elda M., 3, Woodvale.
Stufft, infant, four months, Woodvale.
Suder, Lizzie, 9, Millville.
Suder, James, 5, Millville.
Sullivan, Mrs. Catherine, 55, Millville.
Swank, Leroy, 4, Main street.
Swank, Miss, Morris street.
Sweitzer, William, 35, Morrellville.
Temple, Leroy.
Thoburn, John, 40, Millville.
Thoburn, Mrs. Flora, 36, Millville.
Thoburn, John, Jr., 10, Millville.
Thoburn, Harry, 1, Millville.
Thomas, Tydvil, 19, Millville.
Thomas, Mrs. Annie E., 56, Napoleon street.
Thomas, Mrs. Ann, 41, Woodvale.
Thomas, Albert E., 17, Woodvale.
Thomas, Vivian D., 15, Woodvale.
Thomas, James Roy.
Thomas, Sylvester.
Thomasberger, Fannie, 42, Conemaugh.
Thomasberger, Nellie, 13, Conemaugh.
Thomasberger, Charles, 11, Conemaugh.
Thurin, Levi.
Totas, Jacob, Cambria.
Totas, Sophia, Cambria.
Totas, Michael, Cambria.
Totas, Wavreck, Cambria.
Trefts, William S.
Tross, W. J. Sr., 43, Woodvale.
Tross, Katie, 19, Woodvale.
Tross, William, 17, Woodvale.
Tross, Conrad, 16, Woodvale.

Tross, Charles, 13, Woodvale.
Tross, George, 9, Woodvale.
Tross, Louis, 7, Woodvale.
Tross, Edward, 6, Woodvale.
Tucker, Mrs. Margaret N., 45, Woodvale.
Tucker, Lillian G., 18, Woodvale.
Tucker, Mabel, 6, Woodvale.
Tynan, Michael J., 49, Conemaugh.
Tynan, Mrs. M. J., 47, Conemaugh.
Unverzagt, Lulu, 23, Washington street.
Vallance, David, 55, Conemaugh street.
Vallance, Mrs. Sarah, 66, Conemaugh street.
Vallance, Annie, 21, Conemaugh street.
Valentine, Mrs. Carrie, Market street.
Valentine, Alexander L., 14, Market street.
Valentine, Annie May, 11, Market street.
Valentine, Burt, 7, Market street.
Valentine, Howard, 4, Market street.
Valentine, Ruth, 1½, Market street.
Varner, Viola, 12, Cambria.
Varner, Sarah, 10, Cambria.
Varner, Ida, 7, Cambria.
Varner, Ella, 5, Cambria.
Varner, infant, six weeks, Cambria.
Veith, Mrs. Carrie, 52, Stonycreek street.
Veith, Emma, 14, Stonycreek street.
Voeghtly, Mrs.
Von Alt, Henry, Clinton street.
Wagnor, Mrs. Henry, Cambria.
Wagnor, Frank, Cambria.
Wagnor, John, Cambria.
Walker, Conrad, 27, Clinton street.
Walker, Ida J., 22, Conemaugh.
Walker, Mrs. Ann, Alum Bank, Pa.
Ward, Ella, Cambria.
Warren, Edward, 28, Millville.
Waters, Thomas J., 15, Conemaugh.
Watkins, Mary J., 22, Washington street.
Wearn, Mrs. Priscilla, 66, Walnut street.
Wearn, Richard, 30, King street.
Wearn, Mrs. Ella, 27, King street.
Wearn, Myrtle, 3, King street.
Weaver, Joseph H., 19, Woodvale.
Weaver, Margaret J., Second Ward.
Webber, Christian, 31, Woodvale.
Wehelco, John, Cambria.
Wehn, Casper, 80, Clinton street.
Weinzarl, Annie, 13, Cambria.
Weinzarl, Martua, 11, Cambria.
Weinzarl, Sarah, 7, Cambria.
Weinzarl, Mollie, 5, Cambria.
Weinzarl, John, 3, Cambria.
Weinzarl, George, 4 months, Cambria.
Weisc, Rosa, 10, Cambria.
White, Annie, 23, Market street.
White, Raymond, 4, Youngstown, O.
Wickersham, Richard G., 26, Woodvale.
Wilson, Mrs. Lavina, 38, East Conemaugh.
Wilson, James, 33, Mineral Point.
Wilson, Henry, 58, Millville.
Wilson, Mr., Cambria.
Wiseman, Charles, 26, Conemaugh.
Wiseman, Emma, 4, Conemaugh.
Wiseman, August, 2, Conemaugh.
Witz, Sarah, Third Ward.
Wolf, Anthony, 24, Cambria.
Wolf, Albert, 1½, Cambria.
Wolford, Andrew, Conemaugh.
Wolford, Conemaugh.
Wolford, Conemaugh.
Wolford, Conemaugh.
Woren, Richard, Walnut street.
Woren, Mrs. Richard, Walnut street.
Woren, Willie, 6, Walnut street.
Woren, ——, child, Walnut street.
Woren, ——, child, Walnut street.
Woren, Mrs. Priscilla, 60, Walnut street.
Woren, Miss, 24, Walnut street.
Woren, Mrs. Thomas, Walnut street.
Yocum, Samuel, Third Ward.
Yost, Laura, 18, Grant street.
Yost, Lottie, Jackson street.
Young, Mamie, 12, Broad street.
Young, Katie, 10, Broad street.
Youst, Mr.
Youst, Eddie.
Zellar, Rose.
Zern, Miss.
Zimmerman, Milton, 19, Locust street.
Zimmerman, Morgan, 11, Young's alley.
Zimmerman, Owen N.

Appendix C

When this paper is filled up and executed, it should be returned immediately to the office of the Flood Relief Commission, in the new building, corner Franklin and Locust Streets, opposite Methodist Church, Johnstown, Pa.

Any false statement, wilfully made, of a material fact in this application will render the whole paper void.

APPLICATION FOR RELIEF.

Made by...a sufferer by the Floods of May 31, and June 1, 1889, in the Conemaugh Valley.

STATE OF PENNSYLVANIA, }
   County of Cambria, } ss.

Before me personally appeared the undersigned,...
....who, being duly sworn according to law, makes the following statement:

FIRST—My name is.., age............years. At the time of the flood I resided in.., Cambria County, Pa., at No. ....Street. I was born in .... I have lived in... Cambria County, Pa., for the past......................................years. My occupation or business is... At the time of the flood I was employed by .... as a... My monthly earnings averaged $.......................... Present condition of my health,..

SECOND—I own no real estate except as follows:...
....
....
....worth before the flood $......................
My real estate within the flooded district was injured in the following manner: (See Note.)
....
....

THIRD—At the time of the flood I owned household goods, moneys, debts due from solvent debtors, and other personal property as follows:...
....
....
worth before the flood $........................., which was injured by the flood in the following manner: ....
....
....

FOURTH—At the time of the flood the stock in my store consisting of ....

was worth at cost prices - - - - - - - - - $ ....

which was injured by the flood in the following manner: ....

....

....

FIFTH—My family dependent upon me consists of

.... aged .... years.

.... " .... "

.... " .... "

.... " .... "

.... " .... "

.... " .... "

.... " .... "

.... " .... "

.... " .... "

SIXTH—Members of family lost by flood ....

SEVENTH—My property has been injured or destroyed by the flood as follows:

Real estate to the amount of - - - - - $ ....

Household goods to the amount of - - - - $ ....

Tools, &c., to the amount of - - - - - $ ....

Stock of goods in my store to the amount of - - - $ ....

.... $ _____

Total, - - - - - - - - $ ....

SEVENTH—I have received no aid since the flood except as follows:

.... from ....

.... " ....

.... " ....

.... " ....

Sworn to and subscribed before me, this ⎫

.... day of July, 1889. ⎬ ....

⎭   (Applicant sign here.)

....

(Officer sign here.)

NOTE.—Where house has been totally destroyed or swept away, state size, how many stories high and whether brick or frame.

Appendix D

Clara Barton Letter to Johnstown

BOARD OF CONSULTATION:
PRESIDENT OF THE U. S. AND MEM-
BERS OF THE CABINET.
EXECUTIVE OFFICERS:
CLARA BARTON, PRESIDENT AND ACTING
TREASURER.
WM. LAWRENCE, 1ST VICE-PRESIDENT.
A. S. SOLOMONS, VICE-PRESIDENT.
WALTER P. PHILLIPS, GEN'L SEC'Y.
DR. J. B. HUBBELL, GEN'L FIELD AGENT.
TRUSTEES:
SECRETARY OF THE TREASURY.
SECRETARY OF WAR.
SECRETARY OF THE INTERIOR.

The American National Red Cross,

INCORPORATED UNDER THE LAWS OF THE DISTRICT OF COLUMBIA, OCTOBER 1, 1881.

For the Relief of Suffering by War, Pestilence, Famine, Flood, Fires, and other Calamities of Sufficient magnitude to be
deemed National in extent.   The Organization acts under the Geneva Treaty, the provisions for which were made
in International Convention at Geneva, Switzerland, August 22, 1864, and since signed by nearly all civilized
nations, including the United States, which gave its adhesion by act of Congress, March 1, 1882. Rati-
fied by the Congress of Berne, January 9, 1882. Proclaimed by President Arthur, July 26, 1882.

Washington, D. C., ...March 5th, ...189 2

B. L. Yeagley,

　　Acting Mayor,

　　　　Johnstown, Pa.

Dear Mr. Mayor:

　　　　　Please find enclosed receipt for your second contribution of $839.89, for the famine stricken peasants of Russia, to be dis-
tributed through the Red Cross.

　　　　　I need not, if I could, say to you how gratifying your action
has been in this matter.   The record of Johnstown since its disaster
has been one which any city could be proud.   She has lost no opportunity to show her gratitude to the world.   Before she had even raised to
her feet, she was the first to extend a helping hand to Louisville in her
disaster by tornado, and now, when the children in the far away wastes
of Russia, cry for bread, she has been quick to respond, and the most
generous of any city in proportion to her size and strength.   And if you
will pardon a personal word, it would be that among the memories I could
least afford to lose out of my life, would be that of the months I passed
in Johnstown, and the confidence of her people, evinced through these
later actions are treasured as among life's richest inheritance.

　　　　　With thanks which I can not speak, I remain,

　　　　　　　　Always sincerely yours,

　　　　　　　　　Clara Barton.

　　　　　　　　President American National Red Cross.

Appendix E

Land Title Search

Petoskey Title Company

407 Michigan Street
Petoskey, Michigan 49770
(231) 487-0541 • Fax: (231) 487-0543

March 23, 2000

Name Search furnished to: Michael R. McGough, D.Ed.

Order No. LA-2000 S

1. Beginning Date: January 1, 1889 at 8:00 a.m.

   Covering the names:

   1. Unger, Elias J. (Colonel)
   2. South Fork Fishing and Hunting Club (of Pittsburg)

2. We have searched the records in the office of the Register of Deeds for Emmet County, Michigan, and find no conveyances, liens, lis pendens, levies or attachments describing the said names in said office from said Beginning Date to January 1, 1891 at 8:00 A.M., EXCEPT THE FOLLOWING:

NO ENTRIES FOUND

PETOSKEY TITLE COMPANY

By: _____
        (Authorized signature)

Selected Bibliography

Barton, Clara. *The Red Cross in Peace and War*. Washington, DC: American Historical Press, 1899.

Beale, David J. *Through the Johnstown Flood by a Survivor*. Philadelphia, PA: Hubbard Brothers, 1890.

Burkert, Richard and Cooper, Eileen. *Uphill all the Way: Johnstown and its Inclined Plane*. Johnstown, PA: Cambria County Tourist Council, 1985

Clark, Charles B. *Johnstown Directory and Citizens' Register*. Altoona, NC: Barclay & Sons, 1889.

Connelly, Frank & Jenks, George C. *Official History of the Johnstown Flood*. Journalist Publishing, 1889.

Degan, Carl & Degen, Paula. *The Johnstown Flood of 1889*. Washington, DC: Eastern Acorn Press, 1984.

Dieck, Herman. *The Johnstown Flood*. Philadelphia, PA: private printing, 1889.

Dulles, Foster Rhea. *The American Red Cross A History*. New York, NY: Harper Brothers, 1950.

Ferris, George T. *The Complete History of Johnstown and Conemaugh Valley Flood*. New York, NY: H. S. Goodspeed and Company, 1889.

Heiser, Victor. *An American Doctor's Odyssey*. New York, NY: W. W. Norton, 1936.

Johnson, Willis Fletcher. *History of the Johnstown Flood*. Philadelphia, PA: Edgewood Publishing, 1889.

Landmark Design Associates. *Historic Structures Report Architectural & Historical Data Section Clubhouse, Brown Cottage, Moorhead Cottage, Clubhouse Annex South Fork Fishing and Hunting Club St Michael, Pennsylvania*. Washington, DC: Government Printing Office, 1992.

Law, Anwei Skinsnes. *The Great Flood Johnstown, Pennsylvania 1889*. Johnstown Area Heritage Association, 1997.

McClullough, David G. *The Johnstown Flood*. New York, NY: Simon and Schuster, 1968.

McLaurin, J. J. *The Story of Johnstown*. Harrisburg, PA: James M. Place, 1890.

O'Connor, Richard. *Johnstown: The Day the Dam Broke*. Philadelphia, PA: Lippincott, 1957.

Ogilvie, J. S. *History of the Great Flood in Johnstown PA*. New York, NY: J. S. Ogilvie, 1889.

Rayburn, Ella Sue. *Johnstown Flood National Memorial Elias J. Unger House Historic Structure Report*. Washington, DC: Government Printing Office, 1986.

Sanger, Martha Frick Symington. *Henry Clay Frick an Intimate Portrait*. New York, NY: Abbeville Press, 1998.

Shappee, Nathan D. *A History of Johnstown and the Great Flood of 1889; A Study of Disaster and Rehabilitation*. Pittsburgh, PA: an unpublished doctoral dissertation submitted to the Graduate School of the University of Pittsburgh, 1940.

Slattery, Gertrude Quinn. *Johnstown and Its Flood*. Philadelphia, PA: Dorrance Press, 1936.

Strayer, Harold & London, Irving. *The Photographic Story of the 1889 Johnstown Flood*. Johnstown, PA: Weigel & Barber Printing, 1964.

Unrau, Harlan D. *Historic Structure Report—South Fork Dam*. Washington, DC: Government Printing Office, 1980.

Walker, James H. *The Johnstown Horror: or the Valley of Death*. Chicago, IL: L. P. Miller, 1889.

About the Author

Michael McGough was born in Johnstown in 1951. After graduating from Johnstown High School in 1969, he completed undergraduate work at the University of Pittsburgh at Johnstown. In 1973 he left Johnstown to begin his teaching career at Bermudian Springs High School in Adams County, Pennsylvania. His graduate studies included work at Western Maryland College, where he earned a Master's Degree in 1977, Shippensburg University, where he earned Pennsylvania administrative certification in 1988, and Pennsylvania State University where he earned his doctorate in adult education in 1989. In addition to teaching, McGough has been a building administrator and assistant superintendent of schools. He is currently a professor in the Department of Education at York College of Pennsylvania and the Director of the College's Professional Development Division.

In addition to this volume, McGough has written books on the Battle of Gettysburg, Pennsylvania history, and character development for teens. He is the creator and writer of several long-running newspaper columns and a number of professional articles on a variety of topics. Since 1976, he has been a Licensed Guide with the National Park Service in Gettysburg. McGough is married to the former Christine Wesner, who was also born and raised in Johnstown. They have two grown children, Gregory and Melissa. The McGough's currently live in Adams County.

THOMAS PUBLICATIONS publishes books about the American Colonial era, the Revolutionary War, the Civil War, and other important topics. For a complete list of titles, please visit our website:

http://thomaspublications.com

Or write to:

THOMAS PUBLICATIONS
P.O. Box 3031
Gettysburg, PA 17325